Johnson's Lives of the Poets
A Selection

Edited by **J. P. Hardy**

1971 Clarendon Press · Oxford

·J8
1971

Printed in the United States of America

Contents

Introduction	vii
Chronological Table	xvii
Abbreviations	xix
Reading List	xxi
Cowley	1
Milton	50
Dryden	114
Pope	210
Thomson	316
Collins	327
Gray	331
Appendix: On Religious Poetry (from the Life of Waller)	342
Notes	344
Index	369

Introduction

Edward Dilly's letter (dated 26 Sept. 1777) to James Boswell gives an account of the London booksellers' initial approach to Johnson following their decision to publish a new edition of the English poets:

The edition of the Poets, now printing, will do honour to the English press; and a concise account of the life of each author, by Dr. Johnson, will be a very valuable addition, and stamp the reputation of this edition superior to anything that is gone before. The first cause that gave rise to this undertaking, I believe, was owing to the little trifling edition of the Poets, printing by the Martins, at Edinburgh, and to be sold by Bell, in London. Upon examining the volumes which were printed, the type was found so extremely small that many persons could not read them; not only this inconvenience attended it, but the inaccuracy of the press was very conspicuous. These reasons, as well as the idea of an invasion of what we call our literary property, induced the London booksellers to print an elegant and accurate edition of all the English Poets of reputation, from Chaucer to the present time.

Accordingly a select number of the most respectable booksellers met on the occasion, and on consulting together, agreed that all the proprietors of copyright in the various poets should be summoned together, and when their opinions were given, to proceed immediately on the business. Accordingly a meeting was held, consisting of about forty of the most respectable booksellers of London, when it was agreed that an elegant and uniform edition of 'The English Poets' should be immediately printed, with a concise account of the life of each author by Dr. Samuel Johnson, and that three persons should be deputed to wait upon Dr. Johnson to solicit him to undertake the Lives, viz. T. Davies, Strahan and Cadell. The Doctor very politely undertook it, and seemed exceedingly pleased with the proposal. As to the terms, it was left entirely to the Doctor to name his own; he mentioned two hundred guineas; it was immediately agreed to, and a farther compliment, I believe, will be made him.

It was on the previous Easter Saturday (29 March) that Johnson had briefly met the booksellers and entered into this contract. When an early advertisement in the *Public Advertiser* prompted Boswell to write and ask about the work, Johnson replied (3 May) that he was 'engaged to write little Lives, and little Prefaces, to a little edition of the English Poets'.[1]

Though the completed work was less extensive in scope than Dilly had indicated, its magnitude and importance far exceeded Johnson's own modest reference to it in this letter. Consisting of fifty-two Lives, his detailed 'Prefaces, Biographical and Critical' to the booksellers' *Works of the English Poets* provides a comprehensive account of English poetry from Cowley and the metaphysical school to Gray

---

[1] *Life*, iii. 108, 110–11, 488–9; *YJ*, i. 264; *Letters*, no. 515.

and his contemporaries. It appeared in two instalments. Twenty-two poets, from Cowley to John Hughes, occupied the first four volumes published in March 1779, and thirty poets, from Addison to Gray, the last six published in May 1781.[1]

On Good Friday of that year Johnson wrote in his diary: 'Some time in March I finished the lives of the Poets, which I wrote in my usual way, dilatorily and hastily, unwilling to work, and working with vigour and haste.' Certainly he seems to have been somewhat slow in starting on the project. Much of 1777 was spent, first in efforts on behalf of the unfortunate clergyman William Dodd, executed for forgery in June, and then on an extended visit to Oxford, Lichfield, and Ashbourne (though during his stay in Oxford Johnson had gleaned some material for his Lives from the Bodleian). It was not until November that he was back in London proposing to begin work in good earnest. By the following Easter, according to his diary entry, he had 'written a little of the lives of the poets'; while a letter dated 27 July to the printer John Nichols gives a detailed picture of what had been completed up to that time:

You have now all Cowley. I have been drawn to a great length, but Cowley or Waller never had any critical examination before. I am very far advanced in Dryden, who will be long too. The next great Life I purpose to be Milton's.
It will be kind if you will gather the Lives of Denham, Butler, and Waller, and bind them in half-binding in a small volume, and let me have it to show my friends.

In October he had (apparently after some delay) returned further proof-sheets to Cadell; and later letters to Nichols include the mention of Richard Duke, George Stepney, John Philips, and Edmund Smith.[2]

It is uncertain just when Johnson began work on the last six volumes. During the remainder of 1779 little would seem to have been done. By the following April, however, he was able to write to Mrs. Thrale: 'I have not quite neglected my Lives. Addison is a long one but it is done. Prior is not short, and that is done too. I am upon Rowe, who cannot fill much paper.' Yet the task seemed to hang heavily on his hands. Within the week he wrote again to her at Bath:

You are at all places of high resort, and bring home hearts by dozens; while I am seeking for something to say about men of whom I know

---

[1] Two more London editions were published in Johnson's lifetime: the first in 1781; the second, systematically revised by the author, in 1783.

[2] *YJ*, i. 292, 303–4; *Letters*, nos. 532–3, 581, 584, 597, 603.

nothing but their verses, and sometimes very little of them. Now I have begun, however, I do not despair of making an end.

And again a few days later he alluded to the colds and persistent cough that were to trouble him during the spring and early summer: 'I thought to have finished Rowe's Life today, but I have five or six visitors who hindered me, and I have not been quite well. Next week I hope to dispatch four or five of them.' Small wonder, then, that in reviewing his working-summer in London, he was inclined to be dissatisfied with the amount he had accomplished, and wrote to Boswell in August: 'I have sat at home in Bolt Court all the summer, thinking to write the Lives, and a great part of the time only thinking.' But though at the beginning of September he had the longer Lives of Swift and Pope still to write, it seems probable that by the time he went to Brighton for a short visit in October, much of the work had already been done.[1]

Inevitably in writing such a work, Johnson obtained and solicited different kinds of assistance from a variety of people. Nichols provided not only numerous books, but many factual details as well.[2] Boswell (and probably Lord Hailes) supplied information about Thomson, who, together with John Pomfret, Sir Richard Blackmore, Thomas Yalden, and Isaac Watts, was included in the edition at Johnson's own suggestion.[3] Details of Watts's life were sought from William Sharp, who had some of the poet's letters in his possession; and to Richard Farmer Johnson wrote first in 1777, and again in 1780, stating on the former occasion that if suitable material were available at Cambridge, he would tell the booksellers to employ someone to transcribe it, or even make the journey to consult it himself.[4] From David Garrick he received Dryden's notes on Rymer, and from Dr. William Vyse, rector of Lambeth, Dryden's letter to his sons in Rome; while from the Sheriff of London he hoped for information concerning Settle's office of 'city poet'.[5] When in his earlier years Johnson had intended to write a Life of Dryden, he had sent Samuel Derrick to gather what details he could from the poet's relatives. Indeed, much of Johnson's knowledge, especially of his near-contemporaries, must have come from what he had been told.

---

[1] *Letters*, nos. 654, 657–8, 701; *YJ*, i. 301.

[2] *Letters*, nos. 580.1, 651, 671, 683, 694–6; cf. below, pp. 360, 366.

[3] *Life*, ii. 63–4, iii. 116–17, 133, 359, iv. 35 n. 3; *Life of Watts*, par. 1; *Letters*, nos. 515, 526.

[4] *Letters*, nos. 526, 530, 673; *Life*, iii. 126 n. 1.

[5] *Letters*, nos. 578.1 and n., 582 and n.; cf. below, pp. 140–1, *Lives of the Poets*, ed. G. B. Hill (Oxford, 1905), i. 376 n. 2.

Richard Savage he openly acknowledges as one such source. From Lord Marchmont he was to learn details of Pope; though his most important single source for this Life was undoubtedly the manuscript of Spence's *Anecdotes*, which was lent to him by courtesy of the Duke of Newcastle.[1] Numerous friends, including Joseph Warton, Charles Burney, Mrs. Thrale, and George Steevens, helped him in various other ways as well, though Steevens was the only person thanked by name in Johnson's later Advertisement to the 1783 edition.[2]

Before he returned to London in 1777, Johnson had half-seriously suggested to Mrs. Thrale that she might write some of the Lives for him. Certainly he was disposed to take whatever short-cuts seemed reasonable. He reprinted some of his own earlier work—the *Life of Savage* (1744), *A Dissertation on the Epitaphs written by Pope* (1756), and the account of Collins (1763); and adopted William Oldisworth's memoir of Edmund Smith, and a Life of Young by Herbert Croft of Lincoln's Inn, a friend of the poet's son. He also proposed that the 'historical account' of Lord Lyttelton's life should be the responsibility of the poet's brother Lord Westcote, adding that, to avoid offence, he would confine himself to an examination of the poetry. But Westcote declined his proposal, and within the week Johnson was to write ruefully to Mrs. Thrale: 'I sent to Lord Westcote about his brother's life, but he says he knows not whom to employ, and is sure I shall do him no injury. There is an ingenious scheme to save a day's work or part of a day utterly defeated.'[3]

As a biographer, Johnson made considerable use of printed sources. To Westcote he had replied in the following terms: 'For the life of Lord Lyttelton I shall need no help—it was very public, and I have no need to be minute;' yet he was soon writing to Nichols: 'I expected to have found a Life of Lord Lyttelton prefixed to his Works. Is there not one before the quarto edition? I think there is— if not I am, with respect to him, quite aground.'[4] Johnson's constant debt to such sources can be illustrated by the following paragraph from the Life of Milton, with notes to cite the earliest printed authorities for his statements:

Fortune appears not to have had much of his care. In the civil wars he lent his personal estate to the Parliament; but when, after the contest was decided, he solicited repayment, he met not only with neglect but 'sharp

---

[1] *Life*, i. 456, iii. 392, iv. 63, 482–3.

[2] Ibid. iii. 191, iv. 37; *Letters*, nos. 551, 561.1, 652, 668, 672, 689.1.

[3] *Letters*, nos. 554, 688, 690.

[4] Ibid. nos. 689, 698.

rebuke',[1] and having tired both himself and his friends, was given up to poverty and hopeless indignation till he showed how able he was to do greater service. He was then made Latin Secretary[2] with £200 a year,[3] and had £1000 for his *Defence of the People*.[4] His widow, who after his death retired to Nantwich in Cheshire, and died about 1729,[5] is said to have reported that he lost £2000 by entrusting it to a scrivener, and that in the general depredation upon the Church he had grasped an estate of about £60 a year belonging to Westminster Abbey, which, like other sharers of the plunder of rebellion, he was afterwards obliged to return.[6] Two thousand pounds which he had placed in the Excise Office were also lost.[7] There is yet no reason to believe that he was ever reduced to indigence. His wants being few were competently supplied. He sold his library before his death,[8] and left his family £1500,[9] on which his widow laid hold and only gave £100 to each of his daughters.[10]

1. *Mr John Milton's Character of the Long Parliament and Assembly of Divines* (1681), *CM*, xviii. 247.
2. Wood, *EL*, pp. 39, 43.
3. Newton, i. *liv*.
4. Toland, *EL*, p. 158.
5. Newton, i. *lvi*. [Cf. below, p. 352.]
6. Birch (1738), i. *lxii*.
7. Wood, *EL*, p. 48.
8. Toland, ibid. pp. 192–3.
9. Phillips, ibid. p. 78.
10. Birch (1738), i. *lxii*.

Thus the *Lives* are distinguished not so much by original research, as by the skill and relevance with which their author has reworked and compressed available material.

Yet, though Johnson as a biographer drew freely on printed sources, his final portraits are in no sense derivative. Conscious of the shortcomings of Sprat's undiscriminating and partial estimate of Cowley, he sought to give prominence to such details as would clearly highlight the individual character. And his own insights in this respect were often shrewd and penetrating. He had, after all, been a lifelong student of men and manners, and openly acknowledged both his fondness for biography and the moral importance he attached to it.[1] Sometimes, however, he may be regarded as taking too much upon himself in interpreting fact, and certain portraits, most notably those of Milton and Gray, are coloured by his rather pessimistic view of human nature and his own forthright personality and opinions.

That we value Johnson's work so highly today is primarily because of the literary criticism it contains. Even where we disagree with particular judgements, its combination of percipience and reasoned argument constantly forces us to justify the grounds for advancing a

[1] Cf. *Rambler* 60; *Idler* 84; *Life*, i. 425, iv. 34, v. 79.

different assessment. The modern critic finds such judgements stimulating. Many others are directly illuminating. The *Lives of the Poets* is also of interest because, in its expected affinities with neo-classical criticism, it tends to present us with a definite perspective or viewpoint on a variety of poetic modes.

One might therefore have assumed (as has usually been claimed)[1] that Johnson was most at home in dealing with those poets who wrote within the Augustan tradition. Certainly the Life of Dryden, which is among his best criticism, is discerning and judicious, recognizing not only Dryden's superiority to his immediate predecessors, Denham, Waller, and Cowley, but also inherent limitations in his overall poetic achievement. The Life of Pope, however, for all its excellence as biography, is arguably less successful as criticism. Though Johnson readily appreciates the metrical skill, sophisticated wit, and imaginative brilliance which set Pope so far above his near-contemporaries, he ultimately fails to grapple with those objections to the poet's genius that were already being advanced.

Since Johnson considered Cowley's his best Life,[2] one is naturally prompted to ask how successful is his criticism of other than Augustan poetic modes. In general it must be said that, however lively his critical intelligence, many of his remarks stemmed from neo-classical assumptions about language and poetic form. He condemned most of Gray's poetry—the *Elegy* excepted—for a use of words that seemed to him artificial, affected, and potentially a threat to the stability of the English language. He further held that metaphysical wit in avowedly elegiac poetry was such as to declare the professed emotion counterfeit—a neo-classical criterion of 'sincerity' also largely responsible for his howler in dismissing *Lycidas*. In *Comus* he argued a clash of form and content, describing it as 'a drama in the epic style, inelegantly splendid and tediously instructive'. Yet he was generally a critic who, to adapt his own phrase, knew, but was above the rules.[3] He responded to most forms of poetic originality, and praised not only *The Rape of the Lock*, but achievements as diverse as the intellectual vigour of the metaphysicals, and the quality of perception reflected in Thomson's *Seasons*.

Even where Johnson most obviously employs the analytic method of the neo-classical period, as in discussing *Paradise Lost* under the

[1] Cf. George Watson, *The Literary Critics: A Study of English Descriptive Criticism* (1964), p. 94.

[2] *Life*, iv. 38.

[3] Cf. *Diary & Letters of Madam D'Arblay* (*1778–1840*), ed. Austin Dobson (1904–5), i. 183–4.

conventional headings of fable, characters, sentiments, and diction, he makes us feel the force of his own individual response. What finally differentiates his criticism of Milton's epic from Addison's is the conflict it sets up within his own breast. Though imaginatively committed for moral and religious reasons to the excellence of its grand design, another side of his nature is compelled to acknowledge the poem's 'want of human interest'. And this is but the central paradox in an argument fraught with fascinating contradictions. It has been suggested that in this instance Johnson's critical method resembles that of a 'moderator considering both sides of the argument' in order to reach a judgement;[1] but such a description, though it underlines the attempt at objectivity, only denatures the quality and immediacy of his complex and divided response to the work.

The present selection contains the Lives of seven of the best known poets represented in Johnson's 'Prefaces': Cowley, Milton, Dryden, Pope, Thomson, Collins, and Gray. (The Life of Cowley has been included not only because Johnson himself thought it his best, but because it contains remarks obviously addressed to the work of Donne, the most important poet of the metaphysical school.) Such a principle of selection has meant that other notable Lives—like that of Swift, and the earlier, incomparable Life of Savage—have had to be omitted; but within the space available, the Lives reproduced here do, I believe, give the clearest impression of Johnson's range and achievement as a critic of English poetry.

The previous Oxford text of the *Lives* was that prepared by George Birkbeck Hill, who produced in 1905 what has since remained the standard edition, and to whose informative (though often prolix) annotation every future editor must be indebted. Certainly my own debt to Hill is great. In some places, however, his text is faulty, and it has therefore been necessary to produce a fresh one for this edition. Johnson's first edition (1779–81) has been taken as the copy-text, and all relevant substantive changes introduced from the London editions of 1781 and 1783. Use has also been made of extant proof-sheets bearing the author's manuscript corrections. These authorize, for example, the reading '. . . the pains and the pleasures of other minds' (p. 12), even though all other printed editions read 'pleasure' for 'pleasures'.

In accordance with the editorial policy of this series, Johnson's text has been modernized (except that the original division into sentences and paragraphs has been retained); and notes have been

---

[1] D. M. Hill, 'Johnson as Moderator', *NQ*, cci (1956), 522.

placed at both the foot of the page and the end of the book. Misprints in the text have been silently corrected, but Johnson's misquotations have been reprinted. Examples of misquoted titles are *Virgin Martyr* for *Royal Martyr* (p. 130), and *Albion and Albania* for *Albion and Albanius* (p. 131). Misquotations in passages of both prose and verse are frequent, and some of these are interesting—especially Johnson's 'fecundine' for 'secondine' in Cowley's ode 'The Muse' (p. 34).[1] Proper names are given their accepted modern form; and, wherever necessary, words have been converted to numerals (e.g. '1,750 copies' for 'seventeen hundred and fifty copies', 'Charles I' for 'Charles the first') and vice versa (e.g. 'forty-ninth year' for '49th year').

Footnotes are confined to the glossing of words and allusions which are not included in the *Concise Oxford Dictionary*, or of which the particular sense may not be obvious to a modern reader; short biographical notes; the identification of most quotations and works mentioned in the text; brief literary references; and bibliographical or other material wherever this can be appropriately added to an existing note.[2] Otherwise this material, together with all longer notes, and information of a general or explanatory kind, is relegated to the end-notes, the occurrence of such a note being indicated in the text by a supralinear 'n'. The first end-note to every Life lists the main MS. or printed sources used by Johnson in writing it. All biographical references to Virgil can be found in the *Life* attributed to Donatus. References to Shakespeare's plays are as given in *The London Shakespeare*, ed. John Munro (1958), in 6 vols. In bibliographical references the place of publication, unless specified, is London. Cross-references are not usually given within a single Life.

I wish gratefully to acknowledge the award of a grant from the Myer Foundation Fund of the Australian Humanities Research Council which enabled me to spend two months in Oxford working on this edition, and the kind hospitality of the President and Fellows of Magdalen College during my stay among them. From the staff of the Bodleian Library, the Australian National Library, and the Library of the University of New England, I have received every assistance. Mrs. Karen Jennings, my research assistant, has been

---

[1] Cf. J. D. Fleeman, 'Some Proofs of Johnson's *Prefaces to the Poets*', *The Library*, xvii (1962), 216 n. 1.

[2] Historical or mythological figures as well known as Alexander, Dante, or Venus, are not glossed, and no notes have been given to English kings and princes. Nor has any attempt been made to annotate words or allusions explained in the standard modern editions of the authors from whom Johnson quotes.

conscientious in following up references, as has my secretary Miss Margaret Murray in typing the manuscript. Friends have always been most willing to help. In particular I should like to thank Mr. G. G. Barber, Mr. J. C. Eade, Professor Cecil Grayson, Dr. Mary Hyde, Mr. Emrys Jones, Mr. K. H. P. Lee, Dr. Roger Lonsdale, Professor R. D. Milns, Dr. L. F. Powell (who supervised my first work on Johnson), Dr. Robert Shackleton, and Mr. J. S. G. Simmons. To Miss Mary Lascelles, who has been characteristically generous of her time and knowledge at all stages of the work, and to Mr. John Buxton, who has proved most helpful as the general editor of this series, I owe a special debt of gratitude. My very great thanks are also due to Dr. J. D. Fleeman who, with his wife Isabel, made me so welcome during my stay in Oxford, and has, more recently, willingly supplied many references, and advised me on numerous problems.

Chronological Table

1709	Johnson born at Lichfield, 18 Sept.
1728–9	Undergraduate of Pembroke College, Oxford.
1732	Temporarily usher (or schoolmaster's assistant) at Market Bosworth School.
1733	Translated Lobo's *Voyage to Abyssinia* (published 1735).
1735	Married the widow Elizabeth Porter; opened private school at Edial, near Lichfield.
1737	Moved to London; worked at unfinished tragedy *Irene*.
1738	Began writing for *The Gentleman's Magazine; London.*
1740–43	Reported debates in parliament (published in *The Gentleman's Magazine* 1741–4 as 'Debates in the Senate of Lilliput').
1744	*An Account of the Life of Mr. Richard Savage.*
1745	*Miscellaneous Observations on the Tragedy of Macbeth.*
1747	*The Plan of a Dictionary of the English Language.*
1749	*The Vanity of Human Wishes; Irene.*
1750–52	*The Rambler.*
1752	Death of his wife.
1753–4	Contributed to *The Adventurer.*
1755	*A Dictionary of the English Language.*
1756	*Proposals for an Edition of Shakespeare*; contributed to and probably edited *The Literary Magazine.*
1758–60	*The Idler.*
1759	Death of his mother; *Rasselas.*
1762	Awarded pension of £300 p.a.
1763	Met James Boswell.
1764	The Club founded (other foundation-members included Beauclerk, Burke, Goldsmith, Hawkins, Langton, Reynolds).
1765	Met Thrales; received LL.D. from Dublin; edition of *The Plays of William Shakespeare.*
1770	*The False Alarm.*
1771	*Thoughts on the Late Transactions respecting Falkland's Islands.*
1773	Revised *Dictionary* (4th folio ed.); toured Scotland with Boswell.
1774	Journeyed with Thrales through Midlands into North Wales; *The Patriot.*
1775	*A Journey to the Western Islands of Scotland; Taxation No Tyranny;* received D.C.L. from Oxford; visited France with Thrales.
1779–81	*The Lives of the Poets.*
1781	Death of Henry Thrale.
1783	Revised *Lives of the Poets* (3rd London ed.); founded Essex Head Club.
1784	Died in Bolt Court, Fleet Street, 13 Dec.; buried in Westminster Abbey.

Abbreviations

CM	*The Columbia Edition of the Works of John Milton*, gen. ed. F. A. Patterson (New York, 1931–40), 20 vols.
Cowley: Essays	*Abraham Cowley: Essays, Plays, and Sundry Verses*, ed. A. R. Waller (Cambridge, 1906).
Cowley: Poems	*Abraham Cowley: Poems*, ed. A. R. Waller (Cambridge, 1905).
Dennis	*The Critical Works of John Dennis*, ed. E. N. Hooker (Baltimore, Maryland, 1939–43), 2 vols.
Derrick	*The Miscellaneous Works of John Dryden*, ed. Samuel Derrick (London, 1760), 4 vols.
Dict.	Samuel Johnson, *A Dictionary of the English Language* (London, 1755), 2 vols.
Dryden: DW	*Dryden: The Dramatic Works*, ed. Montague Summers (London, 1931–2), 6 vols.
Dryden: Essays	*John Dryden: Of Dramatic Poesy and other Critical Essays*, ed. George Watson (London, 1962), 2 vols.
Dryden: Letters	*The Letters of John Dryden*, ed. C. E. Ward (Durham, N. C., 1942; repr. New York, 1965).
Dryden: Poems	*The Poems of John Dryden*, ed. James Kinsley (Oxford, 1958), 4 vols.
EL	*The Early Lives of Milton*, ed. Helen Darbishire (London, 1932).
Essay on Pope	Joseph Warton, *An Essay on the Genius and Writings of Pope* (London, 1762, 2nd rev. ed.).
GM	*The Gentleman's Magazine.*
Grant	Douglas Grant, *James Thomson, Poet of the Seasons* (London, 1951).
Gray: Corr.	*The Correspondence of Thomas Gray*, ed. Paget Toynbee and Leonard Whibley (Oxford, 1935), 3 vols.
Letters	*The Letters of Samuel Johnson*, ed. R. W. Chapman (Oxford, 1952), 3 vols.
Life	*Boswell's Life of Johnson* (*Together with Boswell's Journal of a Tour to the Hebrides and Johnson's Diary of a Journey into North Wales*), ed. G. B. Hill, rev. L. F. Powell (Oxford, 1934–50), 6 vols.
LR	*The Life Records of John Milton*, ed. J. Milton French (New Brunswick, N.J., 1949–58), 5 vols.
Mason	William Mason, *Poems of Mr. Gray: to which are prefixed Memoirs of his Life and Writings* (London, 1775, 2nd rev. ed.).
Murdoch	*The Works of James Thomson*, ed. Patrick Murdoch (London, 1762, 4°), 2 vols.
Newton	*Paradise Lost ... A New Edition*, ed. Thomas Newton (London, 1749), 2 vols.
OED	*The Oxford English Dictionary.*
Oeuvres	*Les Oeuvres de M. Boileau Despréaux, Nouvelle édition* (Paris, 1747), 5 vols.

Osborn   James M. Osborn, *John Dryden: Some Biographical Facts and Problems* (Gainesville, Fla., 1965, 2nd rev. ed.).

Parker   W. R. Parker, *Milton: A Biography* (Oxford, 1968), 2 vols.

PL   *Paradise Lost.*

Pope: Corr.   *The Correspondence of Alexander Pope*, ed. George Sherburn (Oxford, 1956), 5 vols.

Pope: Poems   *The Twickenham Edition of the Poems of Alexander Pope*, gen. ed. John Butt (London, 1939–67), 10 vols.

Rehearsal   George Villiers, *The Rehearsal*, ed. Montague Summers (London, 1914).

Ruffhead   Owen Ruffhead, *The Life of Alexander Pope . . . with a Critical Essay on his Writings and Genius* (London, 1769).

Rymer   *The Critical Works of Thomas Rymer*, ed. C. A. Zimansky (New Haven, Conn., 1956).

Sherburn   George Sherburn, *The Early Career of Alexander Pope* (Oxford, 1934; repr. 1968).

Spence   Joseph Spence, *Observations, Anecdotes, and Characters of Books and Men*, ed. J. M. Osborn (Oxford, 1966), 2 vols.

Spingarn   *Critical Essays of the Seventeenth Century*, ed. J. E. Spingarn (Oxford, 1908–9; repr. 1957), 3 vols.

Swift: Corr.   *The Correspondence of Jonathan Swift*, ed. Harold Williams (Oxford, 1963–5), 5 vols.

Thomson: Letters *James Thomson (1700–1748): Letters and Documents*, ed. A. D. McKillop (Lawrence, Mass., 1958).

Walpole: Corr.   *Horace Walpole's Correspondence*, gen. ed. W. S. Lewis (New Haven, Conn., 1937–).

Warburton   *The Works of Alexander Pope . . . with his last Corrections, Additions, and Improvements*, ed. William Warburton (London, 1751, 2nd ed.), 9 vols.

Ward   Charles E. Ward, *The Life of John Dryden* (Chapel Hill, N.C., 1961).

YJ   *The Yale Edition of the Works of Samuel Johnson*, gen. eds. A. T. Hazen and J. H. Middendorf (New Haven, Conn., 1958–).

The standard abbreviations have been used for the titles of modern literary periodicals.

Reading List

I Lives of the Poets

Editions
Prefaces, Biographical and Critical, to the Works of the English Poets (1779–81), 10 vols.
The Lives of the most eminent English Poets (London, 1781), 4 vols.
The Lives of the most eminent English Poets (London, 1783), 4 vols.
Lives of the English Poets, ed. G. B. Hill (Oxford, 1905; repr. New York, 1967), 3 vols.
(Work on the *Lives of the Poets*, as part of the Yale Edition of the Works of Samuel Johnson, is in progress.)

Books
Bate, W. J. *The Achievement of Samuel Johnson* (New York, 1955), chap. V.
Hagstrum, J. H. *Samuel Johnson's Literary Criticism* (Minneapolis, Minn., 1952).
Krutch, J. W. *Samuel Johnson* (New York, 1944), esp. chap. XII.

Articles
Abrams, M. H. 'Unconscious Expectations in the Reading of Poetry', *ELH*, ix (1942), 235–44; repr. as 'Dr. Johnson's Spectacles' in *New Light on Dr. Johnson*, ed. F. W. Hilles (New Haven, Conn., 1959), pp. 177–87.
Boyce, Benjamin. 'Samuel Johnson's Criticism of Pope in the *Life of Pope*', *RES*, n.s. v (1954), 37–46.
Fleischauer, Warren. 'Johnson, *Lycidas*, and the Norms of Criticism', *Johnsonian Studies*, ed. Magdi Wahba (Cairo, 1962), pp. 235–56.
Hilles, F. W. 'The Making of *The Life of Pope*', in *New Light on Dr. Johnson*, pp. 257–84.
Jones, W. P. 'Johnson and Gray: A Study in Literary Antagonism', *MP*, lvi (1958–9), 243–53.
Keast, W. R. 'Johnson's Criticism of the Metaphysical Poets', *ELH*, xvii (1950), 59–70.
Leavis, F. R. 'Johnson as Critic', *Scrutiny*, xii (Summer 1944), 187–204; repr. in *The Importance of Scrutiny*, ed. Eric Bentley (New York, 1948), pp. 55–75, and in *Samuel Johnson: A Collection of Critical Essays*, ed. D. J. Greene (Englewood Cliffs, N.J., 1965), pp. 70–88.
Perkins, David. 'Johnson on Wit and Metaphysical Poetry', *ELH*, xx (1953), 200–17.
Sigworth, O. F. 'Johnson's *Lycidas*: The End of Renaissance Criticism', *ECS*, i (1967–8), 159–68.
Wesling, Donald. 'An Ideal of Greatness: Ethical Implications in Johnson's Critical Vocabulary', *UTQ*, xxxiv (1964–5), 133–45.

II Other Books on Johnson

Bronson, B. H. *Johnson Agonistes and Other Essays* (Cambridge, 1946), esp. pp. 1–52.

Clifford, J. L. *Young Sam Johnson* (New York, 1955).

Greene, D. J. *The Politics of Samuel Johnson* (New Haven, Conn., 1960).

Hodgart, M. J. C. *Samuel Johnson and his Times* (London, 1962).

Lascelles, M. M. *et al.* (ed.) *Johnson, Boswell and their Circle: Essays Presented to L. F. Powell* (Oxford, 1965).

Quinlan, M. J. *Samuel Johnson: A Layman's Religion* (Madison, Wis., 1964).

Sachs, Arieh. *Passionate Intelligence: Imagination and Reason in the Work of Samuel Johnson* (Baltimore, Maryland, 1967).

Sherbo, Arthur. *Samuel Johnson, Editor of Shakespeare; with an Essay on the 'Adventurer'* (Urbana, Ill., 1956).

Sledd, J. H. and Kolb, G. J. *Dr. Johnson's Dictionary: Essays in the Biography of a Book* (Chicago, Ill., 1955).

Voitle, Robert. *Samuel Johnson the Moralist* (Cambridge, Mass., 1961).

Wimsatt, W. K., Jr. *The Prose Style of Samuel Johnson* (New Haven, Conn., 1941).

—— *Philosophic Words: A Study of Style and Meaning in the 'Rambler' and 'Dictionary' of Samuel Johnson* (New Haven, Conn., 1948).

COWLEY[n]

The Life of Cowley, notwithstanding the penury of English biography, has been written by Dr. Sprat, an author whose pregnancy of imagination and elegance of language have deservedly set him high in the ranks of literature; but his zeal of friendship, or ambition of eloquence, has produced a funeral oration rather than a history: he has given the character not the life of Cowley, for he writes with so little detail that scarcely anything is distinctly known, but all is shown confused and enlarged through the mist of panegyric.

Abraham Cowley was born in the year 1618. His father was a grocer, whose condition Dr. Sprat conceals under the general appellation of a citizen;[n] and, what would probably not have been less carefully suppressed, the omission of his name in the register of St. Dunstan's parish gives reason to suspect that his father was a sectary. Whoever he was, he died before the birth of his son, and consequently left him to the care of his mother, whom Wood represents as struggling earnestly to procure him a literary education, and who, as she lived to the age of eighty, had her solicitude rewarded by seeing her son eminent, and, I hope, by seeing him fortunate and partaking his prosperity. We know at least, from Sprat's account,[n] that he always acknowledged her care, and justly paid the dues of filial gratitude.

In the window of his mother's apartment lay Spenser's *Faerie Queene*,[n] in which he very early took delight to read, till by feeling the charms of verse he became, as he relates, irrecoverably a poet. Such are the accidents which, sometimes remembered, and perhaps sometimes forgotten, produce that particular designation of mind and propensity for some certain science or employment which is commonly called genius. The true genius is a mind of large general powers accidentally determined to some particular direction. Sir Joshua Reynolds, the great painter of the present age, had the first fondness for his art excited by the perusal of Richardson's treatise.

Dr. Sprat: Thomas Sprat (1635–1713), Bishop of Rochester and Dean of Westminster.
his father: Thomas Cowley (d. 1618).
his mother: Thomasine Cowley (*fl.* 1618–37).
Wood: Anthony à Wood (1632–95), Oxford antiquary and historian.
Spenser's: Edmund Spenser (1552?–99), poet.
science: branch of knowledge.
Sir Joshua Reynolds: (1723–92). Cf. James Northcote, *Life of Sir Joshua Reynolds* (1818, 2nd rev. ed.), i. 14.
Richardson's: Jonathan Richardson the elder (1665–1745), portrait-painter and author of *An Essay on the Theory of Painting* (1715).

By his mother's solicitation he was admitted into Westminster School, where he was soon distinguished. He was wont, says Sprat, to relate 'that he had this defect in his memory at that time, that his teachers never could bring it to retain the ordinary rules of grammar'.

This is an instance of the natural desire of man to propagate a wonder. It is surely very difficult to tell anything as it was heard, when Sprat could not refrain from amplifying a commodious incident though the book to which he prefixed his narrative contained its confutation. A memory admitting some things and rejecting others, an intellectual digestion that concocted the pulp of learning but refused the husks, had the appearance of an instinctive elegance, of a particular provision made by nature for literary politeness. But in the author's own honest relation the marvel vanishes: he was, he says, such 'an enemy to all constraint that his master never could prevail on him to learn the rules without book'. He does not tell that he could not learn the rules but that, being able to perform his exercises without them, and being an 'enemy to constraint', he spared himself the labour.

Among the English poets, Cowley, Milton and Pope might be said 'to lisp in numbers', and have given such early proofs not only of powers of language but of comprehension of things as to more tardy minds seems scarcely credible. But of the learned puerilities of Cowley there is no doubt, since a volume of his poems was not only written but printed in his thirteenth year,[n] containing, with other poetical compositions, *The Tragical History of Pyramus and Thisbe*, written when he was ten years old, and *Constantia and Philetus*, written two years after.

While he was yet at school he produced a comedy called *Love's Riddle*, though it was not published till he had been some time at Cambridge.[n] This comedy is of the pastoral kind, which requires no acquaintance with the living world, and therefore the time at which it was composed adds little to the wonders of Cowley's minority.

In 1636 he was removed to Cambridge, where he continued his studies with great intenseness, for he is said to have written while he was yet a young student the greater part of his *Davideis*, a work of

---

'*that he had this defect*': Spingarn, ii. 121.

concocted: 'digest[ed] by the stomach, so as to turn food to nutriment' (*Dict.*), a meaning now obs.

'*an enemy*': *Essays*, p. 456.

'*to lisp in numbers*': Pope, *An Epistle to Dr. Arbuthnot*, l. 218.

a volume of his poems: *Poetical Blossomes* (1633).

he is said: Spingarn, ii. 132–3.

which the materials could not have been collected without the study of many years but by a mind of the greatest vigour and activity.

Two years after his settlement at Cambridge he published *Love's Riddle*, with a poetical dedication to Sir Kenelm Digby, of whose acquaintance all his contemporaries seem to have been ambitious, and *Naufragium Joculare*, a comedy written in Latin, but without due attention to the ancient models: for it is not loose verse but mere prose. It was printed with a dedication in verse to Dr. Comber, master of the college, but having neither the facility of a popular nor the accuracy of a learned work, it seems to be now universally neglected.

At the beginning of the Civil War, as the Prince passed through Cambridge in his way to York, he was entertained with the representation of *The Guardian*,[n] a comedy which Cowley says was neither written nor acted, but rough-drawn by him and repeated by the scholars. That this comedy was printed during his absence from his country he appears to have considered as injurious to his reputation; though during the suppression of the theatres[n] it was sometimes privately acted with sufficient approbation.

In 1643, being now Master of Arts, he was by the prevalence of the Parliament ejected from Cambridge,[n] and sheltered himself at St. John's College in Oxford, where, as is said by Wood, he published a satire called *The Puritan and Papist*, which was never inserted in any collection of his works,[n] and so distinguished himself by the warmth of his loyalty and the elegance of his conversation that he gained the kindness and confidence of those who attended the King, and amongst others of Lord Falkland, whose notice cast a lustre on all to whom it was extended.

About the time when Oxford was surrendered to the Parliament[n] he followed the Queen to Paris, where he became secretary to the Lord Jermyn, afterwards Earl of St. Albans, and was employed in such correspondence as the royal cause required, and particularly in ciphering and deciphering the letters that passed between the King and Queen—an employment of the highest confidence and honour.

Sir Kenelm Digby: (1603–65), author, naval commander, and diplomatist.

Dr. Comber: Thomas Comber (1575–1654), Dean of Carlisle and master of Trinity College (1631–44).

which Cowley says: Cowley's 'Preface', Spingarn, ii. 78. Cf. *Essays*, p. 161.

Lord Falkland: Lucius Cary (1610?–43), 2nd Viscount Falkland.

the Queen: Henrietta Maria (1609–69), youngest daughter of Henri IV of France.

Earl of St. Albans: Henry Jermyn (d. 1684) became 1st Earl of St. Albans (1660), having been created Baron Jermyn in 1643.

So wide was his province of intelligence that for several years it filled all his days and two or three nights in the week.

In the year 1647 his *Mistress* was published, for he imagined, as he declared in his preface to a subsequent edition, that 'poets are scarce thought freemen of their company without paying some duties, or obliging themselves to be true to Love'.

This obligation to amorous ditties owes, I believe, its original to the fame of Petrarch, who in an age rude and uncultivated, by his tuneful homage to his Laura, refined the manners of the lettered world and filled Europe with love and poetry. But the basis of all excellence is truth: he that professes love ought to feel its power. Petrarch was a real lover, and Laura doubtless deserved his tenderness. Of Cowley we are told by Barnes, who had means enough of information, that whatever he may talk of his own inflammability, and the variety of characters by which his heart was divided, he in reality was in love but once, and then never had resolution to tell his passion.

This consideration cannot but abate in some measure the reader's esteem for the work and the author. To love excellence is natural; it is natural likewise for the lover to solicit reciprocal regard by an elaborate display of his own qualifications. The desire of pleasing has in different men produced actions of heroism and effusions of wit; but it seems as reasonable to appear the champion as the poet of an 'airy nothing', and to quarrel as to write for what Cowley might have learned from his master Pindar to call the 'dream of a shadow'.

It is surely not difficult in the solitude of a college, or in the bustle of the world, to find useful studies and serious employment. No man needs to be so burdened with life as to squander it in voluntary dreams of fictitious occurrences. The man that sits down to suppose himself charged with treason or peculation, and heats his mind to an elaborate purgation of his character from crimes which he was never within the possibility of committing, differs only by the infrequency of his folly from him who praises beauty which he never saw, complains of jealousy which he never felt, supposes himself sometimes invited and sometimes forsaken, fatigues his fancy and ransacks his

'*poets are*': Spingarn, ii. 85.
Petrarch: Francesco Petrarch (1304–74), Italian poet and humanist.
Barnes: Joshua Barnes (1654–1712), Greek scholar and antiquary; see his *Anacreon* (1705), p. xxxii.
'*airy nothing*': *A Midsummer Night's Dream*, V. i. 16.
Pindar: (518–*c.* 438 B.C.), famous Greek lyric poet; *Pythian Odes*, viii. 95. Cf. Cowley, 'Life and Fame', l. 7 and n.

memory for images which may exhibit the gaiety of hope or the gloominess of despair, and dresses his imaginary Chloris or Phyllis sometimes in flowers fading as her beauty, and sometimes in gems lasting as her virtues.

At Paris, as secretary to Lord Jermyn, he was engaged in transacting things of real importance with real men and real women, and at that time did not much employ his thoughts upon phantoms of gallantry. Some of his letters to Mr. Bennet, afterwards Earl of Arlington, from April to December in 1650,[n] are preserved in *Miscellanea Aulica*, a collection of papers published by Brown. These letters, being written like those of other men whose mind is more on things than words, contribute no otherwise to his reputation than as they show him to have been above the affectation of unseasonable elegance, and to have known that the business of a statesman can be little forwarded by flowers of rhetoric.

One passage, however, seems not unworthy of some notice. Speaking of the Scotch treaty then in agitation:

'The Scotch treaty', says he, 'is the only thing now in which we are vitally concerned; I am one of the last hopers, and yet cannot now abstain from believing that an agreement will be made: all people upon the place incline to that of union. The Scotch will moderate something of the rigour of their demands; the mutual necessity of an accord is visible, the King is persuaded of it. And to tell you the truth (which I take to be an argument above all the rest) Virgil has told the same thing to that purpose'.[n]

This expression from a secretary of the present time would be considered as merely ludicrous, or at most as an ostentatious display of scholarship; but the manners of that time were so tinged with superstition that I cannot but suspect Cowley of having consulted on this great occasion the Virgilian lots,[n] and to have given some credit to the answer of his oracle.

Some years afterwards 'business', says Sprat, 'passed of course into other hands', and Cowley, being no longer useful at Paris, was in 1656 sent back into England, that 'under pretence of privacy and retirement he might take occasion of giving notice of the posture of things in this nation'.

Soon after his return to London, he was seized by some messengers of the usurping powers who were sent out in quest of another man, and being examined, was put into confinement, from which he

---

Mr. Bennet: Henry Bennet (1618–85), 1st Earl of Arlington.
Brown: Thomas Brown (1663–1704), satirist and miscellaneous writer.
says Sprat: Spingarn, ii. 124.

was not dismissed without the security of £1,000 given by Dr. Scarburgh.

This year he published his poems, with a preface, in which he seems to have inserted something, suppressed in subsequent editions,[n] which was interpreted to denote some relaxation of his loyalty. In this preface he declares that 'his desire had been for some years past, and did still very vehemently continue, to retire himself to some of the American plantations, and to forsake this world for ever'.

From the obloquy which the appearance of submission to the usurpers brought upon him his biographer has been very diligent to clear him, and indeed it does not seem to have lessened his reputation. His wish for retirement we can easily believe to be undissembled; a man harassed in one kingdom and persecuted in another, who, after a course of business that employed all his days and half his nights in ciphering and deciphering, comes to his own country and steps into a prison, will be willing enough to retire to some place of quiet and of safety. Yet let neither our reverence for a genius nor our pity for a sufferer dispose us to forget that, if his activity was virtue, his retreat was cowardice.

He then took upon himself the character of physician, still, according to Sprat, with intention 'to dissemble the main design of his coming over', and, as Mr. Wood relates, 'complying with the men then in power (which was much taken notice of by the royal party), he obtained an order to be created Doctor of Physic, which being done to his mind (whereby he gained the ill-will of some of his friends), he went into France again, having made a copy of verses on Oliver's death'.

This is no favourable representation, yet even in this not much wrong can be discovered. How far he complied with the men in power is to be inquired before he can be blamed. It is not said that he told them any secrets, or assisted them by intelligence or any other act. If he only promised to be quiet, that they in whose hands he was might free him from confinement, he did what no law of society prohibits.

The man whose miscarriage in a just cause has put him in the power of his enemy may, without any violation of his integrity, regain his liberty or preserve his life by a promise of neutrality, for the stipulation gives the enemy nothing which he had not before: the neutrality of a captive may be always secured by his imprisonment

Dr. Scarburgh: Sir Charles Scarburgh (1616–94), physician.
'*his desire*': Spingarn, ii. 82.
according to Sprat: ibid. ii. 135.
Oliver's: Oliver Cromwell (1599–1658), the Protector.

or death. He that is at the disposal of another may not promise to aid him in any injurious act, because no power can compel active obedience. He may engage to do nothing, but not to do ill.

There is reason to think that Cowley promised little. It does not appear that his compliance gained him confidence enough to be trusted without security, for the bond of his bail was never cancelled; nor that it made him think himself secure, for at that dissolution of government which followed the death of Oliver he returned into France, where he resumed his former station and stayed till the Restoration.

'He continued', says his biographer, 'under these bonds till the general deliverance'; it is therefore to be supposed that he did not go to France and act again for the King without the consent of his bondsman, that he did not show his loyalty at the hazard of his friend but by his friend's permission.

Of the verses on Oliver's death, in which Wood's narrative seems to imply something encomiastic, there has been no appearance. There is a discourse concerning his government, indeed, with verses intermixed, but such as certainly gained its author no friends among the abettors of usurpation.

A doctor of physic however he was made at Oxford in December 1657; and in the commencement of the Royal Society, of which an account has been published by Dr. Birch, he appears busy among the experimental philosophers with the title of Dr. Cowley.

There is no reason for supposing that he ever attempted practice; but his preparatory studies have contributed something to the honour of his country. Considering botany as necessary to a physician, he retired into Kent to gather plants; and as the predominance of a favourite study affects all subordinate operations of the intellect, botany in the mind of Cowley turned into poetry. He composed in Latin several books on plants, of which the first and second display the qualities of herbs in elegiac verse, the third and fourth the beauties of flowers in various measures, and in the fifth and sixth the uses of trees in heroic numbers.[n]

At the same time were produced from the same university the two great poets Cowley and Milton,[n] of dissimilar genius, of opposite principles, but concurring in the cultivation of Latin poetry, in

'*He continued*': Spingarn, ii. 124.

a discourse: *A Discourse by way of Vision* (*Cowley: Essays*, pp. 342–76).

Dr. Birch: Thomas Birch (1705–66), divine and author, secretary of the Royal Society (1752–65); see *The History of the Royal Society of London* (1756–7), i. 17.

which the English, till their works and May's poem appeared, seemed unable to contest the palm with any other of the lettered nations.

If the Latin performances of Cowley and Milton be compared—for May I hold to be superior to both—the advantage seems to lie on the side of Cowley. Milton is generally content to express the thoughts of the ancients in their language; Cowley, without much loss of purity or elegance, accommodates the diction of Rome to his own conceptions.

At the Restoration, after all the diligence of his long service, and with consciousness not only of the merit of fidelity but of the dignity of great abilities, he naturally expected ample preferments, and that he might not be forgotten by his own fault wrote a Song of Triumph.[n] But this was a time of such general hope that great numbers were inevitably disappointed, and Cowley found his reward very tediously delayed. He had been promised by both Charles I and II the Mastership of the Savoy, but 'he lost it', says Wood, 'by certain persons, enemies to the Muses'.

The neglect of the Court was not his only mortification; having, by such alteration as he thought proper, fitted his old comedy of *The Guardian* for the stage, he produced it to the public under the title of the *Cutter of Coleman Street*. It was treated on the stage with great severity, and was afterwards censured as a satire on the King's party.

Mr. Dryden, who went with Mr. Sprat to the first exhibition, related to Mr. Dennis 'that when they told Cowley how little favour had been shown him, he received the news of his ill success not with so much firmness as might have been expected from so great a man'.

What firmness they expected, or what weakness Cowley discovered, cannot be known. He that misses his end will never be as much pleased as he that attains it, even when he can impute no part of his failure to himself; and when the end is to please the multitude, no man perhaps has a right, in things admitting of gradation and comparison, to throw the whole blame upon his judges and totally to exclude diffidence and shame by a haughty consciousness of his own excellence.

For the rejection of this play it is difficult now to find the reason:

May's: Thomas May (1595–1650), author of *Supplementum Lucani* (1640), a translation of his *Continuation of Lucan's Historicall Poem* (1630).
the Savoy: the Hospital of the Savoy.
Mr. Dennis: John Dennis (1657–1734), critic and lesser playwright; see *The Comical Gallant* (1702), sig. *a2*; cf. *Dennis*, i. 289.

it certainly has, in a very great degree, the power of fixing attention and exciting merriment. From the charge of disaffection he exculpates himself in his preface by observing how unlikely it is that, having followed the royal family through all their distresses, 'he should choose the time of their restoration to begin a quarrel with them'. It appears, however, from the Theatrical Register of Downes the prompter to have been popularly considered as a satire on the Royalists.

That he might shorten this tedious suspense he published his pretensions and his discontent in an ode called 'The Complaint', in which he styles himself the 'melancholy' Cowley. This met with the usual fortune of complaints, and seems to have excited more contempt than pity.

These unlucky incidents are brought maliciously enough together in some stanzas, written about that time, on the choice of a laureate—a mode of satire by which, since it was first introduced by Suckling, perhaps every generation of poets has been teased:[n]

> Savoy-missing Cowley came into the Court,
>   Making apologies for his bad play;
> Everyone gave him so good a report,
>   That Apollo gave heed to all he could say;
> Nor would he have had, 'tis thought, a rebuke,
>   Unless he had done some notable folly;
> Writ verses unjustly in praise of Sam Tuke,[n]
>   Or printed his pitiful Melancholy.

His vehement desire of retirement now came again upon him. 'Not finding', says the morose Wood, 'that preferment conferred upon him which he expected, while others for their money carried away most places, he retired discontented into Surrey.'

'He was now', says the courtly Sprat, 'weary of the vexations and formalities of an active condition. He had been perplexed with a long compliance to foreign manners. He was satiated with the arts of a Court; which sort of life, though his virtue made it innocent to him, yet nothing could make it quiet. Those were the reasons that moved him to follow the violent inclination of his own mind, which, in the

by observing: *Cowley*: *Essays*, p. 261.

Downes: John Downes (*fl.* 1662–1710), prompter to Sir William Davenant's company; see his *Roscius Anglicanus* (1708), p. 25 n.

Suckling: Sir John Suckling (1609–42), poet.

Savoy-missing Cowley: 'The Session of the Poets', *Poems on Affairs of State* (1697), p. 219.

Sam Tuke: Sir Samuel Tuke (d. 1671), 1st Baronet, royalist and playwright.

'*He was now*': Spingarn, ii. 127.

greatest throng of his former business, had still called upon him, and represented to him the true delights of solitary studies, of temperate pleasures, and a moderate revenue below the malice and flatteries of fortune.'

So differently are things seen and so differently are they shown; but actions are visible though motives are secret. Cowley certainly retired, first to Barn-Elms, and afterwards to Chertsey, in Surrey. He seems, however, to have lost part of his dread of the 'hum of men'. He thought himself now safe enough from intrusion without the defence of mountains and oceans, and instead of seeking shelter in America, wisely went only so far from the bustle of life as that he might easily find his way back when solitude should grow tedious. His retreat was at first but slenderly accommodated, yet he soon obtained, by the interest of the Earl of St. Albans and the Duke of Buckingham, such a lease of the Queen's lands as afforded him an ample income.

By the lover of virtue and of wit it will be solicitously asked if he now was happy. Let them peruse one of his letters accidentally preserved by Peck, which I recommend to the consideration of all that may hereafter pant for solitude.

Chertsey 21 May 1665

To Dr. Thomas Sprat

The first night that I came hither I caught so great a cold, with a defluxion of rheum, as made me keep my chamber ten days. And, two after, had such a bruise on my ribs with a fall that I am yet unable to move or turn myself in my bed. This is my personal fortune here to begin with. And besides, I can get no money from my tenants, and have my meadows eaten up every night by cattle put in by my neighbours. What this signifies, or may come to in time, God knows; if it be ominous, it can end in nothing less than hanging. Another misfortune has been, and stranger than all the rest, that you have broke your word with me and failed to come, even though you told Mr. Bois that you would. This is what they call *monstri simile*. I do hope to recover my late hurt so far within five or six days (though it be uncertain yet whether I shall ever recover it) as to walk about again. And then, methinks, you and I and the Dean[n] might be very merry upon St. Anne's Hill. You

'*hum of men*': Milton, 'L'Allegro', l. 118.
Duke of Buckingham: George Villiers (1628–87), 2nd Duke of Buckingham.
Peck: Francis Peck (1692–1743), antiquary; see *Memoirs of the Life and Actions of Oliver Cromwell* (1740), pt. II, pp. 81–2.
Mr. Bois: A Mr. Bois is mentioned by Pepys in his diary entry for 20 Aug. 1664.
monstri simile: Terence, *Eunuchus*, II. iii. 43 or l. 334 ('like an apparition').

might very conveniently come hither the way of Hampton
Town, lying there one night. I write this in pain and can
say no more: *verbum sapienti.*

He did not long enjoy the pleasure or suffer the uneasiness of
solitude, for he died at the Porch House in Chertsey in 1667, in the
forty-ninth year of his age.

He was buried with great pomp near Chaucer and Spenser, and
King Charles pronounced 'that Mr. Cowley had not left a better man
behind him in England'.[n] He is represented by Dr. Sprat as the most
amiable of mankind, and this posthumous praise may be safely credited as it has never been contradicted by envy or by faction.

Such are the remarks and memorials which I have been able to add
to the narrative of Dr. Sprat who, writing when the feuds of the Civil
War were yet recent, and the minds of either party easily irritated,
was obliged to pass over many transactions in general expressions,
and to leave curiosity often unsatisfied. What he did not tell cannot
however now be known. I must therefore recommend the perusal of
his work, to which my narration can be considered only as a slender
supplement.

Cowley, like other poets who have written with narrow views, and
instead of tracing intellectual pleasure to its natural sources in the
mind of man, paid their court to temporary prejudices, has been at
one time too much praised, and too much neglected at another.

Wit, like all other things subject by their nature to the choice of
man, has its changes and fashions, and at different times takes
different forms. About the beginning of the seventeenth century
appeared a race of writers that may be termed the metaphysical
poets,[n] of whom, in a criticism on the works of Cowley, it is not
improper to give some account.

The metaphysical poets were men of learning, and to show their
learning was their whole endeavour; but unluckily resolving to show
it in rhyme, instead of writing poetry they only wrote verses, and very
often such verses as stood the trial of the finger better than of the ear,
for the modulation was so imperfect that they were only found to be
verses by counting the syllables.

If the father of criticism has rightly denominated poetry τέχνη

---

verbum sapienti: a word to the wise.
He is represented: Spingarn, ii. 139 ff.
the father of criticism: i.e. Aristotle, who throughout the *Poetics* speaks of poetry
    as a form of μιμησις, 'imitation'.

μιμητικὴ, 'an imitative art', these writers will, without great wrong, lose their right to the name of poets, for they cannot be said to have imitated anything: they neither copied nature nor life, neither painted the forms of matter nor represented the operations of intellect.[n]

Those however who deny them to be poets allow them to be wits. Dryden confesses of himself and his contemporaries that they fall below Donne in wit, but maintains that they surpass him in poetry.

If wit be well described by Pope as being 'that which has been often thought, but was never before so well expressed', they certainly never attained nor ever sought it, for they endeavoured to be singular in their thoughts, and were careless of their diction. But Pope's account of wit is undoubtedly erroneous: he depresses it below its natural dignity, and reduces it from strength of thought to happiness of language.

If by a more noble and more adequate conception that be considered as wit which is at once natural and new, that which, though not obvious, is upon its first production acknowledged to be just; if it be that which he that never found it wonders how he missed—to wit of this kind the metaphysical poets have seldom risen. Their thoughts are often new but seldom natural; they are not obvious, but neither are they just; and the reader, far from wondering that he missed them, wonders more frequently by what perverseness of industry they were ever found.

But wit, abstracted from its effects upon the hearer, may be more rigorously and philosophically considered as a kind of *discordia concors*, a combination of dissimilar images or discovery of occult resemblances in things apparently unlike. Of wit thus defined they have more than enough. The most heterogeneous ideas are yoked by violence together; nature and art are ransacked for illustrations, comparisons and allusions; their learning instructs and their subtlety surprises, but the reader commonly thinks his improvement dearly bought, and though he sometimes admires, is seldom pleased.

From this account of their compositions it will be readily inferred that they were not successful in representing or moving the affections. As they were wholly employed on something unexpected and surprising, they had no regard to that uniformity of sentiment which enables us to conceive and to excite the pains and the pleasures of

Donne: John Donne (1573–1631), poet and divine. Cf. *Dryden: Essays*, ii. 144.
described by Pope: *An Essay on Criticism*, l. 298.
discordia concors: Manilius, *Astronomicon*, i. 142 ('harmonious discord'). Cf. *Spectator* 62.

other minds: they never inquired what, on any occasion, they should have said or done, but wrote rather as beholders than partakers of human nature, as beings looking upon good and evil impassive and at leisure, as Epicurean deities making remarks on the actions of men and the vicissitudes of life without interest and without emotion. Their courtship was void of fondness and their lamentation of sorrow. Their wish was only to say what they hoped had been never said before.

Nor was the sublime more within their reach than the pathetic,[n] for they never attempted that comprehension and expanse of thought which at once fills the whole mind, and of which the first effect is sudden astonishment, and the second rational admiration. Sublimity is produced by aggregation, and littleness by dispersion. Great thoughts are always general, and consist in positions not limited by exceptions, and in descriptions not descending to minuteness. It is with great propriety that subtlety, which in its original import means exility of particles, is taken in its metaphorical meaning for nicety of distinction. Those writers who lay on the watch for novelty could have little hope of greatness, for great things cannot have escaped former observation. Their attempts were always analytic: they broke every image into fragments, and could no more represent, by their slender conceits and laboured particularities, the prospects of nature or the scenes of life, than he who dissects a sunbeam with a prism can exhibit the wide effulgence of a summer noon.

What they wanted however of the sublime they endeavoured to supply by hyperbole; their amplification had no limits: they left not only reason but fancy behind them, and produced combinations of confused magnificence that not only could not be credited, but could not be imagined.

Yet great labour directed by great abilities is never wholly lost; if they frequently threw away their wit upon false conceits, they likewise sometimes struck out unexpected truth; if their conceits were far-fetched, they were often worth the carriage. To write on their plan it was at least necessary to read and think. No man could be born a metaphysical poet, nor assume the dignity of a writer, by descriptions copied from descriptions, by imitations borrowed from imitations, by traditional imagery and hereditary similes, by readiness of rhyme and volubility of syllables.

In perusing the works of this race of authors, the mind is exercised either by recollection or inquiry: either something already learned

Epicurean deities: Epicurus (341–270 B.C.), Greek philosopher, asserted that the gods existed in perfect repose and were indifferent to human affairs.

is to be retrieved, or something new is to be examined. If their greatness seldom elevates, their acuteness often surprises; if the imagination is not always gratified, at least the powers of reflection and comparison are employed; and in the mass of materials which ingenious absurdity has thrown together, genuine wit and useful knowledge may be sometimes found, buried perhaps in grossness of expression, but useful to those who know their value, and such as, when they are expanded to perspicuity and polished to elegance, may give lustre to works which have more propriety though less copiousness of sentiment.

This kind of writing, which was, I believe, borrowed from Marino and his followers, had been recommended by the example of Donne, a man of very extensive and various knowledge, and by Jonson, whose manner resembled that of Donne more in the ruggedness of his lines than in the cast of his sentiments.

When their reputation was high, they had undoubtedly more imitators than time has left behind. Their immediate successors of whom any remembrance can be said to remain were Suckling, Waller, Denham, Cowley, Cleveland and Milton. Denham and Waller sought another way to fame by improving the harmony of our numbers. Milton tried the metaphysic style only in his lines upon Hobson the carrier. Cowley adopted it and excelled his predecessors, having as much sentiment and more music. Suckling neither improved versification nor abounded in conceits. The fashionable style remained chiefly with Cowley; Suckling could not reach it, and Milton disdained it.

Critical remarks are not easily understood without examples, and I have therefore collected instances of the modes of writing by which this species of poets—for poets they were called by themselves and their admirers—was eminently distinguished.

As the authors of this race were perhaps more desirous of being admired than understood, they sometimes drew their conceits from recesses of learning not very much frequented by common readers of poetry. Thus Cowley on Knowledge:

Marino: Giambattista Marino (1569–1625), the foremost poet of the *secentisti*.
Jonson: Ben Jonson (1573?–1637), dramatist and poet.
Waller: Edmund Waller (1606–87), poet and M.P.
Denham: Sir John Denham (1615–69), poet.
Cleveland: John Cleveland (1613–58), poet.
Hobson the carrier: Thomas Hobson (1544?–1631), Cambridge carrier, commemorated by Milton in two poems, 'On the University Carrier' and 'Another on the Same'.

The sacred tree midst the fair orchard grew;
  The phoenix Truth did on it rest,
  And built his perfumed nest,
That right Porphyrian tree[n] which did true Logic shew.
  Each leaf did learned notions give,
  And th' apples were demonstrative:
  So clear their colour and divine,
The very shade they cast did other lights outshine.

On Anacreon continuing a lover in his old age:

  Love was with thy life entwined,
  Close as heat with fire is joined,
  A powerful brand prescribed the date
  Of thine, like Meleager's fate.
  Th' antiperistasis of age
  More enflamed thy amorous rage.

In the following verses we have an allusion to a Rabbinical opinion concerning manna:

  Variety I ask not: give me one
  To live perpetually upon.
  The person Love does to us fit,
  Like manna, has the taste of all in it.

Thus Donne shows his medicinal knowledge in some encomiastic verses:

  In everything there naturally grows
  A balsamum to keep it fresh and new,
    If 'twere not injured by extrinsic blows;
  Your youth and beauty are this balm in you.
    But you, of learning and religion,
  And virtue and such ingredients, have made
    A mithridate, whose operation
  Keeps off, or cures what can be done or said.

Though the following lines of Donne on the last night of the year have something in them too scholastic, they are not inelegant:

The sacred tree: 'The Tree of Knowledge'. *Poems*, p. 45.
Anacreon: (6th cent. B.C.), Greek lyric poet. 'Elegy upon Anacreon'. *Poems*, p. 60.
Meleager's fate: Meleager's mother Althaea saved him at his birth by snatching from the flames the brand on which the Fates declared his life to depend; but angrily threw it into the fire again on his slaying of her brothers after the boar-hunt.
antiperistasis: 'opposition or contrast of circumstances; the force of contrast or contrariness' (*OED*).
Variety I ask not: 'Resolved to be beloved'. *Poems*, p. 96.
In everything: 'To the Countess of Bedford' ('Reason is our soul's left hand'), ll. 21–8.

This twilight of two years, not past nor next,
  Some emblem is of me, or I of this,
Who, meteor-like, of stuff and form perplexed,
  Whose what and where in disputation is,
  If I should call me anything, should miss.
I sum the years and me, and find me not
  Debtor to th' old, nor creditor to th' new,
That cannot say, my thanks I have forgot,
  Nor trust I this with hopes; and yet scarce true
  This bravery is, since these times showed me you.

Yet more abstruse and profound is Donne's reflection upon man as a microcosm:

If men be worlds, there is in everyone
Something to answer in some proportion
All the world's riches: and in good men, this
Virtue, our form's form, and our soul's soul is.

Of thoughts so far-fetched as to be not only unexpected but unnatural, all their books are full.

To a Lady, who wrote posies for rings

They, who above do various circles find,
Say, like a ring th' equator heaven does bind.
  When heaven shall be adorned by thee
  (Which then more heaven than 'tis, will be),
  'Tis thou must write the poesy there,
  For it wanteth one as yet,
  Though the sun pass through't twice a year,
The sun, which is esteemed the god of wit.

Cowley

The difficulties which have been raised about identity in philosophy are by Cowley with still more perplexity applied to love:

Five years ago (says story) I loved you,
For which you call me most inconstant now;
Pardon me, madam, you mistake the man;
For I am not the same that I was then;
No flesh is now the same 'twas then in me,
And that my mind is changed yourself may see.
The same thoughts to retain still, and intents,
Were more inconstant far; for accidents
Must of all things most strangely inconstant prove,

This twilight: 'To the Countess of Bedford' ('At New Year's Tide'), ll. 1–10.
If men be worlds: 'To Mr. R. W.' ('If, as mine is, thy life'), ll. 29–32.
To a Lady: Poems, p. 31.
poesy: Johnson's original spelling is here left unmodernized as it makes more
  obvious the wit of Cowley's lines.
Five years ago: 'Inconstancy'. Poems, p. 74.

If from one subject they t' another move:
My members then, the father members were
From whence these take their birth, which now are here.
If then this body love what th' other did,
'Twere incest, which by nature is forbid.

The love of different women is in geographical poetry compared to travels through different countries:

Hast thou not found, each woman's breast
(The lands where thou hast travelled)
Either by savages possessed,
Or wild, and uninhabited?
What joy could'st take, or what repose,
In countries so uncivilised as those?

Lust, the scorching dog-star, here
Rages with immoderate heat;
Whilst Pride, the rugged Northern Bear,
In others makes the cold too great.
And where these are temperate known,
The soil's all barren sand, or rocky stone.

COWLEY

A lover, burnt up by his affection, is compared to Egypt:

The fate of Egypt I sustain,
And never feel the dew of rain,
From clouds which in the head appear;
But all my too much moisture owe
To overflowings of the heart below.

COWLEY

The lover supposes his lady acquainted with the ancient laws of augury and rites of sacrifice:

And yet this death of mine, I fear,
Will ominous to her appear,
When sound in every other part,
Her sacrifice is found without an heart.
For the last tempest of my death
Shall sigh out that too, with my breath.

COWLEY

That the chaos was harmonized has been recited of old; but whence the different sounds arose remained for a modern to discover:

Hast thou not found: 'The Welcome'. *Poems*, p. 104.
The fate of Egypt: 'Sleep'. *Poems*, p. 115.
And yet this death: 'The Concealment'. *Poems*, p. 120.
That the chaos: Ovid, *Metamorphoses*, i. 21 ff. Cf. Plato, *Timaeus*, 69b–c.

> Th' ungoverned parts no correspondence knew,
> An artless war from thwarting motions grew;
> Till they to number and fixed rules were brought.
> Water and air he for the tenor chose,
> Earth made the base, the treble flame arose.
>
> COWLEY

The tears of lovers are always of great poetical account, but Donne
has extended them into worlds. If the lines are not easily understood,
they may be read again.

> On a round ball
> A workman, that hath copies by, can lay
> An Europe, Afric, and an Asia,
> And quickly make that, which was nothing, all.
> So doth each tear,
> Which thee doth wear,
> A globe, yea world, by that impression grow,
> Till thy tears mixed with mine do overflow
> This world, by waters sent from thee my heaven dissolved so.

On reading the following lines the reader may perhaps cry out—
'Confusion worse confounded'.

> Here lies a she sun, and a he moon here,
> She gives the best light to his sphere,
> Or each is both, and all, and so
> They unto one another nothing owe.
>
> DONNE

Who but Donne would have thought that a good man is a telescope?

> Though God be our true glass, through which we see
> All, since the being of all things is he,
> Yet are the trunks, which do to us derive
> Things in proportion fit, by perspective,
> Deeds of good men; for by their living here,
> Virtues, indeed remote, seem to be near.

Who would imagine it possible that in a very few lines so many
remote ideas could be brought together?

Th' ungoverned parts: *Davideis*, i. *Poems*, p. 253.
On a round ball: 'A Valediction: of Weeping', ll. 10–18.
'Confusion worse confounded': *PL*, ii. 996.
Here lies: 'An Epithalamion, or Marriage-Song on the Lady Elizabeth and Count
   Palatine being married on St. Valentine's day', ll. 85–8.
Though God: 'Obsequies to the Lord Harrington, brother to the Lady Lucy,
   Countess of Bedford', ll. 35–40.

Since 'tis my doom, Love's undershrieve,
    Why this reprieve?
Why doth my She advowson fly
    Incumbency?
To sell thyself dost thou intend
    By candle's end,
And hold the contract thus in doubt,
    Life's taper out?
Think, but how soon the market fails,
Your sex lives faster than the males;
As if to measure age's span,
The sober Julian were th' account of man,
Whilst you live by the fleet Gregorian.

CLEVELAND

Of enormous and disgusting hyperboles, these may be examples:

By every wind, that comes this way,
Send me at least a sigh or two,
Such and so many I'll repay
As shall themselves make winds to get to you.

COWLEY

In tears I'll waste these eyes,
    By love so vainly fed;
So lust of old the Deluge punished.

COWLEY

All armed in brass, the richest dress of war,
(A dismal glorious sight) he shone afar.
The sun himself started with sudden fright,
To see his beams return so dismal bright.

COWLEY

An universal consternation:

His bloody eyes he hurls round, his sharp paws
Tear up the ground; then runs he wild about,
Lashing his angry tail and roaring out.
Beasts creep into their dens, and tremble there;
Trees, though no wind is stirring, shake with fear;
Silence and horror fill the place around:
Echo itself dares scarce repeat the sound.

COWLEY

Since 'tis my doom: 'To Julia to expedite her Promise', ll. 1–4, 10–18.

Gregorian: Pope Gregory XIII (1502–85) in 1582 reformed the calendar introduced by Julius Caesar in 46 B.C., in order to bring it into closer conformity
with astronomical observation. The Gregorian calendar corrected the excess
of 11 minutes 10 seconds in the Julian year, and was to that extent 'fleet'.

By every wind: 'Friendship in Absence'. *Poems*, p. 28.

In tears I'll waste: 'The Despair'. *Poems*, p. 86.

All armed in brass: *Davideis* iii. *Poems*, pp. 333–4.

His bloody eyes: *Davideis*,   *Poems*, p. 258.

Their fictions were often violent and unnatural.
Of his Mistress bathing:

> The fish around her crowded, as they do
> To the false light that treacherous fishers shew,
> And all with as much ease might taken be,
>   As she at first took me:
>   For ne'er did light so clear
>   Among the waves appear,
> Though every night the sun himself set there.

COWLEY

The poetical effect of a lover's name upon glass:

> My name engraved herein,
> Doth contribute my firmness to this glass;
>   Which, ever since that charm, hath been
>   As hard as that which graved it was.

DONNE

Their conceits were sometimes slight and trifling.
On an inconstant woman:

> He enjoys thy calmy sunshine now,
>   And no breath stirring hears,
> In the clear heaven of thy brow,
>   No smallest cloud appears.
>   He sees thee gentle, fair and gay,
> And trusts the faithless April of thy May.

COWLEY

Upon a paper written with the juice of lemon, and read by the
fire:

> Nothing yet in thee is seen;
> But when a genial heat warms thee within,
> A new-born wood of various lines there grows;
>   Here buds an L, and there a B,
>   Here sprouts a V, and there a T,
> And all the flourishing letters stand in rows.

COWLEY

As they sought only for novelty, they did not much inquire whether
their allusions were to things high or low, elegant or gross; whether
they compared the little to the great or the great to the little.

The fish around her: 'Bathing in the River'. *Poems*, p. 150.
My name engraved: 'A Valediction: of my Name in the Window', ll. 1–4.
On an inconstant woman: 'Ode in imitation of Horace's Ode'. *Poems*, p. 38.
Upon a paper: 'Written in Juice of Lemon'. *Poems*, p. 73.

Physic and Chirurgery for a Lover

Gently, ah gently, madam, touch
   The wound, which you yourself have made;
That pain must needs be very much,
   Which makes me of your hand afraid.
Cordials of pity give me now,
For I too weak for purgings grow.

COWLEY

The World and a Clock.

Mahol, th' inferior world's fantastic face,
Through all the turns of matter's maze did trace;
Great Nature's well-set clock in pieces took;
On all the springs and smallest wheels did look
Of life and motion; and with equal art
Made up again the whole of every part.

COWLEY

A coal-pit has not often found its poet; but that it may not want its
due honour, Cleveland has paralleled it with the sun:

The moderate value of our guiltless ore
Makes no man atheist, and no woman whore;
Yet why should hallowed vestal's sacred shrine
Deserve more honour than a flaming mine?
These pregnant wombs of heat would fitter be
Than a few embers, for a deity.
Had he our pits, the Persian would admire
No sun, but warm's devotion at our fire:
He'd leave the trotting whipster, and prefer
Our profound Vulcan 'bove that waggoner.
For wants he heat, or light? or would have store
Of both? 'tis here: and what can suns give more?
Nay, what's the sun but, in a different name,
A coal-pit rampant, or a mine on flame!
Then let this truth reciprocally run,
The sun's heaven's coalery, and coals our sun.[n]

Death a Voyage:

            No family
Ere rigged a soul for heaven's discovery,
With whom more venturers might boldly dare
Venture their stakes, with him in joy to share.

DONNE

Their thoughts and expressions were sometimes grossly absurd,
and such as no figures or licence can reconcile to the understanding.

Chirurgery: surgery. 'Counsel'. *Poems*, p. 94.
The World and a Clock: *Davideis*, i. *Poems*, pp. 260–1.
Death a Voyage: 'Elegy on the L.C.'. ll. 13–16.

A Lover neither dead nor alive:

> Then down I laid my head,
> Down on cold earth; and for a while was dead,
> And my freed soul to a strange somewhere fled:
>   Ah, sottish soul, said I,
> When back to its cage again I saw it fly:
>   Fool to resume her broken chain!
>   And row her galley here again!
>   Fool, to that body to return
> Where it condemned and destined is to burn!
>   Once dead, how can it be,
> Death should a thing so pleasant seem to thee,
> That thou shoud'st come to live it o'er again in me?

COWLEY

A Lover's heart, a hand grenado.

> Woe to her stubborn heart, if once mine come
>   Into the self-same room,
>   'Twill tear and blow up all within,
> Like a grenado shot into a magazin.
> Then shall Love keep the ashes, and torn parts,
>   Of both our broken hearts:
>   Shall out of both one new one make;
> From hers th' alloy; from mine, the metal take.

COWLEY

The poetical Propagation of Light:

> The prince's favour is diffused o'er all,
> From which all fortunes, names, and natures fall;
> Then from those wombs of stars, the bride's bright eyes,
>   At every glance a constellation flies,
> And sows the court with stars, and doth prevent
>   In light and power, the all-eyed firmament:
> First her eye kindles other ladies' eyes,
>   Then from their beams their jewels' lustres rise;
> And from their jewels torches do take fire,
> And all is warmth, and light, and good desire.

DONNE

They were in very little care to clothe their notions with elegance of dress, and therefore miss the notice and the praise which are often gained by those who think less, but are more diligent to adorn their thoughts.

That a mistress beloved is fairer in idea than in reality is by Cowley thus expressed:

A Lover neither dead: 'The Despair'. *Poems*, p. 87.
A Lover's heart: 'The given Heart'. *Poems*, pp. 100–1.
The poetical Propagation: 'Eclogue, 1613', ll. 23–32.

> Thou in my fancy dost much higher stand,
> Than women can be placed by Nature's hand;
> And I must needs, I'm sure, a loser be,
> To change thee, as thou'rt there, for very thee.

That prayer and labour should co-operate are thus taught by Donne:

> In none but us are such mixed engines found
> As hands of double office: for the ground
> We till with them; and them to heaven we raise;
> Who prayerless labours, or without this, prays,
> Doth but one half, that's none.

By the same author a common topic, the danger of procrastination, is thus illustrated:

> —That which I should have begun
> In my youth's morning, now late must be done;
> And I, as giddy travellers must do,
> Which stray or sleep all day, and having lost
> Light and strength, dark and tired must then ride post.

All that man has to do is to live and die; the sum of humanity is comprehended by Donne in the following lines:

> Think in how poor a prison thou didst lie;
> After, enabled but to suck and cry.
> Think, when 'twas grown to most, 'twas a poor inn,
> A province packed up in two yards of skin,
> And that usurped, or threatened with a rage
> Of sicknesses, or their true mother, age.
> But think that death hath now enfranchised thee;
> Thou hast thy expansion now, and liberty;
> Think, that a rusty piece discharged is flown
> In pieces, and the bullet is his own,
> And freely flies; this to thy soul allow,
> Think thy shell broke, think thy soul hatched but now.

They were sometimes indelicate and disgusting. Cowley thus apostrophizes beauty:

> Thou tyrant, which leav'st no man free!
> Thou subtle thief, from whom nought safe can be!
> Thou murd'rer, which hast killed, and devil, which
> would'st damn me!

Thou in my fancy: 'Against Fruition'. *Poems*, p. 99.
In none but us: 'To the Countess of Bedford' ('T' have w ritten then'), ll. 43–47.
That which I should: 'To Mr. B. B.' ('Is not thy sacred hunger'), ll. 10–14.
Think in how poor: 'The Second Anniversary', ll. 173–84.
Thou tyrant: 'Beauty'. *Poems*, p. 117.

Thus he addresses his mistress:

> Thou, who in many a propriety,
> So truly art the sun to me,
> Add one more likeness, which I'm sure you can,
> And let me and my sun beget a man.

Thus he represents the meditations of a lover:

> Though in thy thoughts scarce any tracts have been
> So much as of original sin,
> Such charms thy beauty wears as might
> Desire in dying confessed saints excite.
> Thou with strange adultery
> Dost in each breast a brothel keep;
> Awake, all men do lust for thee,
> And some enjoy thee when they sleep.

The true taste of Tears:

> Hither with crystal vials, lovers, come,
> And take my tears, which are love's wine,
> And try your mistress' tears at home;
> For all are false that taste not just like mine.

DONNE

This is yet more indelicate:

> As the sweet sweat of roses in a still,
> As that which from chafed musk-cat's pores doth trill,
> As the almighty balm of th' early East,
> Such are the sweet drops of my mistress' breast;
> And on her neck her skin such lustre sets,
> They seem no sweat-drops, but pearl coronets.
> Rank sweaty froth thy mistress' brow defiles.

DONNE

Their expressions sometimes raise horror, when they intend perhaps to be pathetic:

> As men in hell are from diseases free,
> So from all other ills am I,
> Free from their known formality:
> But all pains eminently lie in thee.

COWLEY

Thou, who in many: 'The Parting'. *Poems*, p. 118.
Though in thy thoughts: 'The Innocent Ill'. *Poems*, pp. 145–6.
Hither with crystal: 'Twickenham Garden', ll. 19–22.
As the sweet: 'The Comparison', ll. 1–7.
As men in hell: 'The Usurpation'. *Poems*, p. 128.
formality: 'the characteristic or distinctive property by which a thing is defined. Also, the condition of possessing formal existence' (*OED*), a sense now obs.

They were not always strictly curious whether the opinions from which they drew their illustrations were true; it was enough that they were popular. Bacon remarks that some falsehoods are continued by tradition because they supply commodious allusions.

> It gave a piteous groan, and so it broke;
> In vain it something would have spoke:
> The love within too strong for 't was,
> Like poison put into a Venice glass.

COWLEY

In forming descriptions they looked out not for images but for conceits. Night has been a common subject which poets have contended to adorn. Dryden's Night is well known; Donne's is as follows:

> Thou seest me here at midnight, now all rest:
> Time's dead low-water; when all minds divest
> Tomorrow's business, when the labourers have
> Such rest in bed that their last churchyard grave,
> Subject to change, will scarce be a type of this,
> Now when the client, whose last hearing is
> Tomorrow, sleeps; when the condemned man,
> Who when he opes his eyes, must shut them then
> Again by death, although sad watch he keep,
> Doth practise dying by a little sleep,
> Thou at this midnight seest me.

It must be however confessed of these writers that if they are upon common subjects often unnecessarily and unpoetically subtle, yet where scholastic speculation can be properly admitted their copiousness and acuteness may justly be admired. What Cowley has written upon Hope shows an unequalled fertility of invention:

> Hope, whose weak being ruined is,
> Alike if it succeed, and if it miss;
> Whom good or ill does equally confound,
> And both the horns of Fate's dilemma wound.
>   Vain shadow, which dost vanish quite,
>   Both at full noon and perfect night!
>   The stars have not a possibility
>   Of blessing thee;
> If things then from their end we happy call,
> 'Tis Hope is the most hopeless thing of all.

Bacon: Sir Francis Bacon (1561–1626), 1st Baron Verulam and Viscount St. Alban, Lord Chancellor, essayist; see *The Advancement of Learning* (1605), II. i. 3.
It gave a piteous groan: 'The Heart-Breaking'. *Poems*, p. 126.
Dryden's Night: see below, pp. 117, 178.
Thou seest me here: 'Obsequies to the Lord Harrington', ll. 15–25.
Hope: 'Against Hope'. *Poems*, pp. 109–10.

> Hope, thou bold taster of delight,
> Who, whilst thou should'st but taste, devour'st it quite!
> Thou bring'st us an estate, yet leav'st us poor,
> By clogging it with legacies before!
>   The joys which we entire should wed,
>   Come deflowered virgins to our bed;
> Good fortunes without gain imported be,
>   Such mighty custom's paid to thee:
> For joy, like wine, kept close does better taste;
> If it take air before, its spirits waste.

To the following comparison of a man that travels, and his wife that stays at home, with a pair of compasses, it may be doubted whether absurdity or ingenuity has the better claim:

> Our two souls therefore, which are one,
>   Though I must go, endure not yet
> A breach, but an expansion,
>   Like gold to airy thinness beat.
>
> If they be two, they are two so
>   As stiff twin compasses are two,
> Thy soul the fixed foot, makes no show
>   To move, but doth, if th' other do.
>
> And though it in the centre sit,
>   Yet when the other far doth roam,
> It leans, and hearkens after it,
>   And grows erect, as that comes home.
>
> Such wilt thou be to me, who must
>   Like th' other foot, obliquely run.
> Thy firmness makes my circle just,
>   And makes me end where I begun.
>
>   DONNE

In all these examples it is apparent that whatever is improper or vicious is produced by a voluntary deviation from nature in pursuit of something new and strange, and that the writers fail to give delight by their desire of exciting admiration.

Having thus endeavoured to exhibit a general representation of the style and sentiments of the metaphysical poets, it is now proper to examine particularly the works of Cowley, who was almost the last of that race, and undoubtedly the best.

His *Miscellanies* contain a collection of short compositions, written some as they were dictated by a mind at leisure, and some as they were called forth by different occasions, with great variety of style and sentiment from burlesque levity to awful grandeur. Such

Our two souls: 'A Valediction: forbidding Mourning', ll. 21–36.

an assemblage of diversified excellence no other poet has hitherto afforded. To choose the best among many good is one of the most hazardous attempts of criticism. I know not whether Scaliger himself has persuaded many readers to join with him in his preference of the two favourite odes, which he estimates in his raptures at the value of a kingdom.[n] I will however venture to recommend Cowley's first piece, which ought to be inscribed 'To my Muse', for want of which the second couplet is without reference. When the title is added there will still remain a defect, for every piece ought to contain in itself whatever is necessary to make it intelligible. Pope has some epitaphs without names, which are therefore epitaphs to be let, occupied indeed for the present, but hardly appropriated.

The ode on Wit is almost without a rival. It was about the time of Cowley that *wit*, which had been till then used for 'intellection' in contradistinction to 'will', took the meaning, whatever it be, which it now bears.

Of all the passages in which poets have exemplified their own precepts, none will easily be found of greater excellence than that in which Cowley condemns exuberance of wit:

> Yet 'tis not to adorn and gild each part,
> That shows more cost than art.
> Jewels at nose and lips but ill appear;
> Rather than all things wit, let none be there.
> Several lights will not be seen,
> If there be nothing else between.
> Men doubt, because they stand so thick i' th' sky,
> If those be stars which paint the galaxy.

In his verses to Lord Falkland, whom every man of his time was proud to praise, there are, as there must be in all Cowley's compositions, some striking thoughts; but they are not well wrought. His elegy on Sir Henry Wotton is vigorous and happy, the series of thoughts is easy and natural, and the conclusion, though a little weakened by the intrusion of Alexander, is elegant and forcible.

It may be remarked that in this elegy, and in most of his encomiastic poems, he has forgotten or neglected to name his heroes.

In his poem on the death of Harvey, there is much praise but little passion, a very just and ample delineation of such virtues as a studious privacy admits, and such intellectual excellence as a mind not

Scaliger: Julius Caesar Scaliger (1484–1558), foremost scholar of his day.
Cowley's first piece: This poem is entitled 'The Motto'.
Yet 'tis not to adorn: 'Ode, Of Wit'. *Poems*, p. 17.
Sir Henry Wotton: (1568–1639), diplomat and poet.
Harvey: William Harvey (1578–1657), discoverer of the circulation of the blood.

yet called forth to action can display. He knew how to distinguish and how to commend the qualities of his companion; but when he wishes to make us weep he forgets to weep himself, and diverts his sorrow by imagining how his crown of bays, if he had it, would 'crackle' in the 'fire'. It is the odd fate of this thought to be worse for being true. The bay-leaf crackles remarkably as it burns; as therefore this property was not assigned it by chance, the mind must be thought sufficiently at ease that could attend to such minuteness of physiology. But the power of Cowley is not so much to move the affections as to exercise the understanding.

'The Chronicle' is a composition unrivalled and alone: such gaiety of fancy, such facility of expression, such varied similitude, such a succession of images, and such a dance of words, it is vain to expect except from Cowley. His strength always appears in his agility: his volatility is not the flutter of a light but the bound of an elastic mind. His levity never leaves his learning behind it; the moralist, the politician, and the critic mingle their influence even in this airy frolic of genius. To such a performance Suckling could have brought the gaiety but not the knowledge, Dryden could have supplied the knowledge but not the gaiety.

The verses to Davenant, which are vigorously begun and happily concluded, contain some hints of criticism very justly conceived and happily expressed. Cowley's critical abilities have not been sufficiently observed; the few decisions and remarks which his prefaces and his notes on the *Davideis* supply were at that time accessions to English literature, and show such skill as raises our wish for more examples.

The lines from Jersey are a very curious and pleasing specimen of the familiar descending to the burlesque.

His two metrical disquisitions *for* and *against* Reason are no mean specimens of metaphysical poetry. The stanzas against knowledge produce little conviction. In those which are intended to exalt the human faculties, Reason has its proper task assigned it: that of judging, not of things Revealed, but of the reality of Revelation. In the verses *for* Reason is a passage which Bentley, in the only English verses which he is known to have written, seems to have copied, though with the inferiority of an imitator.

---

when he wishes: cf. Horace, *Ars Poetica*, ll. 102–3.
Davenant: Sir William Davenant (1606–68), poet and dramatist.
for and against Reason: 'Reason'; 'The Tree of Knowledge'.
Bentley: Richard Bentley (1662–1742), scholar and critic.

The holy Book like the eighth sphere does shine
  With thousand lights of truth divine,
So numberless the stars that to our eye
  It makes all but one galaxy:
Yet Reason must assist too; for in seas
  So vast and dangerous as these,
Our course by stars above we cannot know
  Without the compass too below.

After this says Bentley:

Who travels in religious jars,
Truth mixed with error, clouds with rays,
With Whiston wanting pyx and stars,
In the wide ocean sinks or strays.

Cowley seems to have had—what Milton is believed to have wanted—the skill to rate his own performances by their just value, and has therefore closed his *Miscellanies* with the verses upon Crashaw, which apparently excel all that have gone before them, and in which there are beauties which common authors may justly think not only above their attainment, but above their ambition.

To the *Miscellanies* succeed the *Anacreontics*, or paraphrastical translations of some little poems which pass, however justly, under the name of Anacreon. Of those songs dedicated to festivity and gaiety, in which even the morality is voluptuous, and which teach nothing but enjoyment of the present day, he has given rather a pleasing than a faithful representation, having retained their sprightliness but lost their simplicity. The Anacreon of Cowley, like the Homer of Pope, has admitted the decoration of some modern graces, by which he is undoubtedly made more amiable to common readers, and perhaps, if they would honestly declare their own perceptions, to far the greater part of those whom courtesy and ignorance are content to style the learned.

These little pieces will be found more finished in their kind than any other of Cowley's works. The diction shows nothing of the mould of time, and the sentiments are at no great distance from our present habitudes of thought. Real mirth must always be natural, and nature is uniform. Men have been wise in very different modes, but they have always laughed the same way.

Who travels: *The Grove, or a Collection of Original Poems* (1721), p. 228.
Whiston: William Whiston (1667–1752), divine and Lucasian professor, banished
  from Cambridge for his attack on the accepted doctrine of the Trinity.
pyx: 'the mariner's compass. *Obs. rare*' (*OED*).
what Milton: see below, p. 86.
Crashaw: Richard Crashaw (1613?–49), poet.

Levity of thought naturally produced familiarity of language, and the familiar part of language continues long the same: the dialogue of comedy, when it is transcribed from popular manners and real life, is read from age to age with equal pleasure. The artifice of inversion, by which the established order of words is changed, or of innovation, by which new words or new meanings of words are introduced, is practised not by those who talk to be understood, but by those who write to be admired.

The *Anacreontics* therefore of Cowley give now all the pleasure which they ever gave. If he was formed by nature for one kind of writing more than for another, his power seems to have been greatest in the familiar and the festive.

The next class of his poems is called *The Mistress*, of which it is not necessary to select any particular pieces for praise or censure. They have all the same beauties and faults, and nearly in the same proportion. They are written with exuberance of wit and with copiousness of learning, and it is truly asserted by Sprat that the plenitude of the writer's knowledge flows in upon his page so that the reader is commonly surprised into some improvement. But considered as the verses of a lover, no man that has ever loved will much commend them. They are neither courtly nor pathetic, have neither gallantry nor fondness. His praises are too far-sought and too hyperbolical either to express love or to excite it: every stanza is crowded with darts and flames, with wounds and death, with mingled souls, and with broken hearts.

The principal artifice by which *The Mistress* is filled with conceits is very copiously displayed by Addison. Love is by Cowley, as by other poets, expressed metaphorically by flame and fire, and that which is true of real fire is said of love, or figurative fire, the same word in the same sentence retaining both significations. Thus, 'observing the cold regard of his mistress's eyes, and at the same time their power of producing love in him, he considers them as burning-glasses made of ice. Finding himself able to live in the greatest extremities of love, he concludes the torrid zone to be habitable. Upon the dying of a tree, on which he had cut his loves, he observes that his flames had burnt up and withered the tree'.[n]

These conceits Addison calls mixed wit, that is, wit which consists of thoughts true in one sense of the expression and false in the other. Addison's representation is sufficiently indulgent. That confusion of

asserted by Sprat: Spingarn, ii. 131.
Addison: Joseph Addison (1672–1719), essayist, poet, and statesman; see
    Spectator 62.

images may entertain for a moment, but being unnatural it soon grows wearisome. Cowley delighted in it as much as if he had invented it, but not to mention the ancients, he might have found it full-blown in modern Italy.

> Aspice quam variis distringar Vesbia curis,
>   Uror, et heu! nostro manat ab igne liquor;
> Sum Nilus, sumque Aetna simul; restringite flammas
>   O lacrimae, aut lacrimas ebibe flamma meas.[n]

One of the severe theologians of that time censured him as having published 'a book of profane and lascivious verses'.[n] From the charge of profaneness the constant tenor of his life, which seems to have been eminently virtuous, and the general tendency of his opinions, which discover no irreverence of religion, must defend him; but that the accusation of lasciviousness is unjust the perusal of his works will sufficiently evince.

Cowley's *Mistress* has no power of seduction: 'she plays round the head, but comes not at the heart'. Her beauty and absence, her kindness and cruelty, her disdain and inconstancy, produce no correspondence of emotion. His poetical account of the virtues of plants and colours of flowers is not perused with more sluggish frigidity. The compositions are such as might have been written for penance by a hermit, of for hire by a philosophical rhymer who had only heard of another sex, for they turn the mind only on the writer whom, without thinking on a woman but as the subject for his task, we sometimes esteem as learned and sometimes despise as trifling, always admire as ingenious and always condemn as unnatural.

The *Pindaric Odes* are now to be considered, a species of composition which Cowley thinks Pancirolus might have counted 'in his list of the lost inventions of antiquity', and which he has made a bold and vigorous attempt to recover.

The purpose with which he has paraphrased an Olympic and Nemean ode is by himself sufficiently explained. His endeavour was not to show 'precisely what Pindar spoke, but his manner of speaking'. He was therefore not at all restrained to his expressions, nor much to his sentiments; nothing was required of him but not to write as Pindar would not have written.

Of the Olympic Ode the beginning is, I think, above the original in elegance, and the conclusion below it in strength. The connection is

---

One of the severe theologians: Edmund Elys (*fl.* 1707), divine and poet.
'*plays round*': Pope, *Essay on Man*, IV. 254.
Pancirolus: Guido Panciroli (1523–99), jurisconsult and author of an Italian treatise on the lost inventions of antiquity. Cf. *Cowley: Poems*, p. 156.

supplied with great perspicuity, and the thoughts, which to a reader
of less skill seem thrown together by chance, are concatenated
without any abruption. Though the English ode cannot be called a
translation, it may be very properly consulted as a commentary.

The spirit of Pindar is indeed not everywhere equally preserved.
The following pretty lines are not such as his 'deep mouth' was used
to pour:

> Great Rhea's son,
> If in Olympus' top where thou
> Sitt'st to behold thy sacred show,
> If in Alpheus' silver flight,
> If in my verse thou take delight,
> My verse, great Rhea's son, which is
> Lofty as that, and smooth as this.

In the Nemean Ode the reader must, in mere justice to Pindar,
observe that whatever is said of 'the original new moon, her tender
forehead and her horns' is superadded by his paraphrast, who has
many other plays of words and fancy unsuitable to the original, as,

> The table, free for every guest,
> No doubt will thee admit,
> And feast more upon thee, than thou on it.

He sometimes extends his author's thoughts without improving
them. In the Olympionic an oath is mentioned in a single word, and
Cowley spends three lines in swearing by the 'Castalian Stream'. We
are told of Theron's bounty, with a hint that he had enemies, which
Cowley thus enlarges in rhyming prose:

> But in this thankless world the giver
> Is envied even by the receiver;
> 'Tis now the cheap and frugal fashion
> Rather to hide than own the obligation:

'*deep mouth*': Sir Richard Fanshawe, *Select Parts of Horace . . . put into English*
(1652), p. 49 (*Odes*, iv. 2).

Rhea's son: Zeus, whose mother was identified with the Earth or the Asiatic
goddess Cybele. *Poems*, p. 158.

paraphrast: 'one who paraphrases' (*OED*); 'a lax interpreter; one who explains
in many words' (*Dict.*).

The table, free: *Poems*, p. 172.

'*Castalian Stream*': A spring on Mt. Parnassus, sacred to the Muses, into which
the nymph Castalia threw herself when pursued by Apollo.

Theron: tyrant (from 488 B.C.) of Acragas (or Agrigentum), which enjoyed,
during his reign, great wealth and splendour.

But in this thankless: *Poems*, p. 162.

> Nay, 'tis much worse than so;
> It now an artifice does grow
> Wrongs and injuries to do,
> Lest men should think we owe.

It is hard to conceive that a man of the first rank in learning and wit, when he was dealing out such minute morality in such feeble diction, could imagine, either waking or dreaming, that he imitated Pindar.

In the following odes, where Cowley chooses his own subjects, he sometimes rises to dignity truly Pindaric, and if some deficiencies of language be forgiven, his strains are such as those of the Theban bard were to his contemporaries:

> Begin the song, and strike the living lyre:
> Lo how the years to come, a numerous and well-fitted choir,
> All hand in hand do decently advance,
> And to my song with smooth and equal measure dance;
> While the dance lasts, how long soe'er it be,
> My music's voice shall bear it company;
>   Till all gentle notes be drowned
>   In the last trumpet's dreadful sound.

After such enthusiasm, who will not lament to find the poet conclude with lines like these!

> But stop, my Muse—
> Hold thy Pindaric Pegasus closely in,
>   Which does to rage begin—
> 'Tis an unruly and a hard-mouthed horse—
>   'Twill no unskilful touch endure,
> But flings writer and reader too that sits not sure.

The fault of Cowley, and perhaps of all the writers of the metaphysical race, is that of pursuing his thoughts to their last ramifications, by which he loses the grandeur of generality, for of the greatest things the parts are little; what is little can be but pretty, and by claiming dignity becomes ridiculous. Thus all the power of description is destroyed by a scrupulous enumeration, and the force of metaphors is lost when the mind by the mention of particulars is turned more upon the original than the secondary sense, more upon that from which the illustration is drawn than that to which it is applied.

Of this we have a very eminent example in the ode entitled 'The Muse', who goes to 'take the air' in an intellectual chariot to which he harnesses Fancy and Judgement, Wit and Eloquence, Memory and

Begin the song: 'The Resurrection'. *Poems*, pp. 182, 183.

Invention; how he distinguished Wit from Fancy, or how Memory could properly contribute to motion, he has not explained; we are however content to suppose that he could have justified his own fiction, and wish to see the Muse begin her career; but there is yet more to be done.

> Let the *postilion* Nature mount, and let
> The *coachman* Art be set;
> And let the airy *footmen*, running all beside,
> Make a long row of goodly pride;
> Figures, conceits, raptures, and sentences,
> In a well-worded dress,
> And innocent loves, and pleasant truths, and useful lies,
> In all their gaudy *liveries*.

Every mind is now disgusted with this cumber of magnificence; yet I cannot refuse myself the four next lines:

> Mount, glorious queen, thy travelling throne,
>   And bid it to put on;
> For long though cheerful is the way,
> And life alas allows but one ill winter's day.

In the same ode, celebrating the power of the Muse, he gives her prescience, or in poetical language, the foresight of events hatching in futurity; but having once an egg in his mind, he cannot forbear to show us that he knows what an egg contains:

> Thou into the close nests of Time dost peep,
>   And there with piercing eye
> Through the firm shell and the thick white dost spy
>   Years to come a-forming lie,
> Close in their sacred fecundine asleep.

The same thought is more generally, and therefore more poetically, expressed by Casimir, a writer who has many of the beauties and faults of Cowley:

> Omnibus mundi Dóminator horis
> Aptat urgendas per inane pennas,
> Pars adhuc nido latet, et futuros
>   Crescit in annos.[n]

Cowley, whatever was his subject, seems to have been carried by a kind of destiny to the light and the familiar, or to conceits which

---

Let the postilion: *Poems*, pp. 184–5.
Thou into the close nests: *Poems*, p. 186.
Casimir: Maciej Kazimierz Sarbiewski (1595–1640), Latin poet, considered in his day as rivalling Horace.

require still more ignoble epithets. A slaughter in the Red Sea 'new dyes the water's name'; and England, during the Civil War, was 'Albion no more, nor to be named from white'. It is surely by some fascination not easily surmounted that a writer professing to revive 'the noblest and highest writing in verse' makes this address to the New Year:

> Nay, if thou lov'st me, gentle year,
> Let not so much as love be there,
> Vain fruitless love I mean; for, gentle year,
>   Although I fear,
> There's of this caution little need,
>   Yet, gentle year, take heed
>   How thou dost make
>   Such a mistake;
> Such love I mean alone
> As by thy cruel predecessors has been shown;
>   For, though I have too much cause to doubt it,
> I fain would try, for once, if life can live without it.

The reader of this will be inclined to cry out with Prior—

> —Ye critics, say,
> How poor to this was Pindar's style!

Even those who cannot perhaps find in the Isthmian or Nemean songs what antiquity has disposed them to expect will at least see that they are ill represented by such puny poetry, and all will determine that if this be the old Theban strain it is not worthy of revival.

To the disproportion and incongruity of Cowley's sentiments must be added the uncertainty and looseness of his measures. He takes the liberty of using in any place a verse of any length, from two syllables to twelve. The verses of Pindar have, as he observes, very little harmony to a modern ear; yet by examining the syllables we perceive them to be regular, and have reason enough for supposing that the ancient audiences were delighted with the sound. The imitator ought therefore to have adopted what he found and to have added what was wanting, to have preserved a constant return of the same numbers, and to have supplied smoothness of transition and continuity of thought.

'*new dyes*': 'The Plagues of Egypt', st. 17.

'*Albion no more*': 'To Dr. Scarburgh', st. 1.

Nay, if thou lov'st: 'To the New Year'. *Poems*, pp. 207–8.

Prior: Matthew Prior (1664–1721), poet and diplomat. *An English Ballad*, ll. 95–6.

as he observes: Cowley: *Poems*, p. 155.

It is urged by Dr. Sprat that the 'irregularity of numbers is the very thing' which makes 'that kind of poesy fit for all manner of subjects'. But he should have remembered that what is fit for everything can fit nothing well. The great pleasure of verse arises from the known measure of the lines and uniform structure of the stanzas, by which the voice is regulated and the memory relieved.

If the Pindaric style be what Cowley thinks it, 'the highest and noblest kind of writing in verse', it can be adapted only to high and noble subjects; and it will not be easy to reconcile the poet with the critic, or to conceive how that can be the highest kind of writing in verse which, according to Sprat, 'is chiefly to be preferred for its near affinity to prose'.

This lax and lawless versification so much concealed the deficiencies of the barren, and flattered the laziness of the idle, that it immediately overspread our books of poetry; all the boys and girls caught the pleasing fashion, and they that could do nothing else could write like Pindar. The rights of antiquity were invaded, and disorder tried to break into the Latin: a poem on the Sheldonian Theatre, in which all kinds of verse are shaken together, is unhappily inserted in the *Musae Anglicanae*.[n] Pindarism prevailed above half a century, but at last died gradually away, and other imitations supply its place.

The *Pindaric Odes* have so long enjoyed the highest degree of poetical reputation that I am not willing to dismiss them with unabated censure; and surely though the mode of their composition be erroneous, yet many parts deserve at least that admiration which is due to great comprehension of knowledge and great fertility of fancy. The thoughts are often new and often striking; but the greatness of one part is disgraced by the littleness of another, and total negligence of language gives the noblest conceptions the appearance of a fabric august in the plan, but mean in the materials. Yet surely those verses are not without a just claim to praise of which it may be said with truth that no one but Cowley could have written them.

The *Davideis* now remains to be considered, a poem which the author designed to have extended to twelve books, merely, as he makes no scruple of declaring, because the *Aeneid* had that number; but he had leisure or perseverance only to write the third part. Epic poems have been left unfinished by Virgil, Statius, Spenser, and Cowley. That we have not the whole *Davideis* is, however, not much

urged by Dr. Sprat: Spingarn, ii. 132.
as he makes: ibid. ii. 86.
Statius: (*c*. 40–*c*. 96), author of the *Thebaid*, and one book and part of a second of a later epic the *Achilleid*.

to be regretted, for in this undertaking Cowley is, tacitly at least, confessed to have miscarried. There are not many examples of so great a work produced by an author generally read, and generally praised, that has crept through a century with so little regard. Whatever is said of Cowley is meant of his other works. Of the *Davideis* no mention is made: it never appears in books nor emerges in conversation. By the *Spectator* it has once been quoted, by Rymer it has once been praised, and by Dryden, in *Mac Flecknoe*, it has once been imitated;[n] nor do I recollect much other notice from its publication till now in the whole succession of English literature.

Of this silence and neglect, if the reason be inquired, it will be found partly in the choice of the subject, and partly in the performance of the work.

Sacred history has been always read with submissive reverence and an imagination overawed and controlled. We have been accustomed to acquiesce in the nakedness and simplicity of the authentic narrative, and to repose on its veracity with such humble confidence as suppresses curiosity. We go with the historian as he goes, and stop with him when he stops. All amplification is frivolous and vain: all addition to that which is already sufficient for the purposes of religion seems not only useless, but in some degree profane.[n]

Such events as were produced by the visible interposition of Divine Power are above the power of human genius to dignify. The miracle of Creation, however it may teem with images, is best described with little diffusion of language: 'He spake the word, and they were made.'

We are told that Saul 'was troubled with an evil spirit'; from this Cowley takes an opportunity of describing hell and telling the history of Lucifer, who was, he says,

> Once general of a gilded host of sprites,
> Like Hesper leading forth the spangled nights;
> But down like lightning, which him struck, he came,
> And roared at his first plunge into the flame.

Lucifer makes a speech to the inferior agents of mischief in which there is something of heathenism, and therefore of impropriety, and to give efficacy to his words concludes by lashing 'his breast with his

By the Spectator: no. 590.
Rymer: Thomas Rymer (1641–1713), author and archaeologist; see *Rymer*, pp. 7–10, 75.
'*He spake*': Cf. Psalms 33:9; 148:5.
that Saul: I Samuel 16:14.
Once general: *Davideis*, i. *Poems*, p. 244.

long tail'. Envy, after a pause, steps out, and among other declarations of her zeal utters these lines:

> Do thou but threat, loud storms shall make reply,
> And thunder echo to the trembling sky.
> Whilst raging seas swell to so bold an height,
> As shall the fire's proud element affright.
> Th' old drudging sun, from his long-beaten way,
> Shall at thy voice start, and misguide the day.
> The jocund orbs shall break their measured pace,
> And stubborn poles change their allotted place.
> Heaven's gilded troops shall flutter here and there,
> Leaving their boasting songs tuned to a sphere.

Every reader feels himself weary with this useless talk of an allegorical being.

It is not only when the events are confessedly miraculous that fancy and fiction lose their effect: the whole system of life, while the Theocracy was yet visible, has an appearance so different from all other scenes of human action that the reader of the Sacred Volume habitually considers it as the peculiar mode of existence of a distinct species of mankind, that lived and acted with manners uncommunicable, so that it is difficult even for imagination to place us in the state of them whose story is related, and by consequence their joys and griefs are not easily adopted, nor can the attention be often interested in anything that befalls them.

To the subject thus originally indisposed to the reception of poetical embellishments, the writer brought little that could reconcile impatience or attract curiosity. Nothing can be more disgusting than a narrative spangled with conceits, and conceits are all that the *Davideis* supplies.

One of the great sources of poetical delight is description, or the power of presenting pictures to the mind. Cowley gives inferences instead of images, and shows not what may be supposed to have been seen, but what thoughts the sight might have suggested. When Virgil describes the stone which Turnus lifted against Aeneas, he fixes the attention on its bulk and weight:

> Saxum circumspicit ingens,
> Saxum antiquum, ingens, campo quod forte jacebat,
> Limes agro positus, litem ut discerneret arvis.[n]

Cowley says of the stone with which Cain slew his brother,

> I saw him fling the stone, as if he meant
> At once his murder and his monument.

Do thou but threat: Poems, p. 246.   *Saxum*: *Aeneid*, xii. 896–8.
I saw him: *Davideis*, i. *Poems*, p. 247.

Of the sword taken from Goliath, he says,

> A sword so great, that it was only fit
> To cut off his great head that came with it.

Other poets describe death by some of its common appearances; Cowley says, with a learned allusion to sepulchral lamps real or fabulous,

> 'Twixt his right ribs deep pierced the furious blade,
> And opened wide those secret vessels where
> Life's light goes out, when first they let in air.

But he has allusions vulgar as well as learned. In a visionary succession of kings:

> Joas at first does bright and glorious show,
> In life's fresh morn his fame does early crow.

Describing an undisciplined army, after having said with elegance,

> His forces seemed no army, but a crowd
> Heartless, unarmed, disorderly, and loud,

he gives them a fit of the ague.

The allusions however are not always to vulgar things; he offends by exaggeration as much as by diminution:

> The king was placed alone, and o'er his head
> A well-wrought heaven of silk and gold was spread.

Whatever he writes is always polluted with some conceit:

> Where the sun's fruitful beams give metals birth,
> Where he the growth of fatal gold does see,
> Gold, which alone more influence has than he.

In one passage he starts a sudden question to the confusion of philosophy:

> Ye learned heads, whom ivy garlands grace,
> Why does that twining plant the oak embrace?
> The oak, for courtship most of all unfit,
> And rough as are the winds that fight with it.

A sword: *Davideis*, iii. *Poems*, p. 324.
'Twixt his right: *Davideis*, iv. *Poems*, pp. 379–80.
Joas: *Davideis*, ii. *Poems*, p. 299.
His forces: *Davideis*, iv. *Poems*, p. 383.
The king: *Davideis*, ii. *Poems*, p. 293.
Where the sun's: *Davideis*, i. *Poems*, p. 244.
Ye learned heads: *Davideis*, ii. *Poems*, p. 285.

His expressions have sometimes a degree of meanness that surpasses expectation:

> Nay, gentle guests, he cries, since now you're in,
> The story of your gallant friend begin.

In a simile descriptive of the morning:

> As glimmering stars just at th' approach of day,
> Cashiered by troops, at last drop all away.

The dress of Gabriel deserves attention:

> He took for skin a cloud most soft and bright,
> That e'er the midday sun pierced through with light,
> Upon his cheeks a lively blush he spread,
> Washed from the morning beauties' deepest red;
> An harmless flattering meteor shone for hair,
> And fell adown his shoulders with loose care;
> He cuts out a silk mantle from the skies,
> Where the most sprightly azure pleased the eyes;
> This he with starry vapours sprinkles all,
> Took in their prime ere they grow ripe and fall;
> Of a new rainbow, ere it fret or fade,
> The choicest piece cut out, a scarf is made.

This is a just specimen of Cowley's imagery: what might in general expressions be great and forcible he weakens and makes ridiculous by branching it into small parts. That Gabriel was invested with the softest or brightest colours of the sky we might have been told, and been dismissed to improve the idea in our different proportions of conception; but Cowley could not let us go till he had related where Gabriel got first his skin, and then his mantle, then his lace, and then his scarf, and related it in the terms of the mercer and tailor.

Sometimes he indulges himself in a digression, always conceived with his natural exuberance, and commonly, even where it is not long, continued till it is tedious:

> I' th' library a few choice authors stood,
> Yet 'twas well stored, for that small store was good;
> Writing, man's spiritual physic, was not then
> Itself, as now, grown a disease of men.
> Learning (young virgin) but few suitors knew;
> The common prostitute she lately grew,
> And with the spurious brood loads now the press;
> Laborious effects of idleness!

Nay, gentle guests: *Davideis*, iii. *Poems*, p. 332.
As glimmering stars: *Davideis*, iv. *Poems*, p. 375.
He took for skin: *Davideis*, ii. *Poems*, p. 304.
I' th' library: *Davideis*, i. *Poems*, p. 260.

As the *Davideis* affords only four books, though intended to consist of twelve, there is no opportunity for such criticisms as epic poems commonly supply. The plan of the whole work is very imperfectly shown by the third part. The duration of an unfinished action cannot be known. Of characters either not yet introduced, or shown but upon few occasions, the full extent and the nice discriminations cannot be ascertained. The fable is plainly implex, formed rather from the *Odyssey* than the *Iliad*, and many artifices of diversification are employed with the skill of a man acquainted with the best models. The past is recalled by narration and the future anticipated by vision, but he has been so lavish of his poetical art that it is difficult to imagine how he could fill eight books more without practising again the same modes of disposing his matter—and perhaps the perception of this growing encumbrance inclined him to stop. By this abruption posterity lost more instruction than delight. If the continuation of the *Davideis* can be missed, it is for the learning that had been diffused over it, and the notes in which it had been explained.

Had not his characters been depraved like every other part by improper decorations, they would have deserved uncommon praise. He gives Saul both the body and mind of a hero:

His way once chose, he forward thrust outright,
Nor turned aside for danger or delight.

And the different beauties of the lofty Merab and the gentle Michal are very justly conceived and strongly painted.

Rymer has declared the *Davideis* superior to the *Jerusalem* of Tasso, 'which', says he, 'the poet, with all his care, has not totally purged from pedantry'. If by pedantry is meant that minute knowledge which is derived from particular sciences and studies, in opposition to the general notions supplied by a wide survey of life and nature, Cowley certainly errs by introducing pedantry far more frequently than Tasso. I know not, indeed, why they should be compared, for the resemblance of Cowley's work to Tasso's is only that they both exhibit the agency of celestial and infernal spirits, in which however they differ widely: for Cowley supposes them

implex: 'involved; having a complicated plot' (*OED*). Cf. Aristotle, *Poetics*, x. 1, 3; *Spectator* 297.
His way once chose: *Davideis*, iv. *Poems*, p. 374.
he different beauties: *Davideis*, iii. *Poems*, pp. 340–1; cf. I Samuel, 18:17 ff.
Rymer has declared: *Rymer*, p. 10.
Tasso: Torquato Tasso (1544–95), Italian epic poet, author of *La Gerusalemme Liberata*.

commonly to operate upon the mind by suggestion; Tasso represents them as promoting or obstructing events by external agency.

Of particular passages that can be properly compared I remember only the description of heaven, in which the different manner of the two writers is sufficiently discernible. Cowley's is scarcely description, unless it be possible to describe by negatives, for he tells us only what there is not in heaven. Tasso endeavours to represent the splendours and pleasures of the regions of happiness. Tasso affords images, and Cowley sentiments. It happens, however, that Tasso's description affords some reason for Rymer's censure. He says of the Supreme Being,

> Hà sotto i piedi e fato e la natura
> Ministri humili, e'l moto, e ch'il misura.[n]

The second line has in it more of pedantry than perhaps can be found in any other stanza of the poem.

In the perusal of the *Davideis*, as of all Cowley's works, we find wit and learning unprofitably squandered. Attention has no relief; the affections are never moved; we are sometimes surprised but never delighted, and find much to admire but little to approve. Still however it is the work of Cowley, of a mind capacious by nature and replenished by study.

In the general review of Cowley's poetry it will be found that he wrote with abundant fertility but negligent or unskilful selection, with much thought but with little imagery; that he is never pathetic and rarely sublime, but always either ingenious or learned, either acute or profound.

It is said by Denham in his elegy,

> To him no author was unknown;
> Yet what he writ was all his own.

This wide position requires less limitation when it is affirmed of Cowley than perhaps of any other poet. He read much and yet borrowed little.

His character of writing was indeed not his own: he unhappily adopted that which was predominant. He saw a certain way to present praise, and not sufficiently inquiring by what means the ancients have continued to delight through all the changes of human manners, he contented himself with a deciduous laurel, of which the

Cowley's is: *Davideis*, i. *Poems*, pp. 250–1.
Hà sotto i piedi: *Gerusalemme Liberata*, ix. 56.
Denham: 'On Mr. Abraham Cowley', ll. 29–30.

verdure in its spring was bright and gay, but which time has been continually stealing from his brows.

He was in his own time considered as of unrivalled excellence. Clarendon represents him as having taken a flight beyond all that went before him; and Milton is said to have declared that the three greatest English poets were Spenser, Shakespeare and Cowley.

His manner he had in common with others, but his sentiments were his own. Upon every subject he thought for himself, and such was his copiousness of knowledge that something at once remote and applicable rushed into his mind; yet it is not likely that he always rejected a commodious idea merely because another had used it: his known wealth was so great that he might have borrowed without loss of credit.

In his elegy on Sir Henry Wotton, the last lines have such resemblance to the noble epigram of Grotius upon the death of Scaliger that I cannot but think them copied from it, though they are copied by no servile hand.

One passage in his *Mistress* is so apparently borrowed from Donne that he probably would not have written it had it not mingled with his own thoughts so as that he did not perceive himself taking it from another.

> Although I think thou never found wilt be,
>   Yet I'm resolved to search for thee;
>   The search itself rewards the pains.
> So, though the chemic his great secret miss,
> (For neither it in art nor nature is)
>   Yet things well worth his toil he gains:
>   And does his charge and labour pay
> With good unsought experiments by the way.
>
> COWLEY

> Some that have deeper digged Love's mine than I,
> Say where his centric happiness doth lie:
>   I have loved, and got, and told,
> But should I love, get, tell, till I were old,
> I should not find that hidden mystery;
>   Oh, 'tis imposture all:

Clarendon: Edward Hyde (1609–74), 1st Earl of Clarendon; see *The Life of Edward Earl of Clarendon* (Oxford, 1759), pt. I, p. 16.

Milton is said . . .: Newton, i. lvi.

Grotius: Hugo Grotius (1583–1645), Dutch jurist and humanist; see *Poemata* (Leyden, 1617), pp. 358–9 ('Unica lux saecli').

Although I think: 'Maidenhead'. *Poems*, p. 129.

chemic: alchemist.

Some that have: 'Love's Alchemy', ll. 1–12.

> And as no chemic yet th' elixir got,
> But glorifies his pregnant pot,
> If by the way to him befall
> Some odoriferous thing, or medicinal,
> So lovers dream a rich and long delight,
> But get a winter-seeming summer's night.

Jonson and Donne, as Dr. Hurd remarks, were then in the highest esteem.

It is related by Clarendon that Cowley always acknowledged his obligation to the learning and industry of Jonson, but I have found no traces of Jonson in his works; to emulate Donne appears to have been his purpose, and from Donne he may have learned that familiarity with religious images, and that light allusion to sacred things, by which readers far short of sanctity are frequently offended, and which would not be borne in the present age when devotion, perhaps not more fervent, is more delicate.

Having produced one passage taken by Cowley from Donne, I will recompense him by another which Milton seems to have borrowed from him. He says of Goliath,

> His spear, the trunk was of a lofty tree,
> Which nature meant some tall ship's mast should be.

Milton of Satan,

> His spear, to equal which the tallest pine
> Hewn on Norwegian hills, to be the mast
> Of some great admiral, were but a wand,
> He walked with.

His diction was in his own time censured as negligent. He seems not to have known, or not to have considered, that words being arbitrary must owe their power to association, and have the influence, and that only, which custom has given them. Language is the dress of thought, and as the noblest mien or most graceful action would be degraded and obscured by a garb appropriated to the gross employments of rustics or mechanics, so the most heroic sentiments will

---

odoriferous: 'that bears or diffuses scent or smell; odorous; fragrant' (*OED*).
Dr. Hurd: Richard Hurd (1720–1808), Bishop of Worcester; see *Select Works of Mr. A. Cowley*, ed. Hurd (1772, 2nd ed.), i. 168 n.
related by Clarendon: *Life of Clarendon*, pt. 1, p. 16.
His spear, the trunk: *Davideis*, iii. *Poems*, p. 334.
His spear, to equal: *PL*, i. 292–5.
His diction: Cf. Spingarn, ii. 129.
Language is: cf. *Rambler* 168.

lose their efficacy, and the most splendid ideas drop their magnificence, if they are conveyed by words used commonly upon low and trivial occasions, debased by vulgar mouths, and contaminated by inelegant applications.

Truth indeed is always truth, and reason is always reason: they have an intrinsic and unalterable value, and constitute that intellectual gold which defies destruction; but gold may be so concealed in baser matter that only a chemist can recover it; sense may be so hidden in unrefined and plebeian words that none but philosophers can distinguish it; and both may be so buried in impurities as not to pay the cost of their extraction.

The diction, being the vehicle of the thoughts, first presents itself to the intellectual eye, and if the first appearance offends a further knowledge is not often sought. Whatever professes to benefit by pleasing must please at once. The pleasures of the mind imply something sudden and unexpected: that which elevates must always surprise. What is perceived by slow degrees may gratify us with the consciousness of improvement, but will never strike with the sense of pleasure.

Of all this Cowley appears to have been without knowledge or without care. He makes no selection of words, nor seeks any neatness of phrase: he has no elegances either lucky or elaborate; as his endeavours were rather to impress sentences upon the understanding than images on the fancy, he has few epithets, and those scattered without peculiar propriety or nice adaptation. It seems to follow from the necessity of the subject, rather than the care of the writer, that the diction of his heroic poem is less familiar than that of his slightest writings. He has given not the same numbers but the same diction to the gentle Anacreon and the tempestuous Pindar.

His versification seems to have had very little of his care; and if what he thinks be true, that his numbers are unmusical only when they are ill read, the art of reading them is at present lost, for they are commonly harsh to modern ears. He has indeed many noble lines such as the feeble care of Waller never could produce. The bulk of his thoughts sometimes swelled his verse to unexpected and inevitable grandeur, but his excellence of this kind is merely fortuitous: he sinks willingly down to his general carelessness, and avoids with very little care either meanness or asperity.

His contractions are often rugged and harsh:

> One flings a mountain, and its rivers too
> Torn up with't.

that his numbers: Spingarn, ii. 86. *One flings*: *Davideis*, iii. *Poems*, p. 333.

His rhymes are very often made by pronouns or particles, or the like unimportant words, which disappoint the ear and destroy the energy of the line.

His combination of different measures is sometimes dissonant and unpleasing: he joins verses together of which the former does not slide easily into the latter.

The words 'do' and 'did', which so much degrade in present estimation the line that admits them, were in the time of Cowley little censured or avoided; how often he used them, and with how bad an effect, at least to our ears, will appear by a passage in which every reader will lament to see just and noble thoughts defrauded of their praise by inelegance of language:

> Where honour or where conscience *does* not bind,
>   No other law shall shackle me;
>   Slave to myself I ne'er will be;
> Nor shall my future actions be confined
>   By my own present mind.
> Who by resolves and vows engaged *does* stand
>   For days that yet belong to fate,
> *Does* like an unthrift mortgage his estate
>   Before it falls into his hand;
>   The bondman of the cloister so
> All that he *does* receive *does* always owe.
> And still as Time comes in, it goes away,
>   Not to enjoy, but debts to pay.
> Unhappy slave, and pupil to a bell!
> Which his hours' work as well as hours *does* tell:
> Unhappy till the last, the kind releasing knell.

His heroic lines are often formed of monosyllables, but yet they are sometimes sweet and sonorous.[n]

He says of the Messiah,

> Round the whole earth his dreaded name shall sound,
> *And reach to worlds that must not yet be found.*

In another place, of David,

> Yet bid him go securely, when he sends;
> *'Tis Saul that is his foe, and we his friends.*
> *The man who has his God, no aid can lack,*
> *And we who bid him go, will bring him back.*

Yet amidst his negligence he sometimes attempted an improved and scientific versification, of which it will be best to give his own account subjoined to this line,

Where honour: 'Ode: Upon Liberty'. *Essays*, pp. 390–1.
Round the whole earth: *Davideis*, ii. *Poems*, p. 305.
Yet bid him go: *Davideis*, i. *Poems*. p. 252.

Nor can the glory contain itself in th' endless space.

'I am sorry that it is necessary to admonish the most part of readers that it is not by negligence that this verse is so loose, long, and, as it were, vast; it is to paint in the number the nature of the thing which it describes, which I would have observed in divers other places of this poem that else will pass for very careless verses: as before,

And overruns the neighb'ring fields with violent course.

In the second book:

Down a precipice deep, down he casts them all.

And,

And fell a-down his shoulders with loose care.

In the third:

Brass was his helmet, his boots brass, and o'er
His breast a thick plate of strong brass he wore.

In the fourth:

Like some fair pine o'er-looking all th' ignobler wood.

And,

Some from the rocks cast themselves down headlong.

And many more; but it is enough to instance in a few. The thing is that the disposition of words and numbers should be such as that, out of the order and sound of them, the things themselves may be represented. This the Greeks were not so accurate as to bind themselves to; neither have our English poets observed it, for aught I can find. The Latins (*qui musas colunt severiores*) sometimes did it, and their prince, Virgil, always—in whom the examples are innumerable, and taken notice of by all judicious men, so that it is superfluous to collect them.'[n]

I know not whether he has, in many of these instances, attained the representation or resemblance that he purposes. Verse can imitate only sound and motion. A *boundless* verse, a *headlong* verse, and a verse of *brass* or of *strong brass*, seem to comprise very incongruous and unsociable ideas. What there is peculiar in the sound of the line expressing *loose care* I cannot discover, nor why the *pine* is *taller* in an Alexandrine than in ten syllables.

But not to defraud him of his due praise, he has given one example of representative versification which perhaps no other English line can equal:

> Begin, be bold, and venture to be wise.
> He who defers this work from day to day,
> Does on a river's bank expecting stay
> Till the whole stream that stopped him shall be gone,
> *Which runs, and as it runs, for ever shall run on.*

Cowley was, I believe, the first poet that mingled Alexandrines at pleasure with the common heroic of ten syllables, and from him

Nor can the glory: *Davideis*, i. *Poems*, pp. 251, 273.
qui musas: Martial, IX. xi. 17 ('who court Muses more austere').
Begin, be bold: *Essays*, p. 454.

Dryden borrowed the practice, whether ornamental or licentious. He considered the verse of twelve syllables as elevated and majestic, and has therefore deviated into that measure when he supposes the voice heard of the Supreme Being.

The author of the *Davideis* is commended by Dryden for having written it in couplets because he discovered that any staff was too lyrical for an heroic poem; but this seems to have been known before by May and Sandys, the translators of the *Pharsalia* and the *Metamorphoses*.

In the *Davideis* are some hemistichs, or verses left imperfect by the author, in imitation of Virgil, whom he supposes not to have intended to complete them; that this opinion is erroneous may be probably concluded because this truncation is imitated by no subsequent Roman poet, because Virgil himself filled up one broken line in the heat of recitation, because in one the sense is now unfinished, and because all that can be done by a broken verse a line intersected by a caesura and a full stop will equally effect.

Of triplets in his *Davideis* he makes no use, and perhaps did not at first think them allowable; but he appears afterwards to have changed his mind, for in the verses on the government of Cromwell he inserts them liberally[n] with great happiness.

After so much criticism on his poems, the essays which accompany them must not be forgotten. What is said by Sprat of his conversation, that no man could draw from it any suspicion of his excellence in poetry, may be applied to these compositions. No author ever kept his verse and his prose at a greater distance from each other. His thoughts are natural, and his style has a smooth and placid equability which has never yet obtained its due commendation. Nothing is far-sought or hard-laboured, but all is easy without feebleness and familiar without grossness.

It has been observed by Felton, in his essay on the classics, that Cowley was beloved by every Muse that he courted, and that he has rivalled the ancients in every kind of poetry but tragedy.

has therefore deviated: *Davideis*, iv. *Poems*, p. 373.
commended by Dryden: Dryden: *Essays*, ii. 248.
staff: 'stanza or set of lines. *Obs.*' (*OED*).
Sandys: George Sandys (1578–1644), poet, published a translation of Ovid's *Metamorphoses* (1621–6).
whom he supposes: *Davideis*, i, n. 14. *Poems*, pp. 269–70.
filled up: *Aeneid*, vi. 164 and 165.
in one the sense: ibid. iii. 340.   *said by Sprat*: Spingarn, ii. 140.
Felton: Henry Felton (1679–1740), divine; see his *Dissertation on Reading the Classics* (1713), pp. 35–6.

It may be affirmed, without any encomiastic fervour, that he brought to his poetic labours a mind replete with learning, and that his pages are embellished with all the ornaments which books could supply; that he was the first who imparted to English numbers the enthusiasm of the greater ode, and the gaiety of the less; that he was equally qualified for sprightly sallies and for lofty flights; that he was among those who freed translation from servility, and instead of following his author at a distance, walked by his side; and that if he left versification yet improvable, he left likewise from time to time such specimens of excellence as enabled succeeding poets to improve it.

MILTON

The Life of Milton has been already written in so many forms, and with such minute inquiry, that I might perhaps more properly have contented myself with the addition of a few notes to Mr. Fenton's elegant abridgement[n] but that a new narrative was thought necessary to the uniformity of this edition.

John Milton was by birth a gentleman, descended from the proprietors of Milton near Thame in Oxfordshire, one of whom forfeited his estate in the times of York and Lancaster. Which side he took I know not; his descendant inherited no veneration for the White Rose.

His grandfather John was keeper of the forest of Shotover, a zealous Papist who disinherited his son because he had forsaken the religion of his ancestors.

His father John, who was the son disinherited, had recourse for his support to the profession of a scrivener. He was a man eminent for his skill in music, many of his compositions being still to be found; and his reputation in his profession was such that he grew rich, and retired to an estate. He had probably more than common literature as his son addresses him in one of his most elaborate Latin poems. He married a gentlewoman of the name of Caston, a Welsh family, by whom he had two sons, John the poet, and Christopher who studied the law, and adhered, as the law taught him, to the King's party, for which he was awhile persecuted; but having by his brother's interest obtained permission to live in quiet, he supported himself so honourably by chamber-practice that soon after the accession of King James he was knighted and made a judge; but his constitution being too weak for business, he retired before any disreputable compliances became necessary.

He had likewise a daughter Anne, whom he married with a con-

Fenton: Elijah Fenton (1683–1730), poet and editor.
descended from: cf. Parker, ii. 680–1.
His grandfather: Richard Milton (*fl.* 1559–1601), not John, was yeoman of Stanton St. John.
His father: John Milton the elder (1562?–1647); see Parker, i. 5, 11, 18 and nn.
addresses him: 'Ad Patrem'.
He married: Sara(h) Milton (*née* Jeffrey) (1572?–1637) was the poet's mother, some of whose ancestors were probably Castons.
Christopher: Christopher Milton (1615–93) was knighted in 1686.
chamber-practice: 'practice in chambers and not in court, the practice of a chamber-counsel' (*OED*).
Anne: Anne Milton (1602/7–40?) married Edward Phillips (1597–1631) in Nov. 1623.

siderable fortune to Edward Phillips, who came from Shrewsbury, and rose in the Crown Office to be secondary; by him she had two sons, John and Edward, who were educated by the poet, and from whom is derived the only authentic account of his domestic manners.

John, the poet, was born in his father's house at the Spread Eagle in Bread Street, Dec. 9, 1608, between six and seven in the morning. His father appears to have been very solicitous about his education, for he was instructed at first by private tuition under the care of Thomas Young, who was afterwards chaplain to the English merchants at Hamburg, and of whom we have reason to think well since his scholar considered him as worthy of an epistolary elegy.

He was then sent to St. Paul's School, under the care of Mr. Gill, and removed, in the beginning of his sixteenth year, to Christ's College in Cambridge, where he entered a sizar, Feb. 12, 1624.[n]

He was at this time eminently skilled in the Latin tongue; and he himself, by annexing the dates to his first compositions, a boast of which the learned Politian had given him an example, seems to commend the earliness of his own proficiency to the notice of posterity. But the products of his vernal fertility have been surpassed by many, and particularly by his contemporary Cowley. Of the powers of the mind it is difficult to form an estimate: many have excelled Milton in their first essays who never rose to works like *Paradise Lost*.

At fifteen, a date which he uses till he is sixteen, he translated or versified two Psalms, 114 and 136, which he thought worthy of the public eye, but they raise no great expectations; they would in any numerous school have obtained praise but not excited wonder.

Many of his elegies appear to have been written in his eighteenth year,[n] by which it appears that he had then read the Roman authors with very nice discernment. I once heard Mr. Hampton, the translator of Polybius, remark what I think is true, that Milton was the first Englishman who after the revival of letters wrote Latin verses with classic elegance. If any exceptions can be made they are very few.

John: John Phillips (1631–1706?), Milton's amanuensis.
Edward: Edward Phillips (1630–96?), Milton's biographer.
Thomas Young: (1587?–1655), later master of Jesus College, Cambridge (1644–1650), to whom Milton addressed his 'Elegia Quarta'.
Mr. Gill: Alexander Gill the elder (1564–1635).
Politian: Angelo Poliziano (1454–94), Italian poet and humanist.
by his contemporary Cowley: see above, pp. 2, 8.
Mr. Hampton: James Hampton (1721–78).
Polybius: (203? B.C.–c. 120 B.C.), Greek historian.

Haddon and Ascham, the pride of Elizabeth's reign, however they may have succeeded in prose, no sooner attempt verses than they provoke derision.[n] If we produced anything worthy of notice before the elegies of Milton, it was perhaps Alabaster's *Roxana*.

Of these exercises which the rules of the University required, some were published by him in his maturer years.[n] They had been undoubtedly applauded, for they were such as few can perform; yet there is reason to suspect that he was regarded in his college with no great fondness. That he obtained no fellowship is certain; but the unkindness with which he was treated was not merely negative. I am ashamed to relate what I fear is true, that Milton was one of the last students in either university that suffered the public indignity of corporal correction.

It was in the violence of controversial hostility objected to him that he was expelled; this he steadily denies, and it was apparently not true, but it seems plain from his own verses to Diodati that he had incurred 'rustication', a temporary dismission into the country with perhaps the loss of a term:[n]

> Me tenet urbs reflua quam Thamesis alluit unda,
>   Meque nec invitum patria dulcis habet.
> Jam nec arundiferum mihi cura revisere Camum,
>   Nec dudum *vetiti* me *laris* angit amor.—
> Nec duri libet usque minas perferre magistri,
>   Caeteraque ingenio non subeunda meo.
> Si sit hoc *exilium* patrios adiisse penates,
>   Et vacuum curis otia grata sequi,
> Non ego vel *profugi* nomen sortemve recuso,
>   Laetus et *exilii* conditione fruor.[n]

I cannot find any meaning but this which even kindness and reverence can give to the term *vetiti laris*, 'a habitation from which he is excluded', or how 'exile' can be otherwise interpreted. He declares yet more, that he is weary of enduring 'the threats of a rigorous master, and something else which a temper like his cannot undergo'. What was more than threat was probably punishment.

Haddon: Walter Haddon (1516–72) published, with Sir John Cheke, *Reformatio legum ecclesiasticarum* (1571), and defended the Reformation against Jerome Osorio da Fonseca.

Ascham: Roger Ascham (1515–68), author of *Toxophilus* (1545) and *The Schoolmaster* (1570).

Alabaster's: William Alabaster (1567–1640), Latin poet and divine, whose Latin tragedy *Roxana* (written *c.*1592) was not published until 1632.

I am ashamed to relate: cf. Parker, ii. 729.

Diodati: Charles Diodati (1609?–38), physician.

Me tenet: 'Elegia Prima', ll. 9–12, 15–20. For translation, see p. 348.

This poem, which mentions his 'exile', proves likewise that it was not perpetual, for it concludes with a resolution of returning some time to Cambridge. And it may be conjectured from the willingness with which he has perpetuated the memory of his exile that its cause was such as gave him no shame.[n]

He took both the usual degrees: that of Bachelor in 1628,[n] and that of Master in 1632; but he left the University with no kindness for its institution, alienated either by the injudicious severity of his governors or his own captious perverseness. The cause cannot now be known, but the effect appears in his writings. His scheme of education, inscribed to Hartlib, supersedes all academical instruction, being intended to comprise the whole time which men usually spend in literature, from their entrance upon grammar 'till they proceed, as it is called, masters of arts'. And in his discourse *On the likeliest Way to remove Hirelings out of the Church*, he ingeniously proposes that 'the profits of the lands forfeited by the act for superstitious uses, should be applied to such academies all over the land where languages and arts may be taught together, so that youth may be at once brought up to a competency of learning and an honest trade, by which means such of them as had the gift, being enabled to support themselves (without tithes) by the latter, may, by the help of the former, become worthy preachers'.

One of his objections to academical education, as it was then conducted, is that men designed for orders in the Church were permitted to act plays, 'writhing and unboning their clergy limbs to all the antic and dishonest gestures of Trincalos, buffoons and bawds; prostituting the shame of that ministry which they had, or were near having, to the eyes of courtiers and court-ladies, their grooms and mademoiselles'.

This is sufficiently peevish in a man who, when he mentions his exile from the college, relates with great luxuriance the compensation which the pleasures of the theatre afford him. Plays were therefore only criminal when they were acted by academics.

He went to the university with a design of entering into the Church, but in time altered his mind, for he declared that whoever became a clergyman must 'subscribe slave, and take an oath withal, which, unless he took with a conscience that could retch, he must

he left the University: cf. *An Apology against a Pamphlet*, *CM*, iii. 298.
Hartlib: Samuel Hartlib (1596/1600–62), author; see *Of Education*, *CM*, iv. 281.
'*the profits*': *CM*, vi. 79–81.   '*writhing and unboning*': *CM*, iii. 300.
relates with great luxuriance: 'Elegia Prima', ll. 27–46.
'*subscribe slave*': *CM*, iii. 242.

straight perjure himself. He thought it better to prefer a blameless silence before the office of speaking, bought and begun with servitude and forswearing.'

These expressions are, I find, applied to the subscription of the Articles; but it seems more probable that they relate to canonical obedience. I know not any of the Articles which seem to thwart his opinions, but the thoughts of obedience, whether canonical or civil, raised his indignation.

His unwillingness to engage in the ministry, perhaps not yet advanced to a settled resolution of declining it, appears in a letter to one of his friends who had reproved his suspended and dilatory life, which he seems to have imputed to an insatiable curiosity and fantastic luxury of various knowledge. To this he writes a cool and plausible answer in which he endeavours to persuade him that the delay proceeds not from the delights of desultory study, but from the desire of obtaining more fitness for his task, and that he goes on, 'not taking thought of being late, so it give advantage to be more fit'.

When he left the university he returned to his father, then residing at Horton in Buckinghamshire, with whom he lived five years, in which time he is said to have read all the Greek and Latin writers. With what limitations this universality is to be understood who shall inform us?

It might be supposed that he who read so much should have done nothing else, but Milton found time to write the mask of *Comus*,[n] which was presented at Ludlow, then the residence of the Lord President of Wales, in 1634, and had the honour of being acted by the Earl of Bridgewater's sons and daughter. The fiction is derived from Homer's Circe, but we never can refuse to any modern the liberty of borrowing from Homer:

> —a quo ceu fonte perenni
> Vatum Pieriis ora rigantur aquis.

His next production was 'Lycidas', an elegy written in 1637 on the death of Mr. King, the son of Sir John King, Secretary for Ireland

appears in a letter: *CM*, xii. 323–4.

in which time: *Defensio Secunda*, *CM*, viii. 120–1. Cf. ibid. xii. 28–9; *EL*, p. 36.

Earl of Bridgewater's: John Egerton (1579–1649), 1st Earl of Bridgewater, of whom the children referred to here were Alice (1619–89), John (1623–86), and Thomas (1625–48?).   *Homer's Circe*: *Odyssey*, x. 133 ff.

a quo: Ovid, *Amores*, III. ix. 25–6 ('from whom as from fount perennial the lips of bards are bedewed with Pierian waters').

Mr. King: Edward King (1612?–37), whose father Sir John King (d. 1637) held various administrative posts in Ireland, becoming M.P. for Co. Roscommon (1613).

in the time of Elizabeth, James and Charles. King was much a favourite at Cambridge, and many of the wits joined to do honour to his memory.[n] Milton's acquaintance with the Italian writers may be discovered by a mixture of longer and shorter verses, according to the rules of Tuscan poetry,[n] and his malignity to the Church by some lines which are interpreted as threatening its extermination.

He is supposed about this time to have written his 'Arcades', for while he lived at Horton he used sometimes to steal from his studies a few days, which he spent at Harefield, the house of the Countess Dowager of Derby, where the 'Arcades' made part of a dramatic entertainment.[n]

He began now to grow weary of the country, and had some purpose of taking chambers in the Inns of Court, when the death of his mother set him at liberty to travel, for which he obtained his father's consent and Sir Henry Wotton's directions, with the celebrated precept of prudence, *i pensieri stretti, ed il viso sciolto*: 'thoughts close, and looks loose'.

In 1638 he left England[n] and went first to Paris, where by the favour of Lord Scudamore he had the opportunity of visiting Grotius, then residing at the French Court as ambassador from Christina of Sweden. From Paris he hasted into Italy, of which he had with particular diligence studied the language and literature, and though he seems to have intended a very quick perambulation of the country, stayed two months at Florence, where he found his way into the academies, and produced his compositions with such applause as appears to have exalted him in his own opinion, and confirmed him in the hope that 'by labour and intense study, which', says he, 'I take to be my portion in this life, joined with a strong propensity of nature', he might 'leave something so written to after-times as they should not willingly let it die'.

It appears in all his writings that he had the usual concomitant of great abilities—a lofty and steady confidence in himself, perhaps not without some contempt of others, for scarcely any man ever wrote so much and praised so few. Of his praise he was very frugal as he set its value high, and considered his mention of a name as a

---

by some lines: ll. 108–31.

the Countess Dowager of Derby: Alice Spencer (or Spenser) (1559–1637), whose 1st husband was Ferdinando Stanley (1559?–94), 5th Earl of Derby.

Wotton's directions: *CM*, i. 476–7 (Wotton to Milton, 13 Apr. 1638).

Lord Scudamore: John Scudamore (1601–71), 1st Viscount Scudamore, ambassador and joint-ambassador at Paris (1635–9).

Christina: (1626–89), daughter and successor of Gustavus Adolphus.

'by labour': *CM*, iii. 236.

security against the waste of time and a certain preservative from oblivion.

At Florence he could not indeed complain that his merit wanted distinction. Carlo Dati presented him with an encomiastic inscription in the tumid lapidary style, and Francini wrote him an ode of which the first stanza is only empty noise; the rest are perhaps too diffuse on common topics, but the last is natural and beautiful.[n]

From Florence he went to Siena, and from Siena to Rome, where he was again received with kindness by the learned and the great. Holstenius, the keeper of the Vatican Library, who had resided three years at Oxford, introduced him to Cardinal Barberini, and he at a musical entertainment waited for him at the door, and led him by the hand into the assembly. Here Selvaggi praised him in a distich and Salzilli in a tetrastic—neither of them of much value. The Italians were gainers by this literary commerce, for the encomiums with which Milton repaid Salzilli, though not secure against a stern grammarian, turn the balance indisputably in Milton's favour.

Of these Italian testimonies, poor as they are, he was proud enough to publish them before his poems, though he says he cannot be suspected but to have known that they were said *non tam de se, quam supra se.*

At Rome, as at Florence, he stayed only two months, a time indeed sufficient if he desired only to ramble with an explainer of its antiquities or to view palaces and count pictures, but certainly too short for the contemplation of learning, policy or manners.

From Rome he passed on to Naples in company of a hermit, a companion from whom little could be expected, yet to him Milton owed his introduction to Manso, Marquis of Villa, who had been

preservative from oblivion: cf. Sonnet VIII, ll. 5–8.

Carlo Dati: Carlo Roberto Dati (1619–76), author of *Vite de Pittori Antichi* (1667).

Francini: Antonio Francini, lyric poet.

Holstenius: Lucas Holstenius (or Lukas Holste) (1596–1661), German scholar and papal ambassador, secretary and librarian to Barberini, and later Librarian of the Vatican.

Barberini: Francesco Barberini (1597–1679), founder of the Barberini Library and counsellor to his uncle Urban VIII; see *CM*, xii. 40–1 (Milton to Holstenius, 30 March 1639).

Selvaggi: see David Masson, *The Life of John Milton* (London, 1859–94; repr. New York, 1946), i. 806 n.

Salzilli: Giovanni Salzilli (*fl.* 1638), Italian poet.

the encomiums: 'Ad Salsillum poetam Romanum aegrotantem'.

non tam: *CM*, i. 154 ('not so much about him as over him').

Manso: Giovanni Battista Manso (1560?–1645) was addressed in Milton's 'Mansus', and mentioned in *Epitaphium Damonis*, ll. 181–2.

before the patron of Tasso. Manso was enough delighted with his accomplishments to honour him with a sorry distich, in which he commends him for everything but his religion; and Milton, in return, addressed him in a Latin poem which must have raised an high opinion of English elegance and literature.

His purpose was now to have visited Sicily and Greece, but hearing of the differences between the King and Parliament, he thought it proper to hasten home rather than pass his life in foreign amusements while his countrymen were contending for their rights. He therefore came back to Rome, though the merchants informed him of plots laid against him by the Jesuits for the liberty of his conversations on religion. He had sense enough to judge that there was no danger, and therefore kept on his way and acted as before, neither obtruding nor shunning controversy. He had perhaps given some offence by visiting Galileo, then a prisoner in the Inquisition for philosophical heresy, and at Naples he was told by Manso that by his declarations on religious questions he had excluded himself from some distinctions which he should otherwise have paid him. But such conduct, though it did not please, was yet sufficiently safe, and Milton stayed two months more at Rome and went on to Florence without molestation.

From Florence he visited Lucca. He afterwards went to Venice, and having sent away a collection of music and other books, travelled to Geneva, which he probably considered as the metropolis of orthodoxy.[n] Here he reposed as in a congenial element, and became acquainted with John Diodati and Frederick Spanheim,[n] two learned professors of Divinity. From Geneva he passed through France, and came home after an absence of a year and three months.

At his return he heard of the death of his friend Charles Diodati, a man whom it is reasonable to suppose of great merit since he was thought by Milton worthy of a poem entitled *Epitaphium Damonis*,[n] written with the common but childish imitation of pastoral life.

He now hired a lodging at the house of one Russell, a tailor in St. Bride's Churchyard, and undertook the education of John and Edward Phillips, his sister's sons. Finding his rooms too little, he took a house and garden in Aldersgate Street, which was not then so much out of the world as it is now, and chose his dwelling at the

Galileo: (1564–1642); see *CM*, iv. 330; cf. *EL*, p. 95.
John Diodati: Jean (or Giovanni) Diodati (1576–1649), Swiss Calvinist theologian who translated the Bible into Italian, and the uncle of Charles Diodati.
Frederick Spanheim: (1600–49); see below, p. 348.

upper end of a passage that he might avoid the noise of the street. Here he received more boys to be boarded and instructed.

Let not our veneration for Milton forbid us to look with some degree of merriment on great promises and small performance, on the man who hastens home because his countrymen are contending for their liberty, and when he reaches the scene of action, vapours away his patriotism in a private boarding-school. This is the period of his life from which all his biographers seem inclined to shrink. They are unwilling that Milton should be degraded to a schoolmaster, but since it cannot be denied that he taught boys, one finds out that he taught for nothing, and another that his motive was only zeal for the propagation of learning and virtue, and all tell what they do not know to be true only to excuse an act which no wise man will consider as in itself disgraceful. His father was alive, his allowance was not ample, and he supplied its deficiencies by an honest and useful employment.

It is told that in the art of education he performed wonders, and a formidable list is given of the authors, Greek and Latin, that were read in Aldersgate Street by youth between ten and fifteen or sixteen years of age. Those who tell or receive these stories should consider that nobody can be taught faster than he can learn. The speed of the best horseman must be limited by the power of his horse. Every man that has ever undertaken to instruct others can tell what slow advances he has been able to make, and how much patience it requires to recall vagrant inattention, to stimulate sluggish indifference, and to rectify absurd misapprehension.

The purpose of Milton, as it seems, was to teach something more solid than the common literature of schools by reading those authors that treat of physical subjects, such as the Georgic, and astronomical treatises of the ancients. This was a scheme of improvement which seems to have busied many literary projectors of that age. Cowley, who had more means than Milton of knowing what was wanting to the embellishments of life, formed the same plan of education in his imaginary college.[n]

But the truth is that the knowledge of external nature, and the sciences which that knowledge requires or includes, are not the great or the frequent business of the human mind. Whether we provide for action or conversation, whether we wish to be useful or pleasing,

all tell what they do not know: cf. Phillips, Toland, *EL*, pp. 67, 98; Newton, i. *xiii.* Johnson himself had been a schoolmaster.
It is told: Phillips, *EL*, pp. 12 and n. 1, 60.
The purpose: *Of Education, CM*, iv. 277 ff. Cf. *Life*, iii. 358.

the first requisite is the religious and moral knowledge of right and wrong; the next is an acquaintance with the history of mankind, and with those examples which may be said to embody truth, and prove by events the reasonableness of opinions. Prudence and justice are virtues and excellences of all times and of all places: we are perpetually moralists, but we are geometricians only by chance. Our intercourse with intellectual nature is necessary; our speculations upon matter are voluntary and at leisure. Physiological learning is of such rare emergence that one man may know another half his life without being able to estimate his skill in hydrostatics or astronomy; but his moral and prudential character immediately appears.

Those authors, therefore, are to be read at schools that supply most axioms of prudence, most principles of moral truth, and most materials for conversation; and these purposes are best served by poets, orators and historians.

Let me not be censured for this digression as pedantic or paradoxical, for if I have Milton against me I have Socrates on my side. It was his labour to turn philosophy from the study of nature to speculations upon life, but the innovators whom I oppose are turning off attention from life to nature. They seem to think that we are placed here to watch the growth of plants, or the motions of the stars. Socrates was rather of opinion that what we had to learn was how to do good and avoid evil.

$$\ὅττι\ τοι\ ἐν\ μεγάροισι\ κακόν\ τ'\ ἀγαθόν\ τε\ τέτυκται.$$

Of institutions we may judge by their effects. From this wonder-working academy I do not know that there ever proceeded any man very eminent for knowledge; its only genuine product, I believe, is a small history of poetry, written in Latin by his nephew Phillips, of which perhaps none of my readers has ever heard.[n]

That in his school, as in everything else which he undertook, he laboured with great diligence, there is no reason for doubting. One part of his method deserves general imitation. He was careful to instruct his scholars in religion. Every Sunday was spent upon theology, of which he dictated a short system gathered from the writers that were then fashionable in the Dutch universities.[n]

He set his pupils an example of hard study and spare diet, only now and then he allowed himself to pass a day of festivity and indulgence with some gay gentlemen of Gray's Inn.

He now began to engage in the controversies of the times, and lent

Socrates was: cf. *Rambler* 24, 28, 180.

ὅττι τοι: *Odyssey*, iv. 392: ('whatever good or evil has come about in royal halls').

his breath to blow the flames of contention. In 1641 he published a treatise *Of Reformation*, in two books, against the Established Church, being willing to help the Puritans, who were, he says, 'inferior to the prelates in learning'.

Hall, Bishop of Norwich, had published *An Humble Remonstrance* in defence of episcopacy, to which, in 1641, six ministers, of whose names the first letters made the celebrated word *Smectymnuus*, gave their answer.[n] Of this answer a confutation was attempted by the learned Ussher; and to the confutation Milton published a reply entitled *Of Prelatical Episcopacy, and whether it may be deduced from the Apostolical Times, by virtue of those testimonies which are alleged to that purpose in some late treatises, one whereof goes under the name of James Lord Bishop of Armagh.*

I have transcribed this title to show, by his contemptuous mention of Ussher, that he had now adopted the Puritanical savageness of manners. His next work was *The Reason of Church Government urged against Prelacy, by John Milton*, 1642.[n] In this book he discovers, not with ostentatious exultation, but with calm confidence, his high opinion of his own powers, and promises to undertake something, he yet knows not what, that may be of use and honour to his country. 'This', says he, 'is not to be obtained but by devout prayer to that Eternal Spirit that can enrich with all utterance and knowledge, and sends out His seraphim with the hallowed fire of His altar to touch and purify the lips of whom He pleases. To this must be added industrious and select reading, steady observation, and insight into all seemly and generous arts and affairs; till which in some measure be compassed, I refuse not to sustain this expectation.' From a promise like this, at once fervid, pious and rational, might be expected the *Paradise Lost*.

He published the same year two more pamphlets upon the same question. To one of his antagonists who affirms that he was 'vomited out of the university',[n] he answers in general terms: 'The Fellows of the College wherein I spent some years, at my parting, after I had

'*inferior to*': *CM*, viii. 130–1 (where the inferiority is expressed in terms of 'eloquence' not learning).

Hall: Joseph Hall (1574–1656), Bishop of Exeter and Norwich, essayist and poet.

Ussher: James Ussher (1581–1656), Archbishop of Armagh, whose 'confutation' was entitled *The Judgement of Dr. Rainoldes touching the Original of Episcopacy, more largely confirmed out of Antiquity* (1641).

'*This*': *CM*, iii. 241.

two more pamphlets: *Animadversions upon the Remonstrant's Defence against Smectymnuus* (1641); *An Apology against a Pamphlet* (1642).

'*The Fellows*': *CM*, iii. 297–8.

taken two degrees as the manner is, signified many times how much better it would content them that I should stay.... As for the common approbation or dislike of that place as now it is, that I should esteem or disesteem myself the more for that, too simple is the answerer if he think to obtain with me. Of small practice were the physician who could not judge, by what she and her sister have of long time vomited, that the worser stuff she strongly keeps in her stomach, but the better she is ever kecking at, and is queasy: she vomits now out of sickness, but before it be well with her she must vomit by strong physic.... The university, in the time of her better health and my younger judgement, I never greatly admired, but now much less.'

This is surely the language of a man who thinks that he has been injured. He proceeds to describe the course of his conduct and the train of his thoughts, and because he has been suspected of incontinence, gives an account of his own purity: 'That if I be justly charged', says he, 'with this crime, it may come upon me with tenfold shame.'

The style of his piece is rough, and such perhaps was that of his antagonist. This roughness he justifies by great examples in a long digression. Sometimes he tries to be humorous: 'Lest I should take him for some chaplain in hand, some squire of the body to his prelate, one who serves not at the altar only but at the Court-cupboard, he will bestow on us a pretty model of himself, and sets me out half a dozen phthisical mottoes, wherever he had them, hopping short in the measure of convulsion fits; in which labour the agony of his wit having scaped narrowly, instead of well-sized periods he greets us with a quantity of thumb-ring posies.... And thus ends this section, or rather dissection of himself.' Such is the controversial merriment of Milton; his gloomy seriousness is yet more offensive. Such is his malignity 'that hell grows darker at his frown'.

His father, after Reading was taken by Essex, came to reside in his house, and his school increased. At Whitsuntide, in his thirty-fifth year, he married Mary, the daughter of Mr. Powell, a Justice of the Peace in Oxfordshire. He brought her to town with him, and expected all the advantages of a conjugal life. The lady, however, seems not

'*That if I be*': p. 306.   '*Lest I should*': pp. 321, 323.
'*that hell*': *PL*, ii. 719–20.
Essex: Robert Devereux (1591–1646), 3rd Earl of Essex, took Reading on 27 Apr. 1643.
Mary: Mary Powell (1625–52), d. of Richard Powell (d. 1646) was married to Milton in the summer of 1642 (not 1643).

much to have delighted in the pleasures of spare diet and hard study, for, as Phillips relates, 'having for a month led a philosophical life, after having been used at home to a great house, and much company and joviality, her friends, possibly by her own desire, made earnest suit to have her company the remaining part of the summer; which was granted, upon a promise of her return at Michaelmas.'

Milton was too busy to much miss his wife: he pursued his studies, and now and then visited the Lady Margaret Ley, whom he has mentioned in one of his sonnets. At last Michaelmas arrived, but the lady had no inclination to return to the sullen gloom of her husband's habitation, and therefore very willingly forgot her promise. He sent her a letter, but had no answer; he sent more with the same success. It could be alleged that letters miscarry; he therefore dispatched a messenger, being by this time too angry to go himself. His messenger was sent back with some contempt. The family of the lady were Cavaliers.

In a man whose opinion of his own merit was like Milton's, less provocation than this might have raised violent resentment. Milton soon determined to repudiate her for disobedience, and being one of those who could easily find arguments to justify inclination, published (in 1644) *The Doctrine and Discipline of Divorce*,[n] which was followed by *The Judgement of Martin Bucer concerning Divorce*, and the next year his *Tetrachordon: Expositions upon the four chief Places of Scripture which treat of Marriage*.

This innovation was opposed, as might be expected, by the clergy who, then holding their famous Assembly at Westminster, procured that the author should be called before the Lords; 'but that House', says Wood, 'whether approving the doctrine, or not favouring his accusers, did soon dismiss him'.

There seems not to have been much written against him, nor anything by any writer of eminence. The antagonist that appeared is styled by him 'a serving-man turned solicitor'.[n] Howell in his letters mentions the new doctrine with contempt, and it was, I suppose, thought more worthy of derision than of confutation. He complains

as Phillips relates: *EL*, p. 64.
Lady Margaret Ley: Lady Margaret Hobson (*née* Ley) (b. 1608?), d. of 1st Earl of Marlborough, addressed in Sonnet X.
Martin Bucer: (or Butzer) (1491–1551), German protestant divine, Regius Professor of Divinity at Cambridge and author of *De Regno Christi ad Edw. VI* (on part of which Milton's epitome or translation was based).
says Wood: *EL*, p. 41. Cf. *LR*, ii. 116–17; Parker, i. 264.
Howell: James Howell (1594?–1666), author of *Epistolae Ho-Elianae*; see ed. by J. Jacobs (1890–2), p. 569.

of this neglect in two sonnets, of which the first is contemptible, and the second not excellent.

From this time it is observed that he became an enemy to the Presbyterians,[n] whom he had favoured before. He that changes his party by his humour is not more virtuous than he that changes it by his interest: he loves himself rather than truth.

His wife and her relations now found that Milton was not an unresisting sufferer of injuries, and perceiving that he had begun to put his doctrine in practice by courting a young woman of great accomplishments, the daughter of one Dr. Davis, who was however not ready to comply, they resolved to endeavour a reunion. He went sometimes to the house of one Blackborough, his relation, in the lane of St. Martin's Le Grand, and at one of his usual visits was surprised to see his wife come from another room and implore forgiveness on her knees. He resisted her entreaties for a while, 'but partly', says Phillips, 'his own generous nature, more inclinable to reconciliation than to perseverance in anger or revenge, and partly the strong intercession of friends on both sides, soon brought him to an act of oblivion and a firm league of peace'. It were injurious to omit that Milton afterwards received her father and her brothers in his own house, when they were distressed, with other Royalists.

He published about the same time his *Areopagitica, a Speech of Mr. John Milton for the Liberty of unlicensed Printing*. The danger of such unbounded liberty, and the danger of bounding it, have produced a problem in the science of government which human understanding seems hitherto unable to solve. If nothing may be published but what civil authority shall have previously approved, power must always be the standard of truth; if every dreamer of innovations may propagate his projects, there can be no settlement; if every murmurer at government may diffuse discontent, there can be no peace; and if every sceptic in theology may teach his follies, there can be no religion. The remedy against these evils is to punish the authors, for it is yet allowed that every society may punish, though not prevent, the publication of opinions which that society shall think pernicious; but this punishment, though it may crush the author, promotes the book, and it seems not more reasonable to leave the right of printing unrestrained because writers may be afterwards censured, than it

---

two sonnets: XI and XII.   Dr. Davis: see Parker, ii. 926–7.
Blackborough: William Blackborough (Blackborow *or* Blackborrow) (d. 1646?), leatherseller, whose wife Hester was a grand-niece of Milton's maternal grandfather.
says Phillips: EL, p. 67.

would be to sleep with doors unbolted because by our laws we can hang a thief.

But whatever were his engagements, civil or domestic, poetry was never long out of his thoughts. About this time (1645) a collection of his Latin and English poems appeared, in which the 'Allegro' and 'Penseroso', with some others, were first published.

He had taken a larger house in Barbican for the reception of scholars, but the numerous relations of his wife, to whom he generously granted refuge for a while, occupied his rooms. In time, however, they went away, 'and the house again', says Phillips, 'now looked like a house of the Muses only, though the accession of scholars was not great. Possibly his having proceeded so far in the education of youth may have been the occasion of his adversaries calling him pedagogue and schoolmaster, whereas it is well known he never set up for a public school, to teach all the young fry of a parish, but only was willing to impart his learning and knowledge to relations, and the sons of gentlemen who were his intimate friends; and that neither his writings nor his way of teaching ever savoured in the least of pedantry.'

Thus laboriously does his nephew extenuate what cannot be denied, and what might be confessed without disgrace. Milton was not a man who could become mean by a mean employment. This, however, his warmest friends seem not to have found; they therefore shift and palliate. He did not sell literature to all comers at an open shop; he was a chamber-milliner, and measured his commodities only to his friends.

Phillips, evidently impatient of viewing him in this state of degradation, tells us that it was not long continued, and to raise his character again has a mind to invest him with military splendour: 'He is much mistaken', he says, 'if there was not about this time a design of making him an adjutant-general in Sir William Waller's army. But the new-modelling of the army proved an obstruction to the design.' An event cannot be set at a much greater distance than by having been only 'designed, about some time' if a man 'be not much mistaken'. Milton shall be a pedagogue no longer, for if Phillips be not much mistaken, somebody at some time designed him for a soldier.

About the time that the army was new-modelled (1645) he removed to a smaller house in Holborn which opened backward into

says Phillips: *EL*, pp. 67–8.
chamber-milliner: 'a milliner who carries on business in a private house, not in a
  shop' (*OED*).   '*He is much mistaken*': *EL*, p. 68.
Sir William Waller: (1597?–1668), parliamentary general.

Lincoln's Inn Fields.[n] He is not known to have published anything afterwards till the King's death, when, finding his murderers condemned by the Presbyterians, he wrote a treatise to justify it, and 'to compose the minds of the people'.

He made some *Remarks on the Articles of Peace between Ormonde and the Irish Rebels.* While he contented himself to write, he perhaps did only what his conscience dictated; and if he did not very vigilantly watch the influence of his own passions, and the gradual prevalence of opinions first willingly admitted and then habitually indulged—if objections, by being overlooked, were forgotten, and desire superinduced conviction, he yet shared only the common weakness of mankind, and might be no less sincere than his opponents. But as faction seldom leaves a man honest, however it might find him, Milton is suspected of having interpolated the book called *Icon Basilike*, which the Council of State, to whom he was now made Latin Secretary, employed him to censure, by inserting a prayer taken from Sidney's *Arcadia*, and imputing it to the King,[n] whom he charges in his *Iconoclastes* with the use of this prayer as with a heavy crime, in the indecent language with which prosperity had emboldened the advocates for rebellion to insult all that is venerable or great: 'Who would have imagined so little fear in him of the true all-seeing Deity as, immediately before his death, to pop into the hands of the grave bishop that attended him, as a special relic of his saintly exercises, a prayer stolen word for word from the mouth of a heathen woman praying to a heathen god?'

The papers which the King gave to Dr. Juxon on the scaffold the regicides took away, so that they were at least the publishers of this prayer; and Dr. Birch, who had examined the question with great care, was inclined to think them the forgers.[n] The use of it by adaptation was innocent, and they who could so noisily censure it, with a little extension of their malice could contrive what they wanted to accuse.

King Charles II, being now sheltered in Holland, employed Salmasius, professor of Polite Learning at Leyden, to write a defence

---

a treatise: *The Tenure of Kings and Magistrates* (1649).

'*to compose*': *CM*, viii. 136–7.

Ormonde: James Butler (1610–88), 12th Earl and 1st Duke of Ormonde. For Milton's *Observations* see *CM*, vi. 242–71.

Sidney's: Sir Philip Sidney (1554–86), soldier, statesman, poet.

'*Who would have*': *CM*, v. 85–6.

Dr. Juxon: William Juxon (1582–1663), Bishop of London, later Archbishop of Canterbury.

Salmasius: Claude de Saumaise (1588–1653), French humanist and philologist.

of his father and of monarchy, and to excite his industry gave him, as was reported, a hundred jacobuses. Salmasius was a man of skill in languages, knowledge of antiquity, and sagacity of emendatory criticism almost exceeding all hope of human attainment, and having by excessive praises been confirmed in great confidence of himself, though he probably had not much considered the principles of society or the rights of government, undertook the employment without distrust of his own qualifications, and as his expedition in writing was wonderful, in 1649 published *Defensio Regis*.

To this Milton was required to write a sufficient answer, which he performed (1651) in such a manner that Hobbes declared himself unable to decide whose language was best, or whose arguments were worst. In my opinion, Milton's periods are smoother, neater and more pointed, but he delights himself with teasing his adversary as much as with confuting him. He makes a foolish allusion of Salmasius, whose doctrine he considers as servile and unmanly, to the stream of Salmacis, which whoever entered left half his virility behind him. Salmasius was a Frenchman and was unhappily married to a scold. *Tu es Gallus*, says Milton, *et, ut aiunt, nimium gallinaceus*. But his supreme pleasure is to tax his adversary, so renowned for criticism, with vicious Latin. He opens his book with telling that he has used *persona*, which according to Milton signifies only a 'mask', in a sense not known to the Romans by applying it as we apply 'person'. But as Nemesis is always on the watch, it is memorable that he has enforced the charge of a solecism by an expression in itself grossly solecistical when, for one of those supposed blunders, he says, as Ker and I think someone before him has remarked, *propino te grammatistis tuis vapulandum*. From *vapulo*, which has a passive sense, *vapulandus* can never be derived. No man forgets his original trade: the rights of nations and of kings sink into questions of grammar if grammarians discuss them.[n]

Milton when he undertook this answer was weak of body and dim

as was reported: cf. *CM*, vii. 14–15, 280–1, 284–5, 336–7, 428–9.

Hobbes: Thomas Hobbes (1588–1679), philosopher, author of *Leviathan* (1651) and *Behemoth* (1679); q.v. p. 172.

He makes: *CM*, vii. 16–17, 20–1, 280–1.

Salmacis: cf. Ovid, *Metamorphoses*, iv. 285 ff.

Tu es Gallus: you are Gallic, and, as they say, only too gallinaceous.

criticism: 'the critical science which deals with the text, character, composition, and origin of literary documents' (*OED*).

Ker: John Ker, M.D.; see his *Selectarum de Lingua Latina Observationum Libri Duo* (1709), ii. sig. Qq4^v, where it is mentioned that Milton's solecism was noticed by Francis Vavasseur (or Vavassor).

propino te: I hand you over to be cudgelled by your fellow-grammarians.

of sight;[n] but his will was forward, and what was wanting of health was supplied by zeal. He was rewarded with £1,000, and his book was much read,[n] for paradox recommended by spirit and elegance easily gains attention; and he who told every man that he was equal to his king could hardly want an audience.

That the performance of Salmasius was not dispersed with equal rapidity, or read with equal eagerness, is very credible. He taught only the stale doctrine of authority and the unpleasing duty of submission, and he had been so long not only the monarch but the tyrant of literature that almost all mankind were delighted to find him defied and insulted by a new name, not yet considered as anyone's rival. If Christina, as is said, commended the *Defence of the People*,[n] her purpose must be to torment Salmasius who was then at her Court, for neither her civil station nor her natural character could dispose her to favour the doctrine who was by birth a queen, and by temper despotic.

That Salmasius was, from the appearance of Milton's book, treated with neglect, there is not much proof; but to a man so long accustomed to admiration a little praise of his antagonist would be sufficiently offensive, and might incline him to leave Sweden, from which, however, he was dismissed not with any mark of contempt, but with a train of attendance scarce less than regal.[n]

He prepared a reply which, left as it was imperfect, was published by his son in the year of the Restoration. In the beginning, being probably most in pain for his Latinity, he endeavours to defend his use of the word *persona*; but if I remember right, he misses a better authority than any that he has found—that of Juvenal in his fourth satire:

> —Quid agas cum dira et foedior omni
> Crimine *persona* est?

As Salmasius reproached Milton with losing his eyes in the quarrel,[n] Milton delighted himself with the belief that he had shortened Salmasius's life, and both perhaps with more malignity than reason. Salmasius died at the Spa, Sept. 3, 1653, and as controvertists are commonly said to be killed by their last dispute, Milton was flattered with the credit of destroying him.

Cromwell had now dismissed the Parliament by the authority of which he had destroyed monarchy, and commenced monarch

he endeavours: *Ad Johannem Miltonum Responsio* (1660), pp. 25 ff.
Juvenal: (60?–130?), the greatest Roman satirist.
Quid agas: (ll. 14–15) 'What can you do when the person is more foul and monstrous than any charge you can bring against him?'

himself under the title of Protector, but with kingly and more than kingly power.[n] That his authority was lawful never was pretended; he himself founded his right only in necessity; but Milton, having now tasted the honey of public employment, would not return to hunger and philosophy, but continuing to exercise his office under a manifest usurpation, betrayed to his power that liberty which he had defended. Nothing can be more just than that rebellion should end in slavery, that he who had justified the murder of his king for some acts which to him seemed unlawful, should now sell his services and his flatteries to a tyrant of whom it was evident that he could do nothing lawful.

He had now been blind for some years, but his vigour of intellect was such that he was not disabled to discharge his office of Latin Secretary or continue his controversies. His mind was too eager to be diverted, and too strong to be subdued.

About this time his first wife died in childbed, having left him three daughters. As he probably did not much love her, he did not long continue the appearance of lamenting her, but after a short time married Katherine, the daughter of one Captain Woodcock of Hackney, a woman doubtless educated in opinions like his own. She died within a year of childbirth, or some distemper that followed it, and her husband has honoured her memory with a poor sonnet.

The first reply to Milton's *Defensio Populi* was published in 1651, called *Apologia pro Rege et Populo Anglicano, contra Johannis Poly-pragmatici (alias Miltoni) defensionem destructivam Regis et Populi*. Of this the author was not known, but Milton and his nephew Phillips, under whose name he published an answer so much correc-ted by him that it might be called his own,[n] imputed it to Bramhall, and knowing him no friend to regicides, thought themselves at liberty to treat him as if they had known what they only suspected.

Next year appeared *Regii Sanguinis clamor ad Coelum*. Of this the author was Peter Du Moulin, who was afterwards prebendary of Canterbury; but Morus, or More, a French minister, having the

Katherine: Milton's first wife died *c.* 5 May 1652, and was the mother of Anne (1646–77?), Mary (1648–81/94), and Deborah (1652–1727). He married Katherine (1628–58), d. of William Woodcock (d. 1642?) on 12 Nov. 1656, and she was probably the subject of Sonnet XIX.

Apologia pro Rege: 'Apology on behalf of the King and the English People against John Busybody's (alias Milton's) Defence, which would destroy the King and the People.' The author was John Rowland (1606–60).

Bramhall: John Bramhall (1594–1663), Archbishop of Armagh.

Peter Du Moulin: the younger (1601–84), Anglican divine.

Morus: Alexander More (or Morus) (1616–70) delivered the MS. to the printer and composed the dedication to Charles II.

care of its publication, was treated as the writer by Milton in his *Defensio Secunda*, and overwhelmed by such violence of invective that he began to shrink under the tempest, and gave his persecutors the means of knowing the true author. Du Moulin was now in great danger, but Milton's pride operated against his malignity, and both he and his friends were more willing that Du Moulin should escape than that he should be convicted of mistake.

In this second Defence he shows that his eloquence is not merely satirical: the rudeness of his invective is equalled by the grossness of his flattery. 'Deserimur, Cromuelle, tu solus superes, ad te summa nostrarum rerum rediit, in te solo consistit, insuperabili tuae virtuti cedimus cuncti, nemine vel obloquente, nisi qui aequales inaequalis ipse honores sibi quaerit, aut digniori concessos invidet, aut non intelligit nihil esse in societate hominum magis vel Deo gratum, vel rationi consentaneum, esse in civitate nihil aequius, nihil utilius, quam potiri rerum dignissimum. Eum te agnoscunt omnes, Cromuelle, ea tu civis maximus et gloriosissimus,[n] dux publici consilii, exercituum fortissimorum imperator, pater patriae gessisti. Sic tu spontanea bonorum omnium et animitus missa voce salutaris.'

Caesar when he assumed the perpetual dictatorship had not more servile or more elegant flattery. A translation may show its servility, but its elegance is less attainable. Having exposed the unskilfulness or selfishness of the former government, 'We were left', says Milton, 'to ourselves: the whole national interest fell into your hands, and subsists only in your abilities. To your virtue, overpowering and resistless, every man gives way, except some who, without equal qualifications, aspire to equal honours, who envy the distinctions of merit greater than their own, or who have yet to learn that in the coalition of human society nothing is more pleasing to God, or more agreeable to reason, than that the highest mind should have the sovereign power. Such, Sir, are you by general confession; such are the things achieved by you, the greatest and most glorious of our countrymen, the director of our public councils, the leader of unconquered armies, the father of your country—for by that title does every good man hail you with sincere and voluntary praise.'

Next year, having defended all that wanted defence, he found leisure to defend himself. He undertook his own vindication against More, whom he declares in his title to be justly called the author of the *Regii Sanguinis clamor*.[n] In this there is no want of vehemence

---

Deserimur: *CM*, viii. 222.   *Caesar when he assumed*: i.e. 44 B.C.

nor eloquence, nor does he forget his wonted wit. *Morus es? an Momus? an uterque idem est?* He then remembers that *morus* is Latin for a mulberry-tree, and hints at the known transformation:

> —Poma alba ferebat
> Quae post nigra tulit Morus.

With this piece ended his controversies, and he from this time gave himself up to his private studies and his civil employment.[n]

As Secretary to the Protector he is supposed to have written the Declaration of the reasons for a war with Spain.[n] His agency was considered as of great importance, for when a treaty with Sweden was artfully suspended, the delay was publicly imputed to Mr. Milton's indisposition, and the Swedish agent was provoked to express his wonder that only one man in England could write Latin, and that man blind.[n]

Being now forty-seven years old, and seeing himself disencumbered from external interruptions, he seems to have recollected his former purposes, and to have resumed three great works which he had planned for his future employment: an epic poem, the history of his country, and a dictionary of the Latin tongue.

To collect a dictionary seems a work of all others least practicable in a state of blindness because it depends upon perpetual and minute inspection and collation. Nor would Milton probably have begun it after he had lost his eyes, but having had it always before him, he continued it, says Phillips, 'almost to his dying-day; but the papers were so discomposed and deficient that they could not be fitted for the press'. The compilers of the Latin dictionary printed afterwards at Cambridge had the use of those collections in three folios;[n] but what was their fate afterwards is not known.

To compile a history from various authors when they can only be consulted by other eyes is not easy, nor possible, but with more skilful and attentive help than can be commonly obtained; and it was probably the difficulty of consulting and comparing that stopped

Morus es: *CM*, ix. 168–9: 'Are you Morus, or Momus? Or are both one and the same person?' Momus, a son of primeval Night, personifies criticism and fault-finding.

Poma alba: pp. 208–9. Cf. *Metamorphoses*, iv. 51–2. 'Morus, from bearing white fruit, afterwards bore black.' Johnson has changed Milton's *Qui* (masc.) to *Quae* (fem.). The masc. *morus* means fool; the fem., mulberry-tree. The pun is not spoilt in the Latin by this change, but is inevitably lost in translation.

the Swedish agent: Count Christiern Bond(e).

the history of his country: *The History of Britain* (1670).

says Phillips: *EL*, p. 72.

Milton's narrative at the Conquest, a period at which affairs were not yet very intricate nor authors very numerous.

For the subject of his epic poem, after much deliberation, 'long choosing, and beginning late', he fixed upon 'Paradise Lost'—a design so comprehensive that it could be justified only by success. He had once designed to celebrate King Arthur, as he hints in his verses to Mansus, but 'Arthur was reserved', says Fenton, 'to another destiny.'[n]

It appears by some sketches of poetical projects left in manuscript, and to be seen in a library at Cambridge, that he had digested his thoughts on this subject into one of those wild dramas which were anciently called mysteries; and Phillips had seen what he terms part of a tragedy beginning with the first ten lines of Satan's address to the Sun. These mysteries consist of allegorical persons, such as Justice, Mercy, Faith. Of the tragedy or mystery of *Paradise Lost* there are two plans:[n]

THE PERSONS	THE PERSONS
Michael.	Moses.
Chorus of Angels.	Divine Justice, Wisdom, Heavenly Love.
Heavenly Love.	
Lucifer.	The Evening Star, Hesperus.
Adam, ⎫ with the	Chorus of Angels.
Eve, ⎬ Serpent.	Lucifer.
Conscience.	Adam.
Death.	Eve.
Labour, ⎫	Conscience.
Sickness, ⎪	Labour, ⎫
Discontent, ⎬ Mutes.	Sickness, ⎪
Ignorance, ⎪	Discontent, ⎬ Mutes.
with others, ⎭	Ignorance, ⎪
Faith.	Fear, ⎪
Hope.	Death, ⎭
Charity.	Faith.
	Hope.
	Charity.

PARADISE LOST
THE PERSONS

Moses προλογίζει, recounting how he assumed his true body, that it corrupts not, because it is with God in the mount; declares the like of Enoch and Elijah; besides the purity of the

'*long choosing*': *PL*. ix. 26.
as he hints: 'Mansus', ll. 80–1; cf. *Epitaphium Damonis*, ll. 166–8.
προλογίζει: 'delivers the prologue'.
Enoch: Gen. 5:24; Heb. 11:5.   *Elijah*: 2 Kgs. 2:11.

place, that certain pure winds, dews and clouds, preserve it from
corruption; whence exhorts to the sight of God; tells they cannot
see Adam in the state of innocence, by reason of their sin.

Justice,
Mercy,   } debating what should become of man, if he fall.
Wisdom,
Chorus of Angels singing a hymn of the Creation.

ACT II
Heavenly Love.
Evening Star.
Chorus sing the marriage-song, and describe Paradise.

ACT III
Lucifer, contriving Adam's ruin.
Chorus fears for Adam, and relates Lucifer's rebellion and fall.

ACT IV
Adam,   } fallen.
Eve,
Conscience cites them to God's examination.
Chorus bewails, and tells the good Adam has lost.

ACT V
Adam and Eve driven out of Paradise.
——— —— —— presented by an angel with
Labour, Grief, Hatred, Envy, War, Famine,
Pestilence, Sickness, Discontent, Ignorance, } Mutes.
Fear, Death,
To whom he gives their names. Likewise
    Winter, Heat, Tempest, etc.
Faith,
Hope,   } comfort him, and instruct him.
Charity,
Chorus briefly concludes.

Such was his first design, which could have produced only an
allegory or mystery. The following sketch seems to have attained
more maturity.

ADAM UNPARADISED

The angel Gabriel, either descending or entering; showing, since
this globe was created, his frequency as much on earth as in
heaven; describes Paradise. Next, the Chorus, showing the
reason of his coming to keep his watch in Paradise, after Lucifer's
rebellion, by command from God; and withal expressing his
desire to see and know more concerning this excellent new
creature, man. The angel Gabriel, as by his name signifying a
prince of power, tracing Paradise with a more free office, passes
by the station of the Chorus, and, desired by them, relates what
he knew of man; as the creation of Eve, with their love and
marriage. After this, Lucifer appears; after his overthrow, bemoans himself, seeks revenge on man.[n] The Chorus prepare

resistance at his first approach. At last, after discourse of enmity on either side, he departs; whereat the Chorus sings of the battle and victory in heaven, against him and his accomplices: as before, after the first act, was sung a hymn of the creation. Here again may appear Lucifer, relating and insulting in what he had done to the destruction of man. Man next, and Eve having by this time been seduced by the Serpent, appears confusedly covered with leaves. Conscience, in a shape, accuses him; Justice cites him to the place whither Jehovah called for him. In the meanwhile, the Chorus entertains the stage, and is informed by some angel the manner of the Fall. Here the Chorus bewails Adam's fall; Adam then and Eve return; accuse one another; but especially Adam lays the blame to his wife; is stubborn in his offence. Justice appears, reasons with him, convinces him. The Chorus admonisheth Adam, and bids him beware Lucifer's example of impenitence. The angel is sent to banish them out of Paradise; but before causes to pass before his eyes, in shapes, a mask of all the evils of this life and world. He is humbled, relents, despairs: at last appears Mercy, comforts him, promises the Messiah; then calls in Faith, Hope, and Charity; instructs him; he repents, gives God the glory, submits to his penalty. The Chorus briefly concludes. Compare this with the former draught.

These are very imperfect rudiments of *Paradise Lost*, but it is pleasant to see great works in their seminal state, pregnant with latent possibilities of excellence; nor could there be any more delightful entertainment than to trace their gradual growth and expansion, and to observe how they are sometimes suddenly advanced by accidental hints, and sometimes slowly improved by steady meditation.

Invention is almost the only literary labour which blindness cannot obstruct, and therefore he naturally solaced his solitude by the indulgence of his fancy and the melody of his numbers. He had done what he knew to be necessarily previous to poetical excellence: he had made himself acquainted with 'seemly arts and affairs'; his comprehension was extended by various knowledge, and his memory stored with intellectual treasures. He was skilful in many languages, and had by reading and composition attained the full mastery of his own. He would have wanted little help from books had he retained the power of perusing them.

But while his greater designs were advancing, having now, like many other authors, caught the love of publication, he amused himself as he could with little productions. He sent to the press (1658) a manuscript of Raleigh called *The Cabinet Council*, and next year gratified his malevolence to the clergy by *A Treatise of Civil Power in*

Raleigh: Sir Walter Ralegh (or Raleigh) (1552?–1618), military and naval commander and author.

Ecclesiastical Cases and *The Means of removing Hirelings out of the Church.*

Oliver was now dead; Richard was constrained to resign; the system of extemporary government, which had been held together only by force, naturally fell into fragments when that force was taken away, and Milton saw himself and his cause in equal danger. But he had still hope of doing something. He wrote letters, which Toland has published, to such men as he thought friends to the new commonwealth; and even in the year of the Restoration he 'bated no jot of heart or hope', but was fantastical enough to think that the nation, agitated as it was, might be settled by a pamphlet called *A Ready and Easy Way to establish a Free Commonwealth*—which was, however, enough considered to be both seriously and ludicrously answered.[n]

The obstinate enthusiasm of the commonwealth-men was very remarkable. When the King was apparently returning, Harrington, with a few associates as fanatical as himself, used to meet with all the gravity of political importance to settle an equal government by rotation; and Milton, kicking when he could strike no longer, was foolish enough to publish, a few weeks before the Restoration, *Notes* upon a sermon preached by one Griffiths entitled *The Fear of God and the King*. To these notes an answer was written by L'Estrange in a pamphlet petulantly called *No Blind Guides*.

But whatever Milton could write, or men of greater activity could do, the King was now about to be restored with the irresistible approbation of the people. He was therefore no longer Secretary, and was consequently obliged to quit the house which he held by his office;[n] and proportioning his sense of danger to his opinion of the importance of his writings, thought it convenient to seek some shelter, and hid himself for a time in Bartholomew Close by West Smithfield.

I cannot but remark a kind of respect perhaps unconsciously paid to this great man by his biographers: every house in which he

Richard: Richard Cromwell (1626–1712), was proclaimed Protector on 4 Sept. 1658 (the day after his father's death), and forced to abdicate on 25 May 1659.

Toland: John Toland (1670–1722), deist, biographer of Milton; see *Complete Works of Milton* (1698), ii. 779–81, 799–800 (*CM*, vi. 101–9).

'*bated no jot*': 'To Mr. Cyriack Skinner upon his Blindness', ll. 7–8.

Harrington: James Harrington (or Harington) (1611–77), political theorist. Cf. Parker, i. 537–8.

Griffiths: Matthew Griffith (1599?–1665), Royalist divine, whose sermon was preached on 25 March and registered for publication on 31st.

L'Estrange: Sir Roger L'Estrange (1616–1704), Tory pamphleteer.

resided is historically mentioned, as if it were an injury to neglect naming any place that he honoured by his presence.

The King, with lenity of which the world has had perhaps no other example, declined to be the judge or avenger of his own or his father's wrongs, and promised to admit into the Act of Oblivion all except those whom the parliament should except; and the parliament doomed none to capital punishment but the wretches who had immediately co-operated in the murder of the King. Milton was certainly not one of them; he had only justified what they had done.

This justification was indeed sufficiently offensive, and (June 16) an order was issued to seize Milton's *Defence*, and Goodwin's *Obstructors of Justice*, another book of the same tendency, and burn them by the common hangman. The attorney-general was ordered to prosecute the authors, but Milton was not seized, nor perhaps very diligently pursued.

Not long after (August 19) the flutter of innumerable bosoms was stilled by an act which the King, that his mercy might want no recommendation of elegance, rather called an Act of Oblivion than of Grace.[n] Goodwin was named, with nineteen more, as incapacitated for any public trust, but of Milton there was no exception.

Of this tenderness shown to Milton the curiosity of mankind has not forborne to inquire the reason. Burnet thinks he was forgotten, but this is another instance which may confirm Dalrymple's observation who says 'that whenever Burnet's narrations are examined, he appears to be mistaken'.

Forgotten he was not for his prosecution was ordered; it must be therefore by design that he was included in the general oblivion. He is said to have had friends in the House, such as Marvell, Morrice and Sir Thomas Clarges; and undoubtedly a man like him must have had influence. A very particular story of his escape is told by Richardson in his Memoirs,[n] which he received from Pope as

---

Goodwin's: John Goodwin (1594?–1665), republican divine.

The attorney-general: Sir Geoffrey Palmer (1598–1670), 1st Baronet.

Burnet: Gilbert Burnet (1643–1715), Bishop of Salisbury, author of *Bishop Burnet's History of his Own Time* (1724–34); q.v. i. 163.

Dalrymple: Sir John Dalrymple (1726–1810), 4th Baronet of Cranstoun, Scottish judge; see his *Memoirs of Great Britain and Ireland* (Edinburgh, 1771–3), pt. I, p. 34 n. Cf. *Life*, ii. 213.

He is said: See Phillips, Toland, Richardson, *EL*, pp. 74, 175, 271.

Marvell: Andrew Marvell (1621–78), poet and M.P.

Morrice: Sir William Morrice (or Morice) (1602–76), Secretary of State and theologian.

Sir Thomas Clarges: (1619?–95), politician, brother-in-law of General Monck.

delivered by Betterton, who might have heard it from Davenant. In the war between the King and Parliament, Davenant was made prisoner and condemned to die, but was spared at the request of Milton. When the turn of success brought Milton into the like danger, Davenant repaid the benefit by appearing in his favour. Here is a reciprocation of generosity and gratitude so pleasing that the tale makes its own way to credit. But if help were wanted I know not where to find it. The danger of Davenant is certain from his own relation, but of his escape there is no account. Betterton's narration can be traced no higher; it is not known that he had it from Davenant. We are told that the benefit exchanged was life for life, but it seems not certain that Milton's life ever was in danger. Goodwin, who had committed the same kind of crime, escaped with incapacitation; and as exclusion from public trust is a punishment which the power of government can commonly inflict without the help of a particular law, it required no great interest to exempt Milton from a censure little more than verbal. Something may be reasonably ascribed to veneration and compassion—to veneration of his abilities and compassion for his distresses—which made it fit to forgive his malice for his learning. He was now poor and blind, and who would pursue with violence an illustrious enemy depressed by fortune and disarmed by nature?

The publication of the Act of Oblivion put him in the same condition with his fellow-subjects. He was, however, upon some pretence not now known, in the custody of the serjeant in December, and when he was released upon his refusal of the fees demanded, he and the serjeant were called before the House. He was now safe within the shade of Oblivion, and knew himself to be as much out of the power of a griping officer as any other man. How the question was determined is not known. Milton would hardly have contended but that he knew himself to have right on his side.

He then removed to Jewin Street,[n] near Aldersgate Street, and being blind, and by no means wealthy, wanted a domestic companion and attendant, and therefore, by the recommendation of Dr. Paget, married Elizabeth Minshull, of a gentleman's family in Cheshire, probably without a fortune. All his wives were virgins, for he has declared that he thought it gross and indelicate to be a second husband; upon what other principles his choice was made cannot

---

Betterton: Thomas Betterton (1635?–1710), actor and dramatist.
the serjeant: James Norfolk. Cf. Parker, i. 576, ii. 1087–8.
Dr. Paget: Nathan Paget (1615–79), physician.
Elizabeth Minshull: (1638–1727).   *he has declared*: CM, iii. 342.

now be known, but marriage afforded not much of his happiness. The first wife left him in disgust and was brought back only by terror; the second, indeed, seems to have been more a favourite, but her life was short. The third, as Phillips relates, oppressed his children in his lifetime, and cheated them at his death.[n]

Soon after his marriage, according to an obscure story, he was offered the continuance of his employment, and being pressed by his wife to accept it, answered, 'You, like other women, want to ride in your coach; my wish is to live and die an honest man.' If he considered the Latin secretary as exercising any of the powers of government, he that had shared authority either with the Parliament or Cromwell might have forborne to talk very loudly of his honesty; and if he thought the office purely ministerial, he certainly might have honestly retained it under the King. But this tale has too little evidence to deserve a disquisition; large offers and sturdy rejections are among the most common topics of falsehood.

He had so much either of prudence or gratitude that he forbore to disturb the new settlement with any of his political or ecclesiastical opinions, and from this time devoted himself to poetry and literature. Of his zeal for learning in all its parts, he gave a proof by publishing the next year (1661) *Accidence commenced Grammar,*[n] a little book which has nothing remarkable but that its author, who had been lately defending the supreme powers of his country and was then writing *Paradise Lost*, could descend from his elevation to rescue children from the perplexity of grammatical confusion, and the trouble of lessons unnecessarily repeated.

About this time Ellwood the quaker, being recommended to him as one who would read Latin to him for the advantage of his conversation, attended him every afternoon except on Sundays. Milton, who in his letter to Hartlib had declared that 'to read Latin with an English mouth is as ill a hearing as Law French', required that Ellwood should learn and practise the Italian pronunciation, which, he said, was necessary if he would talk with foreigners. This seems to have been a task troublesome without use. There is little reason for preferring the Italian pronunciation to our own except that it is more general; and to teach it to an Englishman is only to make him a foreigner at home. He who travels, if he speaks Latin, may so soon learn the sound which every native gives it that he need make no provision before his journey; and if strangers visit us, it is their business to practise such conformity to our modes as they expect

according to an obscure story: Quoted by Richardson, *EL*, p. 280.
Ellwood: Thomas Ellwood (1639–1713).   '*to read Latin*': *CM*, iv. 281.

from us in their own countries. Ellwood complied with the directions and improved himself by his attendance, for he relates that Milton, having a curious ear, knew by his voice when he read what he did not understand, and would stop him and 'open the most difficult passages'.[n]

In a short time he took a house in the Artillery Walk leading to Bunhill Fields,[n] the mention of which concludes the register of Milton's removals and habitations. He lived longer in this place than in any other.

He was now busied by *Paradise Lost*. Whence he drew the original design has been variously conjectured by men who cannot bear to think themselves ignorant of that which, at last, neither diligence nor sagacity can discover. Some find the hint in an Italian tragedy. Voltaire tells a wild and unauthorised story of a farce seen by Milton in Italy which opened thus: 'Let the rainbow be the fiddlestick of the fiddle of heaven.'[n] It has been already shown that the first conception was a tragedy or mystery, not of a narrative but a dramatic work, which he is supposed to have begun to reduce to its present form about the time (1655) when he finished his dispute with the defenders of the King.

He long before had promised to adorn his native country by some great performance while he had yet perhaps no settled design, and was stimulated only by such expectations as naturally arose from the survey of his attainments and the consciousness of his powers. What he should undertake it was difficult to determine. He was 'long choosing, and began late'.

While he was obliged to divide his time between his private studies and affairs of state, his poetical labour must have been often interrupted, and perhaps he did little more in that busy time than construct the narrative, adjust the episodes, proportion the parts, accumulate images and sentiments, and treasure in his memory or preserve in writing such hints as books or meditation would supply. Nothing particular is known of his intellectual operations while he was a statesman, for having every help and accommodation at hand, he had no need of uncommon expedients.

Being driven from all public stations, he is yet too great not to be traced by curiosity to his retirement, where he has been found by Mr. Richardson, the fondest of his admirers, sitting 'before his door in a grey coat of coarse cloth, in warm sultry weather, to enjoy the

---

Some find: Cf. Newton, i. *xxxv*.

Voltaire: pseud. of François-Marie Arouet (1694–1778), famous French author and philosopher.   *'before his door'*: *EL*, p. 203.

fresh air; and so, as well as in his own room, receiving the visits of people of distinguished parts as well as quality.' His visitors of high quality must now be imagined to be few; but men of parts might reasonably court the conversation of a man so generally illustrious that foreigners are reported by Wood to have visited the house in Bread Street where he was born.

According to another account, he was seen in a small house 'neatly enough dressed in black clothes, sitting in a room hung with rusty green, pale but not cadaverous, with chalkstones in his hands. He said that if it were not for the gout his blindness would be tolerable.'

In the intervals of his pain, being made unable to use the common exercises, he used to swing in a chair, and sometimes played upon an organ.

He was now confessedly and visibly employed upon his poem, of which the progress might be noted by those with whom he was familiar; for he was obliged, when he had composed as many lines as his memory would conveniently retain, to employ some friend in writing them, having, at least for part of the time, no regular attendant. This gave opportunity to observations and reports.

Mr. Phillips observes that there was a very remarkable circumstance in the composure of *Paradise Lost*, 'which I have a particular reason', says he, 'to remember; for whereas I had the perusal of it from the very beginning for some years, as I went from time to time to visit him, in parcels of ten, twenty, or thirty verses at a time (which, being written by whatever hand came next, might possibly want correction as to the orthography and pointing), having, as the summer came on, not been showed any for a considerable while, and desiring the reason thereof, was answered that his vein never happily flowed but from the autumnal equinox to the vernal, and that whatever he attempted at other times was never to his satisfaction, though he courted his fancy never so much; so that, in all the years he was about this poem, he may be said to have spent half his time therein'.

Upon this relation Toland remarks that in his opinion Phillips has mistaken the time of the year, for Milton, in his *Elegies*, declares that with the advance of the spring he feels the increase of his poetical force, *redeunt in carmina vires*. To this it is answered that Phillips

---

reported by Wood: EL, p. 48. Cf. *Burnet's History of his Own Time*, i. 163.
'*neatly enough dressed*': Quoted by Richardson, *EL*, pp. 203–4.
Mr. Phillips observes: EL, p. 73. For the conflicting views expressed subsequently see ibid. pp. 178, 291; Newton, i. *xxxvi*.　　*composure*: composition.
redeunt: 'Elegia Quinta', l. 5 ('strength comes back into my songs').

could hardly mistake time so well marked; and it may be added that Milton might find different times of the year favourable to different parts of life. Mr. Richardson conceives it impossible that 'such a work should be suspended for six months, or for one. It may go on faster or slower, but it must go on.' By what necessity it must continually go on, or why it might not be laid aside and resumed, it is not easy to discover.

This dependence of the soul upon the seasons, those temporary and periodical ebbs and flows of intellect, may, I suppose, justly be derided as the fumes of vain imagination. *Sapiens dominabitur astris*. The author that thinks himself weatherbound will find, with a little help from hellebore, that he is only idle or exhausted. But while this notion has possession of the head, it produces the inability which it supposes. Our powers owe much of their energy to our hopes: *possunt quia posse videntur*. When success seems attainable, diligence is enforced; but when it is admitted that the faculties are suppressed by a cross-wind or a cloudy sky, the day is given up without resistance, for who can contend with the course of nature?

From such prepossessions Milton seems not to have been free. There prevailed in his time an opinion that the world was in its decay, and that we have had the misfortune to be produced in the decrepitude of nature.[n] It was suspected that the whole creation languished, that neither trees nor animals had the height or bulk of their predecessors, and that everything was daily sinking by gradual diminution. Milton appears to suspect that souls partake of the general degeneracy, and is not without some fear that his book is to be written in 'an age too late' for heroic poesy.

Another opinion wanders about the world, and sometimes finds reception among wise men—an opinion that restrains the operations of the mind to particular regions, and supposes that a luckless mortal may be born in a degree of latitude too high or too low for wisdom or for wit. From this fancy, wild as it is, he had not wholly cleared his head when he feared lest the 'climate' of his country might be 'too cold' for flights of imagination.

Into a mind already occupied by such fancies, another not more reasonable might easily find its way. He that could fear lest his genius had fallen upon too old a world, or too chill a climate, might

Sapiens: Burton, *Anatomy of Melancholy*, I. ii. 1. 4 ('a wise man will rule the stars').

from hellebore: cf. Horace, *Epistles*, II. ii. 137.

possunt: *Aeneid*, v. 231 ('they are strong because they deem themselves strong').

'*an age too late*': *PL*, ix. 44.

consistently magnify to himself the influence of the seasons, and believe his faculties to be vigorous only half the year.

His submission to the seasons was at least more reasonable than his dread of decaying nature or a frigid zone, for general causes must operate uniformly in a general abatement of mental power: if less could be performed by the writer, less likewise would content the judges of his work. Among this lagging race of frosty grovellers he might still have risen into eminence by producing something which 'they should not willingly let die'. However inferior to the heroes who were born in better ages, he might still be great among his contemporaries, with the hope of growing every day greater in the dwindle of posterity. He might still be the giant of the pygmies, the one-eyed monarch of the blind.

Of his artifices of study, or particular hours of composition, we have little account, and there was perhaps little to be told. Richardson, who seems to have been very diligent in his inquiries, but discovers always a wish to find Milton discriminated from other men, relates that 'he would sometimes lie awake whole nights, but not a verse could he make; and on a sudden his poetical faculty would rush upon him with an *impetus* or *oestrum*, and his daughter was immediately called to secure what came. At other times he would dictate perhaps forty lines in a breath, and then reduce them to half the number.'

These bursts of light and involutions of darkness, these transient and involuntary excursions and retrocessions of invention, having some appearance of deviation from the common train of nature, are eagerly caught by the lovers of a wonder. Yet something of this inequality happens to every man in every mode of exertion, manual or mental. The mechanic cannot handle his hammer and his file at all times with equal dexterity; there are hours, he knows not why, when 'his hand is out'. By Mr. Richardson's relation, casually conveyed, much regard cannot be claimed. That in his intellectual hour Milton called for his daughter 'to secure what came' may be questioned, for unluckily it happens to be known that his daughters were never taught to write;[n] nor would he have been obliged, as is universally confessed, to have employed any casual visitor in disburdening his memory if his daughter could have performed the office.

The story of reducing his exuberance has been told of other authors, and though doubtless true of every fertile and copious mind, seems to have been gratuitously transferred to Milton.

the one-eyed: Erasmus, *Adagia*, III. iv. 96.   '*he would sometimes*': *EL*, p. 291.
'*his hand is out*': *Love's Labour's Lost*, IV. i. 127.

What he has told us, and we cannot now know more, is that he composed much of his poem in the night and morning, I suppose before his mind was disturbed with common business, and that he poured out with great fluency his 'unpremeditated verse'. Versification free, like his, from the distresses of rhyme must by a work so long be made prompt and habitual, and when his thoughts were once adjusted, the words would come at his command.

At what particular times of his life the parts of his work were written cannot often be known. The beginning of the third book shows that he had lost his sight, and the introduction to the seventh that the return of the King had clouded him with discountenance, and that he was offended by the licentious festivity of the Restoration.[n] There are no other internal notes of time. Milton, being now cleared from all effects of his disloyalty, had nothing required from him but the common duty of living in quiet to be rewarded with the common right of protection; but this, which when he skulked from the approach of his King was perhaps more than he hoped, seems not to have satisfied him, for no sooner is he safe than he finds himself in danger, 'fallen on evil days and evil tongues, and with darkness and with danger compassed round'. This darkness, had his eyes been better employed, had undoubtedly deserved compassion, but to add the mention of danger was ungrateful and unjust. He was fallen indeed on 'evil days': the time was come in which regicides could no longer boast their wickedness. But of 'evil tongues' for Milton to complain required impudence at least equal to his other powers—Milton, whose warmest advocates must allow that he never spared any asperity of reproach or brutality of insolence.

But the charge itself seems to be false, for it would be hard to recollect any reproach cast upon him, either serious or ludicrous, through the whole remaining part of his life. He pursued his studies or his amusements without persecution, molestation or insult. Such is the reverence paid to great abilities, however misused; they who contemplated in Milton the scholar and the wit were contented to forget the reviler of his King.

When the plague (1665) raged in London, Milton took refuge at Chalfont in Bucks., where Ellwood, who had taken the house for him, first saw a complete copy of *Paradise Lost*, and having perused it said to him, 'Thou hast said a great deal upon "Paradise Lost"; what hast thou to say upon "Paradise Found"?'

that he composed: *PL*, iii. 29–32; vii. 28–30; ix. 21–4.
distresses: constraints.
'*Thou hast said*': *Life of Ellwood* (1714), p. 234 (*CM*, xviii. 385).

Next year, when the danger of infection had ceased, he returned to Bunhill Fields and designed the publication of his poem. A licence was necessary, and he could expect no great kindness from a chaplain of the Archbishop of Canterbury. He seems, however, to have been treated with tenderness, for though objections were made to particular passages, and among them to the simile of the sun eclipsed in the first book, yet the licence was granted, and he sold his copy, April 27, 1667, to Samuel Simmons for an immediate payment of £5, with a stipulation to receive £5 more when 1,300 should be sold of the first edition, and again, £5 after the sale of the same number of the second edition, and another £5 after the same sale of the third. None of the three editions were to be extended beyond 1,500 copies.[n]

The first edition was ten books, in a small quarto. The titles were varied from year to year, and an advertisement and the arguments of the books were omitted in some copies, and inserted in others.

The sale gave him in two years a right to his second payment, for which the receipt was signed April 26, 1669.[n] The second edition was not given till 1674; it was printed in small octavo, and the number of books was increased to twelve by a division of the seventh and twelfth, and some other small improvements were made. The third edition was published in 1678, and the widow, to whom the copy was then to devolve, sold all her claims to Simmons for £8, according to her receipt given Dec. 21, 1680. Simmons had already agreed to transfer the whole right to Brabazon Aylmer for £25; and Aylmer sold to Jacob Tonson half, August 17, 1683, and half, March 24, 1690, at a price considerably enlarged. In the history of *Paradise Lost* a deduction thus minute will rather gratify than fatigue.

The slow sale and tardy reputation of this poem have been always mentioned as evidences of neglected merit and of the uncertainty of literary fame, and inquiries have been made and conjectures offered about the causes of its long obscurity and late reception. But has the case been truly stated? Have not lamentation and wonder been lavished on an evil that was never felt?

---

returned to Bunhill Fields: cf. above, p. 78 and n.

a chaplain: Thomas Tomkyns (1637?–75), official licenser of books and chaplain to Gilbert Sheldon (1598–1677), Archbishop of Canterbury.

the simile of the sun: ll. 594 ff.

Samuel Simmons: (or Symmons) (*fl.* 1662–78), printer and publisher.

twelfth: a mistake for 'tenth'.

Brabazon Aylmer: (*fl.* 1671–1707), bookseller of St. Michael, Cornhill.

Jacob Tonson: (1656?–1736), publisher.

March 24, 1690: 24 March 1691 (N.S.).

That in the reigns of Charles and James the *Paradise Lost* received no public acclamations is readily confessed. Wit and literature were on the side of the Court, and who that solicited favour or fashion would venture to praise the defender of the regicides? All that he himself could think his due, from 'evil tongues' in 'evil days', was that reverential silence which was generously preserved. But it cannot be inferred that his poem was not read, or not, however unwillingly, admired.

The sale, if it be considered, will justify the public. Those who have no power to judge of past times but by their own should always doubt their conclusions. The call for books was not in Milton's age what it is in the present. To read was not then a general amusement: neither traders nor often gentlemen thought themselves disgraced by ignorance. The women had not then aspired to literature, nor was every house supplied with a closet of knowledge. Those, indeed, who professed learning were not less learned than at any other time; but of that middle race of students who read for pleasure or accomplishment, and who buy the numerous products of modern typography, the number was then comparatively small. To prove the paucity of readers it may be sufficient to remark that the nation had been satisfied, from 1623 to 1664, that is, forty-one years, with only two editions of the works of Shakespeare,[n] which probably did not together make 1,000 copies.

The sale of 1,300 copies in two years, in opposition to so much recent enmity and to a style of versification new to all and disgusting to many, was an uncommon example of the prevalence of genius. The demand did not immediately increase, for many more readers than were supplied at first the nation did not afford. Only 3,000 were sold in eleven years, for it forced its way without assistance: its admirers did not dare to publish their opinion, and the opportunities now given of attracting notice by advertisements were then very few; the means of proclaiming the publication of new books have been produced by that general literature which now pervades the nation through all its ranks.

But the reputation and price of the copy still advanced, till the Revolution put an end to the secrecy of love and *Paradise Lost* broke into open view with sufficient security of kind reception.[n]

Fancy can hardly forbear to conjecture with what temper Milton surveyed the silent progress of his work, and marked his reputation stealing its way in a kind of subterraneous current through fear and silence. I cannot but conceive him calm and confident, little disappointed, not at all dejected, relying on his own merit with steady consciousness, and waiting without impatience the vicissitudes of opinion and the impartiality of a future generation.

In the meantime he continued his studies and supplied the want of sight by a very odd expedient of which Phillips gives the following account.

Mr. Phillips tells us 'that though our author had daily about him one or other to read, some persons of man's estate, who, of their own accord, greedily catched at the opportunity of being his readers that they might as well reap the benefit of what they read to him, as oblige him by the benefit of their reading, and others of younger years were sent by their parents to the same end; yet excusing only the eldest daughter, by reason of her bodily infirmity and difficult utterance of speech (which, to say truth, I doubt was the principal cause of excusing her), the other two were condemned to the performance of reading and exactly pronouncing of all the languages of whatever book he should, at one time or other, think fit to peruse, viz. the Hebrew (and I think the Syriac), the Greek, the Latin, the Italian, Spanish and French. All which sorts of books to be confined to read, without understanding one word, must needs be a trial of patience almost beyond endurance. Yet it was endured by both for a long time, though the irksomeness of this employment could not be always concealed, but broke out more and more into expressions of uneasiness; so that at length they were all, even the eldest also, sent out to learn some curious and ingenious sorts of manufacture that are proper for women to learn, particularly embroideries in gold or silver.'

In the scene of misery which this mode of intellectual labour sets before our eyes, it is hard to determine whether the daughters or the father are most to be lamented. A language not understood can never be so read as to give pleasure, and very seldom so as to convey meaning. If few men would have had resolution to write books with such embarrassments, few likewise would have wanted ability to find some better expedient.

Three years after his *Paradise Lost* (1667), he published his *History of England*, comprising the whole fable of Geoffrey of Monmouth and continued to the Norman invasion. Why he should have given the first part, which he seems not to believe, and which is universally rejected, it is difficult to conjecture. The style is harsh, but it has

Mr. Phillips tells us: EL, pp. 77–8.
Geoffrey of Monmouth: (1100?–54), Bishop of St. Asaph and chronicler, author of *Historia Regum Britanniae*.
which he seems: CM, x. 30–1.

something of rough vigour, which perhaps may often strike though it cannot please.

On this history the licenser again fixed his claws, and before he would transmit it to the press tore out several parts. Some censures of the Saxon monks were taken away lest they should be applied to the modern clergy, and a character of the Long Parliament and Assembly of Divines was excluded, of which the author gave a copy to the Earl of Anglesey, and which, being afterwards published, has been since inserted in its proper place.[n]

The same year were printed *Paradise Regained* and *Samson Agonistes*, a tragedy written in imitation of the ancients, and never designed by the author for the stage. As these poems were published by another bookseller, it has been asked whether Simmons was discouraged from receiving them by the slow sale of the former.[n] Why a writer changed his bookseller a hundred years ago I am far from hoping to discover. Certainly he who in two years sells 1,300 copies of a volume in quarto, bought for two payments of £5 each, has no reason to repent his purchase.

When Milton showed *Paradise Regained* to Ellwood, 'This', said he, 'is owing to you, for you put it in my head by the question you put to me at Chalfont, which otherwise I had not thought of.'

His last poetical offspring was his favourite. He could not, as Ellwood relates, endure to hear *Paradise Lost* preferred to *Paradise Regained*.[n] Many causes may vitiate a writer's judgement of his own works. On that which has cost him much labour he sets a high value because he is unwilling to think that he has been diligent in vain; what has been produced without toilsome efforts is considered with delight as a proof of vigorous faculties and fertile invention; and the last work, whatever it be, has necessarily most of the grace of novelty. Milton, however it happened, had this prejudice, and had it to himself.

To that multiplicity of attainments and extent of comprehension that entitle this great author to our veneration, may be added a kind of humble dignity which did not disdain the meanest services to literature. The epic poet, the controvertist, the politician, having already descended to accommodate children with a book of rudiments, now, in the last years of his life, composed a book of logic for the initiation of students in philosophy, and published (1672) *Artis Logicae plenior Institutio ad Petri Rami Methodum concinnata*—that

Earl of Anglesey: Arthur Annesley (1614–86), 1st Earl of Anglesey of 2nd creation.
another bookseller: John Starkey (*fl.* 1657–89).
'*This*', *said he*: *Life of Ellwood*, p. 234 (*CM*, xviii. 386).

is, *A New Scheme of Logic, according to the Method of Ramus*. I know not whether, even in this book, he did not intend an act of hostility against the universities, for Ramus was one of the first oppugners of the old philosophy who disturbed with innovations the quiet of the schools.

His polemical disposition again revived. He had now been safe so long that he forgot his fears, and published a treatise *Of True Religion, Heresy, Schism, Toleration, and the best Means to prevent the Growth of Popery*.

But this little tract is modestly written, with respectful mention of the Church of England and an appeal to the Thirty-nine Articles. His principle of toleration is agreement in the sufficiency of the Scriptures, and he extends it to all who, whatever their opinions are, profess to derive them from the sacred books. The Papists appeal to other testimonies, and are therefore in his opinion not to be permitted the liberty of either public or private worship, for though they plead conscience, 'we have no warrant', he says, 'to regard conscience which is not grounded in Scripture'.

Those who are not convinced by his reasons may be perhaps delighted with his wit. The term 'Roman Catholic' is, he says, 'one of the Pope's bulls; it is particular universal, or catholic schismatic'.

He has, however, something better. As the best preservative against popery, he recommends the diligent perusal of the Scriptures —a duty from which he warns the busy part of mankind not to think themselves excused.

He now reprinted his juvenile poems, with some additions.

In the last year of his life he sent to the press, seeming to take delight in publication, a collection of *Familiar Epistles* in Latin, to which, being too few to make a volume, he added some academical exercises[n] which perhaps he perused with pleasure as they recalled to his memory the days of youth, but for which nothing but veneration for his name could now procure a reader.

When he had attained his sixty-sixth year, the gout, with which he had been long tormented, prevailed over the enfeebled powers of nature. He died by a quiet and silent expiration about 10th November 1674, at his house in Bunhill Fields, and was buried next his father in

---

Ramus: Petrus Ramus (Pierre de La Ramée) (1515–72), French humanist and philosopher.

'*we have no warrant*': For this and the other passages cited see *CM*, vi. 173, 167, 175.

He died: On the date of Milton's death, see Parker ii. 1152 n. 80.

the chancel of St. Giles at Cripplegate. His funeral was very splendidly and numerously attended.

Upon his grave there is supposed to have been no memorial, but in our time a monument has been erected in Westminster Abbey 'To the Author of Paradise Lost' by Mr. Benson, who has in the inscription bestowed more words upon himself than upon Milton.[n]

When the inscription for the monument of Philips, in which he was said to be *soli Miltono secundus*, was exhibited to Dr. Sprat, then Dean of Westminster, he refused to admit it; the name of Milton was in his opinion too detestable to be read on the wall of a building dedicated to devotion. Atterbury, who succeeded him, being author of the inscription, permitted its reception. 'And such has been the change of public opinion', said Dr. Gregory, from whom I heard this account, 'that I have seen erected in the church a statue of that man whose name I once knew considered as a pollution of its walls.'

Milton has the reputation of having been in his youth eminently beautiful, so as to have been called the Lady of his college. His hair, which was of a light brown, parted at the foretop and hung down upon his shoulders, according to the picture which he has given of Adam. He was, however, not of the heroic stature but rather below the middle size according to Mr. Richardson, who mentions him as having narrowly escaped from being 'short and thick'. He was vigorous and active, and delighted in the exercise of the sword, in which he is related to have been eminently skilful. His weapon was, I believe, not the rapier, but the backsword, of which he recommends the use in his book on education.

His eyes are said never to have been bright; but if he was a dexterous fencer, they must have been once quick.

His domestic habits, so far as they are known, were those of a severe student. He drank little strong drink of any kind, and fed without excess in quantity, and in his earlier years without delicacy of choice. In his youth he studied late at night, but afterwards

Mr. Benson: William Benson (1682–1754), politician.

Philips: John Philips (1676–1709), poet (*soli Miltono secundus*: 'second only to Milton').

Atterbury: Francis Atterbury (1662–1732), Bishop of Rochester and Dean of Westminster.

Dr. Gregory: David Gregory? (1696–1767), Dean of Christ Church, Oxford.

foretop: 'the fore part of the crown of the head; sometimes, loosely, the top of the head. *Obs.*' (*OED*).

the picture ... of Adam: *PL*, iv. 301–4.   '*short and thick*': *EL*, p. 201.

exercise of the sword: Wood, Richardson, *EL*, pp. 48, 204.

backsword: 'a sword with only one cutting edge' (*OED*); see *CM*, iv. 288.

His eyes: Richardson, *EL*, p. 202.   *In his youth*: *CM*, viii. 118–19.

changed his hours, and rested in bed from nine to four in the summer, and five in winter. The course of his day was best known after he was blind. When he first rose he heard a chapter in the Hebrew Bible, and then studied till twelve; then took some exercise for an hour; then dined; then played on the organ, and sung, or heard another sing; then studied to six; then entertained his visitors till eight; then supped, and after a pipe of tobacco and a glass of water went to bed.

So is his life described; but this even tenor appears attainable only in colleges. He that lives in the world will sometimes have the succession of his practice broken and confused. Visitors, of whom Milton is represented to have had great numbers, will come and stay unseasonably; business, of which every man has some, must be done when others will do it.

When he did not care to rise early, he had something read to him by his bedside; perhaps at this time his daughters were employed. He composed much in the morning, and dictated in the day, sitting obliquely in an elbow-chair, with his leg thrown over the arm.

Fortune appears not to have had much of his care. In the civil wars he lent his personal estate to the Parliament; but when, after the contest was decided, he solicited repayment, he met not only with neglect but 'sharp rebuke', and having tired both himself and his friends, was given up to poverty and hopeless indignation till he showed how able he was to do greater service. He was then made Latin Secretary with £200 a year, and had £1000 for his *Defence of the People*. His widow, who after his death retired to Nantwich in Cheshire, and died about 1729, is said to have reported that he lost £2000 by entrusting it to a scrivener, and that in the general depredation upon the Church he had grasped an estate of about £60 a year belonging to Westminster Abbey, which, like other sharers of the plunder of rebellion, he was afterwards obliged to return.[n] Two thousand pounds which he had placed in the Excise Office were also lost. There is yet no reason to believe that he was ever reduced to indigence. His wants being few were competently supplied. He sold his library before his death, and left his family £1500, on which his widow laid hold and only gave £100 to each of his daughters.

His literature was unquestionably great. He read all the languages which are considered either as learned or polite: Hebrew, with its two dialects, Greek, Latin, Italian, French and Spanish. In Latin his

---

Visitors: Wood, Phillips, *EL*, pp. 48, 74. *elbow-chair*: armchair.
'*sharp rebuke*': *CM*, xviii. 247.

skill was such as places him in the first rank of writers and critics; and he appears to have cultivated Italian with uncommon diligence. The books in which his daughter, who used to read to him, represented him as most delighting (after Homer, which he could almost repeat) were Ovid's *Metamorphoses* and Euripides. His Euripides is, by Mr. Cradock's kindness, now in my hands; the margin is sometimes noted, but I have found nothing remarkable.[n]

Of the English poets he set most value upon Spenser, Shakespeare and Cowley. Spenser was apparently his favourite; Shakespeare he may easily be supposed to like, with every other skilful reader; but I should not have expected that Cowley, whose ideas of excellence were so different from his own, would have had much of his approbation. His character of Dryden, who sometimes visited him, was that he was a good rhymist, but no poet.

His theological opinions are said to have been first Calvinistical, and afterwards, perhaps when he began to hate the Presbyterians, to have tended towards Arminianism. In the mixed questions of theology and government, he never thinks that he can recede far enough from popery or prelacy, but what Baudius says of Erasmus seems applicable to him, *magis habuit quod fugeret, quam quod sequeretur*. He had determined rather what to condemn than what to approve. He has not associated himself with any denomination of Protestants: we know rather what he was not than what he was. He was not of the Church of Rome; he was not of the Church of England.

To be of no church is dangerous. Religion, of which the rewards are distant, and which is animated only by faith and hope, will glide by degrees out of the mind unless it be invigorated and reimpressed by external ordinances, by stated calls to worship, and the salutary influence of example. Milton, who appears to have had full conviction of the truth of Christianity, and to have regarded the Holy Scriptures with the profoundest veneration, to have been untainted by an

---

Ovid: (43 B.C.–A.D. 17 *or* 18), Roman poet.

Euripides: (*c*.484–406? B.C.), Greek tragedian.

Mr. Cradock's: Joseph Cradock (1742–1826), author.

Of the English poets: see above, p. 43.

His character of Dryden: Newton, i. *lvi–lvii*.

theological opinions: Newton, i. *lii*; cf. Toland, *EL*, pp. 176–7, 195.

Arminianism: Jacobus Arminius (1560–1609) was a Dutch theologian who opposed the Calvinist doctrine of predestination.

Baudius: Dominic Baudius (1561–1613), poet, historian, and scholar, author of *Epistolae Semicenturia auctae*; see the Leyden ed. (1650), p. 198 (II. xxvii).

Erasmus: Desiderius Erasmus (1466–1536), famous Dutch scholar and humanist.

heretical peculiarity of opinion, and to have lived in a confirmed belief of the immediate and occasional agency of Providence, yet grew old without any visible worship. In the distribution of his hours there was no hour of prayer either solitary or with his household; omitting public prayers, he omitted all.

Of this omission the reason has been sought upon a supposition which ought never to be made, that men live with their own approbation and justify their conduct to themselves. Prayer certainly was not thought superfluous by him who represents our first parents as praying acceptably in the state of innocence, and efficaciously after their fall. That he lived without prayer can hardly be affirmed; his studies and meditations were an habitual prayer. The neglect of it in his family was probably a fault for which he condemned himself, and which he intended to correct, but that death, as too often happens, intercepted his reformation.

His political notions were those of an acrimonious and surly republican, for which it is not known that he gave any better reason than that 'a popular government was the most frugal, for the trappings of a monarchy would set up an ordinary commonwealth'. It is surely very shallow policy that supposes money to be the chief good—and even this, without considering that the support and expense of a Court is for the most part only a particular kind of traffic by which money is circulated, without any national impoverishment.

Milton's republicanism was, I am afraid, founded in an envious hatred of greatness and a sullen desire of independence, in petulance impatient of control and pride disdainful of superiority. He hated monarchs in the state and prelates in the church, for he hated all whom he was required to obey. It is to be suspected that his predominant desire was to destroy rather than establish, and that he felt not so much the love of liberty as repugnance to authority.

It has been observed that they who most loudly clamour for liberty do not most liberally grant it. What we know of Milton's character in domestic relations is that he was severe and arbitrary. His family consisted of women, and there appears in his books something like a Turkish contempt of females as subordinate and inferior beings. That his own daughters might not break the ranks, he suffered them to be depressed by a mean and penurious education. He thought woman made only for obedience, and man only for rebellion.

the reason has been sought: Newton, i. *liv*, Toland, *EL*, p. 195.
who represents: *PL*, v. 153–210, x. 1098–1104.   '*a popular*': *EL*, p. 186.

Of his family some account may be expected. His sister, first married to Mr. Phillips, afterwards married Mr. Agar, a friend of her first husband who succeeded him in the Crown Office. She had by her first husband Edward and John, the two nephews whom Milton educated, and by her second two daughters.

His brother Sir Christopher had two daughters, Mary and Catherine, and a son Thomas, who succeeded Agar in the Crown Office, and left a daughter, living in 1749 in Grosvenor Street.

Milton had children only by his first wife: Anne, Mary and Deborah. Anne, though deformed, married a master-builder, and died of her first child. Mary died single. Deborah married Abraham Clarke, a weaver in Spitalfields, and lived seventy-six years to August 1727. This is the daughter of whom public mention has been made.[n] She could repeat the first lines of Homer, the *Metamorphoses*, and some of Euripides, by having often read them. Yet here incredulity is ready to make a stand. Many repetitions are necessary to fix in the memory lines not understood; and why should Milton wish or want to hear them so often! These lines were at the beginning of the poems. Of a book written in a language not understood, the beginning raises no more attention than the end; and as those that understand it know commonly the beginning best, its rehearsal will seldom be necessary. It is not likely that Milton required any passage to be so much repeated as that his daughter could learn it; nor likely that he desired the initial lines to be read at all; nor that the daughter, weary of the drudgery of pronouncing unideal sounds, would voluntarily commit them to memory.

To this gentlewoman Addison made a present and promised some establishment, but died soon after. Queen Caroline sent her fifty guineas. She had seven sons and three daughters, but none of them had any children except her son Caleb and her daughter Elizabeth. Caleb went to Fort St. George in the East Indies, and had two sons, of whom nothing is now known. Elizabeth married Thomas Foster, a weaver in Spitalfields, and had seven children who all died. She kept a petty grocer's or chandler's shop, first at Holloway, and after-

Mr. Agar: Thomas Agar (1597?–1673).
by her second two daughters: Mary and Anne (b. 1636?).
Mary (d. of Sir Christopher): (1656–1742).
Catherine: (1656?–1746).   *a son Thomas*: (1647–94).
a daughter: Elizabeth Milton (1690?–1769).   *Abraham Clarke*: (d. 1702?).
unideal: 'of sounds or words: expressing or conveying no idea. *Obs.*' (*OED*).
Queen Caroline: (1683–1737), Queen of George II.
Caleb: Caleb Clarke (d. 1719) had sons Abraham (1703–43?) and Isaac (b. 1711).
Elizabeth: (*née* Clarke) (1688–1754).   *Thomas Foster*: (*fl.* 1719–50).

wards in Cock Lane near Shoreditch Church. She knew little of her grandfather, and that little was not good. She told of his harshness to his daughters, and his refusal to have them taught to write; and in opposition to other accounts, represented him as delicate, though temperate, in his diet.

In 1750, April 5, *Comus* was played for her benefit. She had so little acquaintance with diversion or gaiety that she did not know what was intended when a benefit was offered her. The profits of the night were only £130—though Dr. Newton brought a large contribution, and £20 were given by Tonson, a man who is to be praised as often as he is named. Of this sum £100 was placed in the stocks, after some debate between her and her husband in whose name it should be entered, and the rest augmented their little stock, with which they removed to Islington. This was the greatest benefaction that *Paradise Lost* ever procured the author's descendants, and to this he who has now attempted to relate his life had the honour of contributing a prologue.[n]

In the examination of Milton's poetical works, I shall pay so much regard to time as to begin with his juvenile productions. For his early pieces he seems to have had a degree of fondness not very laudable: what he has once written he resolves to preserve, and gives to the public an unfinished poem which he broke off because he was 'nothing satisfied with what he had done', supposing his readers less nice than himself. These preludes to his future labours are in Italian, Latin and English. Of the Italian I cannot pretend to speak as a critic, but I have heard them commended by a man well qualified to decide their merit.[n] The Latin pieces are lusciously elegant, but the delight which they afford is rather by the exquisite imitation of the ancient writers, by the purity of the diction and the harmony of the numbers, than by any power of invention or vigour of sentiment. They are not all of equal value: the elegies excel the odes, and some of the exercises on Gunpowder Treason[n] might have been spared.

The English poems, though they make no promises of *Paradise Lost*, have this evidence of genius, that they have a cast original and unborrowed. But their peculiarity is not excellence; if they differ from the verses of others they differ for the worse, for they are too often distinguished by repulsive harshness: the combinations of words are

£130: cf. *GM*, xx (1750), 183.

Dr. Newton: Thomas Newton (1704–82), Bishop of Bristol.

Tonson: Jacob Tonson (d. 1767), publisher; great-nephew of the Jacob Tonson mentioned above (p. 83).

'*nothing satisfied*': see Milton's note on 'The Passion'.

new but they are not pleasing; the rhymes and epithets seem to be laboriously sought and violently applied.

That in the early part of his life he wrote with much care appears from his manuscripts happily preserved at Cambridge, in which many of his smaller works are found as they were first written, with the subsequent corrections.[n] Such relics show how excellence is acquired; what we hope ever to do with ease we may learn first to do with diligence.

Those who admire the beauties of this great poet sometimes force their own judgement into false approbation of his little pieces, and prevail upon themselves to think that admirable which is only singular. All that short compositions can commonly attain is neatness and elegance. Milton never learned the art of doing little things with grace: he overlooked the milder excellence of suavity and softness; he was a 'lion' that had no skill 'in dandling the kid'.

One of the poems on which much praise has been bestowed is 'Lycidas', of which the diction is harsh, the rhymes uncertain, and the numbers unpleasing. What beauty there is we must therefore seek in the sentiments and images. It is not to be considered as the effusion of real passion, for passion runs not after remote allusions and obscure opinions. Passion plucks no berries from the myrtle and ivy, nor calls upon Arethuse and Mincius, nor tells of rough 'satyrs' and 'fauns with cloven heel'. Where there is leisure for fiction there is little grief.

In this poem there is no nature for there is no truth; there is no art for there is nothing new. Its form is that of a pastoral, easy, vulgar, and therefore disgusting: whatever images it can supply are long ago exhausted, and its inherent improbability always forces dissatisfaction on the mind. When Cowley tells of Harvey that they studied together, it is easy to suppose how much he must miss the companion of his labours and the partner of his discoveries; but what image of tenderness can be excited by these lines!

> We drove afield, and both together heard
> What time the grey fly winds her sultry horn,
> Battening our flocks with the fresh dews of night.

We know that they never drove afield, and that they had no flocks to batten; and though it be allowed that the representation may be allegorical, the true meaning is so uncertain and remote that it is never sought because it cannot be known when it is found.

'*lion*': *PL*, iv. 343–4.   '*satyrs*': l. 34.
When Cowley: 'On the Death of Mr. William Harvey', st. 5.
We drove: 'Lycidas', ll. 27–9.

Among the flocks and copses and flowers appear the heathen deities, Jove and Phoebus, Neptune and Aeolus, with a long train of mythological imagery such as a college easily supplies. Nothing can less display knowledge, or less exercise invention, than to tell how a shepherd has lost his companion and must now feed his flocks alone, without any judge of his skill in piping, and how one god asks another god what is become of Lycidas, and how neither god can tell. He who thus grieves will excite no sympathy; he who thus praises will confer no honour.

This poem has yet a grosser fault. With these trifling fictions are mingled the most awful and sacred truths, such as ought never to be polluted with such irreverent combinations. The shepherd likewise is now a feeder of sheep, and afterwards an ecclesiastical pastor, a superintendent of a Christian flock. Such equivocations are always unskilful, but here they are indecent and at least approach to impiety, of which, however, I believe the writer not to have been conscious.

Such is the power of reputation justly acquired that its blaze drives away the eye from nice examination. Surely no man could have fancied that he read 'Lycidas' with pleasure had he not known its author.

Of the two pieces 'L'Allegro' and 'Il Penseroso' I believe opinion is uniform: every man that reads them reads them with pleasure. The author's design is not, what Theobald has remarked, merely to show how objects derive their colours from the mind by representing the operation of the same things upon the gay and the melancholy temper, or upon the same man as he is differently disposed, but rather how, among the successive variety of appearances, every disposition of mind takes hold on those by which it may be gratified.

The 'cheerful' man hears the lark in the morning; the 'pensive' man hears the nightingale in the evening. The 'cheerful' man sees the cock strut, and hears the horn and hounds echo in the wood; then walks 'not unseen' to observe the glory of the rising sun, or listen to the singing milkmaid, and view the labours of the ploughman and the mower; then casts his eyes about him over scenes of smiling plenty, and looks up to the distant tower, the residence of some fair inhabitant; thus he pursues rural gaiety through a day of labour or of play, and delights himself at night with the fanciful narratives of superstitious ignorance.

The 'pensive' man at one time walks 'unseen' to muse at midnight,

---

Theobald: Lewis Theobald (1688–1744), editor of *The Works of Shakespeare*; q.v.
i. (1733 ed.), *xix–xx*.   '*not unseen*': 'L'Allegro', l. 57.
'*unseen*': 'Il Penseroso', l. 65.

and at another hears the sullen curfew. If the weather drives him home, he sits in a room lighted only by 'glowing embers'; or by a lonely lamp outwatches the north star to discover the habitation of separate souls, and varies the shades of meditation by contemplating the magnificent or pathetic scenes of tragic and epic poetry. When the morning comes, a morning gloomy with rain and wind, he walks into the dark trackless woods, falls asleep by some murmuring water, and with melancholy enthusiasm expects some dream of prognostication, or some music played by aerial performers.

Both mirth and melancholy are solitary, silent inhabitants of the breast that neither receive nor transmit communication; no mention is therefore made of a philosophical friend or a pleasant companion. The seriousness does not arise from any participation of calamity, nor the gaiety from the pleasures of the bottle.

The man of 'cheerfulness', having exhausted the country, tries what 'towered cities' will afford, and mingles with scenes of splendour, gay assemblies, and nuptial festivities; but he mingles a mere spectator, as when the learned comedies of Jonson or the wild dramas of Shakespeare are exhibited, he attends the theatre.

The 'pensive' man never loses himself in crowds, but walks the cloister or frequents the cathedral. Milton probably had not yet forsaken the Church.

Both his characters delight in music; but he seems to think that cheerful notes would have obtained from Pluto a complete dismission of Eurydice, of whom solemn sounds only procured a conditional release.

For the old age of Cheerfulness he makes no provision, but Melancholy he conducts with great dignity to the close of life. His cheerfulness is without levity, and his pensiveness without asperity.

Through these two poems the images are properly selected and nicely distinguished, but the colours of the diction seem not sufficiently discriminated. I know not whether the characters are kept sufficiently apart. No mirth can indeed be found in his melancholy, but I am afraid that I always meet some melancholy in his mirth. They are two noble efforts of imagination.

The greatest of his juvenile performances is the *Mask of Comus*, in which may very plainly be discovered the dawn or twilight of *Paradise Lost*. Milton appears to have formed very early that system of diction and mode of verse which his maturer judgement approved, and from which he never endeavoured nor desired to deviate.

'*glowing embers*': l. 79.   '*towered cities*': 'L'Allegro', l. 117.

Nor does *Comus* afford only a specimen of his language; it exhibits likewise his power of description and his vigour of sentiment employed in the praise and defence of virtue. A work more truly poetical is rarely found: allusions, images and descriptive epithets embellish almost every period with lavish decoration. As a series of lines, therefore, it may be considered as worthy of all the admiration with which the votaries have received it.

As a drama it is deficient. The action is not probable. A mask, in those parts where supernatural intervention is admitted, must indeed be given up to all the freaks of imagination; but so far as the action is merely human, it ought to be reasonable, which can hardly be said of the conduct of the two Brothers who, when their sister sinks with fatigue in a pathless wilderness, wander both away together in search of berries too far to find their way back, and leave a helpless Lady to all the sadness and danger of solitude. This however is a defect overbalanced by its convenience.

What deserves more reprehension is that the prologue spoken in the wild wood by the Attendant Spirit is addressed to the audience— a mode of communication so contrary to the nature of dramatic representation that no precedents can support it.

The discourse of the Spirit is too long—an objection that may be made to almost all the following speeches: they have not the sprightliness of a dialogue animated by reciprocal contention, but seem rather declamations deliberately composed and formally repeated on a moral question. The auditor therefore listens as to a lecture, without passion, without anxiety.

The song of Comus has airiness and jollity; but, what may recommend Milton's morals as well as his poetry, the invitations to pleasure are so general that they excite no distinct images of corrupt enjoyment, and take no dangerous hold on the fancy.

The following soliloquies of Comus and the Lady are elegant but tedious. The song must owe much to the voice if it ever can delight. At last the Brothers enter, with too much tranquillity; and when they have feared lest their sister should be in danger, and hoped that she is not in danger, the Elder makes a speech in praise of chastity, and the Younger finds how fine it is to be a philosopher.

Then descends the Spirit in form of a shepherd, and the Brother, instead of being in haste to ask his help, praises his singing and inquires his business in that place. It is remarkable that at this interview the Brother is taken with a short fit of rhyming. The Spirit relates that the Lady is in the power of Comus, the Brother moralises again, and the Spirit makes a long narration, of no use because it is false, and therefore unsuitable to a good Being.

In all these parts the language is poetical and the sentiments are generous, but there is something wanting to allure attention.

The dispute between the Lady and Comus is the most animated and affecting scene of the drama, and wants nothing but a brisker reciprocation of objections and replies to invite attention and detain it.

The songs are vigorous and full of imagery, but they are harsh in their diction, and not very musical in their numbers.

Throughout the whole, the figures are too bold and the language too luxuriant for dialogue. It is a drama in the epic style, inelegantly splendid and tediously instructive.

The Sonnets were written in different parts of Milton's life, upon different occasions. They deserve not any particular criticism, for of the best it can only be said that they are not bad, and perhaps only the eighth and the twenty-first are truly entitled to this slender commendation. The fabric of a sonnet, however adapted to the Italian language, has never succeeded in ours, which, having greater variety of termination, requires the rhymes to be often changed.

Those little pieces may be dispatched without much anxiety; a greater work calls for greater care. I am now to examine *Paradise Lost*, a poem which, considered with respect to design, may claim the first place, and with respect to performance, the second among the productions of the human mind.

By the general consent of critics, the first praise of genius is due to the writer of an epic poem, as it requires an assemblage of all the powers which are singly sufficient for other compositions.[n] Poetry is the art of uniting pleasure with truth by calling imagination to the help of reason. Epic poetry undertakes to teach the most important truths by the most pleasing precepts, and therefore relates some great event in the most affecting manner. History must supply the writer with the rudiments of narration, which he must improve and exalt by a nobler art, must animate by dramatic energy, and diversify by retrospection and anticipation; morality must teach him the exact bounds and different shades of vice and virtue; from policy and the practice of life he has to learn the discriminations of character, and the tendency of the passions either single or combined; and physiology must supply him with illustrations and images. To put these materials to poetical use is required an imagination capable of painting nature and realizing fiction. Nor is he yet a poet till he has attained the whole extension of his language, distinguished all the delicacies of phrase and all the colours of words, and learned to adjust their different sounds to all the varieties of metrical modulation.

Bossu is of opinion that the poet's first work is to find a 'moral' which his fable is afterwards to illustrate and establish. This seems to have been the process only of Milton: the moral of other poems is incidental and consequent; in Milton's only it is essential and intrinsic. His purpose was the most useful and the most arduous: 'to vindicate the ways of God to man'; to show the reasonableness of religion, and the necessity of obedience to the Divine Law.

To convey this moral there must be a 'fable', a narration artfully constructed so as to excite curiosity and surprise expectation. In this part of his work Milton must be confessed to have equalled every other poet. He has involved in his account of the Fall of Man the events which preceded and those that were to follow it: he has interwoven the whole system of theology with such propriety that every part appears to be necessary, and scarcely any recital is wished shorter for the sake of quickening the progress of the main action.

The subject of an epic poem is naturally an event of great importance. That of Milton is not the destruction of a city, the conduct of a colony, or the foundation of an empire. His subject is the fate of worlds, the revolutions of heaven and of earth, rebellion against the Supreme King raised by the highest order of created beings, the overthrow of their host and the punishment of their crime, the creation of a new race of reasonable creatures, their original happiness and innocence, their forfeiture of immortality, and their restoration to hope and peace.

Great events can be hastened or retarded only by persons of elevated dignity. Before the greatness displayed in Milton's poem all other greatness shrinks away. The weakest of his agents are the highest and noblest of human beings, the original parents of mankind, with whose actions the elements consented, on whose rectitude or deviation of will depended the state of terrestrial nature and the condition of all the future inhabitants of the globe.

Of the other agents in the poem the chief are such as it is irreverence to name on slight occasions. The rest were lower powers,

> of which the least could wield
> Those elements, and arm him with the force
> Of all their regions;   [vi. 221–3]

Bossu: René Le Bossu (1631–80), French neo-classical critic; see his *Traité du Poëme épique* (Paris, 1675), p. 37.
'*to vindicate*': *PL*, i. 26; cf. *Essay on Man*, i. 16.

powers which only the control of Omnipotence restrains from laying creation waste, and filling the vast expanse of space with ruin and confusion. To display the motives and actions of beings thus superior, so far as human reason can examine them, or human imagination represent them, is the task which this mighty poet has undertaken and performed.

In the examination of epic poems much speculation is commonly employed upon the 'characters'. The characters in the *Paradise Lost* which admit of examination are those of angels and of man: of angels good and evil; of man in his innocent and sinful state.

Among the angels, the virtue of Raphael is mild and placid, of easy condescension and free communication; that of Michael is regal and lofty, and, as may seem, attentive to the dignity of his own nature. Abdiel and Gabriel appear occasionally, and act as every incident requires; the solitary fidelity of Abdiel is very amiably painted.

Of the evil angels the characters are more diversified. To Satan, as Addison observes, such sentiments are given as suit 'the most exalted and most depraved being'. Milton has been censured by Clarke for the impiety which sometimes breaks from Satan's mouth. For there are thoughts, as he justly remarks, which no observation of character can justify because no good man would willingly permit them to pass, however transiently, through his own mind. To make Satan speak as a rebel, without any such expressions as might taint the reader's imagination, was indeed one of the great difficulties in Milton's undertaking, and I cannot but think that he has extricated himself with great happiness. There is in Satan's speeches little that can give pain to a pious ear. The language of rebellion cannot be the same with that of obedience. The malignity of Satan foams in haughtiness and obstinacy; but his expressions are commonly general, and no otherwise offensive than as they are wicked.

The other chiefs of the celestial rebellion are very judiciously discriminated in the first and second books, and the ferocious character of Moloch appears, both in the battle and the council, with exact consistency.

To Adam and to Eve are given, during their innocence, such sentiments as innocence can generate and utter. Their love is pure benevolence and mutual veneration, their repasts are without luxury, and their diligence without toil. Their addresses to their Maker have

---

as Addison observes: *Spectator* 303.
Clarke: John Clarke (1687–1734), schoolmaster and classical scholar; see *An Essay upon Study* (1731), pp. 204–7.

little more than the voice of admiration and gratitude. Fruition left them nothing to ask, and innocence left them nothing to fear.

But with guilt enter distrust and discord, mutual accusation and stubborn self-defence; they regard each other with alienated minds, and dread their Creator as the avenger of their transgression. At last they seek shelter in his mercy, soften to repentance and melt in supplication. Both before and after the Fall the superiority of Adam is diligently sustained.

Of the 'probable' and the 'marvellous', two parts of a vulgar epic poem which immerge the critic in deep consideration, the *Paradise Lost* requires little to be said. It contains the history of a miracle, of Creation and Redemption: it displays the power and the mercy of the Supreme Being; the probable therefore is marvellous, and the marvellous is probable. The substance of the narrative is truth, and as truth allows no choice, it is, like necessity, superior to rule. To the accidental or adventitious parts, as to everything human, some slight exceptions may be made. But the main fabric is immovably supported.

It is justly remarked by Addison that this poem has, by the nature of its subject, the advantage above all others that it is universally and perpetually interesting. All mankind will, through all ages, bear the same relation to Adam and to Eve, and must partake of that good and evil which extend to themselves.

Of the 'machinery', so called from Θεὸς ἀπὸ μηχανῆς, by which is meant the occasional interposition of supernatural power, another fertile topic of critical remarks, here is no room to speak because everything is done under the immediate and visible direction of Heaven; but the rule is so far observed that no part of the action could have been accomplished by any other means.

Of 'episodes' I think there are only two, contained in Raphael's relation of the war in heaven, and Michael's prophetic account of the changes to happen in this world. Both are closely connected with the great action: one was necessary to Adam as a warning, the other as a consolation.

To the completeness or 'integrity' of the design nothing can be objected: it has distinctly and clearly what Aristotle requires, a beginning, a middle, and an end. There is perhaps no poem of the same length from which so little can be taken without apparent

---

Of the 'probable': see *Spectator* 315.
vulgar: 'of the common or usual kind' (*OED*).
remarked by Addison: *Spectator* 267, 273.
Θεὸς: *Poetics*, xv. 10: the god in the car.   *what Aristotle requires*: ibid. vii. 3.

mutilation. Here are no funeral games, nor is there any long description of a shield. The short digressions at the beginning of the third, seventh and ninth books might doubtless be spared; but superfluities so beautiful who would take away, or who does not wish that the author of the *Iliad* had gratified succeeding ages with a little knowledge of himself? Perhaps no passages are more frequently or more attentively read than those extrinsic paragraphs; and since the end of poetry is pleasure, that cannot be unpoetical with which all are pleased.

The questions, whether the action of the poem be strictly 'one', whether the poem can be properly termed 'heroic', and who is the hero, are raised by such readers as draw their principles of judgement rather from books than from reason. Milton, though he entitled *Paradise Lost* only a 'poem', yet calls it himself 'heroic song'. Dryden, petulantly and indecently, denies the heroism of Adam because he was overcome, but there is no reason why the hero should not be unfortunate, except established practice, since success and virtue do not go necessarily together. Cato is the hero of Lucan; but Lucan's authority will not be suffered by Quintilian to decide. However, if success be necessary, Adam's deceiver was at last crushed: Adam was restored to his Maker's favour, and therefore may securely resume his human rank.

After the scheme and fabric of the poem must be considered its component parts, the sentiments and the diction.

The 'sentiments', as expressive of manners or appropriated to characters, are for the greater part unexceptionably just.

Splendid passages, containing lessons of morality or precepts of prudence, occur seldom. Such is the original formation of this poem that, as it admits no human manners till the Fall, it can give little assistance to human conduct. Its end is to raise the thoughts above sublunary cares or pleasures. Yet the praise of that fortitude with which Abdiel maintained his singularity of virtue against the scorn of multitudes may be accommodated to all times; and Raphael's reproof of Adam's curiosity after the planetary motions, with the answer returned by Adam, may be confidently opposed to any rule of life which any poet has delivered.

whether the action: Dennis, ii. 42.   *whether the poem*: Dryden: *Essays*, ii. 84.
who is the hero: ibid. ii. 233; Addison, *Spectator* 297.
'*heroic song*': *PL*, ix. 25.
Cato: of 'Utica' (95–46 B.C.), one of the heroes of the *Pharsalia*, an epic poem by
   Lucan (A.D. 39–65).
Quintilian: (A.D. c. 35–c. 95); see his *Institutio Oratoria*, X. i. 90.
Raphael's reproof: cf. *Rambler* 180.

The thoughts which are occasionally called forth in the progress are such as could only be produced by an imagination in the highest degree fervid and active, to which materials were supplied by incessant study and unlimited curiosity. The heat of Milton's mind might be said to sublimate his learning, to throw off into his work the spirit of science unmingled with its grosser parts.

He had considered creation in its whole extent, and his descriptions are therefore learned. He had accustomed his imagination to unrestrained indulgence, and his conceptions therefore were extensive. The characteristic quality of his poem is sublimity. He sometimes descends to the elegant, but his element is the great. He can occasionally invest himself with grace, but his natural port is gigantic loftiness.[n] He can please when pleasure is required, but it is his peculiar power to astonish.

He seems to have been well acquainted with his own genius, and to know what it was that nature had bestowed upon him more bountifully than upon others: the power of displaying the vast, illuminating the splendid, enforcing the awful, darkening the gloomy, and aggravating the dreadful; he therefore chose a subject on which too much could not be said, on which he might tire his fancy without the censure of extravagance.

The appearances of nature and the occurrences of life did not satiate his appetite of greatness. To paint things as they are requires a minute attention, and employs the memory rather than the fancy. Milton's delight was to sport in the wide regions of possibility; reality was a scene too narrow for his mind. He sent his faculties out upon discovery into worlds where only imagination can travel, and delighted to form new modes of existence and furnish sentiment and action to superior beings, to trace the counsels of hell or accompany the choirs of heaven.

But he could not be always in other worlds: he must sometimes revisit earth and tell of things visible and known. When he cannot raise wonder by the sublimity of his mind, he gives delight by its fertility.

Whatever be his subject, he never fails to fill the imagination. But his images and descriptions of the scenes or operations of nature do not seem to be always copied from original form, nor to have the freshness, raciness and energy of immediate observation. He saw nature, as Dryden expresses it, 'through the spectacles of books',

counsels: Some of the force of Johnson's meaning is lost if the spelling is here modernized to 'councils'.

He saw nature: *Dryden: Essays*, i. 67 (where the reverse is said of Shakespeare).

and on most occasions calls learning to his assistance. The garden of Eden brings to his mind the vale of Enna where Proserpine was gathering flowers. Satan makes his way through fighting elements like 'Argo' between the Cyanean rocks, or Ulysses between the two Sicilian whirlpools, when he shunned Charybdis on the 'larboard'. The mythological allusions have been justly censured as not being always used with notice of their vanity, but they contribute variety to the narration, and produce an alternate exercise of the memory and the fancy.

His similes are less numerous and more various than those of his predecessors. But he does not confine himself within the limits of rigorous comparison: his great excellence is amplitude, and he expands the adventitious image beyond the dimensions which the occasion required. Thus, comparing the shield of Satan to the orb of the moon, he crowds the imagination with the discovery of the telescope, and all the wonders which the telescope discovers.

Of his moral sentiments it is hardly praise to affirm that they excel those of all other poets; for this superiority he was indebted to his acquaintance with the sacred writings. The ancient epic poets, wanting the light of Revelation, were very unskilful teachers of virtue; their principal characters may be great but they are not amiable. The reader may rise from their works with a greater degree of active or passive fortitude, and sometimes of prudence, but he will be able to carry away few precepts of justice, and none of mercy.

From the Italian writers it appears that the advantages of even Christian knowledge may be supposed in vain. Ariosto's pravity is generally known; and though the *Deliverance of Jerusalem* may be considered as a sacred subject, the poet has been very sparing of moral instruction.

In Milton every line breathes sanctity of thought and purity of manners, except when the train of the narration requires the introduction of the rebellious spirits; and even they are compelled to acknowledge their subjection to God in such a manner as excites reverence and confirms piety.

Of human beings there are but two, but those two are the parents of mankind, venerable before their fall for dignity and innocence, and amiable after it for repentance and submission. In their first state their affection is tender without weakness, and their piety sub-

the vale of Enna: iv. 268–9.   *Satan makes his way*: ii. 1014–20.
4. *Argonautica*, ii. 552–611; *Odyssey*, xii. 234–59.
The mythological allusions: *Spectator* 297.   *comparing the shield*: i. 284–91.
Ariosto: Ludovico Ariosto (1474–1533), Italian poet, author of *Orlando Furioso*;
cf. *Dryden: Essays*, ii. 224.

lime without presumption. When they have sinned, they show how discord begins in mutual frailty, and how it ought to cease in mutual forbearance; how confidence of the divine favour is forfeited by sin, and how hope of pardon may be obtained by penitence and prayer. A state of innocence we can only conceive, if indeed in our present misery it be possible to conceive it; but the sentiments and worship proper to a fallen and offending being we have all to learn, as we have all to practise.

The poet, whatever be done, is always great. Our progenitors in their first state conversed with angels; even when folly and sin had degraded them, they had not in their humiliation 'the port of mean suitors'; and they rise again to reverential regard when we find that their prayers were heard.

As human passions did not enter the world before the Fall, there is in the *Paradise Lost* little opportunity for the pathetic, but what little there is has not been lost. That passion which is peculiar to rational nature, the anguish arising from the consciousness of transgression and the horrors attending the sense of the Divine displeasure, are very justly described and forcibly impressed. But the passions are moved only on one occasion; sublimity is the general and prevailing quality in this poem—sublimity variously modified, sometimes descriptive, sometimes argumentative.[n]

The defects and faults of *Paradise Lost*, for faults and defects every work of man must have, it is the business of impartial criticism to discover. As in displaying the excellence of Milton I have not made long quotations, because of selecting beauties there had been no end, I shall in the same general manner mention that which seems to deserve censure; for what Englishman can take delight in transcribing passages which, if they lessen the reputation of Milton, diminish in some degree the honour of our country?

The generality of my scheme does not admit the frequent notice of verbal inaccuracies which Bentley, perhaps better skilled in grammar than in poetry, has often found—though he sometimes made them—and which he imputed to the obtrusions of a reviser whom the author's blindness obliged him to employ.[n] A supposition rash and groundless if he thought it true, and vile and pernicious if, as is said, he in private allowed it to be false.[n]

The plan of *Paradise Lost* has this inconvenience, that it comprises neither human actions nor human manners. The man and woman who act and suffer are in a state which no other man or

'*the port*': xi. 8–9.
argumentative: of or pertaining to the subject-matter, theme or argument.

woman can ever know. The reader finds no transaction in which he can be engaged, beholds no condition in which he can by any effort of imagination place himself; he has, therefore, little natural curiosity or sympathy.

We all, indeed, feel the effects of Adam's disobedience: we all sin like Adam, and like him must all bewail our offences; we have restless and insidious enemies in the fallen angels, and in the blessed spirits we have guardians and friends; in the redemption of mankind we hope to be included; in the description of heaven and hell we are surely interested, as we are all to reside hereafter either in the regions of horror or of bliss.

But these truths are too important to be new: they have been taught to our infancy, they have mingled with our solitary thoughts and familiar conversation, and are habitually interwoven with the whole texture of life. Being therefore not new, they raise no un-accustomed emotion in the mind: what we knew before we cannot learn; what is not unexpected cannot surprise.

Of the ideas suggested by these awful scenes, from some we recede with reverence except when stated hours require their association, and from others we shrink with horror, or admit them only as salutary inflictions, as counterpoises to our interests and passions. Such images rather obstruct the career of fancy than incite it.

Pleasure and terror are indeed the genuine sources of poetry,[n] but poetical pleasure must be such as human imagination can at least conceive, and poetical terror such as human strength and fortitude may combat. The good and evil of eternity are too ponderous for the wings of wit; the mind sinks under them in passive helplessness, content with calm belief and humble adoration.

Known truths, however, may take a different appearance, and be conveyed to the mind by a new train of intermediate images. This Milton has undertaken and performed with pregnancy and vigour of mind peculiar to himself. Whoever considers the few radical positions which the Scriptures afforded him will wonder by what energetic operation he expanded them to such extent, and ramified them to so much variety, restrained as he was by religious reverence from licentiousness of fiction.

Here is a full display of the united force of study and genius, of a great accumulation of materials, with judgement to digest and fancy to combine them: Milton was able to select from nature or from story, from ancient fable or from modern science, whatever could illustrate or adorn his thoughts. An accumulation of knowledge impregnated his mind, fermented by study and exalted by imagination.

It has been therefore said, without an indecent hyperbole, by one of his encomiasts, that in reading *Paradise Lost* we read a book of universal knowledge.

But original deficiency cannot be supplied. The want of human interest is always felt. *Paradise Lost* is one of the books which the reader admires and lays down, and forgets to take up again. None ever wished it longer than it is. Its perusal is a duty rather than a pleasure. We read Milton for instruction, retire harassed and overburdened, and look elsewhere for recreation; we desert our master and seek for companions.

Another inconvenience of Milton's design is that it requires the description of what cannot be described, the agency of spirits. He saw that immateriality supplied no images, and that he could not show angels acting but by instruments of action; he therefore invested them with form and matter. This, being necessary, was therefore defensible, and he should have secured the consistency of his system by keeping immateriality out of sight, and enticing his reader to drop it from his thoughts. But he has unhappily perplexed his poetry with his philosophy. His infernal and celestial powers are sometimes pure spirit and sometimes animated body. When Satan walks with his lance upon the 'burning marle', he has a body; when in his passage between hell and the new world he is in danger of sinking in the vacuity, and is supported by a gust of rising vapours, he has a body; when he animates the toad, he seems to be mere spirit that can penetrate matter at pleasure; when he 'starts up in his own shape', he has at least a determined form; and when he is brought before Gabriel, he has 'a spear and a shield' which he had the power of hiding in the toad, though the arms of the contending angels are evidently material.

The vulgar inhabitants of Pandemonium, being 'incorporeal spirits', are 'at large, though without number' in a limited space; yet in the battle, when they were overwhelmed by mountains, their armour hurt them, 'crushed in upon their substance, now grown gross by sinning'. This likewise happened to the uncorrupted angels, who were overthrown 'the sooner for their arms', for 'unarmed they might easily as spirits have evaded by contraction or remove'. Even

---

one of his encomiasts: Samuel Barrow (1625–82), physician, whose verses 'In Paradisum Amissam' were prefixed to 2nd ed. of the poem.

'*burning marle*': For the passages cited here and below see i. 296, ii. 935–8, iv. 800, 819, 989–90, i. 789–91, vi. 653–61, 595–7, iv. 555–6, ix. 484–7.

as spirits they are hardly spiritual, for 'contraction' and 'remove' are images of matter, but if they could have escaped without their armour, they might have escaped from it, and left only the empty cover to be battered. Uriel, when he rides on a sunbeam, is material; Satan is material when he is afraid of the prowess of Adam.

The confusion of spirit and matter which pervades the whole narration of the war of heaven fills it with incongruity, and the book in which it is related is, I believe, the favourite of children, and gradually neglected as knowledge is increased.

After the operation of immaterial agents, which cannot be explained, may be considered that of allegorical persons which have no real existence. To exalt causes into agents, to invest abstract ideas with form and animate them with activity, has always been the right of poetry. But such airy beings are, for the most part, suffered only to do their natural office and retire. Thus Fame tells a tale, and Victory hovers over a general or perches on a standard; but Fame and Victory can do no more. To give them any real employment, or ascribe to them any material agency, is to make them allegorical no longer, but to shock the mind by ascribing effects to non-entity. In the *Prometheus* of Aeschylus we see Violence and Strength, and in the *Alcestis* of Euripides we see Death brought upon the stage, all as active persons of the drama;[n] but no precedents can justify absurdity.

Milton's allegory of Sin and Death is undoubtedly faulty. Sin is indeed the mother of Death, and may be allowed to be the portress of hell; but when they stop the journey of Satan, a journey described as real, and when Death offers him battle, the allegory is broken. That Sin and Death should have shown the way to hell might have been allowed, but they cannot facilitate the passage by building a bridge because the difficulty of Satan's passage is described as real and sensible, and the bridge ought to be only figurative. The hell assigned to the rebellious spirits is described as not less local than the residence of man. It is placed in some distant part of space, separated from the regions of harmony and order by a chaotic waste and an unoccupied vacuity; but Sin and Death worked up a 'mole' of 'aggregated soil' cemented with 'asphaltus'—a work too bulky for ideal architects.

This unskilful allegory appears to me one of the greatest faults of the poem, and to this there was no temptation but the author's opinion of its beauty.

To the conduct of the narrative some objections may be made.

Aeschylus: (*c.* 525–456 B.C.), Greek tragedian.
a 'mole': x. 293 ff.

Satan is with great expectation brought before Gabriel in Paradise, and is suffered to go away unmolested. The creation of man is represented as the consequence of the vacuity left in heaven by the expulsion of the rebels, yet Satan mentions it as a report 'rife in heaven' before his departure.

To find sentiments for the state of innocence was very difficult, and something of anticipation perhaps is now and then discovered. Adam's discourse of dreams seems not to be the speculation of a new-created being. I know not whether his answer to the angel's reproof for curiosity does not want something of propriety: it is the speech of a man acquainted with many other men. Some philosophical notions, especially when the philosophy is false, might have been better omitted. The angel, in a comparison, speaks of 'timorous deer' before deer were yet timorous and before Adam could understand the comparison.

Dryden remarks that Milton has some flats among his elevations. This is only to say that all the parts are not equal. In every work one part must be for the sake of others: a palace must have passages; a poem must have transitions. It is no more to be required that wit should always be blazing than that the sun should always stand at noon. In a great work there is a vicissitude of luminous and opaque parts, as there is in the world a succession of day and night. Milton, when he has expatiated in the sky, may be allowed sometimes to revisit earth, for what other author ever soared so high, or sustained his flight so long?

Milton, being well versed in the Italian poets, appears to have borrowed often from them, and as every man catches something from his companions, his desire of imitating Ariosto's levity has disgraced his work with the 'Paradise of Fools'—a fiction not in itself ill-imagined, but too ludicrous for its place.

His play on words, in which he delights too often, his equivocations, which Bentley endeavours to defend by the example of the ancients, his unnecessary and ungraceful use of terms of art, it is not necessary to mention because they are easily remarked, and generally censured, and at last bear so little proportion to the whole that they scarcely deserve the attention of a critic.

Such are the faults of that wonderful performance *Paradise Lost*,

expectation: expectancy (on the reader's part).   '*rife in heaven*': i. 650–1.
Adam's discourse: v. 95 ff.   *his answer*: viii. 179 ff.
'*timorous deer*': vi. 857.   *Dryden remarks*: Dryden: *Essays*, ii. 32.
'*Paradise of Fools*': iii. 444–97. Cf. *Orlando Furioso*, xxxiv. 73 ff; *Spectator* 297.
Bentley endeavours to defend: *Milton's Paradise Lost* (1732), p. 204 n.

which he who can put in balance with its beauties must be considered not as nice but as dull, as less to be censured for want of candour than pitied for want of sensibility.

Of *Paradise Regained* the general judgement seems now to be right—that it is in many parts elegant and everywhere instructive. It was not to be supposed that the writer of *Paradise Lost* could ever write without great effusions of fancy, and exalted precepts of wisdom. The basis of *Paradise Regained* is narrow; a dialogue without action can never please like an union of the narrative and dramatic powers. Had this poem been written not by Milton but by some imitator, it would have claimed and received universal praise.

If *Paradise Regained* has been too much depreciated, *Samson Agonistes* has in requital been too much admired. It could only be by long prejudice and the bigotry of learning that Milton could prefer the ancient tragedies, with their encumbrance of a chorus, to the exhibitions of the French and English stages; and it is only by a blind confidence in the reputation of Milton that a drama can be praised in which the intermediate parts have neither cause nor consequence, neither hasten nor retard the catastrophe.

In this tragedy are however many particular beauties, many just sentiments and striking lines; but it wants that power of attracting the attention which a well-connected plan produces.

Milton would not have excelled in dramatic writing; he knew human nature only in the gross, and had never studied the shades of character, nor the combinations of concurring or the perplexity of contending passions. He had read much and knew what books could teach, but had mingled little in the world, and was deficient in the knowledge which experience must confer.

Through all his greater works there prevails an uniform peculiarity of 'diction', a mode and cast of expression which bears little resemblance to that of any former writer, and which is so far removed from common use that an unlearned reader, when he first opens his book, finds himself surprised by a new language.

This novelty has been, by those who can find nothing wrong in Milton, imputed to his laborious endeavours after words suitable to the grandeur of his ideas. 'Our language', says Addison, 'sunk under him.' But the truth is that, both in prose and verse, he had formed his style by a perverse and pedantic principle. He was desirous to use

candour: 'freedom from malice, favourable disposition, kindliness. *Obs.*' (*OED*); 'sweetness of temper, kindness' (*Dict.*).
too much admired: cf. Newton, i. xliv.
the intermediate parts: cf. *Rambler* 139.   '*Our language*': *Spectator* 297.

English words with a foreign idiom. This in all his prose is discovered and condemned, for there judgement operates freely, neither softened by the beauty nor awed by the dignity of his thoughts; but such is the power of his poetry that his call is obeyed without resistance, the reader feels himself in captivity to a higher and a nobler mind, and criticism sinks in admiration.

Milton's style was not modified by his subject: what is shown with greater extent in *Paradise Lost* may be found in *Comus*. One source of his peculiarity was his familiarity with the Tuscan poets: the disposition of his words is, I think, frequently Italian, perhaps sometimes combined with other tongues. Of him, at last, may be said what Jonson says of Spenser, that 'he wrote no language', but has formed what Butler calls 'a Babylonish dialect', in itself harsh and barbarous, but made by exalted genius and extensive learning the vehicle of so much instruction and so much pleasure that, like other lovers, we find grace in its deformity.

Whatever be the faults of his diction, he cannot want the praise of copiousness and variety: he was master of his language in its full extent, and has selected the melodious words with such diligence that from his book alone the Art of English Poetry might be learned.

After his diction, something must be said of his 'versification'. 'The measure', he says, 'is the English heroic verse without rhyme.' Of this mode he had many examples among the Italians, and some in his own country. The Earl of Surrey is said to have translated one of Virgil's books without rhyme; and besides our tragedies, a few short poems had appeared in blank verse, particularly one tending to reconcile the nation to Raleigh's wild attempt upon Guiana, and probably written by Raleigh himself.[n] These petty performances cannot be supposed to have much influenced Milton, who more probably took his hint from Trissino's *Italia Liberata*, and finding blank verse easier than rhyme, was desirous of persuading himself that it is better.

'Rhyme', he says, and says truly, 'is no necessary adjunct of true

---

'*he wrote no language*': *Timber, or Discoveries, Ben Jonson*, ed. Herford and Simpson (Oxford, 1925–52), viii. 618.

Butler: Samuel Butler (1612–80), author of *Hudibras*; q.v. I. i. 93.

'*The measure*': Milton's note on 'The Verse' prefixed to *PL*.

The Earl of Surrey: Henry Howard (1517?–47), Earl of Surrey, whose translations of *Aeneid* ii and iv (published 1557 and 1554 respectively) are the earliest blank-verse poems in English.

Trissino: Giangiorgio Trissino (1478–1550), author of *Sofonisba* (1524), the first Italian tragedy, and *Italia Liberata dai Goti* (1547–8), Italy's first 'serious' epic.

'*Rhyme*': Milton's note on 'The Verse'.

poetry.' But perhaps of poetry as a mental operation metre or music is no necessary adjunct; it is however by the music of metre that poetry has been discriminated in all languages, and in languages melodiously constructed with a due proportion of long and short syllables, metre is sufficient. But one language cannot communicate its rules to another; where metre is scanty and imperfect, some help is necessary. The music of the English heroic line strikes the ear so faintly that it is easily lost unless all the syllables of every line co-operate together; this co-operation can be only obtained by the preservation of every verse unmingled with another as a distinct system of sounds, and this distinctness is obtained and preserved by the artifice of rhyme. The variety of pauses, so much boasted by the lovers of blank verse, changes the measures of an English poet to the periods of a declaimer,[n] and there are only a few skilful and happy readers of Milton who enable their audience to perceive where the lines end or begin. 'Blank verse', said an ingenious critic, 'seems to be verse only to the eye.'

Poetry may subsist without rhyme, but English poetry will not often please; nor can rhyme ever be safely spared but where the subject is able to support itself. Blank verse makes some approach to that which is called the 'lapidary style', has neither the easiness of prose nor the melody of numbers, and therefore tires by long continuance. Of the Italian writers without rhyme whom Milton alleges as precedents, not one is popular; what reason could urge in its defence has been confuted by the ear.

But whatever be the advantage of rhyme, I cannot prevail on myself to wish that Milton had been a rhymer, for I cannot wish his work to be other than it is; yet like other heroes, he is to be admired rather than imitated. He that thinks himself capable of astonishing may write blank verse, but those that hope only to please must condescend to rhyme.

The highest praise of genius is original invention. Milton cannot be said to have contrived the structure of an epic poem, and therefore owes reverence to that vigour and amplitude of mind to which all generations must be indebted for the art of poetical narration, for the texture of the fable, the variation of incidents, the interposition of dialogue, and all the stratagems that surprise and enchain attention. But of all the borrowers from Homer, Milton is perhaps the least indebted. He was naturally a thinker for himself, confident of his own abilities, and disdainful of help or hindrance; he did not refuse

an ingenious critic: William Locke (1732–1810), art amateur and collector; see *Life*, iv. 43.

admission to the thoughts or images of his predecessors, but he did not seek them. From his contemporaries he neither courted nor received support; there is in his writings nothing by which the pride of other authors might be gratified, or favour gained—no exchange of praise, nor solicitation of support. His great works were performed under discountenance and in blindness, but difficulties vanished at his touch; he was born for whatever is arduous, and his work is not the greatest of heroic poems only because it is not the first.

DRYDEN

Of the great poet whose life I am about to delineate, the curiosity which his reputation must excite will require a display more ample than can now be given. His contemporaries, however they reverenced his genius, left his life unwritten, and nothing therefore can be known beyond what casual mention and uncertain tradition have supplied.[n]

John Dryden was born August 9, 1631, at Aldwinckle near Oundle, the son of Erasmus Dryden of Titchmarsh, who was the third son of Sir Erasmus Dryden, Baronet, of Canons Ashby. All these places are in Northamptonshire, but the original stock of the family was in the county of Huntingdon.[n]

He is reported by his last biographer Derrick to have inherited from his father an estate of two hundred a year, and to have been bred, as was said, an Anabaptist. For either of these particulars no authority is given. Such a fortune ought to have secured him from that poverty which seems always to have oppressed him, or if he had wasted it, to have made him ashamed of publishing his necessities. But though he had many enemies who undoubtedly examined his life with a scrutiny sufficiently malicious, I do not remember that he is ever charged with waste of his patrimony. He was indeed sometimes reproached for his first religion. I am therefore inclined to believe that Derrick's intelligence was partly true, and partly erroneous.

From Westminster School, where he was instructed as one of the King's scholars by Dr. Busby, whom he long after continued to reverence, he was in 1650 elected to one of the Westminster scholarships at Cambridge.[n]

Of his school performances has appeared only a poem on the death of Lord Hastings, composed with great ambition of such conceits as, notwithstanding the reformation begun by Waller and Denham, the example of Cowley still kept in reputation. Lord Hastings died of the smallpox, and his poet has made of the pustules first rosebuds and then gems, at last exalts them into stars, and says,

> No comet need foretell his change drew on,
> Whose corpse might seem a constellation. [ll. 65–6]

Erasmus Dryden: (c. 1602/3–54)   *Sir Erasmus Dryden*: (1553–1632).
He is reported: Derrick, i. *xiv*.   *Derrick*: Samuel Derrick (1724–69), author.
Dr. Busby: Richard Busby (1606–95).
Lord Hastings: Henry, Lord Hastings (1630–49).
corpse: living body (obs.).

At the university he does not appear to have been eager of poetical distinction, or to have lavished his early wit either on fictitious subjects or public occasions. He probably considered that he who purposed to be an author ought first to be a student. He obtained, whatever was the reason, no fellowship in the college. Why he was excluded cannot now be known, and it is vain to guess;[n] had he thought himself injured he knew how to complain. In the *Life of Plutarch* he mentions his education in the college with gratitude,[n] but in a prologue at Oxford he has these lines:

> Oxford to him a dearer name shall be
> Than his own mother university;
> Thebes did his rude unknowing youth engage;
> He chooses Athens in his riper age.

It was not till the death of Cromwell, in 1658, that he became a public candidate for fame by publishing 'Heroic Stanzas on the late Lord Protector', which, compared with the verses of Sprat and Waller on the same occasion, were sufficient to raise great expectations of the rising poet.[n]

When the King was restored, Dryden, like the other panegyrists of usurpation, changed his opinion or his profession, and published *Astraea Redux, a Poem on the Happy Restoration and Return of his most Sacred Majesty King Charles the Second*.

The reproach of inconstancy was, on this occasion, shared with such numbers that it produced neither hatred nor disgrace; if he changed, he changed with the nation. It was, however, not totally forgotten when his reputation raised him enemies.[n]

The same year he praised the new King in a second poem on his restoration. In the *Astraea* was the line,

> An horrid *stillness* first *invades* the *ear*,
> And in that silence we a tempest fear,

for which he was persecuted with perpetual ridicule,[n] perhaps with more than was deserved. 'Silence' is indeed mere privation, and so considered, cannot 'invade'; but privation likewise certainly is 'darkness', and probably 'cold'—yet poetry has never been refused the right of ascribing effects or agency to them as to positive powers. No man scruples to say that 'darkness' hinders him from his work, or that 'cold' has killed the plants. Death is also privation—yet who

---

Plutarch: (*c.* 46–*c.* 127), Greek biographer and essayist.
Oxford to him: 'Prologue to the University of Oxford', ('Though Actors cannot'), ll. 35–38.
a second poem: *To His Sacred Majesty, A Panegyric on his Coronation*.

has made any difficulty of assigning to Death a dart and the power of striking?

In settling the order of his works there is some difficulty, for even when they are important enough to be formally offered to a patron, he does not commonly date his dedication; the time of writing and publishing is not always the same; nor can the first editions be easily found, if even from them could be obtained the necessary information.

The time at which his first play was exhibited is not certainly known because it was not printed till it was some years afterwards altered and revived;[n] but since the plays are said to be printed in the order in which they were written,[n] from the dates of some those of others may be inferred, and thus it may be collected that in 1663, in the thirty-second year of his life, he commenced a writer for the stage, compelled undoubtedly by necessity, for he appears never to have loved that exercise of his genius, or to have much pleased himself with his own dramas.

Of the stage when he had once invaded it, he kept possession for many years; not indeed without the competition of rivals who sometimes prevailed, or the censure of critics, which was often poignant and often just, but with such a degree of reputation as made him at least secure of being heard, whatever might be the final determination of the public.

His first piece was a comedy called *The Wild Gallant*. He began with no happy auguries, for his performance was so much disapproved that he was compelled to recall it and change it from its imperfect state to the form in which it now appears, and which is yet sufficiently defective to vindicate the critics.

I wish that there were no necessity of following the progress of his theatrical fame, or tracing the meanders of his mind through the whole series of his dramatic performances; and indeed there is the less as they do not appear in the collection to which this narration is to be annexed.[n] It will be fit however to enumerate them, and to take especial notice of those that are distinguished by any peculiarity intrinsic or concomitant—for the composition and fate of eight and twenty dramas include too much of a poetical life to be omitted.

In 1664 he published *The Rival Ladies*, which he dedicated to the Earl of Orrery, a man of high reputation both as a writer and a statesman. In this play he made his essay of dramatic rhyme, which he defends in his dedication with sufficient certainty of a favourable hearing, for Orrery was himself a writer of rhyming tragedies.[n]

Earl of Orrery: Roger Boyle (1621–79), 1st Earl of Orrery.

He then joined with Sir Robert Howard in *The Indian Queen*, a tragedy in rhyme. The parts which either of them wrote are not distinguished.

The Indian Emperor was published in 1667. It is a tragedy in rhyme intended for a sequel to Howard's *Indian Queen*. Of this connection notice was given to the audience by printed bills, distributed at the door—an expedient supposed to be ridiculed in *The Rehearsal* when Bayes tells how many reams he has printed to instil into the audience some conception of his plot.

In this play is the description of Night which Rymer has made famous by preferring it to those of all other poets.

The practice of making tragedies in rhyme was introduced soon after the Restoration, as it seems, by the Earl of Orrery, in compliance with the opinion of Charles II, who had formed his taste by the French theatre; and Dryden, who wrote, and made no difficulty of declaring that he wrote, only to please, and who perhaps knew that by his dexterity of versification he was more likely to excel others in rhyme than without it, very readily adopted his master's preference. He therefore made rhyming tragedies till, by the prevalence of manifest propriety, he seems to have grown ashamed of making them any longer.

To this play is prefixed a very vehement defence of dramatic rhyme, in confutation of the preface to *The Duke of Lerma* in which Sir Robert Howard had censured it.[n]

In 1667 he published *Annus Mirabilis, the Year of Wonders*, which may be esteemed one of his most elaborate works.

It is addressed to Sir Robert Howard by a letter which is not properly a dedication, and writing to a poet, he has interspersed many critical observations of which some are common, and some perhaps ventured without much consideration. He began, even now, to exercise the domination of conscious genius by recommending his own performance: 'I am satisfied that as the Prince and General [Rupert and Monk] are incomparably the best subjects I ever had, so

---

Sir Robert Howard: (1626–98), dramatist, whose sister, Elizabeth, Dryden married in 1663.

when Bayes: *Rehearsal*, p. 11 (I. ii).

the description of Night: III. ii. 1–5; *Rymer*, pp. 15–16. Cf. *YJ*, vii. 19–20.

the opinion of Charles II: cf. *Dryden*: *DW*, i. 271.

made no difficulty: *Dryden*: *Essays*, i. 120.

'*I am satisfied*': *Dryden*: *Poems*, i. 46.

Rupert: Prince Rupert (1619–82), Count Palatine of Rhine and Duke of Bavaria, Duke of Cumberland and Earl of Holderness.

Monk: George Monck (or Monk) (1608–70), 1st Duke of Albemarle.

what I have written on them is much better than what I have performed on any other. As I have endeavoured to adorn my poem with noble thoughts, so much more to express those thoughts with elocution.'

It is written in quatrains, or heroic stanzas of four lines—a measure which he had learned from the *Gondibert* of Davenant, and which he then thought the most majestic that the English language affords. Of this stanza he mentions the encumbrances, increased as they were by the exactness which the age required. It was, throughout his life, very much his custom to recommend his works by representation of the difficulties that he had encountered, without appearing to have sufficiently considered that where there is no difficulty there is no praise.

There seems to be in the conduct of Sir Robert Howard and Dryden towards each other something that is not now easily to be explained. Dryden, in his dedication to the Earl of Orrery, had defended dramatic rhyme; and Howard, in the preface to a collection of plays, had censured his opinion. Dryden vindicated himself in his *Dialogue on Dramatic Poetry*; Howard, in his preface to *The Duke of Lerma*, animadverted on the vindication; and Dryden, in a preface to *The Indian Emperor*, replied to the animadversions with great asperity, and almost with contumely. The dedication to this play is dated the year in which the *Annus Mirabilis* was published. Here appears a strange inconsistency; but Langbaine affords some help by relating that the answer to Howard was not published in the first edition of the play, but was added when it was afterwards reprinted; and as *The Duke of Lerma* did not appear till 1668, the same year in which the *Dialogue* was published, there was time enough for enmity to grow up between authors who, writing both for the theatre, were naturally rivals.

He was now so much distinguished that in 1668 he succeeded Sir William Davenant as Poet Laureate. The salary of the laureate had been raised in favour of Jonson by Charles I from an hundred marks to £100 a year and a tierce of wine—a revenue in those days not inadequate to the conveniences of life.[n]

The same year he published his *Essay on Dramatic Poetry*, an elegant and instructive dialogue, in which we are told by Prior that the principal character is meant to represent the Duke of Dorset.[n]

---

a collection of plays: *Four New Plays* (1665).

Langbaine: Gerard Langbaine the younger (1656–92), dramatic biographer and critic; see Spingarn, iii. 138.

Duke of Dorset: Charles Sackville (1638–1706), 6th Earl of Dorset and 1st Earl of Middlesex, poet.

This work seems to have given Addison a model for his *Dialogues upon Medals.*

Secret Love, or the Maiden Queen is a tragicomedy. In the preface he discusses a curious question—whether a poet can judge well of his own productions—and determines very justly that of the plan and disposition, and all that can be reduced to principles of science, the author may depend upon his own opinion, but that in those parts where fancy predominates, self-love may easily deceive. He might have observed that what is good only because it pleases cannot be pronounced good till it has been found to please.

Sir Martin Mar-all is a comedy published without preface or dedication, and at first without the name of the author. Langbaine charges it, like most of the rest, with plagiarism, and observes that the song is translated from Voiture, allowing however that both the sense and measure are exactly observed.

The Tempest is an alteration of Shakespeare's play made by Dryden in conjunction with Davenant, 'whom', says he, 'I found of so quick a fancy, that nothing was proposed to him in which he could not suddenly produce a thought extremely pleasant and surprising; and those first thoughts of his, contrary to the Latin proverb, were not always the least happy; and as his fancy was quick, so likewise were the products of it remote and new. He borrowed not of any other, and his imaginations were such as could not easily enter into any other man.'

The effect produced by the conjunction of these two powerful minds was that to Shakespeare's monster Caliban is added a sister-monster Sycorax, and a woman, who in the original play had never seen a man, is in this brought acquainted with a man that had never seen a woman.

About this time, in 1673, Dryden seems to have had his quiet much disturbed by the success of *The Empress of Morocco*, a tragedy written in rhyme by Elkanah Settle, which was so much applauded as to make him think his supremacy of reputation in some danger. Settle had not only been prosperous on the stage but, in the confidence of success, had published his play with sculptures and a preface of

curious question: Dryden: *Essays*, i. 105.

Langbaine charges it: Spingarn, iii. 141–2.

Voiture: Vincent de Voiture (1597–1648), French poet; cf. *Oeuvres de Voiture* (Paris, 1652), ii. 61–3 ('L'Amour sous sa loi').

'*whom*': Dryden: *Essays*, i. 135, where the Latin proverb referred to is cited in n. 2.

Elkanah Settle: (1648–1724), city poet; see pp. 140–1 below.

sculptures: engravings.

defiance. Here was one offence added to another, and for the last blast of inflammation it was acted at Whitehall by the Court ladies.

Dryden could not now repress these emotions, which he called indignation and others jealousy, but wrote upon the play and the dedication such criticism as malignant impatience could pour out in haste.[n]

Of Settle he gives this character. 'He's an animal of a most deplored understanding, without conversation. His being is in a twilight of sense, and some glimmering of thought which he can never fashion into wit or English. His style is boisterous and rough-hewn, his rhyme incorrigibly lewd, and his numbers perpetually harsh and ill-sounding. The little talent which he has is fancy. He sometimes labours with a thought, but with the pudder he makes to bring it into the world, 'tis commonly still-born; so that, for want of learning and elocution, he will never be able to express anything either naturally or justly!'

This is not very decent, yet this is one of the pages in which criticism prevails most over brutal fury. He proceeds: 'He has a heavy hand at fools, and a great felicity in writing nonsense for them. Fools they will be in spite of him. His King, his two Empresses, his villain, and his sub-villain, nay his hero, have all a certain natural cast of the father—their folly was born and bred in them, and something of the Elkanah will be visible.'

This is Dryden's general declamation; I will not withhold from the reader a particular remark. Having gone through the first act he says: 'To conclude this act with the most rumbling piece of nonsense spoken yet,

> To flattering lightning our feigned smiles conform,
> Which backed with thunder do but gild a storm.

"Conform a smile to lightning", make a "smile" imitate "lightning", and "flattering lightning": lightning sure is a threatening thing. And this lightning must "gild a storm". Now if I must conform my smiles to lightning, then my smiles must gild a storm too: to "gild" with "smiles" is a new invention of gilding. And gild a storm by being "backed with thunder". Thunder is part of the storm; so one part of the storm must help to "gild" another part, and help by "backing"; as if a man would gild a thing the better for being backed, or having a load upon his back. So that here is "gilding" by "conforming", "smiling", "lightning", "backing", and

which he called: Notes and Observations on the Empress of Morocco (1674), sig. *A2ᵛ*.   '*He's an animal*': ibid. sig. *A3.*
pudder: pother.   '*He has*': sigg. *A3–A3ᵛ*.   '*To conclude*': pp. 12–13.

"thundering". The whole is as if I should say thus: I will make my counterfeit smiles look like a flattering stone-horse, which, being backed with a trooper, does but gild the battle. I am mistaken if nonsense is not here pretty thick sown. Sure the poet writ these two lines aboard some smack in a storm, and being sea-sick, spewed up a good lump of clotted nonsense at once.'

Here is perhaps a sufficient specimen; but as the pamphlet, though Dryden's, has never been thought worthy of republication, and is not easily to be found, it may gratify curiosity to quote it more largely.

> Whene'er she bleeds,
> He no severer a damnation needs,
> That dares pronounce the sentence of her death,
> Than the infection that attends that breath.

'That attends that breath'. The poet is at 'breath' again; 'breath' can never 'scape him; and here he brings in a 'breath' that must be 'infectious' with 'pronouncing' a sentence; and this sentence is not to be pronounced till the condemned party 'bleeds'—that is, she must be executed first, and sentenced after; and the 'pronouncing' of this 'sentence' will be infectious—that is, others will catch the disease of that sentence, and this infecting of others will torment a man's self. The whole is thus: 'when she bleeds, thou needest no greater hell or torment to thyself than infecting of others by pronouncing a sentence upon her'. What hodge-podge does he make here! Never was Dutch grout such clogging, thick, indigestible stuff. But this is but a taste to stay the stomach; we share a more plentiful mess presently.

Now to dish up the poet's broth that I promised:

> For when we're dead, and our freed souls enlarged,
> Of nature's grosser burden we're discharged,
> Then gently, as a happy lover's sigh,
> Like wandering meteors through the air we'll fly,
> And in our airy walk, as subtle guests,
> We'll steal into our cruel fathers' breasts,
> There read their souls, and track each passion's sphere:
> See how Revenge moves there, Ambition here.
> And in their orbs view the dark characters
> Of sieges, ruins, murders, blood and wars.
> We'll blot out all those hideous draughts, and write
> Pure and white forms; then with a radiant light
> Their breasts encircle, till their passions be
> Gentle as nature in its infancy:
> Till softened by our charms their furies cease,
> And their revenge resolves into a peace.
> Thus by our death their quarrel ends,
> Whom living we made foes, dead we'll make friends.

Whene'er: pp. 5–7.
grout: 'a kind of coarse porridge made from whole meal. *Obs.*' (*OED*).

If this be not a very liberal mess, I will refer myself to the stomach of any moderate guest. And a rare mess it is, far excelling any Westminster white-broth. It is a kind of gibblet porridge, made of the gibblets of a couple of young geese, stodged full of 'meteors', 'orbs', 'spheres', 'track', 'hideous draughts', 'dark characters', 'white forms', and 'radiant light', designed not only to please appetite and indulge luxury; but it is also physical, being an approved medicine to purge choler, for it is propounded by Morena as a receipt to cure their fathers of their choleric humours; and were it written in characters as barbarous as the words, might very well pass for a doctor's bill. To conclude, it is porridge, 'tis a receipt, 'tis a pig with a pudding in the belly, 'tis I know not what; for certainly never anyone that pretended to write sense had the impudence before to put such stuff as this into the mouths of those that were to speak it before an audience whom he did not take to be all fools, and after that to print it too, and expose it to the examination of the world. But let us see what we can make of this stuff:

For when we're dead and our freed souls enlarged—

Here he tells us what it is to be 'dead'; it is to have 'our freed souls set free'. Now if to have a soul set free is to be dead, then to have a 'freed soul' set free is to have a dead man die.

Then gentle as a happy lover's sigh—

They two like one 'sigh', and that one 'sigh' like two wandering meteors,
—shall fly through the air;

that is, they shall mount above like falling stars, or else they shall skip like two Jacks with lanthorns, or Will with a wisp, and Madge with a candle.

And in their airy walk steal into their cruel fathers' breasts, like subtle guests. So that their 'fathers' breasts' must be in an 'airy walk', an airy 'walk' of a 'flier'. *And there they will read their souls, and track the spheres of their passions.* That is, these walking fliers, Jack with a lanthorn, etc. will put on his spectacles and fall a 'reading souls', and put on his pumps and fall a 'tracking of spheres'; so that he will read and run, walk and fly, at the same time! Oh! Nimble Jack. *Then he will see, how revenge here, how ambition there.* The birds will hop about. *And then view the dark characters of sieges, ruins, murders, blood, and wars, in their orbs.* 'Track the characters' to their forms! Oh! rare sport for Jack. Never was place so full of game as these breasts! You cannot stir but flush a sphere, start a character, or unkennel an orb!

Settle's is said to have been the first play embellished with sculptures; those ornaments seem to have given poor Dryden great disturbance. He tries however to ease his pain by venturing his malice in a parody.

The poet has not only been so impudent to expose all this stuff, but so arrogant to defend it with an epistle—like a saucy booth-keeper that, when he had put a cheat upon the people, would wrangle and fight with any that would not like it, or would offer to discover it; for which arro-

white-broth: 'some kind of broth of a white or light colour' (*OED*).
stodged full: filled to distension.
Settle's is said: *Dennis*, ii. 118.   *The poet*: op. cit. pp. 17–18.

gance our poet receives this correction, and to jerk him a little the sharper, I will not transpose his verse, but by the help of his own words trans-non-sense sense, that, by my stuff, people may judge the better what his is:

> Great Boy, thy tragedy and sculptures done
> From press and plates in fleets do homeward come:
> And in ridiculous and humble pride,
> Their course in ballad-singers' baskets guide,
> Whose greasy twigs do all new beauties take,
> From the gay shows thy dainty sculptures make.
> Thy lines a mess of rhyming nonsense yield,
> A senseless tale, with flattering fustian filled.
> No grain of sense does in one line appear,
> Thy words big bulks of boisterous bombast bear.
> With noise they move, and from players' mouths rebound,
> When their tongues dance to thy words' empty sound.
> By thee inspired the rumbling verses roll,
> As if that rhyme and bombast lent a soul:
> And with that soul they seem taught duty too,
> To huffing words does humble nonsense bow,
> As if it would thy worthless worth enhance,
> To th' lowest rank of fops thy praise advance;
> To whom, by instinct, all thy stuff is dear;
> Their loud claps echo to the theatre.
> From breaths of fools thy commendation spreads,
> Fame sings thy praise with mouths of loggerheads.
> With noise and laughing each thy fustian greets,
> 'Tis clapt by choirs of empty-headed cits,
> Who have their tribute sent, and homage given,
> As men in whispers send loud noise to heaven.

Thus I have daubed him with his own puddle; and now we are come from aboard his dancing, masking, rebounding, breathing fleet, and as if we had landed at Gotham, we meet nothing but fools and nonsense.

Such was the criticism to which the genius of Dryden could be reduced between rage and terror—rage with little provocation, and terror with little danger. To see the highest minds thus levelled with the meanest may produce some solace to the consciousness of weakness, and some mortification to the pride of wisdom. But let it be remembered that minds are not levelled in their powers but when they are first levelled in their desires. Dryden and Settle had both placed their happiness in the claps of multitudes.

The Mock Astrologer, a comedy, is dedicated to the illustrious Duke of Newcastle, whom he courts by adding to his praises those

choirs: bands, groups.

Duke of Newcastle: William Cavendish (1592–1676), 1st Duke of Newcastle, author of *La Methode et Invention Nouvelle de dresser les Chevaux* (1658), and *A New Method and Extraordinary Invention to Dress Horses* (1667), also wrote comedies, poems and letters that have survived. Cf. *Dryden: DW*, ii. 238.

of his lady, not only as a lover but a partner of his studies. It is unpleasing to think how many names, once celebrated, are since forgotten. Of Newcastle's works nothing is now known but his treatise
on horsemanship.

The preface seems very elaborately written, and contains many
just remarks on the fathers of the English drama. Shakespeare's
plots, he says, are in the hundred novels of Cinthio, those of Beaumont and Fletcher in Spanish stories; Jonson only made them for
himself. His criticisms upon tragedy, comedy and farce are judicious
and profound. He endeavours to defend the immorality of some of
his comedies by the example of former writers, which is only to say
that he was not the first nor perhaps the greatest offender. Against
those that accused him of plagiarism he alleges a favourable expression of the King: 'He only desired that they, who accuse me of
thefts, would steal him plays like mine'; and then relates how much
labour he spends in fitting for the English stage what he borrows
from others.

Tyrannic Love, or the Virgin Martyr was another tragedy in
rhyme, conspicuous for many passages of strength and elegance,
and many of empty noise and ridiculous turbulence. The rants of
Maximin have been always the sport of criticism, and were at length,
if his own confession may be trusted, the shame of the writer.

Of this play he takes care to let the reader know that it was contrived and written in seven weeks. Want of time was often his excuse,
or perhaps shortness of time was his private boast in the form of an
apology.

It was written before *The Conquest of Granada*, but published after
it.[n] The design is to recommend piety. 'I considered that pleasure
was not the only end of poesy, and that even the instructions of
morality were not so wholly the business of a poet as that precepts
and examples of piety were to be omitted; for to leave that employment altogether to the clergy were to forget that religion was first
taught in verse, which the laziness or dulness of succeeding priesthood turned afterwards into prose.' Thus foolishly could Dryden
write rather than not show his malice to the parsons.

his lady: Margaret Cavendish (*née* Lucas) (1624?–74), author.
Shakespeare's plots: Dryden: *Essays*, i. 150–5.
Cinthio: Giambattista Giraldi Cinthio (1504–73), Italian tragedian, literary
    theorist, and short-story writer, author of *Hecatommithi* (1565).
Beaumont: Francis Beaumont (1584–1616).
Fletcher: John Fletcher (1579–1625).
his own confession: Dryden: *DW*, v. 120.
Of this play: Dryden: *Essays*, i. 140–1.   '*I considered*': ibid. i. 138.

The two parts of *The Conquest of Granada* are written with a seeming determination to glut the public with dramatic wonders, to exhibit in its highest elevation a theatrical meteor of incredible love and impossible valour, and to leave no room for a wilder flight to the extravagance of posterity. All the rays of romantic heat, whether amorous or warlike, glow in Almanzor by a kind of concentration. He is above all laws; he is exempt from all restraints; he ranges the world at will, and governs wherever he appears. He fights without inquiring the cause, and loves in spite of the obligations of justice, of rejection by his mistress, and of prohibition from the dead. Yet the scenes are, for the most part, delightful: they exhibit a kind of illustrious depravity and majestic madness such as, if it is sometimes despised, is often reverenced, and in which the ridiculous is mingled with the astonishing.

In the epilogue to the second part of *The Conquest of Granada*, Dryden indulges his favourite pleasure of discrediting his predecessors; and this epilogue he has defended by a long postscript. He had promised a second dialogue in which he should more fully treat of the virtues and faults of the English poets who have written in the dramatic, epic or lyric way. This promise was never formally performed, but with respect to the dramatic writers he has given us in his prefaces, and in this postscript, something equivalent; but his purpose being to exalt himself by the comparison, he shows faults distinctly and only praises excellence in general terms.

A play thus written in professed defiance of probability naturally drew down upon itself the vultures of the theatre. One of the critics that attacked it was Martin Clifford, to whom Sprat addressed the *Life of Cowley* with such veneration of his critical powers as might naturally excite great expectations of instruction from his remarks. But let honest credulity beware of receiving characters from contemporary writers. Clifford's remarks, by the favour of Dr. Percy, were at last obtained, and that no man may ever want them more, I will extract enough to satisfy all reasonable desire.

In the first Letter his observation is only general: 'You do live', says he, 'in as much ignorance and darkness as you did in the womb; your writings are like a Jack-of-all-trades' shop: they have a variety,

a long postscript: *Defence of the Epilogue, or an Essay on the Dramatic Poetry of the Last Age.*   *He had promised*: Dryden: *Essays*, i. 17.

Martin Clifford: (d. 1677), author; cf. Spingarn, ii. 120.

Dr. Percy: Thomas Percy (1729–1811), Bishop of Dromore and editor of the *Reliques of Ancient English Poetry* (1765).

'*You do live*': *Notes upon Mr. Dryden's Poems, in Four Letters* (1687), pp. 3–4.

but nothing of value; and if thou art not the dullest plant-animal that ever the earth produced, all that I have conversed with are strangely mistaken in thee.'

In the second he tells him that Almanzor is not more copied from Achilles than from Ancient Pistol. 'But I am', says he, 'strangely mistaken if I have not seen this very Almanzor of yours in some disguise about this town, and passing under another name. Prithee tell me true, was not this huffcap once the Indian Emperor, and at another time did he not call himself Maximin? Was not Lyndaraxa once called Almeria? I mean under Montezuma, the Indian Emperor. I protest and vow they are either the same or so alike that I cannot, for my heart, distinguish one from the other. You are therefore a strange unconscionable thief; thou art not content to steal from others, but dost rob thy poor wretched self too.'

Now was Settle's time to take his revenge. He wrote a vindication of his own lines, and if he is forced to yield anything, makes reprisals upon his enemy. To say that his answer is equal to the censure is no high commendation. To expose Dryden's method of analysing his expressions, he tries the same experiment upon the description of the ships in *The Indian Emperor*, of which however he does not deny the excellence, but intends to show that by studied misconstruction everything may be equally represented as ridiculous. After so much of Dryden's elegant animadversions, justice requires that something of Settle's should be exhibited.

The following observations are therefore extracted from a quarto pamphlet of ninety-five pages.

> Fate after him below with pain did move,
> And victory could scarce keep pace above.

These two lines, if he can show me any sense or thought in, or anything but bombast and noise, he shall make me believe every word in his observation on *Morocco* sense.

In *The Empress of Morocco* were these lines:

> I'll travel then to some remoter sphere,
> Till I find out new worlds, and crown you there.

On which Dryden made this remark: 'I believe our learned author takes a sphere for a country—the sphere of Morocco, as if Morocco were the

---

In the second: op. cit. pp. 6–7.
huffcap: 'a swaggering or hectoring blade; a swashbuckler. *Obs.*' (*OED*).
a vindication: *Notes and Observations on The Empress of Morocco Revised* (1674).
the description of the ships: Dryden: *DW*, i. 281 (I. ii); op. cit. pp. 24–5.
Fate after him: ibid. p. 53.
In The Empress of Morocco: p. 70. Cf. Dryden's *Notes and Observations*, p. 56.

globe of earth and water; but a globe is no sphere neither by his leave.' etc.
So 'sphere' must not be sense unless it relate to a circular motion about a
globe, in which sense the astronomers use it. I would desire him to expound
these lines in *Granada*:

> I'll to the turrets of the palace go,
> And add new fire to those that fight below.
> Thence, Hero-like, with torches by my side,
> (Far be the omen though) my Love I'll guide.
> No, like his better fortune I'll appear,
> With open arms, loose veil and flowing hair,
> Just flying forward from my rolling sphere.

I wonder, if he be so strict, how he dares make so bold with 'sphere' himself, and be so critical in other men's writings. Fortune is fancied standing
on a globe, not on a 'sphere', as he told us in the first act.

Because 'Elkanah's similes are the most unlike things to what they are
compared in the world', I'll venture to start a simile in his *Annus Mirabilis*;
he gives this poetical description of the ship called the 'London':

> The goodly London in her gallant trim,
>   The phoenix-daughter of the vanquished old,
> Like a rich bride does to the ocean swim,
>   And on her shadow rides in floating gold.
>
> Her flag aloft spread ruffling in the wind,
>   And sanguine streamers seemed the flood to fire:
> The weaver, charmed with what his loom designed,
>   Goes on to sea, and knows not to retire.
>
> With roomy decks, her guns of mighty strength,
>   Whose low-laid mouths each mounting billow laves,
> Deep in her draught, and warlike in her length,
>   She seems a sea-wasp flying on the waves.

What a wonderful pother is here to make all these poetical beautifications
of a ship! that is, a 'phoenix' in the first stanza, and but a 'wasp' in the
last; nay, to make his humble comparison of a 'wasp' more ridiculous, he
does not say it flies upon the waves as nimbly as a wasp, or the like, but it
seemed a 'wasp'. But our author at the writing of this was not in his
altitudes; to compare ships to floating palaces, a comparison to the purpose, was a perfection he did not arrive to till his *Indian Emperor*'s days.
But perhaps his similitude has more in it than we imagine: this ship had a
great many guns in her, and they, put all together, made the sting in the
wasp's tail—for this is all the reason I can guess why it seemed a 'wasp'.
But because we will allow him all we can to help out, let it be a 'phoenix

---

I'll to the turrets: Dryden: *DW*, iii. 52.

Hero-like: Hero, the beautiful priestess of Aphrodite at Sestos, who used to hold
   up a lighted torch to guide her lover Leander as he swam the Hellespont at
   night to visit her.

Because 'Elkanah's: pp. 74–5. Cf. Dryden's *Notes and Observations*, p. 49.

The goodly: *Annus Mirabilis*, sts. 151–3.

altitudes: 'lofty mood, ways, airs, phrases. *Obs.*' (*OED*).

sea-wasp', and the rarity of such an animal may do much towards the heightening the fancy.

It had been much more to his purpose, if he had designed to render the senseless play little, to have searched for some such pedantry as this:

> Two ifs scarce make one possibility.

> If justice will take all and nothing give,
> Justice, methinks, is not distributive.

> To die or kill you is the alternative;
> Rather than take your life I will not live.

Observe how prettily our author chops logic in heroic verse. Three such fustian canting words as 'distributive', 'alternative', and 'two ifs', no man but himself would have come within the noise of. But he's a man of general learning, and all comes into his play.

'Twould have done well too if he could have met with a rant or two worth the observation: such as

> Move swiftly, Sun, and fly a lover's pace,
> Leave months and weeks behind thee in thy race.

But surely the Sun, whether he flies a lover's or not a lover's pace, leaves weeks and months, nay years too, behind him in his race.

Poor Robin, or any other of the philomathematics, would have given him satisfaction in the point.

> If I could kill thee now, thy fate's so low,
> That I must stoop ere I can give the blow.
> But mine is fixed so far above thy crown,
> That all thy men,
> Piled on thy back, can never pull it down.

Now where that is Almanzor's fate is fixed I cannot guess; but wherever it is, I believe Almanzor, and think that all Abdalla's subjects, piled upon one another, might not pull down his fate so well as without piling; besides, I think Abdalla so wise a man that if Almanzor had told him piling his men upon his back might do the feat, he would scarce bear such a weight for the pleasure of the exploit; but it is a huff, and let Abdalla do it if he dare.

> The people like a headlong torrent go,
> And every dam they break or overflow.
> But, unopposed, they either lose their force,
> Or wind in volumes to their former course.

A very pretty allusion, contrary to all sense or reason. Torrents, I take it, let them wind never so much, can never return to their former course,

---

It had been: op. cit. pp. 77–8.   *Two ifs*: Dryden: *DW*, iii. 41.
If justice: ibid. p. 44.   *To die or kill*: ibid. p. 68.   *Move swiftly*: ibid. p. 163.
Poor Robin: William Winstanley (1628?–98), adopting the pseudonym 'Poor Robin', began to compile in the early 1660s a series of popular almanacs.
If I could kill: Dryden: *DW* iii. 58.
The people: op. cit. pp. 80–1. (Cf. *Dryden: DW*, iii. 59.)

unless he can suppose that fountains can go upwards, which is impossible; nay more, in the foregoing page he tells us so too. A trick of a very unfaithful memory,

> But can no more than fountains upward flow.

Which of a 'torrent', which signifies a rapid stream, is much more impossible. Besides, if he goes to quibble and say that it is possible by art water may be made return, and the same water run twice in one and the same channel, then he quite confutes what he says, for it is by being opposed that it runs into its former course; for all engines that make water so return, do it by compulsion and opposition. Or, if he means a headlong torrent for a tide, which would be ridiculous, yet they do not wind in volumes, but come foreright back (if their upright lies straight to their former course), and that by opposition of the sea-water that drives them back again.

And for fancy, when he lights of anything like it, 'tis a wonder if it be not borrowed. As here, for example of, I find this fanciful thought in his *Ann. Mirab.*

> Old father Thames raised up his reverend head;
> But feared the fate of Simoeis would return;
> Deep in his ooze he sought his sedgy bed;
> And shrunk his waters back into his urn.

This is stolen from Cowley's *Davideis*, p. 9:

> Swift Jordan started, and straight backward fled,
> Hiding amongst thick reeds his aged head.

> And when the Spaniards their assault begin,
> At once beat those without and those within.

This Almanzor speaks of himself, and sure for one man to conquer an army within the city, and another without the city at once, is something difficult; but this flight is pardonable to some we meet with in *Granada*. Osmin, speaking of Almanzor:

> Who, like a tempest that outrides the wind,
> Made a just battle ere the bodies joined.

Pray what does this honourable person mean by a 'tempest that outrides the wind'! A tempest that outrides itself. To suppose a tempest without wind is as bad as supposing a man to walk without feet: for if he supposes the tempest to be something distinct from the wind, yet as being the effect of wind only, to come before the cause is a little preposterous; so that, if he takes it one way, or if he takes it the other, those two 'ifs' will scarce make one 'possibility'.

foreright: 'directly forward, in or towards the front, straight ahead. *Obs.*' (*OED*).
And for fancy: op. cit. pp. 82–3.   *Old father Thames*: *Annus Mirabilis*, st. 232.
Swift Jordan started: Cowley: *Poems*, p. 248.
And when the Spaniards: op. cit. p. 84. Cf. *Dryden: DW*, iii. 46.
Who, like a tempest: *Dryden: DW*, iii. 39.

Enough of Settle.

Marriage à la Mode is a comedy dedicated to the Earl of Rochester, whom he acknowledges not only as the defender of his poetry but the promoter of his fortune. Langbaine places this play in 1673. The Earl of Rochester therefore was the famous Wilmot, whom yet tradition always represents as an enemy to Dryden, and who is mentioned by him with some disrespect in the preface to Juvenal.

The Assignation, or Love in a Nunnery, a comedy, was driven off the stage 'against the opinion', as the author says, 'of the best judges'. It is dedicated, in a very elegant address, to Sir Charles Sedley, in which he finds an opportunity for his usual complaint of hard treatment and unreasonable censure.

Amboyna is a tissue of mingled dialogue in verse and prose, and was perhaps written in less time than *The Virgin Martyr*, though the author thought not fit either ostentatiously or mournfully to tell how little labour it cost him, or at how short a warning he produced it. It was a temporary performance written in the time of the Dutch war to inflame the nation against their enemies, to whom he hopes, as he declares in his epilogue, to make his poetry not less destructive than that by which Tyrtaeus of old animated the Spartans. This play was written in the Second Dutch War in 1673.

Troilus and Cressida is a play altered from Shakespeare, but so altered that even in Langbaine's opinion 'the last scene in the third act is a masterpiece'. It is introduced by a discourse on *The Grounds of Criticism in Tragedy*, to which I suspect that Rymer's book had given occasion.

The Spanish Friar is a tragicomedy eminent for the happy coincidence and coalition of the two plots. As it was written against the Papists, it would naturally at that time have friends and enemies; and partly by the popularity which it obtained at first, and partly by the real power both of the serious and risible part, it continued long a favourite of the public.

It was Dryden's opinion, at least for some time, and he maintains it in the dedication of this play, that the drama required an alternation of comic and tragic scenes, and that it is necessary to mitigate by

Earl of Rochester: John Wilmot (1647–80), 2nd Earl of Rochester, poet and libertine. Cf. *Dryden: DW*, iii. 190; *Dryden: Essays*, ii. 75.

Langbaine: Spingarn, iii. 138.

'*against the opinion*': *Dryden: Essays*, i. 184.

Sir Charles Sedley: (1639?–1701), wit and minor dramatist.

perhaps written in: cf. *Dryden: DW*, iii. 350.

Tyrtaeus: see *Dryden: Poems*, iv. 1859.　　　'*the last scene*': Spingarn, iii. 144.

Rymer's book: *Tragedies of the Last Age* (1678).

alleviations of merriment the pressure of ponderous events and the fatigue of toilsome passions. Whoever, says he, cannot perform both parts 'is but half a writer for the stage'.

The Duke of Guise, a tragedy written in conjunction with Lee as *Oedipus* had been before, seems to deserve notice only for the offence which it gave to the remnant of the Covenanters, and in general to the enemies of the Court, who attacked him with great violence, and were answered by him[n]—though at last he seems to withdraw from the conflict by transferring the greater part of the blame or merit to his partner. It happened that a contract had been made between them by which they were to join in writing a play, and 'he happened', says Dryden, 'to claim the promise just upon the finishing of a poem, when I would have been glad of a little respite. Two-thirds of it belonged to him; and to me only the first scene of the play, the whole fourth act, and the first half or somewhat more of the fifth.'

This was a play written professedly for the party of the Duke of York, whose succession was then opposed. A parallel is intended between the Leaguers of France and the Covenanters of England, and this intention produced the controversy.

Albion and Albania is a musical drama or opera written, like *The Duke of Guise*, against the republicans. With what success it was performed I have not found.

The State of Innocence and Fall of Man is termed by him an opera; it is rather a tragedy in heroic rhyme, but of which the personages are such as cannot decently be exhibited on the stage. Some such production was foreseen by Marvell, who writes thus to Milton:

> Or if a work so infinite be spanned,
> Jealous I was lest some less skilful hand,
> Such as disquiet always what is well,
> And by ill-imitating would excel,
> Might hence presume the whole creation's day
> To change in scenes, and show it in a play.

It is another of his hasty productions, for the heat of his imagination raised it in a month.

This composition is addressed to the Princess of Modena, then

'*is but*': *Dryden: Essays*, i. 279.
Lee: Nathaniel Lee (1653?–92), dramatist; see *Dryden: DW*, v. 327.
'*he happened*': ibid. v. 300.   *Or if*: 'On Mr. Milton's Paradise Lost', ll. 17–22.
a month: *Dryden: Essays*, i. 196.
Princess of Modena: Mary of Modena (1658–1718), d. of Alfonso IV (Duke of Modena), Queen of James II.

Duchess of York, in a strain of flattery which disgraces genius, and which it was wonderful that any man that knew the meaning of his own words could use without self-detestation. It is an attempt to mingle earth and heaven by praising human excellence in the language of religion.

The preface contains an apology for heroic verse and poetic licence, by which is meant not any liberty taken in contracting or extending words, but the use of bold fictions and ambitious figures.

The reason which he gives for printing what was never acted cannot be overpassed: 'I was induced to it in my own defence, many hundred copies of it being dispersed abroad without my knowledge or consent, and everyone gathering new faults, it became at length a libel against me.' These copies, as they gathered faults, were apparently manuscript, and he lived in an age very unlike ours if many hundred copies of 1,400 lines were likely to be transcribed. An author has a right to print his own works, and needs not seek an apology in falsehood; but he that could bear to write the dedication felt no pain in writing the preface.

Aureng-Zebe is a tragedy founded on the actions of a great prince then reigning, but over nations not likely to employ their critics upon the transactions of the English stage. If he had known and disliked his own character, our trade was not in those times secure from his resentment. His country is at such a distance that the manners might be safely falsified and the incidents feigned, for remoteness of place is remarked by Racine to afford the same conveniences to a poet as length of time.

This play is written in rhyme, and has the appearance of being the most elaborate of all the dramas. The personages are imperial, but the dialogue is often domestic and therefore susceptible of sentiments accommodated to familiar incidents. The complaint of life is celebrated, and there are many other passages that may be read with pleasure.

This play is addressed to the Earl of Mulgrave, afterwards Duke of Buckingham, himself, if not a poet, yet a writer of verses and a

---

'*I was induced*': *Dryden: Essays*, i. 195–6.

a great prince: Aurangzeb (1618–1707), one of the greatest of the Mogul emperors of India.

Racine: Jean Racine (1639–99), French tragic poet; see his *Bajazet*, ed. Cuthbert Girdlestone (Oxford, 1955), p. 4.

but the dialogue: cf. *Rambler* 125.

The complaint of life: Dryden: *DW*, iv. 129 (IV. i). Cf. *Life*, iv. 303.

Earl of Mulgrave: John Sheffield (1648–1721), 3rd Earl of Mulgrave and 1st Duke of Buckingham and Normanby.

critic. In this address Dryden gave the first hints of his intention to write an epic poem. He mentions his design in terms so obscure that he seems afraid lest his plan should be purloined, as, he says, happened to him when he told it more plainly in his preface to Juvenal. 'The design', says he, 'you know is great, the story English, and neither too near the present times, nor too distant from them.'

All for Love, or the World well Lost, a tragedy founded upon the story of Antony and Cleopatra, he tells us 'is the only play which he wrote for himself'; the rest were given to the people. It is by universal consent accounted the work in which he has admitted the fewest improprieties of style or character, but it has one fault equal to many, though rather moral than critical, that by admitting the romantic omnipotence of love he has recommended as laudable and worthy of imitation that conduct which, through all ages, the good have censured as vicious, and the bad despised as foolish.

Of this play the prologue and the epilogue, though written upon the common topics of malicious and ignorant criticism, and without any particular relation to the characters or incidents of the drama, are deservedly celebrated for their elegance and sprightliness.

Limberham, or the Kind Keeper is a comedy which, after the third night, was prohibited as too indecent for the stage. What gave offence was in the printing, as the author says, altered or omitted. Dryden confesses that its indecency was objected to, but Langbaine, who yet seldom favours him, imputes its expulsion to resentment, because it 'so much exposed the keeping part of the town'.

Oedipus is a tragedy formed by Dryden and Lee in conjunction, from the works of Sophocles, Seneca and Corneille. Dryden planned the scenes, and composed the first and third acts.

Don Sebastian is commonly esteemed either the first or second of his dramatic performances.[n] It is too long to be all acted, and has many characters and many incidents; and though it is not without sallies of frantic dignity and more noise than meaning, yet as it makes approaches to the possibilities of real life, and has some sentiments which leave a strong impression, it continued long to attract attention. Amidst the distresses of princes and the vicissitudes

He mentions: *Dryden: Essays*, i. 191.   *as, he says*: ibid. ii. 292–3.
he tells us: ibid. ii. 207.   *as the author says*: *Dryden: DW*, iv. 271.
but Langbaine: Spingarn, iii. 137.
from the works: *Dryden: Essays*, i. 232–4.
Sophocles: (c. 496–406 B.C.), Greek tragedian.
Seneca: the younger (4 B.C.–A.D. 65), Roman statesman, philosopher, and author of various works (including nine tragedies).
Corneille: Pierre Corneille (1606–84), French dramatist.

of empire are inserted several scenes which the writer intended for comic, but which, I suppose, that age did not much commend, and this would not endure. There are, however, passages of excellence universally acknowledged: the dispute and the reconciliation of Dorax and Sebastian has always been admired.

This play was first acted in 1690, after Dryden had for some years discontinued dramatic poetry.

Amphitryon is a comedy derived from Plautus and Molière. The dedication is dated Oct. 1690. This play seems to have succeeded at its first appearance, and was, I think, long considered as a very diverting entertainment.

Cleomenes is a tragedy, only remarkable as it occasioned an incident related in the *Guardian*, and allusively mentioned by Dryden in his preface. As he came out from the representation, he was accosted thus by some airy stripling: 'Had I been left alone with a young beauty, I would not have spent my time like your Spartan.' 'That, Sir', said Dryden, 'perhaps is true; but give me leave to tell you that you are no hero.'

King Arthur is another opera. It was the last work that Dryden performed for King Charles, who did not live to see it exhibited; and it does not seem to have been ever brought upon the stage.[n] In the dedication to the Marquis of Halifax, there is a very elegant character of Charles, and a pleasing account of his latter life.

His last drama was *Love Triumphant*, a tragicomedy. In his dedication to the Earl of Salisbury he mentions 'the lowness of fortune to which he has voluntarily reduced himself, and of which he has no reason to be ashamed'.

This play appeared in 1694. It is said to have been unsuccessful. The catastrophe, proceeding merely from a change of mind, is confessed by the author to be defective.[n] Thus he began and ended his dramatic labours with ill success.

From such a number of theatrical pieces it will be supposed by most readers that he must have improved his fortune; at least, that

several scenes: cf. *Rambler* 125.   *the dispute*: Dryden: *DW*, vi. 106 ff.
derived from Plautus: ibid. vi. 149.
Plautus: (*c.* 254–184 B.C.), Roman comic poet.
Molière: *nom de théâtre* of Jean-Baptiste Poquelin (1622–73), the creator of French classical comedy.
an incident: *Guardian* 45; Dryden: *DW*, vi. 300.
Marquis of Halifax: Sir George Savile (1633–95), 1st Marquis of Halifax.
Earl of Salisbury: James Cecil (d. 1693), 4th Earl of Salisbury; see Dryden: *DW*, vi. 403.
It is said: ibid. vi. 402.

such diligence with such abilities must have set penury at defiance. But in Dryden's time the drama was very far from that universal approbation which it has now obtained. The playhouse was abhorred by the Puritans, and avoided by those who desired the character of seriousness or decency. A grave lawyer would have debased his dignity, and a young trader would have impaired his credit, by appearing in those mansions of dissolute licentiousness. The profits of the theatre, when so many classes of the people were deducted from the audience, were not great, and the poet had for a long time but a single night. The first that had two nights was Southerne, and the first that had three was Rowe.[n] There were, however, in those days, arts of improving a poet's profit which Dryden forbore to practise, and a play therefore seldom produced him more than £100 by the accumulated gain of the third night, the dedication, and the copy.

Almost every piece had a dedication written with such elegance and luxuriance of praise as neither haughtiness nor avarice could be imagined able to resist. But he seems to have made flattery too cheap. That praise is worth nothing of which the price is known.

To increase the value of his copies, he often accompanied his work with a preface of criticism—a kind of learning then almost new in the English language, and which he, who had considered with great accuracy the principles of writing, was able to distribute copiously as occasions arose. By these dissertations the public judgement must have been much improved, and Swift, who conversed with Dryden, relates that he regretted the success of his own instructions, and found his readers made suddenly too skilful to be easily satisfied.

His prologues had such reputation that for some time a play was considered as less likely to be well received if some of his verses did not introduce it. The price of a prologue was two guineas, till being asked to write one for Mr. Southerne he demanded three—'Not', said he, 'young man, out of disrespect to you, but the players have had my goods too cheap.'[n]

Though he declares that in his own opinion his genius was not

---

Southerne: Thomas Southerne (1660–1746), dramatist, best known for *The Fatal Marriage* (1694) and *Oroonoko* (1696).
Rowe: Nicholas Rowe (1674–1718), poet and dramatist.
arts of improving: i.e. 'the drudgery of sollicitation'; see Cibber, *Lives of the Poets* (1753), v. 329.
Swift: Jonathan Swift (1667–1745), Dean of St. Patrick's and great prose satirist; cf. *A Tale of a Tub*, §5 (where Swift is in fact satirizing Dryden).
Though he declares: Dryden: *Essays*, ii. 91.

dramatic, he had great confidence in his own fertility, for he is said to have engaged by contract to furnish four plays a year.[n]

It is certain that in one year, 1678, he published *All for Love, Assignation*, two parts of *The Conquest of Granada, Sir Martin Mar-all*, and *The State of Innocence*,[n] six complete plays, with a celerity of performance which, though all Langbaine's charges of plagiarism should be allowed, shows such facility of composition, such readiness of language, and such copiousness of sentiment, as since the time of Lope de Vega perhaps no other author has possessed.

He did not enjoy his reputation, however great, nor his profits, however small, without molestation. He had critics to endure and rivals to oppose. The two most distinguished wits of the nobility, the Duke of Buckingham and Earl of Rochester, declared themselves his enemies.

Buckingham characterised him in 1671 by the name of Bayes in *The Rehearsal*, a farce which he is said to have written with the assistance of Butler, the author of *Hudibras*, Martin Clifford of the Charterhouse, and Dr. Sprat, the friend of Cowley, then his chaplain.[n] Dryden and his friends laughed at the length of time and the number of hands employed upon this performance,[n] in which, though by some artifice of action it yet keeps possession of the stage, it is not possible now to find anything that might not have been written without so long delay or a confederacy so numerous.

To adjust the minute events of literary history is tedious and troublesome; it requires indeed no great force of understanding, but often depends upon inquiries which there is no opportunity of making, or is to be fetched from books and pamphlets not always at hand.

The Rehearsal was played in 1671, and yet is represented as ridiculing passages in *The Conquest of Granada* and *Assignation*, which were not published till 1678, in *Marriage à la Mode*, published in 1673, and in *Tyrannic Love* of 1677. These contradictions show how rashly satire is applied.[n]

It is said that this farce was originally intended against Davenant, who in the first draught was characterised by the name of Bilboa.[n] Davenant had been a soldier and an adventurer.

There is one passage in *The Rehearsal* still remaining which seems to have related originally to Davenant. Bayes hurts his nose, and comes in with brown paper applied to the bruise; how this affected

Lope de Vega: Félix Lope de Vega Carpio (1562–1635), poet and Spain's first great dramatist, prolific author of plays.
Bayes hurts his nose: *Rehearsal*, pp. 28–9 (II. v, III. i).

Dryden does not appear. Davenant's nose had suffered such diminution by mishaps among the women that a patch upon that part evidently denoted him.

It is said likewise that Sir Robert Howard was once meant.[n] The design was probably to ridicule the reigning poet, whoever he might be.

Much of the personal satire to which it might owe its first reception is now lost or obscured. Bayes probably imitated the dress and mimicked the manner of Dryden: the cant words which are so often in his mouth may be supposed to have been Dryden's habitual phrases or customary exclamations. Bayes, when he is to write, is blooded and purged; this, as Lamotte relates himself to have heard, was the real practice of the poet.

There were other strokes in *The Rehearsal* by which malice was gratified: the debate between love and honour, which keeps Prince Volscius in a single boot, is said to have alluded to the misconduct of the Duke of Ormonde, who lost Dublin to the rebels while he was toying with a mistress.

The Earl of Rochester, to suppress the reputation of Dryden, took Settle into his protection,[n] and endeavoured to persuade the public that its approbation had been to that time misplaced. Settle was a while in high reputation: his *Empress of Morocco*, having first delighted the town, was carried in triumph to Whitehall, and played by the ladies of the Court. Now was the poetical meteor at the highest; the next moment began its fall. Rochester withdrew his patronage, seeming resolved, says one of his biographers, 'to have a judgement contrary to that of the town'.[n] Perhaps being unable to endure any reputation beyond a certain height, even when he had himself contributed to raise it.

Neither critics nor rivals did Dryden much mischief, unless they gained from his own temper the power of vexing him, which his frequent bursts of resentment give reason to suspect. He is always angry at some past or afraid of some future censure; but he lessens the smart of his wounds by the balm of his own approbation, and endeavours to repel the shafts of criticism by opposing a shield of adamantine confidence.

The perpetual accusation produced against him was that of

Lamotte: Charles Lamotte (d. 1742); see his *Essay upon Poetry and Painting* (1730), p. 103 n.; cf. *Rehearsal*, p. 18.

the debate: *Rehearsal*, pp. 41–2.

Duke of Ormonde: royalist commander in Ireland; see above, p. 65 n.

plagiarism, against which he never attempted any vigorous defence; for though he was perhaps sometimes injuriously censured, he would by denying part of the charge have confessed the rest, and as his adversaries had the proof in their own hands, he, who knew that wit had little power against facts, wisely left in that perplexity which generality produces a question which it was his interest to suppress, and which, unless provoked by vindication, few were likely to examine.

Though the life of a writer, from about thirty-five to sixty-three, may be supposed to have been sufficiently busied by the composition of eight-and-twenty pieces for the stage, Dryden found room in the same space for many other undertakings.

But how much soever he wrote, he was at least once suspected of writing more, for in 1679 a paper of verses called *An Essay on Satire* was shown about in manuscript, by which the Earl of Rochester, the Duchess of Portsmouth, and others, were so much provoked that, as was supposed, for the actors were never discovered, they procured Dryden, whom they suspected as the author, to be waylaid and beaten.[n] This incident is mentioned by the Duke of Buckinghamshire, the true writer, in his Art of Poetry, where he says of Dryden,

> Though praised and beaten for another's rhymes,
> His own deserves as great applause sometimes.

His reputation in time was such that his name was thought necessary to the success of every poetical or literary performance, and therefore he was engaged to contribute something, whatever it might be, to many publications. He prefixed the *Life of Polybius* to the translation of Sir Henry Sheeres, and those of Lucian and Plutarch to versions of their works by different hands.[n] Of the English *Tacitus* he translated the first book, and if Gordon be credited, translated it from the French. Such a charge can hardly be mentioned without some degree of indignation, but it is not, I suppose, so much to be inferred that Dryden wanted the literature

Duchess of Portsmouth: Louise Renée de Kéroualle (1649–1734), Charles II's mistress, created Duchess of Portsmouth in 1673.

Though praised: *An Essay upon Poetry* (1682), Spingarn, ii. 290.

Sir Henry Sheeres: (d. 1710), military engineer and author, whose translation of Polybius appeared in 1693.

Lucian: (c.115?–c.180), Greek author of essays, speeches, dialogues, letters, and stories.

Tacitus: (b. c. A.D. 55), Roman historian. Cf. *Annals and History of Tacitus ... made English by Several Hands* (1698).

Gordon: Thomas Gordon (1691?–1750), author; see *The Works of Tacitus*, transl. by Gordon (1728–31), i. 1–2.

necessary to the perusal of Tacitus as that, considering himself as hidden in a crowd, he had no awe of the public, and writing merely for money was contented to get it by the nearest way.

In 1680 the *Epistles* of Ovid being translated by the poets of the time, among which one was the work of Dryden, and another of Dryden and Lord Mulgrave,[n] it was necessary to introduce them by a preface; and Dryden, who on such occasions was regularly summoned, prefixed a discourse upon translation, which was then struggling for the liberty that it now enjoys. Why it should find any difficulty in breaking the shackles of verbal interpretation, which must for ever debar it from elegance, it would be difficult to conjecture, were not the power of prejudice every day observed. The authority of Jonson, Sandys and Holyday had fixed the judgement of the nation,[n] and it was not easily believed that a better way could be found than they had taken, though Fanshawe, Denham, Waller and Cowley had tried to give examples of a different practice.[n]

In 1681 Dryden became yet more conspicuous by uniting politics with poetry in the memorable satire called *Absalom and Achitophel*, written against the faction which, by Lord Shaftesbury's incitement, set the Duke of Monmouth at its head.

Of this poem, in which personal satire was applied to the support of public principles, and in which therefore every mind was interested, the reception was eager and the sale so large that my father, an old bookseller, told me he had not known it equalled but by Sacheverell's trial.

The reason of this general perusal Addison has attempted to derive from the delight which the mind feels in the investigation of secrets, and thinks that curiosity to decipher the names procured readers to the poem. There is no need to inquire why those verses were read which, to all the attractions of wit, elegance and harmony, added the co-operation of all the factious passions, and filled every mind with triumph or resentment.

Holyday: Barten Holyday (or Holiday) (1593–1661), divine and translator of Juvenal and Persius.

Fanshawe: Sir Richard Fanshawe (1608–66), diplomatist and author.

Lord Shaftesbury: Anthony Ashley Cooper (1621–83), 1st Baron Ashley and 1st Earl of Shaftesbury.

Duke of Monmouth: James Scott (1649–85), Duke of Monmouth and Buccleuch, natural son of Charles II.   *my father*: Michael Johnson (1656–1731).

Sacheverell's trial: Henry Sacheverell (1674?–1724), political preacher, favoured non-resistance, and condemned toleration and occasional conformity. Cf. *The Tryal of Dr. Henry Sacheverell ... 27 February 1709/10 ... until 23 March following* (1710).   *Addison has attempted*: Spectator 512.

It could not be supposed that all the provocation given by Dryden would be endured without resistance or reply. Both his person and his party were exposed in their turns to the shafts of satire which, though neither so well pointed nor perhaps so well aimed, undoubtedly drew blood.

One of these poems is called *Dryden's Satire on his Muse*, ascribed (though, as Pope says, falsely) to Somers, who was afterwards Chancellor.[n] The poem, whosesoever it was, has much virulence and some sprightliness. The writer tells all the ill that he can collect both of Dryden and his friends.

The poem of *Absalom and Achitophel* had two answers, now both forgotten—one called *Azaria and Hushai*, the other *Absalom Senior*. Of these hostile compositions Dryden apparently imputes *Absalom Senior* to Settle by quoting in his verses against him the second line. *Azaria and Hushai* was, as Wood says, imputed to him,[n] though it is somewhat unlikely that he should write twice on the same occasion. This is a difficulty which I cannot remove for want of a minuter knowledge of poetical transactions.

The same year he published *The Medal*, of which the subject is a medal struck on Lord Shaftesbury's escape from a prosecution by the *ignoramus* of a grand jury of Londoners.

In both poems he maintains the same principles, and saw them both attacked by the same antagonist. Elkanah Settle, who had answered *Absalom*, appeared with equal courage in opposition to *The Medal* and published an answer called *The Medal Reversed*, with so much success in both encounters that he left the palm doubtful, and divided the suffrages of the nation. Such are the revolutions of fame, or such is the prevalence of fashion, that the man whose works have not yet been thought to deserve the care of collecting them, who died forgotten in an hospital, and whose latter years were spent in contriving shows for fairs, and carrying an elegy or epithalamium, of which the beginning and end were occasionally varied but the intermediate parts were always the same, to every house where there was a funeral or a wedding, might with truth have had inscribed upon his stone,

Here lies the Rival and Antagonist of Dryden.

Settle was for this rebellion severely chastised by Dryden under the name of Doeg in the second part of *Absalom and Achitophel*, and was perhaps for his factious audacity made the city poet, whose

Somers: John Somers (or Sommers) (1651–1716), Baron Somers.
by quoting: *The Second Part of Absalom and Achitophel*, l. 446.

annual office was to describe the glories of the Mayor's day. Of these bards he was the last, and seems not much to have deserved even this degree of regard if it was paid to his political opinions, for he afterwards wrote a panegyric on the virtues of Judge Jeffreys—and what more could have been done by the meanest zealot for prerogative?

Of translated fragments or occasional poems, to enumerate the titles, or settle the dates, would be tedious with little use. It may be observed that as Dryden's genius was commonly excited by some personal regard, he rarely writes upon a general topic.

Soon after the accession of King James, when the design of reconciling the nation to the Church of Rome became apparent, and the religion of the Court gave the only efficacious title to its favours, Dryden declared himself a convert to popery. This at any other time might have passed with little censure. Sir Kenelm Digby embraced popery; the two Rainolds reciprocally converted one another; and Chillingworth himself was a while so entangled in the wilds of controversy as to retire for quiet to an infallible church. If men of argument and study can find such difficulties, or such motives, as may either unite them to the Church of Rome or detain them in uncertainty, there can be no wonder that a man, who perhaps never inquired why he was a Protestant, should by an artful and experienced disputant be made a Papist, overborne by the sudden violence of new and unexpected arguments, or deceived by a representation which shows only the doubts on one part, and only the evidence on the other.

That conversion will always be suspected that apparently concurs with interest. He that never finds his error till it hinders his progress towards wealth or honour will not be thought to love Truth only for herself. Yet it may easily happen that information may come at a commodious time, and, as truth and interest are not by any fatal necessity at variance, that one may by accident introduce the other. When opinions are struggling into popularity, the arguments by which they are opposed or defended become more known, and he that changes his profession would perhaps have changed it before with the like opportunities of instruction. This was then the state of popery: every artifice was used to show it in its fairest form; and it

Judge Jeffreys: George Jeffreys (1644–89), 1st Baron Jeffreys of Wem, celebrated in Settle's *Panegyrick on the Loyal and Honourable Sir George Jeffries Lord Chief Justice of England* (1683), and notorious for his brutality.

Rainolds: William (1544?–94) and John (1549–1607) Rainolds (or Reynolds). Cf. Thomas Fuller, *Church History of Britain*, x. 47.

Chillingworth: William Chillingworth (1602–44), theologian, who embraced Romanism in 1630 and abjured it in 1634.

must be owned to be a religion of external appearance sufficiently attractive.

It is natural to hope that a comprehensive is likewise an elevated soul, and that whoever is wise is also honest. I am willing to believe that Dryden, having employed his mind, active as it was, upon different studies, and filled it, capacious as it was, with other materials, came unprovided to the controversy, and wanted rather skill to discover the right than virtue to maintain it. But inquiries into the heart are not for man; we must now leave him to his Judge.

The priests, having strengthened their cause by so powerful an adherent, were not long before they brought him into action. They engaged him to defend the controversial papers found in the strong-box of Charles II, and, what yet was harder, to defend them against Stillingfleet.[n]

With hopes of promoting popery, he was employed to translate Maimbourg's *History of the League*, which he published with a large introduction.[n] His name is likewise prefixed to the English *Life of Francis Xavier*, but I know not that he ever owned himself the translator. Perhaps the use of his name was a pious fraud, which however seems not to have had much effect, for neither of the books, I believe, was ever popular.

The version of Xavier's *Life* is commended by Brown in a pamphlet[n] not written to flatter, and the occasion of it is said to have been that the Queen, when she solicited a son, made vows to him as her tutelary saint.

He was supposed to have undertaken to translate Varillas's *History of Heresies*, and when Burnet published remarks upon it to have written an *Answer*;[n] upon which Burnet makes the following observation:

I have been informed from England that a gentleman, who is famous both for poetry and several other things, had spent three months in translating M. Varillas's *History*, but that, as soon as my *Reflections* appeared, he discontinued his labour, finding the credit of his author was gone. Now, if he thinks it is recovered by his *Answer*, he will perhaps go on with his transla-

Stillingfleet: Edward Stillingfleet (1635–99), Bishop of Worcester, formerly chaplain to Charles II.

Maimbourg: Louis Maimbourg (1610–86), French Jesuit and historian.

Francis Xavier: St. Francis Xavier (1506–52), Basque Jesuit missionary, whose *Life* Dryden translated from the French of Dominic Bouhours.

pious fraud: cf. *Hudibras*, I. iii. 1145.

Varillas: Antoine Varillas (1624–96), French historian.

I have been informed: *A Defence of the Reflections on Mr. Varillas's History of Heresies* (Amsterdam, 1687), pp. 138–40.

tion; and this may be, for aught I know, as good an entertainment for him as the conversation that he had set on between the Hinds and Panthers, and all the rest of animals, for whom M. Varillas may serve well enough as an author; and this history and that poem are such extraordinary things of their kind that it will be but suitable to see the author of the worst poem become likewise the translator of the worst history that the age has produced. If his grace and his wit improve both proportionably, he will hardly find that he has gained much by the change he has made, from having no religion to choose one of the worst. It is true he had somewhat to sink from in matter of wit; but as for his morals, it is scarce possible for him to grow a worse man than he was. He has lately wreaked his malice on me for spoiling his three months' labour, but in it he has done me all the honour that any man can receive from him, which is to be railed at by him. If I had ill-nature enough to prompt me to wish a very bad wish for him, it should be that he would go on and finish his translation. By that it will appear whether the English nation, which is the most competent judge in this matter, has, upon the seeing our debate, pronounced in M. Varillas's favour or in mine. It is true Mr. D. will suffer a little by it; but at least it will serve to keep him in from other extravagances; and if he gains little honour by this work, yet he cannot lose so much by it as he has done by his last employment.

Having probably felt his own inferiority in theological controversy, he was desirous of trying whether, by bringing poetry to aid his arguments, he might become a more efficacious defender of his new profession. To reason in verse was, indeed, one of his powers; but subtlety and harmony united are still feeble when opposed to truth.

Actuated therefore by zeal for Rome, or hope of fame, he published *The Hind and Panther*, a poem in which the Church of Rome, figured by the 'milk-white Hind', defends her tenets against the Church of England, represented by the 'Panther', a beast beautiful but spotted.

A fable which exhibits two beasts talking theology appears at once full of absurdity, and it was accordingly ridiculed in *The City Mouse and Country Mouse*, a parody written by Montagu, afterwards Earl of Halifax, and Prior, who then gave the first specimen of his abilities.

The conversion of such a man at such a time was not likely to pass uncensured. Three dialogues were published by the facetious Thomas Brown, of which the two first were called *Reasons of Mr. Bayes's changing his Religion*, and the third *The Reasons of Mr. Hains the Player's Conversion and Reconversion*. The first was printed in 1688,

---

wreaked his malice on me: see *The Hind and the Panther*, iii. 1121 ff., where the Buzzard represents Burnet.
Montagu: Charles Montagu (1661–1715), 1st Earl of Halifax.

the second not till 1690, the third in 1691. The clamour seems to have been long continued, and the subject to have strongly fixed the public attention.

In the two first dialogues Bayes is brought into the company of Crites and Eugenius, with whom he had formerly debated on dramatic poetry. The two talkers in the third are Mr. Bayes and Mr. Hains.

Brown was a man not deficient in literature nor destitute of fancy, but he seems to have thought it the pinnacle of excellence to be a 'merry fellow', and therefore laid out his powers upon small jests or gross buffoonery, so that his performances have little intrinsic value, and were read only while they were recommended by the novelty of the event that occasioned them.

These dialogues are like his other works: what sense or knowledge they contain is disgraced by the garb in which it is exhibited. One great source of pleasure is to call Dryden 'little Bayes'. Ajax, who happens to be mentioned, is 'he that wore as many cowhides upon his shield as would have furnished half the king's army with shoe-leather'.

Being asked whether he has seen *The Hind and Panther*, Crites answers: 'Seen it! Mr. Bayes, why I can stir nowhere but it pursues me; it haunts me worse than a pewter-buttoned serjeant does a decayed cit. Sometimes I meet it in a bandbox, when my laundress brings home my linen; sometimes, whether I will or no, it lights my pipe at a coffee-house; sometimes it surprises me in a trunkmaker's shop; and sometimes it refreshes my memory for me on the backside of a Chancery Lane parcel. For your comfort too, Mr. Bayes, I have not only seen it, as you may perceive, but have read it too, and can quote it as freely upon occasion as a frugal tradesman can quote that noble treatise *The Worth of a Penny* to his extravagant 'prentice, that revels in stewed apples and penny custards.'

The whole animation of these compositions arises from a profusion of ludicrous and affected comparisons. 'To secure one's chastity', says Bayes, 'little more is necessary than to leave off a correspondence with the other sex, which, to a wise man, is no greater a punishment than it would be to a fanatic parson to be forbid

'*merry fellow*': *Twelfth Night*, III. i. 23.
'*little Bayes*': cf. *The Reasons of Mr. Bays Changing his Religion* (1688), p. 1.
'*he that wore*': *The Late Converts Exposed* (1690), p. 2. For the shield of Ajax, son of Telamon, see Pope's *Iliad*, vii. 267–8.
'*Seen it*': *The Late Converts Exposed*, p. 1.
The Worth of a Penny: by Henry Peacham the younger, published 1647.
'*To secure*': op. cit. p. 9.

seeing *The Cheats* and *The Committee*, or for my Lord Mayor and aldermen to be interdicted the sight of *The London Cuckold.*' This is the general strain, and therefore I shall be easily excused the labour of more transcription.

Brown does not wholly forget past transactions: 'You began', says Crites to Bayes, 'with a very indifferent religion, and have not mended the matter in your last choice. It was but reason that your Muse, which appeared first in a tyrant's quarrel, should employ her last efforts to justify the usurpations of the Hind.'

Next year the nation was summoned to celebrate the birth of the Prince. Now was the time for Dryden to rouse his imagination and strain his voice. Happy days were at hand, and he was willing to enjoy and diffuse the anticipated blessings. He published a poem filled with predictions of greatness and prosperity—predictions of which it is not necessary to tell how they have been verified.

A few months passed after these joyful notes and every blossom of popish hope was blasted for ever by the Revolution. A Papist now could be no longer laureate. The revenue which he had enjoyed with so much pride and praise was transferred to Shadwell, an old enemy whom he had formerly stigmatised by the name of Og. Dryden could not decently complain that he was deposed, but seemed very angry that Shadwell succeeded him, and has therefore celebrated the intruder's inauguration in a poem exquisitely satirical called *Mac Flecknoe*,[n] of which *The Dunciad*, as Pope himself declares, is an imitation, though more extended in its plan and more diversified in its incidents.

It is related by Prior[n] that Lord Dorset, when as chamberlain he was constrained to eject Dryden from his office, gave him from his own purse an allowance equal to the salary. This is no romantic or incredible act of generosity; an hundred a year is often enough given to claims less cogent by men less famed for liberality. Yet Dryden always represented himself as suffering under a public infliction, and once particularly demands respect for the patience with which he endured the loss of his little fortune. His patron might, indeed, enjoin

The Cheats: by John Wilson, first performed in 1663.
The Committee: by Sir Robert Howard, first performed in 1662.
The London Cuckold: by Edward Ravenscroft, probably first performed in 1681.
'*You began*'; op. cit. p. 4.
a poem: *Britannia Rediviva* (1688).
Shadwell: Thomas Shadwell (1642?–92), dramatist and poet; cf. *The Second Part of Absalom and Achitophel*, ll. 408–11, 457–509.
as Pope himself declares: cf. *Pope: Poems*, v. xxxviii, 61, 96.
once particularly demands: *Dryden: Essays*, ii. 92.

him to suppress his bounty; but if he suffered nothing he should not have complained.

During the short reign of King James he had written nothing for the stage, being in his own opinion more profitably employed in controversy and flattery. Of praise he might perhaps have been less lavish without inconvenience, for James was never said to have much regard for poetry; he was to be flattered only by adopting his religion.

Times were now changed: Dryden was no longer the Court poet, and was to look back for support to his former trade, and having waited about two years, either considering himself as discountenanced by the public, or perhaps expecting a second revolution, he produced *Don Sebastian* in 1690, and in the next four years four dramas more.

In 1693 appeared a new version of Juvenal and Persius. Of Juvenal he translated the first, third, sixth, tenth and sixteenth satires, and of Persius the whole work. On this occasion he introduced his two sons to the public as nurselings of the Muses. The fourteenth of Juvenal was the work of John, and the seventh of Charles Dryden. He prefixed a very ample preface in the form of a dedication to Lord Dorset, and there gives an account of the design which he had once formed to write an epic poem on the actions either of Arthur or the Black Prince. He considered the epic as necessarily including some kind of supernatural agency, and had imagined a new kind of contest between the guardian angels of kingdoms, of whom he conceived that each might be represented zealous for his charge without any intended opposition to the purposes of the Supreme Being, of which all created minds must in part be ignorant.

This is the most reasonable scheme of celestial interposition that ever was formed. The surprises and terrors of enchantments, which have succeeded to the intrigues and oppositions of pagan deities, afford very striking scenes and open a vast extent to the imagination, but, as Boileau observes, and Boileau will be seldom found mistaken, with this incurable defect, that in a contest between heaven and hell we know at the beginning which is to prevail; for this reason we follow Rinaldo to the enchanted wood with more curiosity than terror.

Persius: (A.D. 34–62), Roman satirist.
two sons: John Dryden (1668–1701), writer, second son of the poet; Charles
    Dryden (1666–1704), Chamberlain to Pope Innocent XII, eldest son of the poet.
He considered: see *Dryden: Essays*, ii. 86–91.
Boileau: Nicholas Boileau-Despréaux (1636–1711), French poet and critic; see
    L'Art poétique (1674), iii. 193 ff.
we follow Rinaldo: *Gerusalemme Liberata*, can. xviii.

In the scheme of Dryden there is one great difficulty which yet he would perhaps have had address enough to surmount. In a war justice can be but on one side, and to entitle the hero to the protection of angels he must fight in the defence of indubitable right. Yet some of the celestial beings thus opposed to each other must have been represented as defending guilt.

That this poem was never written is reasonably to be lamented. It would doubtless have improved our numbers and enlarged our language, and might perhaps have contributed by pleasing instruction to rectify our opinions and purify our manners.

What he required as the indispensable condition of such an undertaking, a public stipend, was not likely in those times to be obtained. Riches were not become familiar to us, nor had the nation yet learned to be liberal.

This plan he charged Blackmore with stealing, 'only', says he, 'the guardian angels of kingdoms were machines too ponderous for him to manage'.

In 1694 he began the most laborious and difficult of all his works, the translation of Virgil,[n] from which he borrowed two months that he might turn Fresnoy's 'Art of Painting' into English prose. The preface, which he boasts to have written in twelve mornings, exhibits a parallel of poetry and painting, with a miscellaneous collection of critical remarks such as cost a mind stored like his no labour to produce them.

In 1697 he published his version of the works of Virgil, and that no opportunity of profit might be lost, dedicated the *Pastorals* to the Lord Clifford, the *Georgics* to the Earl of Chesterfield, and the *Aeneid* to the Earl of Mulgrave. This economy of flattery, at once lavish and discreet, did not pass without observation.

This translation was censured by Milbourne, a clergyman, styled by Pope 'the fairest of critics' because he exhibited his own version to be compared with that which he condemned.

Blackmore: Sir Richard Blackmore (*c.* 1655–1729), physician and author; see *Dryden: Essays*, ii. 292–3.

from which he borrowed: ibid. ii. 183.

Fresnoy: Charles Alphonse Du Fresnoy (1611–65), French painter and critic, author of *De arte graphica* (1668).

which he boasts: *Dryden: Essays*, ii. 207–8.

Lord Clifford: Hugh Clifford (1663–1730), 2nd Baron Chudleigh.

Earl of Chesterfield: Philip Stanhope (1633–1713), 2nd Earl of Chesterfield.

did not pass: cf. *A Tale of a Tub*, §1.

Milbourne: Luke Milbourne (1649–1720), poet, author of *Notes on Dryden's Virgil* (1698). Cf. *Pope: Poems*, v. 141.

His last work was his *Fables*, published in 1699,[n] in consequence, as is supposed, of a contract now in the hands of Mr. Tonson by which he obliged himself, in consideration of £300, to finish for the press 10,000 verses.

In this volume is comprised the well-known 'Ode on St. Cecilia's Day' which, as appeared by a letter communicated to Dr. Birch, he spent a fortnight in composing and correcting.[n] But what is this to the patience and diligence of Boileau, whose 'Equivoque', a poem of only 346 lines, took from his life eleven months to write it and three years to revise it!

Part of this book of *Fables* is the first *Iliad* in English, intended as a specimen of a version of the whole. Considering into what hands Homer was to fall, the reader cannot but rejoice that this project went no further.

The time was now at hand which was to put an end to all his schemes and labours. On 1 May, 1701, having been some time, as he tells us, a cripple in his limbs, he died in Gerard Street of a mortification in his leg.[n]

There is extant a wild story relating to some vexatious events that happened at his funeral, which, at the end of Congreve's *Life* by a writer of I know not what credit, are thus related, as I find the account transferred to a biographical dictionary:[n]

Mr. Dryden dying on the Wednesday morning, Dr. Thomas Sprat, then Bishop of Rochester and Dean of Westminster, sent the next day to the Lady Elizabeth Howard, Mr. Dryden's widow, that he would make a present of the ground, which was £40, with all the other Abbey fees. The Lord Halifax likewise sent to the Lady Elizabeth, and Mr. Charles Dryden her son, that if they would give him leave to bury Mr. Dryden, he would inter him with a gentleman's private funeral, and afterwards bestow £500 on a monument in the Abbey; which, as they had no reason to refuse, they accepted. On the Saturday following the company came; the corpse was put into a velvet hearse, and eighteen mourning coaches, filled with company, attended. When they were just ready to move, the Lord Jeffreys, son of the Lord Chancellor Jeffreys, with some of his rakish companions coming by, asked whose funeral it was, and being told Mr. Dryden's, he said, 'What, shall Dryden, the greatest honour and ornament of the nation, be buried after this private manner! No, gentlemen, let all that loved Mr. Dryden, and honour his memory, alight and join with me in gaining my Lady's consent to let me have the honour of his interment,

whose 'Equivoque': *Oeuvres*, i. 233 n. 5.
as he tells us: *Dryden: Letters*, pp. 135–6 (Dryden to Elizabeth Steward, 11 Apr. 1700).
Congreve: William Congreve (1670–1729), dramatist.
Lady Elizabeth Howard: Elizabeth Dryden (*née* Howard) (1636/8?–1714).
Lord Jeffreys: John Jeffreys (1670?–1702), 2nd Baron Jeffreys of Wem.

which shall be after another manner than this; and I will bestow £1,000 on a monument in the Abbey for him'. The gentlemen in the coaches, not knowing of the Bishop of Rochester's favour, nor of the Lord Halifax's generous design (they both having, out of respect to the family, enjoined the Lady Elizabeth and her son to keep their favour concealed to the world, and let it pass for their own expense), readily came out of the coaches, and attended Lord Jeffreys up to the lady's bedside, who was then sick; he repeated the purport of what he had before said, but she absolutely refusing, he fell on his knees, vowing never to rise till his request was granted. The rest of the company by his desire kneeled also, and the lady, being under a sudden surprize, fainted away. As soon as she recovered her speech, she cried, 'No, no'. 'Enough, gentlemen', replied he; 'my Lady is very good, she says, "Go, go".' She repeated her former words with all her strength, but in vain, for her feeble voice was lost in their acclamations of joy; and the Lord Jeffreys ordered the hearsemen to carry the corpse to Mr. Russell's, an undertaker's in Cheapside, and leave it there till he should send orders for the embalment, which, he added, should be after the royal manner. His directions were obeyed, the company dispersed, and Lady Elizabeth and her son remained inconsolable. The next day Mr. Charles Dryden waited on the Lord Halifax and the Bishop, to excuse his mother and himself by relating the real truth. But neither his Lordship nor the Bishop would admit of any plea—especially the latter, who had the Abbey lighted, the ground opened, the choir attending, an anthem ready set, and himself waiting for some time without any corpse to bury. The undertaker, after three days' expectance of orders for embalment without receiving any, waited on the Lord Jeffreys, who, pretending ignorance of the matter, turned it off with an ill-natured jest, saying, That those who observed the orders of a drunken frolic deserved no better; that he remembered nothing at all of it; and that he might do what he pleased with the corpse. Upon this, the undertaker waited upon the Lady Elizabeth and her son, and threatened to bring the corpse home, and set it before the door. They desired a day's respite, which was granted. Mr. Charles Dryden wrote a handsome letter to the Lord Jeffreys, who returned it with this cool answer, That he knew nothing of the matter, and would be troubled no more about it. He then addressed the Lord Halifax and the Bishop of Rochester, who absolutely refused to do anything in it. In this distress Dr. Garth sent for the corpse to the College of Physicians, and proposed a funeral by subscription, to which himself set a most noble example. At last a day, about three weeks after Mr. Dryden's decease, was appointed for the interment: Dr. Garth pronounced a fine Latin oration at the college over the corpse, which was attended to the Abbey by a numerous train of coaches. When the funeral was over, Mr. Charles Dryden sent a challenge to the Lord Jeffreys, who refusing to answer it, he sent several others, and went often himself, but could neither get a letter delivered, nor admittance to speak to him—which so incensed him that he resolved, since his lordship refused to answer him like a gentleman, that he would watch an opportunity to meet and fight off-hand, though with all the rules of honour; which his lordship hearing, left the town, and Mr.

Mr. Russell's: William Russell (*fl.* 1684–1700), coffin-maker and embalmer.
Dr. Garth: Samuel Garth (1661–1719), physician and poet. Cf. Ward, p. 318.

Charles Dryden could never have the satisfaction of meeting him, though he sought it till his death with the utmost application.

This story I once intended to omit, as it appears with no great evidence; nor have I met with any confirmation but in a letter of Farquhar, and he only relates that the funeral of Dryden was tumultuary and confused.[n]

Supposing the story true, we may remark that the gradual change of manners, though imperceptible in the process, appears great when different times, and those not very distant, are compared. If at this time a young drunken lord should interrupt the pompous regularity of a magnificent funeral, what would be the event but that he would be jostled out of the way and compelled to be quiet? If he should thrust himself into a house he would be sent roughly away; and what is yet more to the honour of the present time, I believe that those who had subscribed to the funeral of a man like Dryden would not, for such an accident, have withdrawn their contributions.

He was buried among the poets in Westminster Abbey where, though the Duke of Newcastle had, in a general dedication prefixed by Congreve to his dramatic works, accepted thanks for his intention of erecting him a monument, he lay long without distinction, till the Duke of Buckinghamshire gave him a tablet inscribed only with the name of DRYDEN.

He married the Lady Elizabeth Howard, daughter of the Earl of Berkshire, with circumstances, according to the satire imputed to Lord Somers, not very honourable to either party; by her he had three sons, Charles, John and Henry. Charles was usher of the palace to Pope Clement XI, and visiting England in 1704 was drowned in an attempt to swim cross the Thames at Windsor.

John was author of a comedy called *The Husband his own Cuckold.* He is said to have died at Rome. Henry entered into some religious order. It is some proof of Dryden's sincerity in his second religion that he taught it to his sons. A man conscious of hypocritical profession in himself is not likely to convert others, and as his sons were

Farquhar: George Farquhar (1678–1707), dramatist; see *The Complete Works of George Farquhar*, ed. Charles Stonehill (1930), ii. 321.

Duke of Newcastle: Sir Thomas Pelham-Holles (1693–1768), 1st Duke of Newcastle-upon-Tyne and Newcastle-under-Lyme. See *The Dramatick Works of John Dryden*, ed. Congreve (1717–18), i. sigg. *a–a^v*.

Earl of Berkshire: Thomas Howard (*c.* 1580–1669), 1st Earl of Berkshire.

satire imputed to Lord Somers: *Satyr to his Muse* (1682) sig. B2^v.

Henry: Erasmus Henry Dryden (1669–1710).

Pope Clement XI: (1649–1721).

died at Rome: Birch, *General Dictionary*, iv. 684.

qualified in 1693 to appear among the translators of Juvenal, they must have been taught some religion before their father's change.

Of the person of Dryden I know not any account; of his mind the portrait which has been left by Congreve, who knew him with great familiarity, is such as adds our love of his manners to our admiration of his genius. 'He was', we are told, 'of a nature exceedingly humane and compassionate, ready to forgive injuries, and capable of a sincere reconciliation with those that had offended him. His friendship, where he professed it, went beyond his professions. He was of a very easy, of very pleasing access, but somewhat slow, and, as it were, diffident in his advances to others; he had that in his nature which abhorred intrusion into any society whatever. He was therefore less known, and consequently his character became more liable to misapprehensions and misrepresentations; he was very modest, and very easily to be discountenanced in his approaches to his equals or superiors. As his reading had been very extensive, so was he very happy in a memory tenacious of everything that he had read. He was not more possessed of knowledge than he was communicative of it, but then his communication was by no means pedantic, or imposed upon the conversation, but just such, and went so far as, by the natural turn of the conversation in which he was engaged, it was necessarily promoted or required. He was extreme ready and gentle in his correction of the errors of any writer who thought fit to consult him, and full as ready and patient to admit of the reprehensions of others in respect of his own oversights or mistakes.'

To this account of Congreve nothing can be objected but the fondness of friendship; and to have excited that fondness in such a mind is no small degree of praise. The disposition of Dryden, however, is shown in this character rather as it exhibited itself in cursory conversation than as it operated on the more important parts of life. His placability and his friendship indeed were solid virtues, but courtesy and good humour are often found with little real worth. Since Congreve, who knew him well, has told us no more, the rest must be collected as it can from other testimonies, and particularly from those notices which Dryden has very liberally given us of himself.

The modesty which made him so slow to advance, and so easy to be repulsed, was certainly no suspicion of deficient merit or unconsciousness of his own value: he appears to have known in its whole extent the dignity of his character, and to have set a very high value on his own powers and performances. He probably did not

we are told: *Dramatick Works of Dryden* (1717), i. sigg. *a6ᵛ–a8ᵛ*.

offer his conversation because he expected it to be solicited, and he retired from a cold reception not submissive but indignant, with such reverence of his own greatness as made him unwilling to expose it to neglect or violation.

His modesty was by no means inconsistent with ostentatiousness: he is diligent enough to remind the world of his merit, and expresses with very little scruple his high opinion of his own powers; but his self-commendations are read without scorn or indignation; we allow his claims, and love his frankness.

Tradition, however, has not allowed that his confidence in himself exempted him from jealously of others. He is accused of envy and insidiousness, and is particularly charged with inciting Creech to translate Horace that he might lose the reputation which Lucretius had given him.

Of this charge we immediately discover that it is merely conjectural; the purpose was such as no man would confess, and a crime that admits no proof why should we believe?

He has been described as magisterially presiding over the younger writers, and assuming the distribution of poetical fame; but he who excels has a right to teach, and he whose judgement is incontestable may, without usurpation, examine and decide.

Congreve represents him as ready to advise and instruct; but there is reason to believe that his communication was rather useful than entertaining. He declares of himself that he was saturnine, and not one of those whose sprightly sayings diverted company; and one of his censurers makes him say,

> Nor wine nor love could ever see me gay;
> To writing bred, I knew not what to say.

There are men whose powers operate only at leisure and in retirement, and whose intellectual vigour deserts them in conversation, whom merriment confuses and objection disconcerts, whose bashfulness restrains their exertion and suffers them not to speak till the time of speaking is past, or whose attention to their own character makes them unwilling to utter at hazard what has not been considered, and cannot be recalled.

Creech: Thomas Creech (1659–1700), translator, whose versions of Lucretius and
    Horace appeared in 1682 and 1684 respectively. Cf. *The Late Converts Exposed*
    (1690), pp. 53–54.   *Horace*: (65–8 B.C.), Roman lyric poet and satirist.
Lucretius: (c. 99–c. 55 B.C.), Roman philosophical poet.
He has been described: cf. *Dryden: Letters*, p. 69 (Dennis to Dryden, 3 March
    1694).   *He declares*: *Dryden: Essays*, i. 116.
Nor wine: *Satyr to his Muse* (1682), sig. B2ᵛ.

Of Dryden's sluggishness in conversation it is vain to search or to guess the cause. He certainly wanted neither sentiments nor language: his intellectual treasures were great though they were locked up from his own use. 'His thoughts', when he wrote, 'flowed in upon him so fast that his only care was which to choose, and which to reject.' Such rapidity of composition naturally promises a flow of talk, yet we must be content to believe what an enemy says of him when he likewise says it of himself. But whatever was his character as a companion, it appears that he lived in familiarity with the highest persons of his time. It is related by Carte of the Duke of Ormonde that he used often to pass a night with Dryden, and those with whom Dryden consorted; who they were Carte has not told, but certainly the convivial table at which Ormonde sat was not surrounded with a plebeian society. He was indeed reproached with boasting of his familiarity with the great, and Horace will support him in the opinion that to please superiors is not the lowest kind of merit.

The merit of pleasing must, however, be estimated by the means. Favour is not always gained by good actions or laudable qualities. Caresses and preferments are often bestowed on the auxiliaries of vice, the procurers of pleasure, or the flatterers of vanity. Dryden has never been charged with any personal agency unworthy of a good character; he abetted vice and vanity only with his pen. One of his enemies has accused him of lewdness in his conversation, but if accusation without proof be credited, who shall be innocent?

His works afford too many examples of dissolute licentiousness and abject adulation, but they were probably, like his merriment, artificial and constrained, the effects of study and meditation, and his trade rather than his pleasure.

Of the mind that can trade in corruption, and can deliberately pollute itself with ideal wickedness for the sake of spreading the contagion in society, I wish not to conceal or excuse the depravity. Such degradation of the dignity of genius, such abuse of superlative abilities, cannot be contemplated but with grief and indignation. What consolation can be had Dryden has afforded by living to repent, and to testify his repentance.

Of dramatic immorality he did not want examples among his predecessors or companions among his contemporaries; but in the

'*His thoughts*': *Dryden: Essays*, ii. 272.

Carte: Thomas Carte (1686–1754), historian; see *An History of the Life of James Duke of Ormonde* (1736), ii. 554.   *to please superiors*: *Epistles*, I. xvii. 35.
One of his enemies: *Satyr to his Muse*, sigg. B2–B2ᵛ.

meanness and servility of hyperbolical adulation I know not whether, since the days in which the Roman emperors were deified, he has been ever equalled, except by Afra Behn in an address to Eleanor Gwyn. When once he has undertaken the task of praise, he no longer retains shame in himself nor supposes it in his patron. As many odoriferous bodies are observed to diffuse perfumes from year to year without sensible diminution of bulk or weight, he appears never to have impoverished his mint of flattery by his expenses, however lavish. He had all the forms of excellence, intellectual and moral, combined i n his mind with endless variation, and when he had scattered on the hero of the day the golden shower of wit and virtue, he had ready for him whom he wished to court on the morrow new wit and virtue with another stamp. Of this kind of meanness he never seems to decline the practice or lament the necessity; he considers the great as entitled to encomiastic homage, and brings praise rather as a tribute than a gift, more delighted with the fertility of his invention than mortified by the prostitution of his judgement. It is indeed not certain that on these occasions his judgement much rebelled against his interest. There are minds which easily sink into submission, that look on grandeur with undistinguishing reverence, and discover no defect where there is elevation of rank and affluence of riches.

With his praises of others and of himself is always intermingled a strain of discontent and lamentation, a sullen growl of resentment or a querulous murmur of distress. His works are undervalued, his merit is unrewarded, and 'he has few thanks to pay his stars that he was born among Englishmen'. To his critics he is sometimes contemptuous, sometimes resentful, and sometimes submissive. The writer who thinks his works formed for duration mistakes his interest when he mentions his enemies. He degrades his own dignity by showing that he was affected by their censures, and gives lasting importance to names which, left to themselves, would vanish from remembrance. From this principle Dryden did not oft depart: his complaints are for the greater part general; he seldom pollutes his page with an adverse name. He condescended indeed to a controversy with Settle, in which he perhaps may be considered rather as assaulting than repelling; and since Settle is sunk into oblivion, his libel remains injurious only to himself.

Afra (Aphra or Ayfara) *Behn*: (1640–89), dramatist and novelist; see *The Works of Aphra Behn*, ed. Montague Summers (1915), ii. 305–6 (dedicatory epistle to *The Feigned Courtesans*).
Eleanor Gwyn: (1650–87), actress, and mistress of Charles II.
'*he has*': *Dryden: Essays*, ii. 63.

Among answers to critics, no poetical attacks or altercations are to be included; they are, like other poems, effusions of genius, produced as much to obtain praise as to obviate censure. These Dryden practised and in these he excelled.

Of Collier, Blackmore and Milbourne, he has made mention in the preface to his *Fables*. To the censure of Collier, whose remarks may be rather termed admonitions than criticisms, he makes little reply, being at the age of sixty-eight attentive to better things than the claps of a playhouse. He complains of Collier's rudeness and the 'horseplay of his raillery', and asserts that 'in many places he has perverted by his glosses the meaning' of what he censures; but in other things he confesses that he is justly taxed, and says with great calmness and candour: 'I have pleaded guilty to all thoughts or expressions of mine that can be truly accused of obscenity, immorality or profaneness, and retract them. If he be my enemy, let him triumph; if he be my friend, he will be glad of my repentance.' Yet as our best dispositions are imperfect, he left standing in the same book a reflection on Collier of great asperity, and indeed of more asperity than wit.

Blackmore he represents as made his enemy by the poem of *Absalom and Achitophel*, which 'he thinks a little hard upon his fanatic patrons', and charges him with borrowing the plan of his *Arthur* from the preface to Juvenal, 'though he had', says he, 'the baseness not to acknowledge his benefactor, but instead of it to traduce me in a libel'.

The libel in which Blackmore traduced him was *A Satire upon Wit*,[n] in which, having lamented the exuberance of false wit and the deficiency of true, he proposes that all wit should be recoined before it is current, and appoints masters of assay who shall reject all that is light or debased.

> 'Tis true, that when the coarse and worthless dross
> Is purged away, there will be mighty loss;
> Ev'n Congreve, Southerne, manly Wycherley,
> When thus refined, will grievous sufferers be;
> Into the melting-pot when Dryden comes,
> What horrid stench will rise, what noisome fumes!

Collier: Jeremy Collier (1650–1726), nonjuror, author of *A Short View of the Immorality and Profaneness of the English Stage* (1698). Cf. *Dryden: Essays*, ii. 293.

a reflection on Collier: Epilogue to *The Pilgrim*, ll. 1–4 (*Dryden: Poems*, iv. 1759).

Blackmore he represents: *Dryden: Essays*, ii. 292–3.

'Tis true: Spingarn, iii. 329.

Wycherley: William Wycherley (1640?–1716), dramatist.

> How will he shrink, when all his lewd allay
> And wicked mixture shall be purged away!

Thus stands the passage in the last edition, but in the original there was an abatement of the censure beginning thus:

> But what remains will be so pure, 'twill bear
> Th' examination of the most severe.

Blackmore finding the censure resented, and the civility disregarded, ungenerously omitted the softer part. Such variations discover a writer who consults his passions more than his virtue, and it may be reasonably supposed that Dryden imputes his enmity to its true cause.

Of Milbourne he wrote only in general terms, such as are always ready at the call of anger, whether just or not; a short extract will be sufficient. 'He pretends a quarrel to me that I have fallen foul upon priesthood; if I have, I am only to ask pardon of good priests, and am afraid his share of the reparation will come to little. Let him be satisfied that he shall never be able to force himself upon me for an adversary; I contemn him too much to enter into competition with him . . . As for the rest of those who have written against me, they are such scoundrels that they deserve not the least notice to be taken of them. Blackmore and Milbourne are only distinguished from the crowd by being remembered to their infamy.'

Dryden indeed discovered, in many of his writings, an affected and absurd malignity to priests and priesthood which naturally raised him many enemies, and which was sometimes as unseasonably resented as it was exerted. Trapp is angry that he calls the sacrificer in the *Georgics* the 'holy butcher'; the translation is indeed ridiculous, but Trapp's anger arises from his zeal not for the author, but the priest—as if any reproach of the follies of paganism could be extended to the preachers of truth.

Dryden's dislike of the priesthood is imputed by Langbaine, and I think by Brown, to a repulse which he suffered when he solicited ordination,[n] but he denies in the preface to his *Fables* that he ever designed to enter into the Church; and such a denial he would not have hazarded if he could have been convicted of falsehood.

allay: alloy.
'*He pretends*': *Dryden: Essays*, ii. 291, 294.
Trapp: Joseph Trapp (1679–1747), poet and pamphleteer; see *The Aeneis of Virgil translated into Blank verse* (1718–20), i. *lii*.
by Langbaine: Spingarn, iii. 142.
by Brown: *The Late Converts Exposed* (1690), sig. [2]*A* ('Preface to Mr. Bays').
he denies: *Dryden: Essays*, ii. 292.

Malevolence to the clergy is seldom at a great distance from irreverence of religion, and Dryden affords no exception to this observation. His writings exhibit many passages which, with all the allowance that can be made for characters and occasions, are such as piety would not have admitted, and such as may vitiate light and un-principled minds. But there is no reason for supposing that he dis-believed the religion which he disobeyed. He forgot his duty rather than disowned it. His tendency to profaneness is the effect of levity, negligence, and loose conversation, with a desire of accommodating himself to the corruption of the times by venturing to be wicked as far as he durst. When he professed himself a convert to popery, he did not pretend to have received any new conviction of the funda-mental doctrines of Christianity.

The persecution of critics was not the worst of his vexations: he was much more disturbed by the importunities of want. His com-plaints of poverty are so frequently repeated, either with the dejection of weakness sinking in helpless misery, or the indignation of merit claiming its tribute from mankind, that it is impossible not to detest the age which could impose on such a man the necessity of such solicitations, or not to despise the man who could submit to such solicitations without necessity.

Whether by the world's neglect or his own imprudence, I am afraid that the greatest part of his life was passed in exigencies. Such outcries were surely never uttered but in severe pain. Of his supplies or his expenses no probable estimate can now be made. Except the salary of the Laureate, to which King James added the office of Historiographer, perhaps with some additional emoluments,[n] his whole revenue seems to have been casual; and it is well known that he seldom lives frugally who lives by chance. Hope is always liberal, and they that trust her promises make little scruple of revelling today on the profits of the morrow.

Of his plays the profit was not great, and of the produce of his other works very little intelligence can be had. By discoursing with the late amiable Mr. Tonson, I could not find that any memorials of the transactions between his predecessor and Dryden had been pre-served except the following papers:

I do hereby promise to pay John Dryden, Esq. or order, on the 25th of March 1699, the sum of 250 guineas, in consideration of 10,000 verses which the said John Dryden, Esq. is to deliver to me Jacob Tonson, when finished, whereof 7,500 verses, more or less, are already in the said Jacob Tonson's possession. And I do hereby farther promise and engage myself

Mr. Tonson: Jacob Tonson (d. 1767).

to make up the said sum of 250 guineas £300 sterling to the said John Dryden, Esq. his executors, administrators, or assigns, at the beginning of the second impression of the said 10,000 verses.

In witness whereof I have hereunto set my hand and seal, this twentieth day of March, 1698/9.

JACOB TONSON

Sealed and delivered, being first
duly stamped, pursuant to the acts
of parliament for that purpose, in
the presence of

> BEN. PORTLOCK
> WILL. CONGREVE

March 24th, 1698.

Received then of Mr. Jacob Tonson the sum of £268.15s., in pursuance of an agreement for 10,000 verses, to be delivered by me to the said Jacob Tonson, whereof I have already delivered to him about 7,500, more or less; he the said Jacob Tonson being obliged to make up the foresaid sum of £268.15s., £300 at the beginning of the second impression of the foresaid 10,000 verses;

I say, received by me
JOHN DRYDEN

Witness CHARLES DRYDEN

Two hundred and fifty guineas at £1. 1s. 6d. is £268. 15s.[n]

It is manifest from the dates of this contract that it relates to the volume of *Fables*, which contains about 12,000 verses, and for which therefore the payment must have been afterwards enlarged.

I have been told of another letter yet remaining in which he desires Tonson to bring him money to pay for a watch which he had ordered for his son, and which the maker would not leave without the price.

The inevitable consequence of poverty is dependence. Dryden had probably no recourse in his exigencies but to his bookseller. The particular character of Tonson I do not know, but the general conduct of traders was much less liberal in those times than in our own; their views were narrower, and their manners grosser. To the mercantile ruggedness of that race the delicacy of the poet was sometimes exposed. Lord Bolingbroke, who in his youth had cultivated poetry, related to Dr. King of Oxford that one day when he visited Dryden, they heard, as they were conversing, another person entering the house. 'This', said Dryden, 'is Tonson. You will take care not to

another letter: Dryden: *Letters*, pp. 82–3.
Lord Bolingbroke: Henry St. John (1678–1751), 1st Viscount Bolingbroke, statesman.
Dr. King: William King (1685–1763), principal of St. Mary Hall, whom Johnson knew as early as 1755.

depart before he goes away, for I have not completed the sheet which I promised him, and if you leave me unprotected, I must suffer all the rudeness to which his resentment can prompt his tongue.'

What rewards he obtained for his poems, besides the payment of the bookseller, cannot be known; Mr. Derrick, who consulted some of his relations, was informed that his *Fables* obtained £500 from the Duchess of Ormonde—a present not unsuitable to the magnificence of that splendid family; and he quotes Moyle as relating that £40 were paid by a musical society for the use of *Alexander's Feast*.

In those days the economy of government was yet unsettled, and the payments of the Exchequer were dilatory and uncertain; of this disorder there is reason to believe that the laureate sometimes felt the effects, for in one of his prefaces he complains of those who, being entrusted with the distribution of the Prince's bounty, suffer those that depend upon it to languish in penury.

Of his petty habits or slight amusements, tradition has retained little. Of the only two men whom I have found to whom he was personally known, one told me that at the house which he frequented, called Will's Coffee-house, the appeal upon any literary dispute was made to him; and the other related that his armed chair, which in the winter had a settled and prescriptive place by the fire, was in the summer placed in the balcony, and that he called the two places his winter and his summer seat. This is all the intelligence which his two survivors afforded me.

One of his opinions will do him no honour in the present age, though in his own time, at least in the beginning of it, he was far from having it confined to himself. He put great confidence in the prognostications of judicial astrology. In the appendix to the *Life of Congreve* is a narrative of some of his predictions wonderfully fulfilled,[n] but I know not the writer's means of information or character of veracity. That he had the configurations of the horoscope in his mind, and considered them as influencing the affairs of men, he does not forbear to hint.

> The utmost malice of the stars is past.—

> Now frequent *trines* the happier lights among,
> And *high-raised Jove*, from his dark prison freed,

Mr. Derrick . . . was informed: Derrick, i. *xxviii*. But cf. Osborn, pp. 18–19.

the Duchess of Ormonde: Lady Mary Somerset (*c.* 1665–1733), 2nd w. of 2nd Duke of Ormonde.   *Moyle*: Walter Moyle (1672–1721), politician.

he complains: Dryden: *Essays*, ii. 92.

the only two men: Colley Cibber (1671–1757) and Owen MacSwinney (d. 1754); cf. *Life*, iii. 71.   *The utmost malice*: *Annus Mirabilis*, sts. 291–2.

Those weights took off that on his planet hung,
Will gloriously the new-laid works succeed.

He has elsewhere shown his attention to the planetary powers, and
in the preface to his *Fables* has endeavoured obliquely to justify his
superstition by attributing the same to some of the ancients. The
letter added to this narrative leaves no doubt of his notions or practice.

So slight and so scanty is the knowledge which I have been able to
collect concerning the private life and domestic manners of a man
whom every English generation must mention with reverence as a
critic and a poet.

Dryden may be properly considered as the father of English
criticism, as the writer who first taught us to determine upon principles the merit of composition. Of our former poets, the greatest
dramatist wrote without rules, conducted through life and nature by
a genius that rarely misled and rarely deserted him. Of the rest, those
who knew the laws of propriety had neglected to teach them.

Two Arts of English Poetry were written in the days of Elizabeth
by Webbe and Puttenham, from which something might be learned,
and a few hints had been given by Jonson and Cowley; but Dryden's
Essay on Dramatic Poetry was the first regular and valuable treatise
on the art of writing.

He who, having formed his opinions in the present age of English
literature, turns back to peruse this dialogue, will not perhaps find
much increase of knowledge or much novelty of instruction; but he
is to remember that critical principles were then in the hands of a
few, who had gathered them partly from the ancients, and partly
from the Italians and French. The structure of dramatic poems was
not then generally understood. Audiences applauded by instinct,
and poets perhaps often pleased by chance.

A writer who obtains his full purpose loses himself in his own
lustre. Of an opinion which is no longer doubted the evidence ceases
to be examined. Of an art universally practised the first teacher is
forgotten. Learning once made popular is no longer learning: it has
the appearance of something which we have bestowed upon ourselves, as the dew appears to rise from the field which it refreshes.

in the preface: Dryden: *Essays*, ii. 277.

Webbe: William Webbe (*fl.* 1586–91), author of *A Discourse of English Poetry*
(1586).

Puttenham: Richard Puttenham (1520?–1601?), reputed author of *The Art of
English Poesy* (1589), which has, however, been ascribed to his brother George
(d. 1590).

To judge rightly of an author we must transport ourselves to his time and examine what were the wants of his contemporaries, and what were his means of supplying them. That which is easy at one time was difficult at another. Dryden at least imported his science, and gave his country what it wanted before, or rather, he imported only the materials, and manufactured them by his own skill.

The dialogue on the drama was one of his first essays of criticism, written when he was yet a timorous candidate for reputation, and therefore laboured with that diligence which he might allow himself somewhat to remit when his name gave sanction to his positions, and his awe of the public was abated partly by custom, and partly by success. It will not be easy to find, in all the opulence of our language, a treatise so artfully variegated with successive representations of opposite probabilities, so enlivened with imagery, so brightened with illustrations. His portraits of the English dramatists are wrought with great spirit and diligence. The account of Shakespeare may stand as a perpetual model of encomiastic criticism, exact without minuteness, and lofty without exaggeration. The praise lavished by Longinus on the attestation of the heroes of Marathon by Demosthenes, fades away before it. In a few lines is exhibited a character so extensive in its comprehension, and so curious in its limitations, that nothing can be added, diminished or reformed; nor can the editors and admirers of Shakespeare, in all their emulation of reverence, boast of much more than of having diffused and paraphrased this epitome of excellence, of having changed Dryden's gold for baser metal, of lower value though of greater bulk.

In this, and in all his other essays on the same subject, the criticism of Dryden is the criticism of a poet—not a dull collection of theorems nor a rude detection of faults, which perhaps the censor was not able to have committed, but a gay and vigorous dissertation where delight is mingled with instruction, and where the author proves his right of judgement by his power of performance.

The different manner and effect with which critical knowledge may be conveyed was perhaps never more clearly exemplified than in the performances of Rymer and Dryden. It was said of a dispute between

The account of Shakespeare: *Dryden: Essays*, i. 67, quoted by Johnson in his own *Preface* (*YJ*, vii. 112).

Longinus: (3rd cent. A.D.), Greek rhetorician, wrongly supposed to be the author of *On the Sublime*; q.v. xvi.

Demosthenes: (384–22 B.C.), statesman, the greatest of Greek orators; see *De Corona*, 208.

censor: a critic able to or even prone to find faults.

committed: put down in writing.

two mathematicians, 'malim cum Scaligero errare, quam cum Clavio recte sapere', that 'it was more eligible to go wrong with one than right with the other'. A tendency of the same kind every mind must feel at the perusal of Dryden's prefaces and Rymer's discourses. With Dryden we are wandering in quest of Truth, whom we find, if we find her at all, dressed in the graces of elegance, and if we miss her, the labour of the pursuit rewards itself: we are led only through fragrance and flowers; Rymer, without taking a nearer, takes a rougher way: every step is to be made through thorns and brambles, and Truth, if we meet her, appears repulsive by her mien and ungraceful by her habit. Dryden's criticism has the majesty of a queen, Rymer's has the ferocity of a tyrant.

As he had studied with great diligence the art of poetry, and enlarged or rectified his notions by experience perpetually increasing, he had his mind stored with principles and observations; he poured out his knowledge with little labour, for of labour, notwithstanding the multiplicity of his productions, there is sufficient reason to suspect that he was not a lover. To write *con amore*, with fondness for the employment, with perpetual touches and retouches, with unwillingness to take leave of his own idea, and an unwearied pursuit of unattainable perfection, was, I think, no part of his character.

His criticism may be considered as general or occasional. In his general precepts, which depend upon the nature of things and the structure of the human mind, he may doubtless be safely recommended to the confidence of the reader; but his occasional and particular positions were sometimes interested, sometimes negligent, and sometimes capricious. It is not without reason that Trapp, speaking of the praises which he bestows on *Palamon and Arcite*, says, 'Novimus judicium Drydeni de poemate quodam Chauceri, pulchro sane illo, et admodum laudando, nimirum quod non modo vere epicum sit, sed *Iliada* etiam atque *Aeneida* aequet, imo superet. Sed novimus eodem tempore viri illius maximi non semper accuratissimas esse censuras, nec ad severissimam critices normam exactas: illo judice id plerumque optimum est, quod nunc prae manibus habet, et in quo nunc occupatur.'[n]

He is therefore by no means constant to himself. His defence and

malim: cf. *Life*, ii. 444; Cicero, *Tusculanae Disputationes*, I. xvii. 39.

Scaligero: Joseph Justus Scaliger (1540–1609), the greatest classical scholar of his day, disputed the variations in the Gregorian Calendar.

Clavio: Christopher Clavius (1537?–1612), Jesuit mathematician and astronomer, one of the principal collaborators in devising the Gregorian Calendar.

his occasional: cf. *Rambler* 93.

His defence and desertion: cf. Dryden: *Essays*, i. 156–7, 231.

desertion of dramatic rhyme is generally known. Spence, in his remarks on Pope's *Odyssey*, produces what he thinks an unconquerable quotation from Dryden's preface to the *Aeneid* in favour of translating an epic poem into blank verse; but he forgets that when his author attempted the *Iliad* some years afterwards, he departed from his own decision and again translated into rhyme.

When he has any objection to obviate, or any licence to defend, he is not very scrupulous about what he asserts, nor very cautious, if the present purpose be served, not to entangle himself in his own sophistries. But when all arts are exhausted, like other hunted animals he sometimes stands at bay; when he cannot disown the grossness of one of his plays, he declares that he knows not any law that prescribes morality to a comic poet.

His remarks on ancient or modern writers are not always to be trusted. His parallel of the versification of Ovid with that of Claudian has been very justly censured by Sewell. His comparison of the first line of Virgil with the first of Statius is not happier. Virgil, he says, is soft and gentle, and would have thought Statius mad if he had heard him thundering out

> Quae superimposito moles geminata colosso.

Statius perhaps heats himself, as he proceeds, to exaggerations somewhat hyperbolical, but undoubtedly Virgil would have been too hasty if he had condemned him to straw for one sounding line. Dryden wanted an instance, and the first that occurred was impressed into the service.

What he wishes to say he says at hazard; he cited *Gorbuduc*, which he had never seen, gives a false account of Chapman's versification, and discovers in the preface to his *Fables* that he translated the first book of the *Iliad* without knowing what was in the second.

Spence: Joseph Spence (1699–1768), anecdotist; see his *Essay on Pope's Odyssey* (1726–7), pt. I, pp. 121–2. Cf. *Dryden: Essays*, ii. 240.

he declares: *Dryden: Essays*, i. 150.   *His parallel*: ibid. ii. 21–2.

Claudian: (c. 370–404), the last major classical poet of Rome.

Sewell: George Sewell (d. 1726), controversialist and hack writer, author of the dedication in *Ovid's Metamorphoses, a New Translation by Several Hands* (1717), i. *viii–ix*.

His comparison: *Dryden: Essays*, i. 277, ii. 204–5; cf. also ii. 274.

Quae superimposito: *Sylvae*, I. i. 1 ('What a mighty mass redoubled by the huge form surmounting it').

he cited: *Dryden: Essays*, i. 5–6.

Chapman: George Chapman (1559?–1634), poet and playwright. Cf. ibid. i. 96.

and discovers: cf. ibid. ii. 270, 274–7; though Johnson's inference seems unjustified.

It will be difficult to prove that Dryden ever made any great advances in literature. As having distinguished himself at Westminster under the tuition of Busby, who advanced his scholars to a height of knowledge very rarely attained in grammar schools, he resided afterwards at Cambridge, it is not to be supposed that his skill in the ancient languages was deficient compared with that of common students; but his scholastic acquisitions seem not proportionate to his opportunities and abilities. He could not, like Milton or Cowley, have made his name illustrious merely by his learning. He mentions but few books, and those such as lie in the beaten track of regular study, from which if ever he departs he is in danger of losing himself in unknown regions.

In his dialogue on the drama, he pronounces with great confidence that the Latin tragedy of *Medea* is not Ovid's because it is not sufficiently interesting and pathetic. He might have determined the question upon surer evidence, for it is quoted by Quintilian as the work of Seneca, and the only line which remains of Ovid's play, for one line is left us, is not there to be found. There was therefore no need of the gravity of conjecture, or the discussion of plot or sentiment, to find what was already known upon higher authority than such discussions can ever reach.

His literature, though not always free from ostentation, will be commonly found either obvious, and made his own by the art of dressing it, or superficial, which by what he gives shows what he wanted, or erroneous, hastily collected, and negligently scattered.

Yet it cannot be said that his genius is ever unprovided of matter, or that his fancy languishes in penury of ideas. His works abound with knowledge, and sparkle with illustrations. There is scarcely any science or faculty that does not supply him with occasional images and lucky similitudes: every page discovers a mind very widely acquainted both with art and nature, and in full possession of great stores of intellectual wealth. Of him that knows much it is natural to suppose that he has read with diligence; yet I rather believe that the knowledge of Dryden was gleaned from accidental intelligence and various conversation by a quick apprehension, a judicious selection, and a happy memory, a keen appetite of knowledge and a powerful digestion, by vigilance that permitted nothing to pass without notice, and a habit of reflection that suffered nothing useful to be lost. A mind like Dryden's, always curious, always active, to which every understanding was proud to be associated, and of which

he pronounces: Dryden: *Essays*, i. 41.
quoted by Quintilian: *Institutio Oratoria*, IX. ii. 9.

everyone solicited the regard by an ambitious display of himself, had a more pleasant, perhaps a nearer, way to knowledge than by the silent progress of solitary reading. I do not suppose that he despised books or intentionally neglected them, but that he was carried out, by the impetuosity of his genius, to more vivid and speedy instructors, and that his studies were rather desultory and fortuitous than constant and systematical.

It must be confessed that he scarcely ever appears to want book-learning but when he mentions books, and to him may be transferred the praise which he gives his master Charles:

> His conversation, wit, and parts,
> His knowledge in the noblest useful arts,
> Were such, dead authors could not give,
> But habitudes of those that live;
> Who, lighting him, did greater lights receive.
> He drained from all, and all they knew,
> His apprehension quick, his judgement true:
> That the most learned with shame confess
> His knowledge more, his reading only less.

Of all this, however, if the proof be demanded, I will not undertake to give it; the atoms of probability, of which my opinion has been formed, lie scattered over all his works, and by him who thinks the question worth his notice, his works must be perused with very close attention.

Criticism either didactic or defensive occupies almost all his prose, except those pages which he has devoted to his patrons; but none of his prefaces were ever thought tedious. They have not the formality of a settled style, in which the first half of the sentence betrays the other. The clauses are never balanced nor the periods modelled; every word seems to drop by chance, though it falls into its proper place. Nothing is cold or languid: the whole is airy, animated and vigorous; what is little is gay; what is great is splendid. He may be thought to mention himself too frequently, but while he forces himself upon our esteem, we cannot refuse him to stand high in his own. Everything is excused by the play of images and the sprightliness of expression. Though all is easy nothing is feeble; though all seems careless there is nothing harsh; and though, since his earlier works, more than a century has passed, they have nothing yet uncouth or obsolete.

He who writes much will not easily escape a manner—such a recurrence of particular modes as may be easily noted. Dryden is

His conversation: *Threnodia Augustalis*, ll. 337–45.

always 'another and the same': he does not exhibit a second time the same elegances in the same form, nor appears to have any art other than that of expressing with clearness what he thinks with vigour. His style could not easily be imitated, either seriously or ludicrously, for being always equable and always varied it has no prominent or discriminative characters. The beauty who is totally free from disproportion of parts and features cannot be ridiculed by an overcharged resemblance.

From his prose, however, Dryden derives only his accidental and secondary praise: the veneration with which his name is pronounced by every cultivator of English literature is paid to him as he refined the language, improved the sentiments, and tuned the numbers of English poetry.

After about half a century of forced thoughts and rugged metre, some advances towards nature and harmony had been already made by Waller and Denham; they had shown that long discourses in rhyme grew more pleasing when they were broken into couplets, and that verse consisted not only in the number but the arrangement of syllables.

But though they did much, who can deny that they left much to do? Their works were not many, nor were their minds of very ample comprehension. More examples of more modes of composition were necessary for the establishment of regularity, and the introduction of propriety in word and thought.

Every language of a learned nation necessarily divides itself into diction scholastic and popular, grave and familiar, elegant and gross, and from a nice distinction of these different parts arises a great part of the beauty of style. But if we except a few minds, the favourites of nature, to whom their own original rectitude was in the place of rules, this delicacy of selection was little known to our authors; our speech lay before them in a heap of confusion, and every man took for every purpose what chance might offer him.

There was therefore before the time of Dryden no poetical diction, no system of words at once refined from the grossness of domestic use and free from the harshness of terms appropriated to particular arts. Words too familiar or too remote defeat the purpose of a poet. From those sounds which we hear on small or on coarse occasions, we do not easily receive strong impressions or delightful images; and words to which we are nearly strangers, whenever they occur, draw that attention on themselves which they should transmit to things.

Those happy combinations of words which distinguish poetry

'*another*': Pope, *Dunciad*, iii. 40.   *From those sounds*: cf. *Rambler* 168.

from prose had been rarely attempted; we had few elegances or flowers of speech: the roses had not yet been plucked from the bramble, or different colours had not been joined to enliven one another.

It may be doubted whether Waller and Denham could have overborne the prejudices which had long prevailed, and which even then were sheltered by the protection of Cowley. The new versification, as it was called, may be considered as owing its establishment to Dryden, from whose time it is apparent that English poetry has had no tendency to relapse to its former savageness.

The affluence and comprehension of our language is very illustriously displayed in our poetical translations of ancient writers—a work which the French seem to relinquish in despair, and which we were long unable to perform with dexterity. Ben Jonson thought it necessary to copy Horace almost word by word; Felltham, his contemporary and adversary, considers it as indispensably requisite in a translation to give line for line. It is said that Sandys, whom Dryden calls the best versifier of the last age, has struggled hard to comprise every book of his English *Metamorphoses* in the same number of verses with the original. Holyday had nothing in view but to show that he understood his author—with so little regard to the grandeur of his diction or the volubility of his numbers that his metres can hardly be called verses; they cannot be read without reluctance, nor will the labour always be rewarded by understanding them. Cowley saw that such 'copiers' were a 'servile race'; he asserted his liberty and spread his wings so boldly that he left his authors. It was reserved for Dryden to fix the limits of poetical liberty, and give us just rules and examples of translation.

When languages are formed upon different principles, it is impossible that the same modes of expression should always be elegant in both. While they run on together, the closest translation may be considered as the best; but when they divaricate, each must take its natural course. Where correspondence cannot be obtained, it is necessary to be content with something equivalent. 'Translation therefore', says Dryden, 'is not so loose as paraphrase, nor so close as metaphrase.'

All polished languages have different styles: the concise, the

---

Felltham: Owen Felltham (or Feltham) (1602?–68); see his *Lusoria, or Occasional Pieces, with a Taste of Some Letters* (1661), pp. 17–18 ('An Answer to the Ode of "Come leave the loathed stage"').

whom Dryden calls: *Dryden: Essays*, ii. 270; cf. ibid. ii. 164.

Cowley saw: *Cowley: Poems*, pp. 155–6.

'*Translation therefore*': *Dryden: Essays*, ii. 246.

diffuse, the lofty, and the humble. In the proper choice of style consists the resemblance which Dryden principally exacts from the translator. He is to exhibit his author's thoughts in such a dress of diction as the author would have given them had his language been English: rugged magnificence is not to be softened, hyperbolical ostentation is not to be repressed, nor sententious affectation to have its points blunted. A translator is to be like his author; it is not his business to excel him.

The reasonableness of these rules seems sufficient for their vindication, and the effects produced by observing them were so happy that I know not whether they were ever opposed but by Sir Edward Sherburne, a man whose learning was greater than his powers of poetry, and who, being better qualified to give the meaning than the spirit of Seneca, has introduced his version of three tragedies by a defence of close translation. The authority of Horace, which the new translators cited in defence of their practice, he has by a judicious explanation taken fairly from them; but reason wants not Horace to support it.

It seldom happens that all the necessary causes concur to any great effect; will is wanting to power, or power to will, or both are impeded by external obstructions. The exigencies in which Dryden was condemned to pass his life are reasonably supposed to have blasted his genius, to have driven out his works in a state of immaturity, and to have intercepted the full-blown elegance which longer growth would have supplied.

Poverty, like other rigid powers, is sometimes too hastily accused. If the excellence of Dryden's works was lessened by his indigence, their number was increased; and I know not how it will be proved that if he had written less he would have written better, or that indeed he would have undergone the toil of an author if he had not been solicited by something more pressing than the love of praise.

But as is said by his Sebastian,

> What had been, is unknown; what is, appears.

We know that Dryden's several productions were so many successive expedients for his support; his plays were therefore often borrowed, and his poems were almost all occasional.

In an occasional performance no height of excellence can be expected from any mind, however fertile in itself, and however

Sir Edward Sherburne: (1618–1702), Clerk of the Ordnance and translator; see
    The Tragedies of Seneca, translated in English Verse (1701), pp. *xxxvi–xxxix*.
are reasonbly supposed: cf. *Pope: Poems*, vii. 88.
What had been: Dryden: *DW*, vi. 111.

stored with acquisitions. He whose work is general and arbitrary has the choice of his matter, and takes that which his inclination and his studies have best qualified him to display and decorate. He is at liberty to delay his publication till he has satisfied his friends and himself, till he has reformed his first thoughts by subsequent examination, and polished away those faults which the precipitance of ardent composition is likely to leave behind it. Virgil is related to have poured out a great number of lines in the morning, and to have passed the day in reducing them to fewer.

The occasional poet is circumscribed by the narrowness of his subject. Whatever can happen to man has happened so often that little remains for fancy or invention. We have been all born, we have most of us been married, and so many have died before us that our deaths can supply but few materials for a poet. In the fate of princes the public has an interest, and what happens to them of good or evil the poets have always considered as business for the Muse. But after so many inauguratory gratulations, nuptial hymns, and funeral dirges, he must be highly favoured by nature or by fortune who says anything not said before. Even war and conquest, however splendid, suggest no new images: the triumphal chariot of a victorious monarch can be decked only with those ornaments that have graced his predecessors.

Not only matter but time is wanting. The poem must not be delayed till the occasion is forgotten. The lucky moments of animated imagination cannot be attended: elegances and illustrations cannot be multiplied by gradual accumulation; the composition must be dispatched while conversation is yet busy and admiration fresh, and haste is to be made lest some other event should lay hold upon mankind.

Occasional compositions may however secure to a writer the praise both of learning and facility, for they cannot be the effect of long study, and must be furnished immediately from the treasures of the mind.

The death of Cromwell was the first public event which called forth Dryden's poetical powers. His 'Heroic Stanzas' have beauties and defects: the thoughts are vigorous, and though not always proper, show a mind replete with ideas; the numbers are smooth; and the diction, if not altogether correct, is elegant and easy.

Davenant was perhaps at this time his favourite author, though *Gondibert* never appears to have been popular, and from Davenant he learned to please his ear with the stanza of four lines alternately rhymed.

Dryden very early formed his versification: there are in this early production no traces of Donne's or Jonson's ruggedness; but he did not so soon free his mind from the ambition of forced conceits. In his verses on the Restoration, he says of the King's exile:

> He, tossed by Fate—
> Could taste no sweets of youth's desired age,
> But found his life too true a pilgrimage.

And afterwards, to show how virtue and wisdom are increased by adversity, he makes this remark:

> Well might the ancient poets then confer
> On Night the honoured name of *counsellor*,
> Since, struck with rays of prosperous fortune blind,
> We light alone in dark afflictions find.

His praise of Monk's dexterity comprises such a cluster of thoughts unallied to one another as will not elsewhere be easily found:

> 'Twas Monk, whom Providence designed to loose
> Those real bonds false freedom did impose.
> The blessed saints that watched this turning scene,
> Did from their stars with joyful wonder lean,
> To see small clews draw vastest weights along,
> Not in their bulk, but in their order strong.
> Thus pencils can by one slight touch restore
> Smiles to that changed face that wept before.
> With ease such fond chimeras we pursue,
> As fancy frames for fancy to subdue;
> But when ourselves to action we betake,
> It shuns the mint like gold that chemists make;
> How hard was then his task, at once to be
> What in the body natural we see!
> Man's Architect distinctly did ordain
> The charge of muscles, nerves, and of the brain,
> Through viewless conduits spirits to dispense
> The springs of motion from the seat of sense.
> 'Twas not the hasty product of a day,
> But the well-ripened fruit of wise delay.
> He, like a patient angler, ere he strook,
> Would let them play awhile upon the hook.
> Our healthful food the stomach labours thus,
> At first embracing what it straight doth crush.
> Wise leeches will not vain receipts obtrude,
> While growing pains pronounce the humours crude;
> Deaf to complaints, they wait upon the ill,
> Till some safe crisis authorize their skill.

He, tossed by Fate: Astraea Redux, ll. 51, 53–4.
Well might: ll. 93–6.   *'Twas Monk*: ll. 151–78.

He had not yet learned, indeed he never learned well, to forbear the improper use of mythology. After having rewarded the heathen deities for their care,

> With alga who the sacred altar strows?
> To all the sea-gods Charles an offering owes;
> A bull to thee, Portunus, shall be slain;
> A ram to you, ye Tempests of the Main,

he tells us, in the language of religion,

> Prayer stormed the skies, and ravished Charles from thence,
> As heaven itself is took by violence.

And afterwards mentions one of the most awful passages of Sacred History.

Other conceits there are too curious to be quite omitted, as,

> For by example most we sinned before,
> And, glass-like, clearness mixed with frailty bore.

How far he was yet from thinking it necessary to found his sentiments on nature appears from the extravagance of his fictions and hyperboles:

> The winds, that never moderation knew,
> Afraid to blow too much, too faintly blew;
> Or, out of breath with joy, could not enlarge
> Their straitened lungs.—
> It is no longer motion cheats your view;
> As you meet it, the land approacheth you;
> The land returns, and in the white it wears
> The marks of penitence and sorrow bears.

I know not whether this fancy, however little be its value, was not borrowed. A French poet read to Malherbe some verses in which he represents France as moving out of its place to receive the king. 'Though this', said Malherbe, 'was in my time, I do not remember it.'

His poem on the Coronation has a more even tenor of thought. Some lines deserve to be quoted:

> You have already quenched sedition's brand,
> And zeal, that burnt it, only warms the land;
> The jealous sects that durst not trust their cause

With alga: ll. 119–22.   *Prayer stormed*: ll. 143–4.
afterwards mentions: ll. 262–5. Cf. Exodus 33: 18–23, 34: 1–6.
For by example: ll. 207–8.   *The winds*: ll. 242–5, 252–5.
Malherbe: François de Malherbe (1555–1628), French poet and critic. Cf. A. H.
   de Sallengre, *Mémoires de littérateur* (The Hague, 1715–17), ii. 72–3.
His poem: *To His Sacred Majesty, A Panegyric on his Coronation.*
You have: ll. 79–84.

> So far from their own will as to the laws,
> Him for their umpire and their synod take,
> And their appeal alone to Caesar make.

Here may be found one particle of that old versification of which,
I believe, in all his works there is not another:

> Nor is it duty, or our hope alone,
> Creates that joy, but full *fruition*.

In the verses to the Lord Chancellor Clarendon, two years afterwards, is a conceit so hopeless at the first view that few would have
attempted it, and so successfully laboured that though at last it gives
the reader more perplexity than pleasure, and seems hardly worth
the study that it costs, yet it must be valued as a proof of a mind at
once subtle and comprehensive:

> In open prospect nothing bounds our eye,
> Until the earth seems joined unto the sky:
> So in this hemisphere our outmost view
> Is only bounded by our king and you:
> Our sight is limited where you are joined,
> And beyond that no farther heaven can find.
> So well your virtues do with his agree,
> That, though your orbs of different greatness be,
> Yet both are for each other's use disposed,
> His to enclose, and yours to be enclosed.
> Nor could another in your room have been,
> Except an emptiness had come between.

The comparison of the Chancellor to the Indies leaves all resemblance too far behind it:

> And as the Indies were not found before
> Those rich perfumes which from the happy shore
> The winds upon their balmy wings conveyed,
> Whose guilty sweetness first their world betrayed;
> So by your counsels we are brought to view
> A new and undiscovered world in you.

There is another comparison, for there is little else in the poem, of
which, though perhaps it cannot be explained into plain prosaic
meaning, the mind perceives enough to be delighted, and readily
forgives its obscurity for its magnificence:

> How strangely active are the arts of peace,
> Whose restless motions less than wars do cease!
> Peace is not freed from labour, but from noise;

Nor is it duty: ll. 69–70. *In open prospect*: *To my Lord Chancellor*, ll. 31–42.
And as the Indies: ll. 73–8. *How strangely*: ll. 105–18.

> And war more force, but not more pains employs.
> Such is the mighty swiftness of your mind,
> That, like the earth's, it leaves our sense behind,
> While you so smoothly turn and roll our sphere,
> That rapid motion does but rest appear.
> For as in nature's swiftness, with the throng
> Of flying orbs while ours is borne along,
> All seems at rest to the deluded eye,
> Moved by the soul of the same harmony;
> So carried on by your unwearied care,
> We rest in peace, and yet in motion share.

To this succeed four lines which perhaps afford Dryden's first attempt at those penetrating remarks on human nature for which he seems to have been peculiarly formed:

> Let envy then those crimes within you see,
> From which the happy never must be free;
> Envy that does with misery reside,
> The joy and the revenge of ruined pride.

Into this poem he seems to have collected all his powers, and after this he did not often bring upon his anvil such stubborn and unmalleable thoughts; but as a specimen of his abilities to unite the most unsociable matter, he has concluded with lines of which I think not myself obliged to tell the meaning:

> Yet unimpaired with labours, or with time,
> Your age but seems to a new youth to climb.
> Thus heavenly bodies do our time beget,
> And measure change, but share no part of it:
> And still it shall without a weight increase,
> Like this new year, whose motions never cease.
> For since the glorious course you have begun
> Is led by Charles, as that is by the sun,
> It must both weightless and immortal prove,
> Because the centre of it is above.

In the *Annus Mirabilis* he returned to the quatrain, which from that time he totally quitted, perhaps from this experience of its inconvenience, for he complains of its difficulty. This is one of his greatest attempts. He had subjects equal to his abilities, a great naval war, and the Fire of London. Battles have always been described in heroic poetry, but a sea-fight and artillery had yet something of novelty. New arts are long in the world before poets describe them, for they borrow everything from their predecessors, and commonly derive very little from nature or from life. Boileau was the

---

Let envy: ll. 119–22.   *Yet unimpaired*: ll. 147–56.
Boileau: *Epître* IV (composed 1672), *Oeuvres*, i. 305–19; cf. ibid. v. 52–3.

first French writer that had ever hazarded in verse the mention of modern war or the effects of gunpowder. We, who are less afraid of novelty, had already possession of those dreadful images: Waller had described a sea-fight. Milton had not yet transferred the invention of firearms to the rebellious angels.

This poem is written with great diligence, yet does not fully answer the expectation raised by such subjects and such a writer. With the stanza of Davenant he has sometimes his vein of parenthesis and incidental disquisition, and stops his narrative for a wise remark.

The general fault is that he affords more sentiment than description, and does not so much impress scenes upon the fancy as deduce consequences and make comparisons.

The initial stanzas have rather too much resemblance to the first lines of Waller's poem on the war with Spain; perhaps such a beginning is natural, and could not be avoided without affectation. Both Waller and Dryden might take their hint from the poem on the civil war of Rome, *Orbem jam totum*, etc.

Of the King collecting his navy, he says,

> It seems as every ship their sovereign knows,
> His awful summons they so soon obey;
> So hear the scaly herds when Proteus blows,
> And so to pasture follow through the sea.

It would not be hard to believe that Dryden had written the two first lines seriously, and that some wag had added the two latter in burlesque. Who would expect the lines that immediately follow, which are indeed perhaps indecently hyperbolical, but certainly in a mode totally different?

> To see this fleet upon the ocean move,
> Angels drew wide the curtains of the skies;
> And heaven, as if there wanted lights above,
> For tapers made two glaring comets rise.

The description of the attempt at Bergen[n] will afford a very complete specimen of the descriptions in this poem:

> And now approached their fleet from India, fraught
> With all the riches of the rising sun;
> And precious sand from southern climates brought,
> The fatal regions where the war begun.

Waller: 'Of a War with Spain, and a Fight at Sea' (published 1658 or 1659).
Orbem: Petronius, *Satyricon*, 119, l. 1.   *It seems*: st. 15.
Proteus: an 'ancient one of sea', herded the seals, etc. (*Odyssey*, iv. 351 ff.).
And now approached: sts. 24–30.

> Like hunted castors, conscious of their store,
>   Their waylaid wealth to Norway's coast they bring:
> Then first the North's cold bosom spices bore,
>   And winter brooded on the eastern spring.
>
> By the rich scent we found our perfumed prey,
>   Which, flanked with rocks, did close in covert lie:
> And round about their murdering canon lay,
>   At once to threaten and invite the eye.
>
> Fiercer than canon, and than rocks more hard,
>   The English undertake th' unequal war:
> Seven ships alone, by which the port is barred,
>   Besiege the Indies, and all Denmark dare.
>
> These fight like husbands, but like lovers those:
>   These fain would keep, and those more fain enjoy;
> And to such height their frantic passion grows,
>   That what both love, both hazard to destroy.
>
> Amidst whole heaps of spices lights a ball,
>   And now their odours armed against them fly:
> Some preciously by shattered porcelain fall,
>   And some by aromatic splinters die.
>
> And though by tempests of the prize bereft,
>   In heaven's inclemency some ease we find:
> Our foes we vanquished by our valour left,
>   And only yielded to the seas and wind.

In this manner is the sublime too often mingled with the ridiculous. The Dutch seek a shelter for a wealthy fleet; this surely needed no illustration; yet they must fly, not like all the rest of mankind on the same occasion, but 'like hunted castors'; and they might with strict propriety be hunted, for we winded them by our noses—their 'perfumes' betrayed them. The 'husband' and the 'lover', though of more dignity than the 'castor', are images too domestic to mingle properly with the horrors of war. The two quatrains that follow are worthy of the author.

The account of the different sensations with which the two fleets retired when the night parted them, is one of the fairest flowers of English poetry.

> The night comes on, we eager to pursue
>   The combat still, and they ashamed to leave;
> Till the last streaks of dying day withdrew,
>   And doubtful moonlight did our rage deceive.
>
> In th' English fleet each ship resounds with joy,
>   And loud applause of their great leader's fame;
> In fiery dreams the Dutch they still destroy,
>   And, slumbering, smile at the imagined flame.

castors: beavers.   *The night*: sts. 68–71.

> Not so the Holland fleet, who, tired and done,
>   Stretched on their decks like weary oxen lie;
> Faint sweats all down their mighty members run,
>   (Vast bulks, which little souls but ill supply).
>
> In dreams they fearful precipices tread,
>   Or, shipwrecked, labour to some distant shore,
> Or, in dark churches, walk among the dead;
>   They wake with horror, and dare sleep no more.

It is a general rule in poetry that all appropriated terms of art should be sunk in general expressions, because poetry is to speak an universal language. This rule is still stronger with regard to arts not liberal, or confined to few, and therefore far removed from common knowledge; and of this kind, certainly, is technical navigation. Yet Dryden was of opinion that a sea-fight ought to be described in the nautical language, 'and certainly', says he, 'as those who in a logical disputation keep to general terms would hide a fallacy, so those who do it in any poetical description would veil their ignorance'.

Let us then appeal to experience, for by experience at last we learn as well what will please as what will profit. In the battle his terms seem to have been blown away, but he deals them liberally in the dock:

> So here some pick out bullets from the side,
>   Some drive old *oakum* through each *seam* and rift:
> Their left hand does the *caulking-iron* guide
>   The rattling *mallet* with the right they lift.
>
> With boiling pitch another near at hand
>   (From friendly Sweden brought) the *seams instops*:
> Which, well laid o'er, the salt-sea waves withstand,
>   And shake them from the rising beak in drops.
>
> Some the *galled* ropes with dauby *marline* bind,
>   Or cerecloth masts with strong *tarpaulin* coats;
> To try new *shrouds* one mounts into the wind,
>   And one below, their ease or stiffness notes.

I suppose here is not one term which every reader does not wish away.

His digression to the original and progress of navigation, with his prospect of the advancement which it shall receive from the Royal Society, then newly instituted, may be considered as an example seldom equalled of seasonable excursion and artful return.

'*and certainly*': Dryden: *Essays*, i. 96.   *So here*: sts. 146–8.
caulking-iron: 'an instrument resembling a chisel used for driving the oakum into the seams of ships' (*OED*).   *instops*: stops or closes up.
cerecloth: 'apply a "cerecloth" or cerate to' (*OED*).
His digression: sts. 155–66.

One line, however, leaves me discontented; he says that by the help of the philosophers

> Instructed ships shall sail to quick commerce,
> By which remotest regions are allied.—

Which he is constrained to explain in a note, 'By a more exact measure of longitude'. It had better become Dryden's learning and genius to have laboured science into poetry, and have shown, by explaining longitude, that verse did not refuse the ideas of philosophy.

His description of the Fire is painted by resolute meditation, out of a mind better formed to reason than to feel. The conflagration of a city, with all its tumults of concomitant distress, is one of the most dreadful spectacles which this world can offer to human eyes; yet it seems to raise little emotion in the breast of the poet: he watches the flame coolly from street to street, with now a reflection, and now a simile, till at last he meets the King, for whom he makes a speech rather tedious in a time so busy, and then follows again the progress of the fire.

There are, however, in this part some passages that deserve attention, as in the beginning:

> The diligence of trades and noiseful gain
> And luxury more late asleep were laid;
> All was the night's, and in her silent reign
> No sound the rest of Nature did invade.
>
> In this deep quiet—.

The expression 'All was the night's' is taken from Seneca, who remarks on Virgil's line,

> Omnia noctis erant placida composta quiete,[n]

that he might have concluded better,

> Omnia noctis erant.

The following quatrain is vigorous and animated:

> The ghosts of traitors from the bridge descend
> With bold fanatic spectres to rejoice;
> About the fire into a dance they bend,
> And sing their sabbath notes with feeble voice.

His prediction of the improvements which shall be made in the new city is elegant and poetical, and, with an event which poets

---

Instructed ships: st. 163.   *a speech*: 262–70.
The diligence: sts. 216–17.
Seneca: the elder (55 B.C.–A.D. 40?), Roman rhetorician. Cf. *Controversiae*, ed.
    H. J. Müller (Hildesheim, 1963 repr.), VII. i. 27.   *The ghosts*: st. 223.
His prediction: sts. 293–8.

cannot always boast, has been happily verified. The poem concludes with a simile that might have better been omitted.

Dryden, when he wrote this poem, seems not yet fully to have formed his versification, or settled his system of propriety.

From this time he addicted himself almost wholly to the stage, 'to which', says he, 'my genius never much inclined me', merely as the most profitable market for poetry. By writing tragedies in rhyme he continued to improve his diction and his numbers. According to the opinion of Harte, who had studied his works with great attention, he settled his principles of versification in 1676 when he produced the play of *Aureng-Zebe*; and according to his own account of the short time in which he wrote *Tyrannic Love* and *The State of Innocence*, he soon obtained the full effect of diligence, and added facility to exactness.

Rhyme has been so long banished from the theatre that we know not its effect upon the passions of an audience; but it has this convenience, that sentences stand more independent on each other, and striking passages are therefore easily selected and retained. Thus the description of Night in *The Indian Emperor*, and the rise and fall of empire in *The Conquest of Granada*, are more frequently repeated than any lines in *All for Love* or *Don Sebastian*.

To search his plays for vigorous sallies and sententious elegances, or to fix the dates of any little pieces which he wrote by chance or by solicitation, were labour too tedious and minute.

His dramatic labours did not so wholly absorb his thoughts but that he promulgated the laws of translation in a preface to the English *Epistles* of Ovid, one of which he translated himself, and another in conjunction with the Earl of Mulgrave.

Absalom and Achitophel is a work so well known that particular criticism is superfluous. If it be considered as a poem political and controversial, it will be found to comprise all the excellences of which the subject is susceptible: acrimony of censure, elegance of praise, artful delineation of characters, variety and vigour of sentiment, happy turns of language, and pleasing harmony of numbers—and all these raised to such a height as can scarcely be found in any other English composition.

It is not, however, without faults: some lines are inelegant or

'*to which*': *Dryden: Essays*, ii. 91.
Harte: Walter Harte (1709–74), miscellaneous writer known to Johnson.
the rise and fall of empire: *Dryden: DW*, iii. 93 (*2 Conquest of Granada*, I. i).
he promulgated: *Dryden: Essays*, i. 268–73.
one of which: see above, p. 139 and n.

improper, and too many are irreligiously licentious. The original structure of the poem was defective: allegories drawn to great length will always break; Charles could not run continually parallel with David.

The subject had likewise another inconvenience: it admitted little imagery or description, and a long poem of mere sentiments easily becomes tedious; though all the parts are forcible and every line kindles new rapture, the reader, if not relieved by the interposition of something that soothes the fancy, grows weary of admiration and defers the rest.

As an approach to historical truth was necessary, the action and catastrophe were not in the poet's power; there is therefore an unpleasing disproportion between the beginning and the end. We are alarmed by a faction formed out of many sects various in their principles but agreeing in their purpose of mischief, formidable for their numbers and strong by their supports, while the King's friends are few and weak. The chiefs on either part are set forth to view; but when expectation is at the height, the King makes a speech, and

> Henceforth a series of new times began.

Who can forbear to think of an enchanted castle, with a wide moat and lofty battlements, walls of marble and gates of brass, which vanishes at once into air when the destined knight blows his horn before it?[n]

In the second part, written by Tate, there is a long insertion which, for poignancy of satire, exceeds any part of the former. Personal resentment, though no laudable motive to satire, can add great force to general principles. Self-love is a busy prompter.

The Medal, written upon the same principles with *Absalom and Achitophel* but upon a narrower plan, gives less pleasure, though it discovers equal abilities in the writer. The superstructure cannot extend beyond the foundation; a single character or incident cannot furnish as many ideas as a series of events or multiplicity of agents. This poem therefore, since time has left it to itself, is not much read, nor perhaps generally understood, yet it abounds with touches both of humorous and serious satire. The picture of a man whose propensions to mischief are such that his best actions are but inability of wickedness, is very skilfully delineated and strongly coloured.

> Power was his aim: but, thrown from that pretence,
> The wretch turned loyal in his own defence,

Henceforth: l. 1028.
Tate: Nahum Tate (1652–1715), poetaster and dramatist.
Power was his aim: ll. 50–64.

And malice reconciled him to his prince.
Him, in the anguish of his soul, he served;
Rewarded faster still than he deserved.
Behold him now exalted into trust;
His counsels oft convenient, seldom just.
Ev'n in the most sincere advice he gave,
He had a grudging still to be a knave.
The frauds he learnt in his fanatic years,
Made him uneasy in his lawful gears:
At least as little honest as he could;
And, like white witches, mischievously good.
To his first bias, longingly, he leans;
And rather would be great by wicked means.

The *Threnodia*, which, by a term I am afraid neither authorized nor analogical, he calls *Augustalis*, is not among his happiest productions. Its first and obvious defect is the irregularity of its metre, to which the ears of that age, however, were accustomed. What is worse, it has neither tenderness nor dignity, it is neither magnificent nor pathetic. He seems to look round him for images which he cannot find, and what he has he distorts by endeavouring to enlarge them. He is, he says, 'petrified with grief'; but the marble sometimes relents and trickles in a joke.

> The sons of art all med'cines tried,
> And every noble remedy applied;
> With emulation each essayed
> His utmost skill; *nay more they prayed*:
> Was never losing game with better conduct played.

He had been a little inclined to merriment before upon the prayers of a nation for their dying sovereign, nor was he serious enough to keep heathen fables out of his religion.

> With him th' innumerable crowd of armed prayers
> Knocked at the gates of heaven, and knocked aloud;
> *The first well-meaning rude petitioners*,
> All for his life assailed the throne,
> All would have bribed the skies by offering up their own.
> So great a throng not heaven itself could bar;
> 'Twas almost borne by force *as in the giants' war*.
> The prayers, at least, for his reprieve were heard;
> His death, like Hezekiah's, was deferred.

There is throughout the composition a desire of splendour without wealth. In the conclusion he seems too much pleased with the prospect of the new reign to have lamented his old master with much sincerity.

'*petrified*': l. 8.   *The sons*: ll. 160–4.   *With him*: ll. 97–106.

He did not miscarry in this attempt for want of skill either in lyric or elegiac poetry. His poem 'On the Death of Mrs. Killigrew' is undoubtedly the noblest ode that our language ever has produced. The first part flows with a torrent of enthusiasm. *Fervet immensusque ruit.* All the stanzas indeed are not equal. An imperial crown cannot be one continued diamond: the gems must be held together by some less valuable matter.

In his first 'Ode for Cecilia's Day', which is lost in the splendour of the second, there are passages which would have dignified any other poet. The first stanza is vigorous and elegant, though the word 'diapason' is too technical, and the rhymes are too remote from one another.

> From harmony, from heavenly harmony,
>   This universal frame began:
>   When nature underneath a heap
>   Of jarring atoms lay,
>   And could not heave her head,
> The tuneful voice was heard from high,
>   Arise ye more than dead.
> Then cold and hot, and moist and dry,
> In order to their stations leap,
>   And music's power obey.
> From harmony, from heavenly harmony,
>   This universal frame began:
>   From harmony to harmony
> Through all the compass of the notes it ran,
> The diapason closing full in man.

The conclusion is likewise striking, but it includes an image so awful in itself that it can owe little to poetry; and I could wish the antithesis of 'music untuning' had found some other place.

> As from the power of sacred lays
>   The spheres began to move,
> And sung the great Creator's praise
>   To all the blessed above.
> So when the last and dreadful hour
> This crumbling pageant shall devour,
> The trumpet shall be heard on high,
> The dead shall live, the living die,
> And music shall untune the sky.

Of his skill in elegy he has given a specimen in his *Eleonora*, of which the following lines discover their author.

> Though all these rare endowments of the mind
> Were in a narrow space of life confined,

Fervet: Horace, *Odes*, IV. ii. 7.   *Though all*: ll. 270–90.

> The figure was with full perfection crowned;
> Though not so large an orb, as truly round.
> As when in glory, through the public place,
> The spoils of conquered nations were to pass,
> And but one day for triumph was allowed,
> The consul was constrained his pomp to crowd,
> And so the swift procession hurried on,
> That all, though not distinctly, might be shown;
> So in the straitened bounds of life confined,
> She gave but glimpses of her glorious mind;
> And multitudes of virtues passed along,
> Each pressing foremost in the mighty throng,
> Ambitious to be seen, and then make room
> For greater multitudes that were to come.
> Yet unemployed no minute slipped away;
> Moments were precious in so short a stay.
> The haste of heaven to have her was so great, ⎫
> That some were single acts, though each complete; ⎬
> And every act stood ready to repeat. ⎭

This piece, however, is not without its faults: there is so much likeness in the initial comparison that there is no illustration. As a king would be lamented Eleonora was lamented.

> As when some great and gracious monarch dies,
> Soft whispers, first, and mournful murmurs rise
> Among the sad attendants; then the sound
> Soon gathers voice, and spreads the news around
> Through town and country, till the dreadful blast
> Is blown to distant colonies at last,
> Who then, perhaps, were offering vows in vain
> For his long life, and for his happy reign;
> So slowly by degrees, unwilling fame ⎫
> Did matchless Eleonora's fate proclaim, ⎬
> Till public as the loss the news became. ⎭

This is little better than to say in praise of a shrub that it is as green as a tree, or of a brook that it waters a garden as a river waters a country.

Dryden confesses that he did not know the lady whom he celebrates; the praise being therefore inevitably general fixes no impression upon the reader, nor excites any tendency to love, nor much desire of imitation. Knowledge of the subject is to the poet what durable materials are to the architect.

The *Religio Laici*, which borrows its title from the *Religio Medici* of Browne, is almost the only work of Dryden which can be considered as a voluntary effusion; in this, therefore, it might be hoped

Dryden confesses: Dryden: *Essays*, ii. 61–2.
Browne: Sir Thomas Browne (1605–82), physician and author.

that the full effulgence of his genius would be found. But unhappily the subject is rather argumentative than poetical; he intended only a specimen of metrical disputation:

> And this unpolished rugged verse I chose,
> As fittest for discourse, and nearest prose.

This, however, is a composition of great excellence in its kind, in which the familiar is very properly diversified with the solemn and the grave with the humorous, in which metre has neither weakened the force nor clouded the perspicuity of argument; nor will it be easy to find another example equally happy of this middle kind of writing which, though prosaic in some parts, rises to high poetry in others, and neither towers to the skies nor creeps along the ground.

Of the same kind, or not far distant from it, is *The Hind and Panther*, the longest of all Dryden's original poems—an allegory intended to comprise and to decide the controversy between the Romanists and Protestants. The scheme of the work is injudicious and incommodious, for what can be more absurd than that one beast should counsel another to rest her faith upon a pope and council? He seems well enough skilled in the usual topics of argument, endeavours to show the necessity of an infallible judge, and reproaches the reformers with want of unity, but is weak enough to ask why, since we see without knowing how, we may not have an infallible judge without knowing where.

The Hind at one time is afraid to drink at the common brook because she may be worried, but walking home with the Panther, talks by the way of the Nicene Fathers,[n] and at last declares herself to be the Catholic Church.

This absurdity was very properly ridiculed in the *City Mouse and Country Mouse* of Montagu and Prior, and in the detection and censure of the incongruity of the fiction chiefly consists the value of their performance, which, whatever reputation it might obtain by the help of temporary passions, seems to readers almost a century distant not very forcible or animated.

Pope, whose judgement was perhaps a little bribed by the subject, used to mention this poem as the most correct specimen of Dryden's versification. It was indeed written when he had completely formed his manner, and may be supposed to exhibit, negligence excepted, his deliberate and ultimate scheme of metre.

And this: ll. 453–4.
to rest her faith: For the passages alluded to here see ii. 80 ff., 72–6; i. 528–30; ii. 156, 394 ff.

We may therefore reasonably infer that he did not approve the perpetual uniformity which confines the sense to couplets, since he has broken his lines in the initial paragraph.

> A milk-white Hind, immortal and unchanged,
> Fed on the lawns, and in the forest ranged;
> Without unspotted, innocent within,
> She feared no danger, for she knew no sin.
> Yet had she oft been chased with horns and hounds
> And Scythian shafts, and many winged wounds
> Aimed at her heart; was often forced to fly,
> And doomed to death, though fated not to die.

These lines are lofty, elegant and musical, notwithstanding the interruption of the pause, of which the effect is rather increase of pleasure by variety than offence by ruggedness.

To the first part it was his intention, he says, 'to give the majestic turn of heroic poesy'; and perhaps he might have executed his design not unsuccessfully had not an opportunity of satire, which he cannot forbear, fallen sometimes in his way. The character of a Presbyterian, whose emblem is the Wolf, is not very heroically majestic.

> More haughty than the rest, the wolfish race
> Appear with belly gaunt and famished face:
> Never was so deformed a beast of grace.
> His ragged tail betwixt his legs he wears,
> Close clapped for shame; but his rough crest he rears,
> And pricks up his predestinating ears.

His general character of the other sorts of beasts that never go to church, though sprightly and keen, has, however, not much of heroic poesy.

> These are the chief; to number o'er the rest,
> And stand, like Adam, naming every beast,
> Were weary work; nor will the Muse describe
> A slimy-born, and sun-begotten tribe,
> Who, far from steeples and their sacred sound,
> In fields their sullen conventicles found.
> These gross, half-animated, lumps I leave;
> Nor can I think what thoughts they can conceive;
> But if they think at all, 'tis sure no higher
> Than matter, put in motion, may aspire;
> Souls that can scarce ferment their mass of clay;
> So drossy, so divisible are they,
> As would but serve pure bodies for allay:
> Such souls as shards produce, such beetle things

'*to give*': *Dryden: Poems*, ii. 469.   *More haughty*: i. 160–5.
clapped: held in.   *These are the chief*: i. 308–26.

> As only buzz to heaven with evening wings;
> Strike in the dark, offending but by chance;
> Such are the blindfold blows of ignorance.
> They know not beings, and but hate a name;
> To them the Hind and Panther are the same.

One more instance, and that taken from the narrative part, where style was more in his choice, will show how steadily he kept his resolution of heroic dignity.

> For when the herd, sufficed, did late repair
> To ferny heaths, and to their forest lair,
> She made a mannerly excuse to stay,
> Proffering the Hind to wait her half the way:
> That since the sky was clear, an hour of talk
> Might help her to beguile the tedious walk.
> With much goodwill the motion was embraced,
> To chat awhile on their adventures past;
> Nor had the grateful Hind so soon forgot
> Her friend and fellow-sufferer in the plot.
> Yet wondering how of late she grew estranged,
> Her forehead cloudy and her count'nance changed,
> She thought this hour th' occasion would present
> To learn her secret cause of discontent,
> Which well she hoped might be with ease redressed,⎤
> Considering her a well-bred civil beast,   ⎬
> And more a gentlewoman than the rest.   ⎦
> After some common talk what rumours ran,
> The lady of the spotted muff began.

The second and third parts he professes to have reduced to diction more familiar and more suitable to dispute and conversation; the difference is not, however, very easily perceived: the first has familiar and the two others have sonorous lines. The original incongruity runs through the whole; the King is now Caesar and now the Lion, and the name Pan is given to the Supreme Being.

But when this constitutional absurdity is forgiven, the poem must be confessed to be written with great smoothness of metre, a wide extent of knowledge, and an abundant multiplicity of images; the controversy is embellished with pointed sentences, diversified by illustrations, and enlivened by sallies of invective. Some of the facts to which allusions are made are now become obscure, and perhaps there may be many satirical passages little understood.

As it was by its nature a work of defiance, a composition which would naturally be examined with the utmost acrimony of criticism,

For when: ì. 554–72. *he professes*: loc. cit.
now Caesar: cf. iii. 60; i. 531. *the name Pan*: ii. 711.

it was probably laboured with uncommon attention; and there are, indeed, few negligences in the subordinate parts. The original impropriety, and the subsequent unpopularity of the subject added to the ridiculousness of its first elements, has sunk it into neglect; but it may be usefully studied as an example of poetical ratiocination in which the argument suffers little from the metre.

In the poem on 'The Birth of the Prince of Wales', nothing is very remarkable but the exorbitant adulation, and that insensibility of the precipice on which the King was then standing which the laureate apparently shared with the rest of the courtiers. A few months cured him of controversy, dismissed him from Court, and made him again a playwright and translator.

Of Juvenal there had been a translation by Stapylton, and another by Holyday; neither of them is very poetical. Stapylton is more smooth, and Holyday's is more esteemed for the learning of his notes. A new version was proposed to the poets of that time, and undertaken by them in conjunction. The main design was conducted by Dryden, whose reputation was such that no man was unwilling to serve the Muses under him.

The general character of this translation will be given when it is said to preserve the wit but to want the dignity of the original. The peculiarity of Juvenal is a mixture of gaiety and stateliness, of pointed sentences and declamatory grandeur. His points have not been neglected, but his grandeur none of the band seemed to consider as necessary to be imitated except Creech, who undertook the thirteenth satire. It is therefore perhaps possible to give a better representation of that great satirist even in those parts which Dryden himself has translated, some passages excepted which will never be excelled.

With Juvenal was published Persius, translated wholly by Dryden. This work, though like all the other productions of Dryden it may have shining parts, seems to have been written merely for wages in an uniform mediocrity, without any eager endeavour after excellence or laborious effort of the mind.

There wanders an opinion among the readers of poetry that one of these satires is an exercise of the school. Dryden says that he once

---

'*The Birth*': i.e. *Britannia Rediviva* (1688); cf. ll. 114–17.

Stapylton: Sir Robert Stapleton (or Stapylton) (d. 1669), dramatist and translator; see *Juvenal's Sixteen Satyrs* (1647).

another by Holyday: *Juvenal and Persius, translated and illustrated* (1673).

There wanders an opinion: Cf. Derrick, i. *xiv*.

Dryden says that: headnote to the 'Third Satire'.

translated it at school, but not that he preserved or published the juvenile performance.

Not long afterwards he undertook perhaps the most arduous work of its kind, a translation of Virgil, for which he had shown how well he was qualified by his version of the 'Pollio', and two episodes, one of Nisus and Euryalus, the other of Mezentius and Lausus.[n]

In the comparison of Homer and Virgil, the discriminative excellence of Homer is elevation and comprehension of thought, and that of Virgil is grace and splendour of diction. The beauties of Homer are therefore difficult to be lost, and those of Virgil difficult to be retained. The massy trunk of sentiment is safe by its solidity, but the blossoms of elocution easily drop away. The author, having the choice of his own images, selects those which he can best adorn; the translator must, at all hazards, follow his original, and express thoughts which perhaps he would not have chosen. When to this primary difficulty is added the inconvenience of a language so much inferior in harmony to the Latin, it cannot be expected that they who read the *Georgic* and the *Aeneid* should be much delighted with any version.

All these obstacles Dryden saw, and all these he determined to encounter. The expectation of his work was undoubtedly great: the nation considered its honour as interested in the event. One gave him the different editions of his author, and another helped him in the subordinate parts. The arguments of the several books were given him by Addison.

The hopes of the public were not disappointed. He produced, says Pope, 'the most noble and spirited translation that I know in any language'. It certainly excelled whatever had appeared in English, and appears to have satisfied his friends, and for the most part to have silenced his enemies. Milbourne, indeed, a clergyman, attacked it, but his outrages seem to be the ebullitions of a mind agitated by stronger resentment than bad poetry can excite, and previously resolved not to be pleased.

---

the 'Pollio': *Eclogue* iv, dedicated to Gaius Asinius Pollio (consul 40 B.C.).

Nisus and Euryalus: faithful friends of Aeneas, who take part in the foot-race (bk. v).

Mezentius and Lausus: Mezentius, a cruel tyrant, and his son Lausus were killed by Aeneas (bk. x).

One gave him: Sir Gilbert Dolben (1658–1722), judge. Cf. *Dryden: Essays*, ii. 260.

and another: Knightly Chetwood (1650–1720), Dean of Gloucester, contributed the preface to the *Pastorals* and the 'Life of Virgil' (*Dryden: Essays*, ii. 254 and n. 1).

The arguments: ibid.   '*the most noble*': *Pope: Poems*, vii. 22.

His criticism extends only to the Preface, *Pastorals*, and *Georgics*,
and as he professes to give his antagonist an opportunity of reprisal,
he has added his own version of the first and fourth *Pastorals*, and
the first *Georgic*. The world has forgotten his book, but since his
attempt has given him a place in literary history, I will preserve a
specimen of his criticism by inserting his remarks on the invocation
before the first *Georgic*, and of his poetry by annexing his own
version.

Ver. 1.   What makes a plenteous harvest, when to turn,
           The fruitful soil, and when to sow the corn.

It's *unlucky*, they say, *to stumble at the threshold*, but what has a 'plenteous
harvest' to do here? Virgil would not pretend to prescribe *rules* for *that*
which depends not on the *husbandman's* care, but the *disposition of
Heaven* altogether. Indeed, the 'plenteous crop' depends somewhat on the
good method of tillage, and where the land's ill-manured, the 'corn',
without a miracle, can be but *indifferent*; but the 'harvest' may be *good*,
which is its *properest* epithet, though the *husbandman's skill* were never so
indifferent. The next *sentence* is *too literal*, and 'when to plough' had been
Virgil's meaning, and intelligible to everybody, and 'when to sow the
corn' is a needless *addition*.

Ver. 3.   The care of sheep, of oxen, and of kine;
           And when to geld the lambs, and sheer the swine,

would as well have fallen under the *cura boum, qui cultus habendo sit
pecori*, as Mr. D.'s *deduction* of particulars.

Ver. 5.   The birth and genius of the frugal bee,
           I sing, Maecenas, and I sing to thee.

But where did *experientia* ever signify 'birth and genius'? or what ground
was there for such a *figure* in this place? How much more manly is Mr.
Ogilby's version![n]

       What makes rich grounds, in what celestial signs,
       'Tis good to plough, and marry elms with vines.
       What best fits cattle, what with sheep agrees,
       And several arts improving frugal bees,
          I sing, Maecenas.

Which four lines, though faulty enough, are yet much more to the purpose
than Mr. D.'s six.

Ver. 22.   From fields and mountains to my song repair.

For *patrium linquens nemus, saltusque Lycaei*—Very well explained!

Ver. 1: *Notes on Dryden's Virgil* (1698), pp. 108–11.
cura boum: *Georgics*, i. 3–4.
Maecenas: (74/64–8 B.C.), literary patron under Augustus.
experientia: *Georgics*, i. 4: . . . *apibus quanta experientia parcis* ('what skill the
    thrifty bees').
Mr. Ogilby's: John Ogilby (1600–76), author and printer.
Lycaeus: a mountain in Arcadia.

Ver. 23, 24.   Inventor Pallas, of the fattening oil,
       Thou founder of the plough, and ploughman's toil!

Written as if *these* had been Pallas's 'invention'. The 'ploughman's toil's' impertinent.

Ver. 25.   —The shroud-like cypress—

Why 'shroud-like'? Is a 'cypress' pulled up by the *roots*, which the *sculpture* in the *last Eclogue* fills Silvanus's hand with, so very like a 'shroud'? Or did not Mr. D. think of that kind of 'cypress' used often for *scarves and hatbands* at funerals formerly, or for *widow's veils*, etc. If so, 'twas a *deep good thought*.

Ver. 26.   —that wear
       The rural honours, and increase the year.

What's meant by 'increasing the year'? Did the *gods or goddesses* add more *months*, or *days*, or *hours* to it? Or how can *arva tueri* signify to 'wear rural honours'? Is this to *translate*, or *abuse* an *author*? The next *couplet* are borrowed from Ogilby, I suppose, because *less to the purpose* than ordinary.

Ver. 33.   The patron of the world, and Rome's peculiar guard.

Idle, and none of Virgil's, no more than the sense of the *precedent couplet*; so again, he *interpolates* Virgil with that

       And the round circle of the year to guide;
       Powerful of blessings, which thou strew'st around.

A ridiculous *Latinism*, and an *impertinent addition*; indeed the whole *period* is but one piece of *absurdity* and *nonsense*, as those who lay it with the *original* must find.

Ver. 42, 43.   And Neptune shall resign the fasces of the sea.

Was he *consul* or *dictator* there?

       And watery virgins for thy bed shall strive.

Both absurd *interpolations*.

Ver. 47, 48.   Where in the void of heaven a place is free.
       Ah Happy D—n, were that place for thee!

But where is 'that void'? Or what does our *translator* mean by it? He knows what Ovid says God did to prevent such a 'void' in heaven; perhaps this was then forgotten; but Virgil talks more sensibly.

Ver. 49.   The scorpion ready to receive thy laws.

No, he would not then have *gotten out of his way* so fast.

Ver. 56.   Though Proserpine affects her silent seat.

Pallas: Pallas Athene, daughter of Zeus, with whom the Romans identified Minerva (see *Georgics*, i. 18).
Silvanus: in Roman religion a spirit of the woods.
He knows: Dryden: *Poems*, ii. 802; *Metamorphoses*, i. 72–5.
Proserpine: perhaps originally an Italian goddess of the earth, identified with Persephone, a beautiful goddess who was carried off from the fields of Enna in Sicily by the god of the underworld to be his queen.

What made *her* then so *angry* with Ascalaphus for preventing her return? She was now mused to patience under the *determinations of Fate*, rather than *fond* of her *residence*.

Ver. 61, 62, 63.   Pity the poet's, and the ploughman's cares,
Interest thy greatness in our mean affairs,
And use thyself betimes to hear our prayers.

Which is such a wretched *perversion* of Virgil's *noble thought* as *vicars* would have blushed at; but Mr. Ogilby makes us some amends by his better lines:

O whereso'er thou art, from thence incline,
And grant assistance to my bold design!
Pity with me, poor husbandmen's affairs,
And now, as if translated, hear our prayers.

This is *sense*, and *to the purpose*; the other, poor *mistaken stuff*.

Such were the strictures of Milbourne, who found few abettors, and of whom it may be reasonably imagined that many who favoured his design were ashamed of his insolence.

When admiration had subsided, the translation was more coolly examined, and found like all others to be sometimes erroneous and sometimes licentious. Those who could find faults thought they could avoid them, and Dr. Brady attempted in blank verse a translation of the *Aeneid* which, when dragged into the world, did not live long enough to cry. I have never seen it, but that such a version there is, or has been, perhaps some old catalogue informed me.

With not much better success Trapp, when his tragedy and his *Prelections* had given him reputation, attempted another blank version of the *Aeneid*, to which, notwithstanding the slight regard with which it was treated, he had afterwards perseverance enough to add the *Eclogues* and *Georgics*.[n] His book may continue its existence as long as it is the clandestine refuge of schoolboys.

Since the English ear has been accustomed to the mellifluence of Pope's numbers, and the diction of poetry has become more splendid, new attempts have been made to translate Virgil, and all his works have been attempted by men better qualified to contend with Dryden. I will not engage myself in an invidious comparison by opposing one passage to another—a work of which there would be no end, and which might be often offensive without use.

It is not by comparing line with line that the merit of great works

Ascalaphus: son of Acheron, who revealed that Persephone had eaten some pomegranate seeds in the underworld, which therefore made it impossible for her to leave it.

Dr. Brady: Nicholas Brady the elder (1659–1726), divine and poet, who published the first book of *Virgil's Aeneis, translated into Blank Verse* (1714), and the complete poem in four instalments (1716 to 1726).

is to be estimated, but by their general effects and ultimate result. It is easy to note a weak line and write one more vigorous in its place, to find a happiness of expression in the original and transplant it by force into the version; but what is given to the parts may be subducted from the whole, and the reader may be weary though the critic may commend. Works of imagination excel by their allurement and delight, by their power of attracting and detaining the attention. That book is good in vain which the reader throws away. He only is the master who keeps the mind in pleasing captivity, whose pages are perused with eagerness, and in hope of new pleasure are perused again, and whose conclusion is perceived with an eye of sorrow such as the traveller casts upon departing day.

By his proportion of this predomination I will consent that Dryden should be tried—of this which, in opposition to reason, makes Ariosto the darling and the pride of Italy; of this which, in defiance of criticism, continues Shakespeare the sovereign of the drama.

His last work was his *Fables,* in which he gave us the first example of a mode of writing which the Italians call *rifacimento,* a renovation of ancient writers by modernizing their language. Thus the old poem of Boiardo has been new-dressed by Domenichi and Berni. The works of Chaucer, upon which this kind of rejuvenescence has been bestowed by Dryden, require little criticism. The tale of the Cock seems hardly worth revival, and the story of Palamon and Arcite, containing an action unsuitable to the times in which it is placed, can hardly be suffered to pass without censure of the hyperbolical commendation which Dryden has given it in the general preface, and in a poetical dedication, a piece where his original fondness of remote conceits seems to have revived.

Of the three pieces borrowed from Boccace, 'Sigismonda' may be defended by the celebrity of the story. 'Theodore and Honoria', though it contains not much moral, yet afforded opportunities of striking description. And 'Cymon' was formerly a tale of such

predomination: 'the action, fact, or condition of predominating' (*OED*).

Boiardo: Matteo Maria Boiardo (1441–94), Count of Scandiano and Italian poet, author of the first three books of *Orlando Innamorato.*

Domenichi: Lodovico Domenichi (d. 1564), Italian man of letters; cf. *Orlando Innamorato . . . nuovamente riformato* (1545).

Berni: Francesco Berni (1497?–1536), Italian poet; cf. *Orlando Innamorato, nuovamente composto da M. F. Berni* (1541).

a poetical dedication: 'To Her Grace the Duchess of Ormonde'.

Boccace: Giovanni Boccaccio (1313–75), Italian story-writer and poet; see *Il Decamerone,* IV. i, V. i, viii.

reputation that, at the revival of letters, it was translated into Latin by one of the Beroalds.

Whatever subjects employed his pen, he was still improving our measures and embellishing our language.

In this volume are interspersed some short original poems which, with his prologues, epilogues and songs, may be comprised in Congreve's remark that even those, if he had written nothing else, would have entitled him to the praise of excellence in his kind.[n]

One composition must however be distinguished. The 'Ode for St. Cecilia's Day', perhaps the last effort of his poetry, has been always considered as exhibiting the highest flight of fancy, and the exactest nicety of art. This is allowed to stand without a rival. If indeed there is any excellence beyond it, in some other of Dryden's works that excellence must be found. Compared with the 'Ode on Killigrew', it may be pronounced perhaps superior in the whole, but without any single part equal to the first stanza of the other.

It is said to have cost Dryden a fortnight's labour, but it does not want its negligences: some of the lines are without correspondent rhymes—a defect which I never detected but after an acquaintance of many years, and which the enthusiasm of the writer might hinder him from perceiving.

His last stanza has less emotion than the former, but is not less elegant in the diction. The conclusion is vicious: the music of Timotheus, which 'raised a mortal to the skies', had only a metaphorical power; that of Cecilia, which 'drew an angel down', had a real effect; the crown therefore could not reasonably be divided.

In a general survey of Dryden's labours, he appears to have a mind very comprehensive by nature, and much enriched with acquired knowledge. His compositions are the effects of a vigorous genius operating upon large materials.

The power that predominated in his intellectual operations was rather strong reason than quick sensibility. Upon all occasions that were presented he studied rather than felt, and produced sentiments not such as nature enforces but meditation supplies. With the simple and elemental passions as they spring separate in the mind, he seems not much acquainted, and seldom describes them but as they are complicated by the various relations of society, and confused in the tumults and agitations of life.

one of the Beroalds: Philip Beroald the elder (1453–1505), Italian man of letters, professor at Bologna; cf. Varia Philippi Beroaldi opuscula (Basle, 1513), fos. 33^v–36^v.   perhaps the last effort: see above, p. 148 and n.
Timotheus: (447–357 B.C.), poet and musician of Miletus.
the crown: see Alexander's Feast, l. 178.

What he says of love may contribute to the explanation of his character:

> Love various minds does variously inspire;
> It stirs in gentle bosoms gentle fire,
> Like that of incense on the altar laid;
> But raging flames tempestuous souls invade;
> A fire which every windy passion blows,
> With pride it mounts, or with revenge it glows.

Dryden's was not one of the 'gentle bosoms': love, as it subsists in itself, with no tendency but to the person loved, and wishing only for correspondent kindness, such love as shuts out all other interest, the Love of the Golden Age, was too soft and subtle to put his faculties in motion. He hardly conceived it but in its turbulent effervescence with some other desires, when it was inflamed by rivalry or obstructed by difficulties, when it invigorated ambition or exasperated revenge.

He is therefore with all his variety of excellence not often pathetic, and had so little sensibility of the power of effusions purely natural that he did not esteem them in others. Simplicity gave him no pleasure, and for the first part of his life he looked on Otway with contempt; though at last, indeed very late, he confessed that in his play 'there was nature, which is the chief beauty'.

We do not always know our own motives. I am not certain whether it was not rather the difficulty which he found in exhibiting the genuine operations of the heart than a servile submission to an injudicious audience, that filled his plays with false magnificence. It was necessary to fix attention, and the mind can be captivated only by recollection or by curiosity, by reviving natural sentiments or impressing new appearances of things; sentences were readier at his call than images: he could more easily fill the ear with some splendid novelty than awaken those ideas that slumber in the heart.

The favourite exercise of his mind was ratiocination, and that argument might not be too soon at an end, he delighted to talk of liberty and necessity, destiny and contingence; these he discusses in the language of the school with so much profundity that the terms which he uses are not always understood. It is indeed learning, but learning out of place.

When once he had engaged himself in disputation, thoughts flowed in on either side: he was now no longer at a loss; he had

Love various: *Dryden: DW*, ii. 351 (*Tyrannic Love*, act II).

Otway: Thomas Otway (1652–85), dramatist. Cf. Charles Gildon, *The Laws of Poetry* (1721), p. 211.

'*there was nature*': *Dryden: Essays*, ii. 201 (where *Venice Preserved* is the play referred to).

always objections and solutions at command; *verbaque provisam rem*—give him matter for his verse and he finds without difficulty verse for his matter.

In comedy, for which he professes himself not naturally qualified, the mirth which he excites will perhaps not be found so much to arise from any original humour or peculiarity of character nicely distinguished and diligently pursued, as from incidents and circumstances, artifices and surprises—from jests of action rather than of sentiment. What he had of humorous or passionate he seems to have had not from nature but from other poets, if not always as a plagiary, at least as an imitator.

Next to argument his delight was in wild and daring sallies of sentiment, in the irregular and eccentric violence of wit. He delighted to tread upon the brink of meaning, where light and darkness begin to mingle, to approach the precipice of absurdity, and hover over the abyss of unideal vacancy. This inclination sometimes produced nonsense, which he knew, as,

> Move swiftly, Sun, and fly a lover's pace,
> Leave weeks and months behind thee in thy race.

> Amariel flies
> To guard thee from the demons of the air;
> My flaming sword above them to display,
> All keen and ground upon the edge of day.

And sometimes it issued in absurdities, of which perhaps he was not conscious:

> Then we upon our orb's last verge shall go,
> And see the ocean leaning on the sky;
> From thence our rolling neighbours we shall know,
> And on the lunar world securely pry.

These lines have no meaning; but may we not say, in imitation of Cowley on another book,

> 'Tis so like *sense* 'twill serve the turn as well?

This endeavour after the grand and the new produced many sentiments either great or bulky, and many images either just or splendid:

verbaque: *Ars Poetica*, l. 311.   *unideal*: see above, p. 92.
Move swiftly: Dryden: *DW*. iii. 163.
Amariel flies: ibid. ii. 363 (*Tyrannic Love*, act IV).
Then we: *Annus Mirabilis*, st. 164.
'Tis so like: 'To Mr. Hobbes', *Cowley: Poems*, p. 188 (''Tis so like Truth 'twill serve our turn as well').

> I am as free as Nature first made man, ⎫
> Ere the base laws of servitude began, ⎬
> When wild in woods the noble savage ran. ⎭

> —'Tis but because the living death ne'er knew,
> They fear to prove it as a thing that's new:
> Let me th' experiment before you try,
> I'll show you first how easy 'tis to die.

> —There with a forest of their darts he strove,
> And stood like Capaneus defying Jove,
> With his broad sword the boldest beating down,
> While Fate grew pale lest he should win the town,
> And turned the iron leaves of his dark book
> To make new dooms, or mend what it mistook.

> —I beg no pity for this mouldering clay;
> For if you give it burial, there it takes
> Possession of your earth;
> If burnt, and scattered in the air, the winds
> That strew my dust diffuse my royalty,
> And spread me o'er your clime; for where one atom
> Of mine shall light, know there Sebastian reigns.

Of these quotations the two first may be allowed to be great, the two latter only tumid.

Of such selection there is no end. I will add only a few more passages, of which the first, though it may perhaps not be quite clear in prose, is not too obscure for poetry, as the meaning that it has is noble:

> No, there is a necessity in Fate,
> Why still the brave bold man is fortunate;
> He keeps his object ever full in sight,
> And that assurance holds him firm and right;
> True, 'tis a narrow way that leads to bliss, ⎫
> But right before there is no precipice; ⎬
> Fear makes men look aside, and so their footing miss. ⎭

Of the images which the two following citations afford, the first is elegant, the second magnificent; whether either be just let the reader judge:

> What precious drops are these,
> Which silently each other's track pursue,
> Bright as young diamonds in their infant dew?

I am as free: Dryden: *DW*, iii. 34 (*1 Conquest of Granada*, act I).
'Tis but: ibid. ii. 382 (*Tyrannic Love*, act V).
There with: ibid. ii. 341 (ibid. act I).
Capaneus: one of the Seven before Thebes, who was struck with lightning by
    Jupiter.   *I beg*: Dryden: *DW*, vi. 38 (*Don Sebastian*, act I).
No, there: ibid. iii. 72–3 (*1 Conquest of Granada*, IV. ii).
What precious: ibid. iii. 116 (*2 Conquest of Granada*, III. i).

> —Resign your castle—
> —Enter, brave Sir; for when you speak the word,
> The gates shall open of their own accord;
> The genius of the place its Lord shall meet,
> And bow its towery forehead at your feet.

These bursts of extravagance Dryden calls the 'Dalilahs' of the theatre, and owns that many noisy lines of Maximin and Almanzor call out for vengeance upon him; but 'I knew', says he, 'that they were bad enough to please even when I wrote them'. There is surely reason to suspect that he pleased himself as well as his audience, and that these, like the harlots of other men, had his love, though not his approbation.

He had sometimes faults of a less generous and splendid kind. He makes, like almost all other poets, very frequent use of mythology, and sometimes connects religion and fable too closely without distinction.

He descends to display his knowledge with pedantic ostentation, as when, in translating Virgil, he says, 'tack to the larboard' and 'veer starboard', and talks in another work of 'virtue spooming before the wind'. His vanity now and then betrays his ignorance:

> They nature's King through nature's optics viewed;
> Reversed they viewed Him lessened to their eyes.

He had heard of reversing a telescope, and unluckily reverses the object.

He is sometimes unexpectedly mean. When he describes the Supreme Being as moved by prayer to stop the Fire of London, what is his expression?

> A hollow crystal pyramid He takes,
> In firmamental waters dipped above,
> Of this a broad *extinguisher* He makes,
> And *hoods* the flames that to their quarry strove.

When he describes the Last Day and the decisive tribunal, he intermingles his image:

> When rattling bones together fly,
> From the four quarters of the sky.

Resign your castle: Dryden: *DW*, iii. 126 (*2 Conquest of Granada*, III. iii).
These bursts: Dryden: *Essays*, i. 276.   '*tack to*': *Aeneis*, iii. 526–7.
'*virtue spooming*': *The Hind and the Panther*, iii. 96.
spooming: scudding, running before the wind.
They nature's: *Hind and the Panther*, i. 57–8.
A hollow: *Annus Mirabilis*, st. 281.
When rattling: 'To the Memory of Mrs. Anne Killigrew', ll. 184–5.

It was indeed never in his power to resist the temptation of a jest. In his elegy on Cromwell:

> No sooner was the Frenchman's cause embraced,
> Than the *light Monsieur* the *grave Don* outweighed.
> His fortune turned the scale—.

He had a vanity unworthy of his abilities to show, as may be suspected, the rank of the company with whom he lived by the use of French words which had then crept into conversation—such as *fraîcheur* for 'coolness', *fougue* for 'turbulence', and a few more, none of which the language has incorporated or retained. They continue only where they stood first, perpetual warnings to future innovators.

These are his faults of affectation; his faults of negligence are beyond recital. Such is the unevenness of his compositions that ten lines are seldom found together without something of which the reader is ashamed.[n] Dryden was no rigid judge of his own pages: he seldom struggled after supreme excellence, but snatched in haste what was within his reach, and when he could content others was himself contented. He did not keep present to his mind an idea of pure perfection, nor compare his works, such as they were, with what they might be made. He knew to whom he should be opposed. He had more music than Waller, more vigour than Denham, and more nature than Cowley; and from his contemporaries he was in no danger. Standing therefore in the highest place, he had no care to rise by contending with himself, but while there was no name above his own was willing to enjoy fame on the easiest terms.

He was no lover of labour. What he thought sufficient he did not stop to make better, and allowed himself to leave many parts unfinished in confidence that the good lines would overbalance the bad. What he had once written he dismissed from his thoughts, and I believe there is no example to be found of any correction or improvement made by him after publication. The hastiness of his productions might be the effect of necessity, but his subsequent neglect could hardly have any other cause than impatience of study.

What can be said of his versification will be little more than a dilatation of the praise given it by Pope:

> Waller was smooth; but Dryden taught to join⎫
> The varying verse, the full-resounding line, ⎬
> The long majestic march, and energy divine. ⎭

No sooner: 'Heroic Stanzas', st. 23.
fraîcheur: *To his Sacred Majesty*, l. 102.   *fougue*: *Astraea Redux*, l. 203.
Waller was smooth: *Imit. Hor. Ep.* II. i. 267–9.

Some improvements had been already made in English numbers, but the full force of our language was not yet felt; the verse that was smooth was commonly feeble. If Cowley had sometimes a finished line, he had it by chance. Dryden knew how to choose the flowing and the sonorous words, to vary the pauses and adjust the accents, to diversify the cadence and yet preserve the smoothness of his metre.

Of triplets and alexandrines, though he did not introduce the use, he established it. The triplet has long subsisted among us. Dryden seems not to have traced it higher than to Chapman's *Homer*, but it is to be found in Phaer's *Virgil*, written in the reign of Mary, and in Hall's *Satires*, published five years before the death of Elizabeth.

The alexandrine was, I believe, first used by Spenser for the sake of closing his stanza with a fuller sound. We had a longer measure of fourteen syllables into which the *Aeneid* was translated by Phaer, and other works of the ancients by other writers, of which Chapman's *Iliad* was, I believe, the last.

The two first lines of Phaer's third *Aeneid* will exemplify this measure:

> When Asia's state was overthrown, and Priam's kingdom stout,
> All guiltless, by the power of gods above was rooted out.

As these lines had their break or caesura always at the eighth syllable, it was thought in time commodious to divide them, and quatrains of lines alternately consisting of eight and six syllables make the most soft and pleasing of our lyric measures, as,

> Relentless Time, destroying power,
> Which stone and brass obey,
> Who giv'st to every flying hour
> To work some new decay.

In the alexandrine, when its power was once felt, some poems, as Drayton's *Polyolbion*, were wholly written, and sometimes the

---

Dryden seems not: *Dryden: Essays*, ii. 247 and n. 2.

Phaer's: Thomas Phaer (or Phayer) (1510?–60), lawyer, physician, and translator; see *The Seven first Bookes of the Eneidos of Virgil, converted into Englishe meter* (1558).

Hall's Satires: *Virgidemiarum, Sixe Bookes of . . . Satyrs* (1597–8).

Priam's: Priam, in Greek mythology the son of Laomedon, was king of Troy at the time of the Trojan war.

Relentless Time: Thomas Parnell, *Poems on Several Occasions* (1722), p. 148 ('An Imitation of Some French Verses').

Drayton's: Michael Drayton (1563–1631), poet, who finished his *Polyolbion* in 1622.

measures of twelve and fourteen syllables were interchanged with one another. Cowley was the first that inserted the alexandrine at pleasure among the heroic lines of ten syllables, and from him Dryden professes to have adopted it.

The triplet and alexandrine are not universally approved. Swift always censured them, and wrote some lines to ridicule them. In examining their propriety, it is to be considered that the essence of verse is regularity, and its ornament is variety. To write verse is to dispose syllables and sounds harmonically by some known and settled rule—a rule however lax enough to substitute similitude for identity, to admit change without breach of order, and to relieve the ear without disappointing it. Thus a Latin hexameter is formed from dactyls and spondees differently combined; the English heroic admits of acute or grave syllables variously disposed. The Latin never deviates into seven feet, or exceeds the number of seventeen syllables; but the English alexandrine breaks the lawful bounds, and surprises the reader with two syllables more than he expected.

The effect of the triplet is the same: the ear has been accustomed to expect a new rhyme in every couplet, but is on a sudden surprised with three rhymes together, to which the reader could not accommodate his voice did he not obtain notice of the change from the braces of the margins. Surely there is something unskilful in the necessity of such mechanical direction.

Considering the metrical art simply as a science and consequently excluding all casualty, we must allow that triplets and alexandrines inserted by caprice are interruptions of that constancy to which science aspires. And though the variety which they produce may very justly be desired, yet to make our poetry exact there ought to be some stated mode of admitting them.

But till some such regulation can be formed, I wish them still to be retained in their present state. They are sometimes grateful to the reader, and sometimes convenient to the poet. Fenton was of opinion that Dryden was too liberal and Pope too sparing in their use.[n]

The rhymes of Dryden are commonly just, and he valued himself for his readiness in finding them; but he is sometimes open to objection.

It is the common practice of our poets to end the second line with a weak or grave syllable:

Dryden professes: cf. *Dryden: Essays*, ii. 247.

Swift . . . wrote some lines to ridicule them: see 'A Description of a City Shower', ll. 61–3 and n.

he valued himself: *Dryden: Essays*, ii. 240.

> Together o'er the Alps methinks we fly,
> Filled with ideas of fair Italy.

Dryden sometimes puts the weak rhyme in the first:

> Laugh all the powers that favour *tyranny*,
> And all the standing army of the sky.

Sometimes he concludes a period or paragraph with the first line of a couplet, which, though the French seem to do it without irregularity, always displeases in English poetry.

The alexandrine, though much his favourite, is not always very diligently fabricated by him. It invariably requires a break at the sixth syllable—a rule which the modern French poets never violate, but which Dryden sometimes neglected:

> And with paternal thunder vindicates his throne.

Of Dryden's works it was said by Pope that 'he could select from them better specimens of every mode of poetry than any other English writer could supply'.[n] Perhaps no nation ever produced a writer that enriched his language with such variety of models. To him we owe the improvement, perhaps the completion of our metre, the refinement of our language, and much of the correctness of our sentiments. By him we were taught *sapere et fari*, to think naturally and express forcibly. Though Davies has reasoned in rhyme before him, it may be perhaps maintained that he was the first who joined argument with poetry. He showed us the true bounds of a translator's liberty. What was said of Rome adorned by Augustus, may be applied by an easy metaphor to English poetry embellished by Dryden—*lateritiam invenit, marmoream reliquit*, he found it brick, and he left it marble.

The invocation before the *Georgics* is here inserted from Mr. Milbourne's version that, according to his own proposal, his verses may be compared with those which he censures.

> What makes the richest tilth, beneath what signs
> To plough, and when to match your elms and vines;
> What care with flocks and what with herds agrees,
> And all the management of frugal bees,

Together o'er: Pope, 'Epistle to Mr. Jervas', ll. 25–6.
Laugh all: *Palamon and Arcite*, iii. 671–2.
And with: *Hind and the Panther*, ii. 537.   *sapere*: Horace, *Epistles*, I. iv. 9.
Davies: Sir John Davies (1569–1626), Attorney-General for Ireland and poet, author of *Nosce Teipsum* (1599).
lateritiam: Suetonius, *Divus Augustus*, 28.
What makes: *Notes on Dryden's Virgil*, pp. 206–9.

I sing, Maecenas! Ye immensely clear,
Vast orbs of light which guide the rolling year;
Bacchus, and mother Ceres, if by you
We fatt'ning corn for hungry mast pursue,
If, taught by you, we first the cluster pressed,
And thin cold streams with sprightly juice refreshed.
Ye fawns the present numens of the field,
Wood-nymphs and fawns, your kind assistance yield,
Your gifts I sing! and thou, at whose feared stroke
From rending earth the fiery courser broke,
Great Neptune, O assist my artful song!
And thou to whom the woods and groves belong,
Whose snowy heifers on her flowery plains
In mighty herds the Caean Isle maintains!
Pan, happy shepherd, if thy cares divine,
E'er to improve thy Maenalus incline;
Leave thy Lycaean wood and native grove,
And with thy lucky smiles our work approve!
Be Pallas too, sweet oil's inventor, kind;
And he, who first the crooked plough designed!
Sylvanus, god of all the woods appear,
Whose hands a new-drawn tender cypress bear!
Ye gods and goddesses whoe'er with love,
Would guard our pastures, and our fields improve!
You, who new plants from unsown lands supply;
And with condensing clouds obscure the sky,
And drop 'em softly thence in fruitful showers,
Assist my enterprize, ye gentler powers!

And thou, great Caesar! though we know not yet
Among what gods thou'lt fix thy lofty seat,
Whether thou'lt be the kind tutelar god
Of thy own Rome; or with thy awful nod,
Guide the vast world, while thy great hand shall bear, ⎫
The fruits and seasons of the turning year, ⎬
And thy bright brows thy mother's myrtles wear; ⎭
Whether thou'lt all the boundless ocean sway,

Ceres: goddess of corn, agriculture in general, and of the earth.
sprightly: 'having lively qualities or properties, suggestive of animation or gaiety', used of liquors (*OED*).
numens: divinities, presiding spirits.
at whose feared stroke: Neptune was said to have produced the horse in Thessaly by a stroke of his trident.
And thou to whom: Aristaeus, a god of husbandry, delivered the isle of Ceos from drought and was honoured there with the attributes of Zeus.
Maenalus: a mountain in Arcadia sacred to Pan.
And he: Triptolemus, son of Celeus (?) of Eleusis and favourite of Demeter.
thy mother's myrtles: The myrtle was identified with Venus, with whom the Julian family was supposed to be connected.

And seamen only to thyself shall pray,
Thule, the farthest island, kneel to thee,
And, that thou may'st her son by marriage be,
Tethys will for the happy purchase yield
To make a dowry of her watery field;
Whether thou'lt add to heaven a brighter sign,
And o'er the summer months serenely shine;
Where between Cancer and Erigone,
There yet remains a spacious room for thee.
Where the hot Scorpion too his arms declines,
And more to thee than half his arch resigns;
Whate'er thou'lt be; for sure the realms below
No just pretence to thy command can show:
No such ambition sways thy vast desires,
Though Greece her own Elysian fields admires.
And now, at last, contented Proserpine
Can all her mother's earnest prayers decline.
Whate'er thou'lt be, O guide our gentle course,
And with thy smiles our bold attempts enforce;
With me th' unknowing rustics' wants relieve,
And, though on earth, our sacred vows receive!

Mr. Dryden, having received from Rymer his *Remarks on the Tragedies of the Last Age*, wrote observations on the blank leaves, which, having been in the possession of Mr. Garrick, are by his favour communicated to the public that no particle of Dryden may be lost.[n]

That we may the less wonder why pity and terror are not now the only springs on which our tragedies move, and that Shakespeare may be more excused, Rapin confesses that the French tragedies now all run on the *tendre*, and gives the reason, because love is the passion which most predominates in our souls, and that therefore the passions represented become insipid unless they are conformable to the thoughts of the audience. But it is to be concluded that this passion works not now amongst the French so strongly as the other two did amongst the ancients. Amongst us, who have a stronger genius for writing, the operations from the writing are much stronger, for the raising of Shakespeare's passions is more from the excellency of the words and thoughts than the justness of the occasion; and if he has been able to pick single occasions, he has never founded the whole reasonably; yet by the genius of poetry in writing, he has succeeded.

Tethys: the consort of Oceanus, parent of the rivers of the world and of the ocean nymphs.
Erigone: daughter of Icarius, who hanged herself through grief for her father's death and became the constellation Virgo.
her mother's: Demeter (Ceres) wished to recover her lost daughter Persephone (Proserpine).
Mr. Garrick: David Garrick (1717–79), the greatest actor of his day, and friend of Johnson.
Rapin: René Rapin (1621–87), French Jesuit, critic, and author of *De Hortis*.

Rapin attributes more to the *dictio*, that is, to the words and discourse of a tragedy, than Aristotle has done, who places them in the last rank of beauties—perhaps only last in order, because they are the last product of the design, of the disposition or connection of its parts: of the characters, of the manners of those characters, and of the thoughts proceeding from those manners. Rapin's words are remarkable: 'Tis not the admirable intrigue, the surprising events, and extraordinary incidents, that make the beauty of a tragedy; 'tis the discourses when they are natural and passionate; so are Shakespeare's.

The parts of a poem, tragic or heroic, are,

1. The fable itself.
2. The order or manner of its contrivance in relation of the parts to the whole.
3. The manners, or decency of the characters in speaking or acting what is proper for them, and proper to be shown by the poet.
4. The thoughts which express the manners.
5. The words which express those thoughts.

In the last of these, Homer excels Virgil, Virgil all other ancient poets, and Shakespeare all modern poets.

For the second of these, the order, the meaning is that a fable ought to have a beginning, middle, and an end, all just and natural; so that that part, e.g. which is the middle, could not naturally be the beginning or end, and so of the rest; all depend on one another, like the links of a curious chain. If terror and pity are only to be raised, certainly this author follows Aristotle's rules, and Sophocles' and Euripides's example; but joy may be raised too, and that doubly, either by seeing a wicked man punished, or a good man at last fortunate; or perhaps indignation, to see wickedness prosperous and goodness depressed; both these may be profitable to the end of tragedy, reformation of manners, but the last improperly, only as it begets pity in the audience—though Aristotle, I confess, places tragedies of this kind in the second form.

He who undertakes to answer this excellent critique of Mr. Rymer in behalf of our English poets against the Greek, ought to do it in this manner. Either by yielding to him the greatest part of what he contends for, which consists in this, that the μῦθος, i.e. the design and conduct of it, is more conducing in the Greeks to those ends of tragedy which Aristotle and he propose, namely, to cause terror and pity; yet the granting this does not set the Greeks above the English poets.

But the answerer ought to prove two things: first, that the fable is not the greatest masterpiece of a tragedy, though it be the foundation of it.

Secondly, that other ends as suitable to the nature of tragedy may be found in the English which were not in the Greek.

Aristotle places the fable first, not *quoad dignitatem, sed quoad fundamentum*; for a fable, never so movingly contrived to those ends of his, pity and terror, will operate nothing on our affections except the characters, manners, thoughts and words are suitable.

---

quoad dignitatem: 'on account of its merit, but on account of its importance as the foundation'.

So that it remains for Mr. Rymer to prove that in all those, or the greatest part of them, we are inferior to Sophocles and Euripides: and this he has offered at in some measure, but, I think, a little partially to the ancients.

For the fable itself, 'tis in the English more adorned with episodes, and larger than in the Greek poets; consequently more diverting. For, if the action be but one, and that plain, without any counter-turn of design or episode, i.e. underplot, how can it be so pleasing as the English, which have both underplot and a turned design, which keeps the audience in expectation of the catastrophe? whereas in the Greek poets we see through the whole design at first.

For the characters, they are neither so many nor as various in Sophocles and Euripides as in Shakespeare and Fletcher; only they are more adapted to those ends of tragedy which Aristotle commends to us, pity and terror.

The manners flow from the characters, and consequently must partake of their advantages and disadvantages.

The thoughts and words, which are the fourth and fifth beauties of tragedy, are certainly more noble and more poetical in the English than in the Greek; which must be proved by comparing them somewhat more equitably than Mr. Rymer has done.

After all, we need not yield that the English way is less conducing to move pity and terror, because they often show virtue oppressed and vice punished; where they do not both, or either, they are not to be defended.

And if we should grant that the Greeks performed this better, perhaps it may admit of dispute whether pity and terror are either the prime, or at least the only ends of tragedy.

'Tis not enough that Aristotle has said so, for Aristotle drew his models of tragedy from Sophocles and Euripides, and if he had seen ours, might have changed his mind. And chiefly we have to say (what I hinted on pity and terror, in the last paragraph save one) that the punishment of vice and reward of virtue are the most adequate ends of tragedy because most conducing to good example of life. Now pity is not so easily raised for a criminal—and the ancient tragedy always represents its chief person such—as it is for an innocent man; and the suffering of innocence and punishment of the offender is of the nature of English tragedy; contrarily, in the Greek, innocence is unhappy often, and the offender escapes. Then we are not touched with the sufferings of any sort of men so much as of lovers; and this was almost unknown to the ancients: so that they neither administered poetical justice, of which Mr. Rymer boasts, so well as we; neither knew they the best commonplace of pity, which is love.

He therefore unjustly blames us for not building on what the ancients left us, for it seems, upon consideration of the premises, that we have wholly finished what they began.

My judgement on this piece is this, that it is extremely learned, but that the author of it is better read in the Greek than in the English poets; that all writers ought to study this critique as the best account I have ever seen of the ancients; that the model of tragedy he has here given is excellent, and extreme correct; but that it is not the only model of all tragedy because it is too much circumscribed in plot, characters, etc.; and lastly, that we may be taught here justly to admire and imitate the ancients, without giving them the preference with this author in prejudice to our own country.

Want of method in this excellent treatise makes the thoughts of the author sometimes obscure.

His meaning, that pity and terror are to be moved, is that they are to be moved as the means conducing to the ends of tragedy, which are pleasure and instruction.

And these two ends may be thus distinguished. The chief end of the poet is to please, for his immediate reputation depends on it.

The great end of the poem is to instruct, which is performed by making pleasure the vehicle of that instruction; for poesy is an art, and all arts are made to profit. *Rapin.*

The pity which the poet is to labour for is for the criminal, not for those or him whom he has murdered, or who have been the occasion of the tragedy. The terror is likewise in the punishment of the same criminal, who, if he be represented too great an offender, will not be pitied; if altogether innocent, his punishment will be unjust.

Another obscurity is where he says Sophocles perfected tragedy by introducing the third actor—that is, he meant, three kinds of action: one company singing, or another playing on the music, a third dancing.

To make a true judgement in this competition betwixt the Greek poets and the English in tragedy:

Consider, first, how Aristotle has defined a tragedy. Secondly, what he assigns the end of it to be. Thirdly, what he thinks the beauties of it. Fourthly, the means to attain the end proposed.

Compare the Greek and English tragic poets justly, and without partiality, according to those rules.

Then, secondly, consider whether Aristotle has made a just definition of tragedy: of its parts, of its ends, and of its beauties; and whether he, having not seen any others but those of Sophocles, Euripides, etc., had or truly could determine what all the excellences of tragedy are, and wherein they consist.

Next show in what ancient tragedy was deficient: for example, in the narrowness of its plots, and fewness of persons; and try whether that be not a fault in the Greek poets; and whether their excellency was so great, when the variety was visibly so little; or whether what they did was not very easy to do.

Then make a judgement on what the English have added to their beauties, as, for example, not only more plot, but also new passions, as, namely, that of love, scarce touched on by the ancients, except in this one example of *Phaedra*, cited by Mr. Rymer; and in that how short they were of Fletcher!

Prove also that love, being an heroic passion, is fit for tragedy, which cannot be denied because of the example alleged of *Phaedra*; and how far Shakespeare has outdone them in friendship, etc.

To return to the beginning of this inquiry, consider if pity and terror be enough for tragedy to move; and I believe upon a true definition of tragedy it will be found that its work extends farther, and that it is to reform manners by a delightful representation of human life in great persons, by way of dialogue. If this be true, then not only pity and terror are to be moved, as the only means to bring us to virtue, but generally love to virtue and hatred to vice, by showing the rewards of one, and punishments of the other; at least, by rendering virtue always amiable, though it be shown unfortunate, and vice detestable, though it be shown triumphant.

If, then, the encouragement of virtue and discouragement of vice be the proper ends of poetry in tragedy, pity and terror, though good means, are not the only. For all the passions, in their turns, are to be set in a ferment: as joy, anger, love, fear are to be used as the poet's commonplaces; and a general concernment for the principal actors is to be raised by making them appear such in their characters, their words, and actions, as will interest the audience in their fortunes.

And if, after all, in a larger sense, pity comprehends this concernment for the good, and terror includes detestation for the bad, then let us consider whether the English have not answered this end of tragedy as well as the ancients, or perhaps better.

And here Mr. Rymer's objections against these plays are to be impartially weighed, that we may see whether they are of weight enough to turn the balance against our countrymen.

'Tis evident those plays which he arraigns, have moved both those passions in a high degree upon the stage.

To give the glory of this away from the poet, and to place it upon the actors, seems unjust.

One reason is, because whatever actors they have found, the event has been the same; that is, the same passions have been always moved; which shows that there is something of force and merit in the plays themselves conducing to the design of raising these two passions; and suppose them ever to have been excellently acted, yet action only adds grace, vigour, and more life upon the stage, but cannot give it wholly where it is not first. But secondly, I dare appeal to those who have never seen them acted if they have not found these two passions move within them; and if the general voice will carry it, Mr. Rymer's prejudice will take off his single testimony.

This, being matter of fact, is reasonably to be established by this appeal; as if one man says 'tis night, the rest of the world conclude it to be day; there needs no farther argument against him that it is so.

If he urge that the general taste is depraved, his arguments to prove this can at best but evince that our poets took not the best way to raise those passions; but experience proves against him, that these means, which they have used, have been successful and have produced them.

And one reason of that success is, in my opinion, this, that Shakespeare and Fletcher have written to the genius of the age and nation in which they lived; for though nature, as he objects, is the same in all places, and reason too the same, yet the climate, the age, the disposition of the people to whom a poet writes, may be so different that what pleased the Greeks would not satisfy an English audience.

And if they proceeded upon a foundation of truer reason to please the Athenians than Shakespeare and Fletcher to please the English, it only shows that the Athenians were a more judicious people; but the poet's business is certainly to please the audience.

Whether our English audience have been pleased hitherto with acorns, as he calls it, or with bread, is the next question; that is, whether the means which Shakespeare and Fletcher have used in their plays to raise those passions before named, be better applied to the ends by the Greek poets than by them. And perhaps we shall not grant him this wholly; let it be granted that a writer is not to run down with the stream, or to please the people by their own usual methods, but rather to reform their judgements, it still remains to prove that our theatre needs this total reformation.

The faults which he has found in their designs are rather wittily aggravated in many places than reasonably urged, and as much may be returned on the Greeks by one who were as witty as himself.

2. They destroy not, if they are granted, the foundation of the fabric, only take away from the beauty of the symmetry; for example, the faults in the character of the *King and No King* are not as he makes them, such as render him detestable, but only imperfections which accompany human nature, and are for the most part excused by the violence of his love, so that they destroy not our pity or concernment for him; this answer may be applied to most of his objections of that kind.

And Rollo committing many murders, when he is answerable but for one, is too severely arraigned by him; for it adds to our horror and detestation of the criminal; and poetic justice is not neglected neither, for we stab him in our minds for every offence which he commits—and the point which the poet is to gain on the audience is not so much in the death of an offender as the raising an horror of his crimes.

That the criminal should neither be wholly guilty, nor wholly innocent, but so participating of both as to move both pity and terror, is certainly a good rule, but not perpetually to be observed; for that were to make all tragedies too much alike, which objection he foresaw, but has not fully answered.

To conclude, therefore; if the plays of the ancients are more correctly plotted, ours are more beautifully written. And if we can raise passions as high on worse foundations, it shows our genius in tragedy is greater; for, in all other parts of it, the English have manifestly excelled them.

The original of the following letter is preserved in the library at Lambeth, and was kindly imparted to the public by the reverend Dr. Vyse.

Copy of an original Letter from John Dryden, Esq. to his sons in Italy, from a MS. in the Lambeth Library, marked No 933. p. 56.

>   (*Superscribed*)

>   Al Illustrissimo Sig^{re}
>   Carlo Dryden Camariere
>   d'Honore A.S.S.
>   In Roma.

Franca per Mantova.

>   Sept. the 3d, our style.

Dear Sons,

Being now at Sir William Bowyer's in the country, I cannot write at large because I find myself somewhat indisposed with a cold, and am thick of hearing, rather worse

---

Vyse: Dr. William Vyse (1742–1816), rector of Lambeth.
Being now: Dryden: Letters, pp. 92–4 and nn. (pp. 178–9).
Sir William Bowyer: (1639–1722) of Denham Court, Bucks.

than I was in town. I am glad to find, by your letter of July
26th, your style, that you are both in health; but wonder
you should think me so negligent as to forget to give you an
account of the ship in which your parcel is to come. I have
written to you two or three letters concerning it, which I
have sent by safe hands, as I told you, and doubt not but
you have them before this can arrive to you. Being out of
town, I have forgotten the ship's name, which your mother
will inquire, and put it into her letter, which is joined with
mine. But the master's name I remember: he is called Mr.
Ralph Thorp; the ship is bound to Leghorn, consigned to
Mr. Peter and Mr. Tho. Ball, merchants. I am of your
opinion, that by Tonson's means almost all our letters have
miscarried for this last year. But, however, he has missed of
his design in the Dedication, though he had prepared the
book for it; for in every figure of Aeneas he has caused
him to be drawn like King William, with a hooked nose.
After my return to town, I intend to alter a play of Sir
Robert Howard's, written long since, and lately put by him
into my hands: 'tis called *The Conquest of China by the
Tartars*. It will cost me six weeks' study, with the probable
benefit of £100. In the meantime I am writing a song for
St. Cecilia's Feast, who, you know, is the patroness of
music. This is troublesome, and no way beneficial; but I
could not deny the Stewards of the Feast, who came in a
body to me to desire that kindness, one of them being Mr.
Bridgman, whose parents are your mother's friends. I hope
to send you thirty guineas between Michaelmas and
Christmas, of which I will give you an account when I come
to town. I remember the counsel you give me in your
letter; but dissembling, though lawful in some cases, is not
my talent; yet, for your sake, I will struggle with the plain
openness of my nature, and keep in my just resentments
against that degenerate order. In the meantime, I flatter
not myself with any manner of hopes, but do my duty, and
suffer for God's sake, being assured, beforehand, never to
be rewarded, though the times should alter. Towards the
latter end of this month, September, Charles will begin to
recover his perfect health, according to his nativity which,
casting it myself, I am sure is true, and all things hitherto
have happened accordingly to the very time that I predicted
them; I hope at the same time to recover more health,
according to my age. Remember me to poor Harry, whose
prayers I earnestly desire. My *Virgil* succeeds in the world
beyond its desert or my expectation. You know the profits
might have been more; but neither my conscience nor my
honour would suffer me to take them; but I never can
repent of my constancy, since I am thoroughly persuaded

he has missed: cf. *Lives of the Poets*, ed. Hill, i. 480 n. 2.

of the justice of the cause for which I suffer. It has pleased God to raise up many friends to me amongst my enemies, though they who ought to have been my friends are negligent of me. I am called to dinner, and cannot go on with this letter, which I desire you to excuse; and am

Your most affectionate father,

JOHN DRYDEN

POPE

Alexander Pope was born in London, May 22, 1688,[n] of parents whose rank or station was never ascertained; we are informed that they were of 'gentle blood', that his father was of a family of which the Earl of Downe was the head, and that his mother was the daughter of William Turner, Esquire, of York, who had likewise three sons, one of whom had the honour of being killed, and the other of dying, in the service of Charles I; the third was made a general officer in Spain, from whom the sister inherited what sequestrations and forfeitures had left in the family.[n]

This, and this only, is told by Pope, who is more willing, as I have heard observed, to show what his father was not than what he was. It is allowed that he grew rich by trade, but whether in a shop or on the Exchange was never discovered till Mr. Tyers told, on the authority of Mrs. Rackett, that he was a linen-draper in the Strand. Both parents were Papists.

Pope was from his birth of a constitution tender and delicate, but is said to have shown remarkable gentleness and sweetness of disposition. The weakness of his body continued through his life, but the mildness of his mind perhaps ended with his childhood. His voice, when he was young, was so pleasing that he was called in fondness the 'little Nightingale'.[n]

Being not sent early to school, he was taught to read by an aunt, and when he was seven or eight years old became a lover of books. He first learned to write by imitating printed books—a species of penmanship in which he retained great excellence through his whole life, though his ordinary hand was not elegant.

When he was about eight, he was placed in Hampshire under Taverner, a Romish priest, who by a method very rarely practised taught him the Greek and Latin rudiments together. He was now first regularly initiated in poetry by the perusal of Ogilby's *Homer*, and Sandys's *Ovid*; Ogilby's assistance he never repaid with any

'*gentle blood*': *Epistle to Arbuthnot*, l. 388.
his father: Alexander Pope senior (1646–1717).
the Earl of Downe: William Pope (1573–1631), 1st Earl, was not Pope's ancestor.
his mother: Editha Pope (*née* Turner) (1642–1733).
Mr. Tyers: Thomas Tyers (1726–87), writer; see his *Historical Rhapsody on Mr. Pope* (1782), p. 5. (This fact was added in 1783.)
Mrs. Rackett: Magdalen Rackett, Pope's half-sister.
is said to have shown: Spence, § 8; Ruffhead, pp. 10–11.
an aunt: probably Elizabeth Turner (1636–1710).
Taverner: John Banister (alias 'Taverner') (d. 1745), master of Twyford School.

praise, but of Sandys he declared, in his notes to the *Iliad*, that English poetry owed much of its present beauty to his translations. Sandys very rarely attempted original composition.

From the care of Taverner, under whom his proficiency was considerable, he was removed to a school at Twyford near Winchester, and again to another school about Hyde Park Corner, from which he used sometimes to stroll to the playhouse, and was so delighted with theatrical exhibitions that he formed a kind of play from Ogilby's *Iliad*, with some verses of his own intermixed, which he persuaded his schoolfellows to act with the addition of his master's gardener, who personated Ajax.

At the two last schools he used to represent himself as having lost part of what Taverner had taught him, and on his master at Twyford he had already exercised his poetry in a lampoon. Yet under those masters he translated more than a fourth part of the *Metamorphoses*. If he kept the same proportion in his other exercises, it cannot be thought that his loss was great.

He tells of himself in his poems that 'he lisped in numbers', and used to say that he could not remember the time when he began to make verses. In the style of fiction it might have been said of him as of Pindar, that when he lay in his cradle 'the bees swarmed about his mouth'.

About the time of the Revolution his father, who was undoubtedly disappointed by the sudden blast of popish prosperity, quitted his trade and retired to Binfield in Windsor Forest[n] with about £20,000, for which, being conscientiously determined not to entrust it to the government, he found no better use than that of locking it up in a chest, and taking from it what his expenses required; and his life was long enough to consume a great part of it before his son came to the inheritance.

To Binfield Pope was called by his father when he was about twelve years old, and there he had for a few months the assistance of one Deane, another priest, of whom he learned only to construe a little of Tully's *Offices*. How Mr. Deane could spend with a boy who

of Sandys he declared: *Pope: Poems*, viii. 463.
had already exercised: Cf. Spence §§ 14 n., 19, 20 n.
'*he lisped in numbers*': *Epistle to Arbuthnot*, l. 128.
used to say: Spence, § 32; Warburton, iv. 17 n.
'*the bees*': Pausanias, *Boeotia*, xxiii. 2; Antipater of Sidon, *Anthologia Graeca*, xvi. 305.
one Deane: William Mannock (1677–1749), not Thomas Deane (1651–1735), may have been the priest under whom Pope studied at Binfield.
Tully's: Cicero (106–43 B.C.), great Roman orator and statesman.

had translated so much of Ovid some months over a small part of Tully's *Offices*, it is now vain to inquire.

Of a youth so successfully employed, and so conspicuously improved, a minute account must be naturally desired, but curiosity must be contented with confused, imperfect, and sometimes improbable intelligence. Pope, finding little advantage from external help, resolved thenceforward to direct himself, and at twelve formed a plan of study which he completed with little other incitement than the desire of excellence.

His primary and principal purpose was to be a poet, with which his father accidentally concurred by proposing subjects, and obliging him to correct his performances by many revisals, after which the old gentleman, when he was satisfied, would say, 'These are good rhymes'.

In his perusal of the English poets he soon distinguished the versification of Dryden, which he considered as the model to be studied, and was impressed with such veneration of his instructor that he persuaded some friends to take him to the coffee-house which Dryden frequented, and pleased himself with having seen him.

Dryden died May 1, 1701, some days before Pope was twelve; so early must he therefore have felt the power of harmony and the zeal of genius. Who does not wish that Dryden could have known the value of the homage that was paid him, and foreseen the greatness of his young admirer?

The earliest of Pope's productions is his 'Ode on Solitude', written before he was twelve,[n] in which there is nothing more than other forward boys have attained, and which is not equal to Cowley's performances at the same age.

His time was now spent wholly in reading and writing. As he read the classics, he amused himself with translating them, and at fourteen made a version of the first book of the *Thebais* which, with some revision, he afterwards published.[n] He must have been at this time, if he had no help, a considerable proficient in the Latin tongue.

By Dryden's *Fables*, which had then been not long published and were much in the hands of poetical readers, he was tempted to try his own skill in giving Chaucer a more fashionable appearance, and put 'January and May' and the 'Prologue of the Wife of Bath' into modern English. He translated likewise the 'Epistle of Sappho to

'These are': Warburton, iv. 18 n. Cf. Spence, § 11.
which he considered: Warburton, iv. 18 n.; Spence, § 55.
May 1, 1701: see below, p. 357.

Phaon' from Ovid to complete the version which was before imperfect, and wrote some other small pieces which he afterwards
printed.

He sometimes imitated the English poets, and professed to have
written at fourteen his poem upon 'Silence', after Rochester's
'Nothing'. He had now formed his versification, and in the smoothness of his numbers surpassed his original, but this is a small part of
his praise; he discovers such acquaintance both with human life and
public affairs as is not easily conceived to have been attainable by a
boy of fourteen in Windsor Forest.

Next year he was desirous of opening to himself new sources of
knowledge by making himself acquainted with modern languages,
and removed for a time to London that he might study French and
Italian, which, as he desired nothing more than to read them, were by
diligent application soon dispatched. Of Italian learning he does not
appear to have ever made much use in his subsequent studies.

He then returned to Binfield, and delighted himself with his own
poetry. He tried all styles and many subjects. He wrote a comedy, a
tragedy, an epic poem, with panegyrics on all the princes of Europe,
and, as he confesses, 'thought himself the greatest genius that ever
was'. Self-confidence is the first requisite to great undertakings; he,
indeed, who forms his opinion of himself in solitude, without
knowing the powers of other men, is very liable to error, but it was
the felicity of Pope to rate himself at his real value.

Most of his puerile productions were, by his maturer judgement,
afterwards destroyed: 'Alcander' the epic poem, was burnt by the
persuasion of Atterbury. The tragedy was founded on the legend of
St. Genevieve. Of the comedy there is no account.

Concerning his studies it is related that he translated Tully *On Old
Age*, and that, besides his books of poetry and criticism, he read
Temple's *Essays* and Locke *On Human Understanding*. His reading,
though his favourite authors are not known, appears to have been
sufficiently extensive and multifarious, for his early pieces show with
sufficient evidence his knowledge of books.

He that is pleased with himself easily imagines that he shall please

which was before imperfect: see above, p. 139.
professed to have written: *Pope: Poems*, vi. 19.
'thought himself': Warburton, i. *xi.
St. Genevieve: (c. 422–c. 500), patron saint of Paris.
it is related: Spence, §§ 42, 48.
Temple's: Sir William Temple (1628–99), statesman and author.
Locke: John Locke (1632–1704), philosopher.

others. Sir William Trumbull, who had been ambassador at Constantinople and Secretary of State, when he retired from business fixed his residence in the neighbourhood of Binfield. Pope, not yet sixteen, was introduced to the statesman of sixty, and so distinguished himself that their interviews ended in friendship and correspondence. Pope was, through his whole life, ambitious of splendid acquaintance, and he seems to have wanted neither diligence nor success in attracting the notice of the great, for from his first entrance into the world, and his entrance was very early, he was admitted to familiarity with those whose rank or station made them most conspicuous.

From the age of sixteen the life of Pope as an author may be properly computed. He now wrote his *Pastorals*, which were shown to the poets and critics of that time; as they well deserved, they were read with admiration, and many praises were bestowed upon them and upon the Preface, which is both elegant and learned in a high degree; they were, however, not published till five years afterwards.

Cowley, Milton and Pope are distinguished among the English poets by the early exertion of their powers, but the works of Cowley alone were published in his childhood, and therefore of him only can it be certain that his puerile performances received no improvement from his maturer studies.

At this time began his acquaintance with Wycherley, a man who seems to have had among his contemporaries his full share of reputation, to have been esteemed without virtue, and caressed without good humour. Pope was proud of his notice; Wycherley wrote verses in his praise which he was charged by Dennis with writing to himself, and they agreed for a while to flatter one another. It is pleasant to remark how soon Pope learned the cant of an author and began to treat critics with contempt, though he had yet suffered nothing from them.

But the fondness of Wycherley was too violent to last. His esteem of Pope was such that he submitted some poems to his revision, and when Pope, perhaps proud of such confidence, was sufficiently bold in his criticisms and liberal in his alterations, the old scribbler was angry to see his pages defaced, and felt more pain from the detection than content from the amendment of his faults. They parted; but

Sir William Trumbull: (1639–1716).

among his contemporaries: cf. *Dryden*: *Essays*, ii. 200.

verses in his praise: 'To my friend Mr. Pope, on his Pastorals'. Cf. *Dennis*, i. 417; ii. 356.

began to treat: cf. *Pope: Corr.* i. 2 and n. 4. (Pope to Wycherley, 26 Dec. 1704).

Pope always considered him with kindness, and visited him a little time before he died.

Another of his early correspondents was Mr. Cromwell, of whom I have learned nothing particular but that he used to ride a-hunting in a tie-wig. He was fond, and perhaps vain, of amusing himself with poetry and criticism, and sometimes sent his performances to Pope, who did not forbear such remarks as were now and then unwelcome. Pope, in his turn, put the juvenile version of Statius into his hands for correction.

Their correspondence afforded the public its first knowledge of Pope's epistolary powers, for his letters were given by Cromwell to one Mrs. Thomas, and she many years afterwards sold them to Curll, who inserted them in a volume of his *Miscellanies*.

Walsh, a name yet preserved among the minor poets, was one of his first encouragers. His regard was gained by the *Pastorals*, and from him Pope received the counsel by which he seems to have regulated his studies. Walsh advised him to correctness which, as he told him, the English poets had hitherto neglected, and which therefore was left to him as a basis of fame, and being delighted with rural poems, recommended to him to write a pastoral comedy like those which are read so eagerly in Italy—a design which Pope probably did not approve as he did not follow it.

Pope had now declared himself a poet, and thinking himself entitled to poetical conversation, began at seventeen to frequent Will's, a coffee-house on the north side of Russell Street in Covent Garden where the wits of that time used to assemble, and where Dryden had, when he lived, been accustomed to preside.

During this period of his life he was indefatigably diligent and insatiably curious; wanting health for violent, and money for expensive pleasures, and having certainly excited in himself very strong desires of intellectual eminence, he spent much of his time over his books; but he read only to store his mind with facts and images, seizing all that his authors presented with undistinguishing voracity and with an appetite for knowledge too eager to be nice. In a mind like

Mr. Cromwell: Henry Cromwell (1659?–1728), critic and man about town. Cf. John Gay, 'Mr. Pope's Welcome from Greece', l. 136.

tie-wig: 'a wig having the hair gathered together behind and tied with a knot of ribbon' (*OED*).

Mrs. Thomas: Elizabeth Thomas (1677–1731), poetaster.

Curll: Edmund Curll (1675–1747), bookseller.

Walsh: William Walsh (1663–1708), poet and critic.

recommended to him: Pope: *Corr*. i. 18 (Walsh to Pope, 24 June 1706). Cf. ibid. p. 19.

his, however, all the faculties were at once involuntarily improving. Judgement is forced upon us by experience. He that reads many books must compare one opinion or one style with another, and when he compares must necessarily distinguish, reject and prefer. But the account given by himself of his studies was that from fourteen to twenty he read only for amusement, from twenty to twenty-seven for improvement and instruction, that in the first part of this time he desired only to know, and in the second he endeavoured to judge.

The *Pastorals*, which had been for some time handed about among poets and critics, were at last printed (1709) in Tonson's *Miscellany*, in a volume which began with the pastorals of Philips and ended with those of Pope.

The same year was written the *Essay on Criticism*, a work which displays such extent of comprehension, such nicety of distinction, such acquaintance with mankind, and such knowledge both of ancient and modern learning, as are not often attained by the maturest age and longest experience. It was published about two years afterwards, and being praised by Addison in the *Spectator* with sufficient liberality, met with so much favour as enraged Dennis, 'who', he says, 'found himself attacked, without any manner of provocation on his side, and attacked in his person, instead of his writings, by one who was wholly a stranger to him, at a time when all the world knew he was persecuted by fortune; and not only saw that this was attempted in a clandestine manner, with the utmost falsehood and calumny, but found that all this was done by a little affected hypocrite who had nothing in his mouth at the same time but truth, candour, friendship, good-nature, humanity and magnanimity.'

How the attack was clandestine is not easily perceived, nor how his person is depreciated;[n] but he seems to have known something of Pope's character, in whom may be discovered an appetite to talk too frequently of his own virtues.

The pamphlet is such as rage might be expected to dictate. He supposes himself to be asked two questions: whether the *Essay* will succeed, and who or what is the author.

Its success he admits to be secured by the false opinions then prevalent; the author he concludes to be 'young and raw'.

First, because he discovers a sufficiency beyond his little ability, and hath rashly undertaken a task infinitely above his force. Secondly, while this

the account: Warburton, iv. 211 n. Cf. Spence, §§ 24, 42, 578.
Philips: Ambrose Philips (1674–1749), poet.
being praised by Addison: *Spectator* 253.
'*who*', *he says*: Dennis, i. 396–7.   *Its success*: ibid. i. 397–9, 401–2.

little author struts and affects the dictatorian air, he plainly shows that at the same time he is under the rod, and while he pretends to give law to others is a pedantic slave to authority and opinion. Thirdly, he hath, like schoolboys, borrowed both from living and dead. Fourthly, he knows not his own mind, and frequently contradicts himself. Fifthly, he is almost perpetually in the wrong.

All these positions he attempts to prove by quotations and remarks, but his desire to do mischief is greater than his power. He has, however, justly criticised some passages. In these lines,

> There are whom heaven has blessed with store of wit,
> Yet want as much again to manage it;
> For wit and judgement ever are at strife—

it is apparent that 'wit' has two meanings, and that what is wanted, though called wit, is truly judgement. So far Dennis is undoubtedly right, but not content with argument, he will have a little mirth, and triumphs over the first couplet in terms too elegant to be forgotten. 'By the way, what rare numbers are here! Would not one swear that this youngster had espoused some antiquated muse, who had sued out a divorce on account of impotence from some superannuated sinner, and having been p–xed by her former spouse, has got the gout in her decrepit age, which makes her hobble so damnably.' This was the man who would reform a nation sinking into barbarity.

In another place Pope himself allowed that Dennis had detected one of those blunders which are called 'bulls'. The first edition had this line:

> What is this wit—
> Where wanted, scorned; and envied where acquired?

'How', says the critic, 'can wit be *scorned* where it is not? Is not this a figure frequently employed in Hibernian land? The person that wants this wit may indeed be scorned, but the scorn shows the honour which the contemner has for wit.' Of this remark Pope made the proper use by correcting the passage.

I have preserved, I think, all that is reasonable in Dennis's criticism; it remains that justice be done to his delicacy. 'For his acquaintance (says Dennis) he names Mr. Walsh, who had by no means the qualification which this author reckons absolutely necessary to a

There are whom: ll. 80–2.   'By the way': *Dennis*. i. 404.
Pope himself allowed: *Pope: Corr*. i. 121 (Pope to Caryll, 25 June 1711).
'*How*', *says the critic*: *Dennis* i. 411.
'*For his acquaintance*': ibid. i. 416–17.

critic, it being very certain that he was, like this Essayer, a very indifferent poet; he loved to be well-dressed; and I remember a little young gentleman whom Mr. Walsh used to take into his company, as a double foil to his person and capacity. . . . Inquire between Sunninghill and Oakingham for a young, short, squab gentleman, the very bow of the God of Love, and tell me whether he be a proper author to make personal reflections? . . . He may extol the ancients, but he has reason to thank the gods that he was born a modern; for had he been born of Grecian parents, and his father consequently had by law had the absolute disposal of him, his life had been no longer than that of one of his poems, the life of half a day. . . . Let the person of a gentleman of his parts be never so contemptible, his inward man is ten times more ridiculous, it being impossible that his outward form, though it be that of downright monkey, should differ so much from human shape as his unthinking immaterial part does from human understanding.' Thus began the hostility between Pope and Dennis which, though it was suspended for a short time, never was appeased. Pope seems at first to have attacked him wantonly; but though he always professed to despise him, he discovers, by mentioning him very often, that he felt his force or his venom.

Of this *Essay* Pope declared that he did not expect the sale to be quick because 'not one gentleman in sixty, even of liberal education, could understand it'. The gentlemen and the education of that time seem to have been of a lower character than they are of this. He mentioned a thousand copies as a numerous impression.

Dennis was not his only censurer: the zealous Papists thought the monks treated with too much contempt and Erasmus too studiously praised, but to these objections he had not much regard.[n]

The *Essay* has been translated into French by Hamilton, author of the *Comte de Grammont*, whose version was never printed, by Robothon, secretary to the King for Hanover, and by Resnel, and commented by Dr. Warburton, who has discovered in it such order

Pope declared: *Pope: Corr*. i. 128 (Pope to Caryll, 19 July 1711).

Hamilton: Anthony Hamilton (1646?–1720), privy councillor and general, author of *Memoires du Comte de Grammont* [Hamilton's brother-in-law] (1713). Cf. *Pope: Corr*. i. 192–3, esp. n. 2 (Pope to Hamilton, 10 Oct. 1713).

Robothon: John Robothon (or Robethon) (d. 1722), Huguenot refugee who came to England *c*. 1689 and was later secretary to George I.

Resnel: Jean-François du Bellay Du Resnel (1692–1761), abbé and man of letters, whose translation of Pope's *Essay* appeared in 1730.

Dr. Warburton: William Warburton (1698–1779), Bishop of Gloucester, later friend and editor of Pope. Cf. Warburton, i. 137–8 n.; *Spectator* 253; *Richardsoniana* (1776), p. 264.

and connection as was not perceived by Addison nor, as is said, intended by the author.

Almost every poem consisting of precepts is so far arbitrary and immethodical that many of the paragraphs may change places with no apparent inconvenience, for of two or more positions depending upon some remote and general principle, there is seldom any cogent reason why one should precede the other. But for the order in which they stand, whatever it be, a little ingenuity may easily give a reason. 'It is possible', says Hooker, 'that by long circumduction, from any one truth all truth may be inferred.' Of all homogeneous truths at least, of all truths respecting the same general end, in whatever series they may be produced, a concatenation by intermediate ideas may be formed such as, when it is once shown, shall appear natural; but if this order be reversed, another mode of connection equally specious may be found or made. Aristotle is praised for naming Fortitude first of the cardinal virtues as that without which no other virtue can steadily be practised, but he might with equal propriety have placed Prudence and Justice before it, since without Prudence Fortitude is mad, without Justice it is mischievous.

As the end of method is perspicuity, that series is sufficiently regular that avoids obscurity; and where there is no obscurity it will not be difficult to discover method.

In the *Spectator* was published the 'Messiah', which he first submitted to the perusal of Steele, and corrected in compliance with his criticisms.

It is reasonable to infer from his letters that the verses on the 'Unfortunate Lady' were written about the time when his *Essay* was published.[n] The lady's name and adventures I have sought with fruitless inquiry.

I can therefore tell no more than I have learned from Mr. Ruffhead, who writes with the confidence of one who could trust his information.[n] She was a woman of eminent rank and large fortune, the ward of an uncle who, having given her a proper education, expected like other guardians that she should make at least an equal

---

Hooker: Richard Hooker (1554?–1600), theologian; see *The Laws of Ecclesiastical Polity*, II. i. 2.

circumduction: 'the action of leading round or about, a roundabout or circuitous course. *Obs.*' (*OED*).

for naming Fortitude: *Nicomachean Ethics*, iii. 6.

Steele: Sir Richard Steele (1672–1729), author and politician. Cf. *Spectator* 378; *Pope: Corr.* i. 146 (Steele to Pope, 1 June 1712).

Mr. Ruffhead: Owen Ruffhead (1723–69), miscellaneous writer; see his *Life of Alexander Pope* (1769), pp. 133–5.

match; and such he proposed to her, but found it rejected in favour of a young gentleman of inferior condition.

Having discovered the correspondence between the two lovers, and finding the young lady determined to abide by her own choice, he supposed that separation might do what can rarely be done by arguments, and sent her into a foreign country where she was obliged to converse only with those from whom her uncle had nothing to fear.

Her lover took care to repeat his vows, but his letters were intercepted and carried to her guardian, who directed her to be watched with still greater vigilance, till of this restraint she grew so impatient that she bribed a woman-servant to procure her a sword, which she directed to her heart.

From this account, given with evident intention to raise the lady's character, it does not appear that she had any claim to praise, nor much to compassion. She seems to have been impatient, violent and ungovernable. Her uncle's power could not have lasted long: the hour of liberty and choice would have come in time. But her desires were too hot for delay, and she liked self-murder better than suspense.

Nor is it discovered that the uncle, whoever he was, is with much justice delivered to posterity as a 'false guardian': he seems to have done only that for which a guardian is appointed—he endeavoured to direct his niece till she should be able to direct herself. Poetry has not often been worse employed than in dignifying the amorous fury of a raving girl.

Not long after he wrote *The Rape of the Lock*, the most airy, the most ingenious, and the most delightful of all his compositions, occasioned by a frolic of gallantry rather too familiar in which Lord Petre cut off a lock of Mrs. Arabella Fermor's hair. This, whether stealth or violence, was so much resented that the commerce of the two families, before very friendly, was interrupted. Mr. Caryll, a gentleman who, being secretary to King James's Queen, had followed

---

condition: 'position with reference to the grades of society; social position, estate, rank' (*OED*).   '*false guardian*': l. 29.

Lord Petre: Robert Petre (1690–1713), 7th Baron Petre.

Mrs. Arabella Fermor's: Arabella Fermor (1690?–1738). ('Mrs' was used of young, unmarried ladies since 'Miss' could have derogatory overtones; cf. *Life*, v. 185 n. 1.)

Mr. Caryll: John Caryll (1625–1711), titular Baron Caryll, secretary to Queen Mary of Modena (from 1681) and author of *Sir Salomon Single* (1671), was the uncle of John Caryll (1667–1736), the friend who requested Pope to write the poem.

his mistress into France, and who being the author of *Sir Solomon Single*, a comedy, and some translations, was entitled to the notice of a wit, solicited Pope to endeavour a reconciliation by a ludicrous poem which might bring both the parties to a better temper. In compliance with Caryll's request, though his name was for a long time marked only by the first and last letter, C—l, a poem of two cantos was written (1711), as is said in a fortnight, and sent to the offended lady, who liked it well enough to show it, and with the usual process of literary transactions, the author, dreading a surreptitious edition, was forced to publish it.

The event is said to have been such as was desired—the pacification and diversion of all to whom it related, except Sir George Browne, who complained with some bitterness that in the character of Sir Plume he was made to talk nonsense. Whether all this be true I have some doubt, for at Paris a few years ago a niece of Mrs. Fermor, who presided in an English convent, mentioned Pope's work with very little gratitude rather as an insult than an honour, and she may be supposed to have inherited the opinion of her family.

At its first appearance it was termed by Addison *merum sal*. Pope, however, saw that it was capable of improvement, and having luckily contrived to borrow his machinery from the Rosicrucians, imparted the scheme with which his head was teeming to Addison, who told him that his work as it stood was 'a delicious little thing', and gave him no encouragement to retouch it.

This has been too hastily considered as an instance of Addison's jealousy, for as he could not guess the conduct of the new design, or the possibilities of pleasure comprised in a fiction of which there had been no examples, he might very reasonably and kindly persuade the author to acquiesce in his own prosperity, and forbear an attempt which he considered as an unnecessary hazard.

Addison's counsel was happily rejected. Pope foresaw the future efflorescence of imagery then budding in his mind, and resolved to spare no art or industry of cultivation. The soft luxuriance of his fancy was already shooting, and all the gay varieties of diction were ready at his hand to colour and embellish it.

His attempt was justified by its success. *The Rape of the Lock*

in a fortnight: *Pope: Poems*, ii. 144 n.; cf. Spence, § 107.
Sir George Browne: (d. 1730).
a niece: Mrs. Fermor (*fl.* 1775), Abbess of the Austin Nuns, Paris. Cf. *Life*, ii. 392–3 and n.
merum sal: pure wit; Warburton, iv. 26 n. Cf. Lucretius, *De Rerum Natura*, iv. 1162.
too hastily considered: *Essay on Pope*, pp. 155–6. Cf. Warburton iv. 26 n.

stands forward, in the classes of literature, as the most exquisite example of ludicrous poetry. Berkeley congratulated him upon the display of powers more truly poetical than he had shown before; with elegance of description and justness of precepts, he had now exhibited boundless fertility of invention.

He always considered the intermixture of the machinery with the action as his most successful exertion of poetical art. He indeed could never afterwards produce anything of such unexampled excellence. Those performances which strike with wonder are combinations of skilful genius with happy casualty, and it is not likely that any felicity, like the discovery of a new race of preternatural agents, should happen twice to the same man.

Of this poem the author was, I think, allowed to enjoy the praise for a long time without disturbance. Many years afterwards Dennis published some remarks upon it, with very little force, and with no effect, for the opinion of the public was already settled, and it was no longer at the mercy of criticism.

About this time he published *The Temple of Fame* which, as he tells Steele in their correspondence, he had written two years before,[n] that is, when he was only twenty-two years old, an early time of life for so much learning and so much observation as that work exhibits.

On this poem Dennis afterwards published some remarks, of which the most reasonable is that some of the lines represent 'motion' as exhibited by 'sculpture'.

Of the 'Epistle from Eloisa to Abelard' I do not know the date.[n] His first inclination to attempt a composition of that tender kind arose, as Mr. Savage told me, from his perusal of Prior's *Nut-brown Maid*. How much he has surpassed Prior's work it is not necessary to mention when perhaps it may be said with justice that he has excelled every composition of the same kind. The mixture of religious hope and resignation gives an elevation and dignity to disappointed love which images merely natural cannot bestow. The gloom of a convent strikes the imagination with far greater force than the solitude of a grove.

This piece was, however, not much his favourite in his latter years,[n] though I never heard upon what principle he slighted it.

Berkeley: George Berkeley (1685–1753), philosopher, Bishop of Cloyne. Cf. *Pope: Corr.* i. 221 (Berkeley to Pope, 1 May 1714).
some remarks upon it: *Remarks on Mr. Pope's Rape of the Lock* (1728).
the most reasonable: Dennis, ii. 142–3.
Mr. Savage: Richard Savage (1698–1743), poet.
Nut-brown Maid: *Henry and Emma, a Poem upon the Model of The Nut-brown Maid* (1709).

In the next year (1713) he published *Windsor Forest*, of which part was, as he relates, written at sixteen, about the same time as his *Pastorals*, and the latter part was added afterwards; where the addition begins we are not told. The lines relating to the Peace confess their own date. It is dedicated to Lord Lansdowne, who was then high in reputation and influence among the Tories, and it is said that the conclusion of the poem gave great pain to Addison both as a poet and a politician. Reports like this are often spread with boldness very disproportionate to their evidence. Why should Addison receive any particular disturbance from the last lines of *Windsor Forest*? If contrariety of opinion could poison a politician, he would not live a day; and as a poet, he must have felt Pope's force of genius much more from many other parts of his works.

The pain that Addison might feel it is not likely that he would confess, and it is certain that he so well suppressed his discontent that Pope now thought himself his favourite, for having been consulted in the revisal of *Cato*, he introduced it by a prologue, and when Dennis published his *Remarks* undertook not indeed to vindicate but to revenge his friend by a *Narrative of the Frenzy of John Dennis*.

There is reason to believe that Addison gave no encouragement to this disingenuous hostility, for, says Pope, in a letter to him, 'indeed your opinion, that 'tis entirely to be neglected, would be my own in my own case; but I felt more warmth here than I did when I first saw his book against myself (though indeed in two minutes it made me heartily merry).' Addison was not a man on whom such cant of sensibility could make much impression. He left the pamphlet to itself, having disowned it to Dennis, and perhaps did not think Pope to have deserved much by his officiousness.

This year was printed in the *Guardian* the ironical comparison between the *Pastorals* of Philips and Pope—a composition of artifice, criticism and literature to which nothing equal will easily be found. The superiority of Pope is so ingeniously dissembled, and the feeble lines of Philips so skilfully preferred, that Steele, being deceived, was

of which part was: *Pope: Poems*, i. 148 n. Cf. ibid. i. 175 n.

lines relating to the Peace: ll. 355 ff.

Lord Lansdowne: George Granville (or Grenville) (1666–1735), Baron Lansdowne, poet and dramatist, who in 1710 became the Tory Secretary-at-War.

it is said: *Essay on Pope*, pp. 29–30.

his Remarks: *Remarks upon Cato, a Tragedy* (1713).

'indeed your opinion': *Pope: Corr.* i. 183 (Pope to Addison, 30 July 1713— fabricated from Pope to Caryll, 19 Nov. 1712).

having disowned it: ibid. i. 184 (Steele to Lintot, 4 Aug. 1713).

in the Guardian: no. 40 (written by Pope).

unwilling to print the paper lest Pope should be offended. Addison immediately saw the writer's design and, as it seems, had malice enough to conceal his discovery, and to permit a publication which, by making his friend Philips ridiculous, made him for ever an enemy to Pope.

It appears that about this time Pope had a strong inclination to unite the art of painting with that of poetry, and put himself under the tuition of Jervas. He was near-sighted, and therefore not formed by nature for a painter; he tried, however, how far he could advance, and sometimes persuaded his friends to sit. A picture of Betterton, supposed to be drawn by him, was in the possession of Lord Mansfield; if this was taken from the life, he must have begun to paint earlier, for Betterton was now dead.[n] Pope's ambition of this new art produced some encomiastic verses to Jervas, which certainly show his power as a poet, but I have been told that they betray his ignorance of painting.[n]

He appears to have regarded Betterton with kindness and esteem, and after his death published under his name a version into modern English of Chaucer's *Prologues* and one of his *Tales*, which, as was related by Mr. Harte, were believed to have been the performance of Pope himself by Fenton, who made him a gay offer of £5 if he would show them in the hand of Betterton.

The next year (1713) produced a bolder attempt by which profit was sought as well as praise. The poems which he had hitherto written, however they might have diffused his name, had made very little addition to his fortune. The allowance which his father made him, though proportioned to what he had it might be liberal, could not be large; his religion hindered him from the occupation of any civil employment, and he complained that he wanted even money to buy books.

He therefore resolved to try how far the favour of the public extended by soliciting a subscription to a version of the *Iliad*, with large notes.

To print by subscription was, for some time, a practice peculiar to the English. The first considerable work for which this expedient was employed is said to have been Dryden's *Virgil*; and it had been tried again with great success when the *Tatlers* were collected into volumes.

Jervas: Charles Jervas (1675–1739), painter and friend of Pope.
Lord Mansfield: William Murray (1705–93), 1st Earl of Mansfield, Lord Chief
    Justice.   *some encomiastic verses*: 'Epistle to Mr. Jervas'.
he complained: Spence, § 192.
The first considerable work: cf. ibid. § 62 and n.

There was reason to believe that Pope's attempt would be successful. He was in the full bloom of reputation, and was personally known to almost all whom dignity of employment or splendour of reputation had made eminent; he conversed indifferently with both parties, and never disturbed the public with his political opinions; and it might be naturally expected as each faction then boasted its literary zeal that the great men, who on other occasions practised all the violence of opposition, would emulate each other in their encouragement of a poet who had delighted all, and by whom none had been offended.

With those hopes he offered an English *Iliad* to subscribers, in six volumes in quarto, for six guineas—a sum, according to the value of money at that time, by no means inconsiderable, and greater than I believe to have been ever asked before. His proposal, however, was very favourably received, and the patrons of literature were busy to recommend his undertaking and promote his interest. Lord Oxford, indeed, lamented that such a genius should be wasted upon a work not original, but proposed no means by which he might live without it; Addison recommended caution and moderation, and advised him not to be content with the praise of half the nation when he might be universally favoured.

The greatness of the design, the popularity of the author, and the attention of the literary world, naturally raised such expectations of the future sale that the booksellers made their offers with great eagerness, but the highest bidder was Bernard Lintot, who became proprietor on condition of supplying, at his own expense, all the copies which were to be delivered to subscribers or presented to friends, and paying £200 for every volume.[n]

Of the quartos it was, I believe, stipulated that none should be printed but for the author, that the subscription might not be depreciated; but Lintot impressed the same pages upon a small folio, and paper perhaps a little thinner, and sold exactly at half the price, for half a guinea each volume, books so little inferior to the quartos that, by a fraud of trade, those folios, being afterwards shortened by cutting away the top and bottom, were sold as copies printed for the subscribers.[n]

Lintot printed 250 on royal paper in folio for two guineas a volume;

he offered: cf. *Pope: Poems*, vii. *xxxvi* n. 5.
Lord Oxford: Robert Harley (1661–1724), 1st Earl of Oxford, statesman; cf.
  Spence, §§ 226–7; Warburton, iv. 66–7 n.
Addison: Spence, §§ 146–7; *Pope: Corr.* i. 196–7 (Addison to Pope, 2 Nov. 1713).
Lintot: Barnaby Bernard Lintot (1675–1736), publisher.

of the small folio, having printed 1,750 copies of the first volume, he reduced the number in the other volumes to 1,000.[n]

It is unpleasant to relate that the bookseller, after all his hopes and all his liberality, was by a very unjust and illegal action defrauded of his profit. An edition of the English *Iliad* was printed in Holland in duodecimo, and imported clandestinely for the gratification of those who were impatient to read what they could not yet afford to buy. This fraud could only be counteracted by an edition equally cheap and more commodious, and Lintot was compelled to contract his folio at once into a duodecimo, and lose the advantage of an intermediate gradation. The notes, which in the Dutch copies were placed at the end of each book as they had been in the large volumes, were now subjoined to the text in the same page, and are therefore more easily consulted. Of this edition 2,500 were first printed, and 5,000 a few weeks afterwards; but indeed great numbers were necessary to produce considerable profit.

Pope, having now emitted his proposals, and engaged not only his own reputation but in some degree that of his friends who patronised his subscription, began to be frighted at his own undertaking, and finding himself at first embarrassed with difficulties which retarded and oppressed him, he was for a time timorous and uneasy, had his nights disturbed by dreams of long journeys through unknown ways, and wished, as he said, 'that somebody would hang him'.

This misery, however, was not of long continuance; he grew by degrees more acquainted with Homer's images and expressions, and practice increased his facility of versification. In a short time he represents himself as dispatching regularly fifty verses a day, which would show him by an easy computation the termination of his labour.

His own diffidence was not his only vexation. He that asks a subscription soon finds that he has enemies. All who do not encourage him defame him. He that wants money will rather be thought angry than poor, and he that wishes to save his money conceals his avarice by his malice. Addison had hinted his suspicion that Pope was too much a Tory, and some of the Tories suspected his principles because he had contributed to the *Guardian*, which was carried on by Steele.

'that somebody': Spence, § 197.

he represents himself: Pope: *Corr.* i. 254 (Pope to Gay, 23 Sept. 1714); cf. Spence, §§ 107, 198.

Addison had hinted: Pope: *Corr.* i. 196–7 (Addison to Pope, 2 Nov. 1713).

some of the Tories: ibid. i. 197 (Pope to Addison, Dec. 1713?), 220 (Pope to Caryll, 1 May 1714).

To those who censured his politics were added enemies yet more dangerous who called in question his knowledge of Greek, and his qualifications for a translator of Homer. To these he made no public opposition, but in one of his letters escapes from them as well as he can. At an age like his, for he was not more than twenty-five, with an irregular education, and a course of life of which much seems to have passed in conversation, it is not very likely that he overflowed with Greek.[n] But when he felt himself deficient he sought assistance, and what man of learning would refuse to help him? Minute inquiries into the force of words are less necessary in translating Homer than other poets because his positions are general and his representations natural, with very little dependence on local or temporary customs, on those changeable scenes of artificial life which, by mingling original with accidental notions, and crowding the mind with images which time effaces, produce ambiguity in diction and obscurity in books. To this open display of unadulterated nature it must be ascribed that Homer has fewer passages of doubtful meaning than any other poet either in the learned or in modern languages. I have read of a man who, being by his ignorance of Greek compelled to gratify his curiosity with the Latin printed on the opposite page, declared that from the rude simplicity of the lines literally rendered he formed nobler ideas of the Homeric majesty than from the laboured elegance of polished versions.

Those literal translations were always at hand, and from them he could easily obtain his author's sense with sufficient certainty; and among the readers of Homer the number is very small of those who find much in the Greek more than in the Latin, except the music of the numbers.

If more help was wanting, he had the poetical translation of Eobanus Hessus, an unwearied writer of Latin verses; he had the French *Homers* of La Valterie and Dacier, and the English of Chapman, Hobbes and Ogilby.[n] With Chapman, whose work, though now totally neglected, seems to have been popular almost to the end of the

who called in question: cf. *Dennis*, ii. 122–4.
one of his letters: Pope: *Corr.* i. 209 (Pope to Addison, 30 Jan. 1714).
I have read: cf. *Life*, iii. 333.
Hessus: Helius Eobanus Hessus (1488–1540), German scholar and Latin poet, author of *Poetarum ... principis Homeri Ilias ... Latino carmine reddita* (1540).
La Valterie: Abbé de la Valterie (*fl.* 1678–82), whose *L'Iliade d'Homère, nouvelle traduction* appeared in 1681.
Dacier: Anne Lefèvre Dacier (1654–1720), classical scholar, author of *L'Iliade d'Homère, traduite en François, avec des remarques* (1711).

last century, he had very frequent consultations, and perhaps never translated any passage till he had read his version, which indeed he has been sometimes suspected of using instead of the original.

Notes were likewise to be provided, for the six volumes would have been very little more than six pamphlets without them. What the mere perusal of the text could suggest Pope wanted no assistance to collect or methodize, but more was necessary: many pages were to be filled, and learning must supply materials to wit and judgement. Something might be gathered from Dacier, but no man loves to be indebted to his contemporaries, and Dacier was accessible to common readers. Eustathius was therefore necessarily consulted. To read Eustathius, of whose work there was then no Latin version,[n] I suspect Pope, if he had been willing, not to have been able; some other was therefore to be found who had leisure as well as abilities, and he was doubtless most readily employed who would do much work for little money.

The history of the notes has never been traced. Broome, in his preface to his poems, declares himself the commentator 'in part upon the *Iliad*', and it appears from Fenton's letter, preserved in the Museum, that Broome was at first engaged in consulting Eustathius, but that after a time, whatever was the reason, he desisted; another man of Cambridge was then employed, who soon grew weary of the work; and a third that was recommended by Thirlby is now discovered to have been Jortin, a man since well known to the learned world, who complained that Pope, having accepted and approved his performance, never testified any curiosity to see him, and who professed to have forgotten the terms on which he worked. The terms which Fenton uses are very mercantile: 'I think at first sight that his performance is very commendable, and have sent word for him to finish the 17th book, and to send it with his demands for his trouble. I have here enclosed the specimen; if the rest come before you return, I will keep them till I receive your order.'

Broome then offered his service a second time, which was probably

---

pamphlets: Johnson argued that 'a few sheets of poetry unbound are a pamphlet, as much as a few sheets of prose' (*Life*, iii. 319). Cf. *Dict*.

Eustathius: (12th cent.), Bishop of Thessalonica and commentator on Homer.

Broome: William Broome (1689–1745), poet and translator; see *Poems on Several Occasions* (1727), p. 3.

Fenton's letter: *Pope: Corr*. i. 496–7 (Fenton to Pope, Sept. 1718).

Thirlby: Styan Thirlby (1686?–1753), critic and theologian of Jesus College, Cambridge.

Jortin: John Jortin (1698–1770), ecclesiastical historian.

Broome then offered: *Pope: Corr*. i. 497 (Fenton to Pope, Sept. 1718).

accepted, as they had afterwards a closer correspondence. Parnell contributed the Life of Homer, which Pope found so harsh that he took great pains in correcting it; and by his own diligence, with such help as kindness or money could procure him, in somewhat more than five years he completed his version of the *Iliad*, with the notes. He began it in 1712, his twenty-fifth year, and concluded it in 1718, his thirtieth year.

When we find him translating fifty lines a day, it is natural to suppose that he would have brought his work to a more speedy conclusion. The *Iliad*, containing less than 16,000 verses, might have been dispatched in less than 320 days by 50 verses in a day. The notes, compiled with the assistance of his mercenaries, could not be supposed to require more time than the text. According to this calculation, the progress of Pope may seem to have been slow; but the distance is commonly very great between actual performances and speculative possibility. It is natural to suppose that as much as has been done today may be done tomorrow, but on the morrow some difficulty emerges or some external impediment obstructs. Indolence, interruption, business and pleasure all take their turns of retardation, and every long work is lengthened by a thousand causes that can, and ten thousand that cannot, be recounted. Perhaps no extensive and multifarious performance was ever effected within the term originally fixed in the undertaker's mind. He that runs against Time has an antagonist not subject to casualties.

The encouragement given to this translation, though report seems to have overrated it, was such as the world has not often seen. The subscribers were 575. The copies for which subscriptions were given were 654; and only 660 were printed. For those copies Pope had nothing to pay; he therefore received, including the £200 a volume, £5,320. 4s., without deduction, as the books were supplied by Lintot.[n]

By the success of his subscription Pope was relieved from those pecuniary distresses with which, notwithstanding his popularity, he had hitherto struggled. Lord Oxford had often lamented his disqualification for public employment, but never proposed a pension. While the translation of Homer was in its progress, Mr. Craggs, then Secretary of State, offered to procure him a pension which, at least during his ministry, might be enjoyed with secrecy. This was not accepted by Pope, who told him, however, that if he should be pressed

Parnell: Thomas Parnell (1679–1718), poet.
began it in 1712: cf. *Pope: Poems*, vii. xxxv–xxxvii.
Mr. Craggs: James Craggs the younger (1686–1721). Cf. Warburton, iv. 68 n.

with want of money he would send to him for occasional supplies. Craggs was not long in power, and was never solicited for money by Pope, who disdained to beg what he did not want.

With the product of this subscription, which he had too much discretion to squander, he secured his future life from want by considerable annuities. The estate of the Duke of Buckingham was found to have been charged with £500 a year, payable to Pope, which doubtless his translation enabled him to purchase.[n]

It cannot be unwelcome to literary curiosity that I deduce thus minutely the history of the English *Iliad*. It is certainly the noblest version of poetry which the world has ever seen, and its publication must therefore be considered as one of the great events in the annals of learning.

To those who have skill to estimate the excellence and difficulty of this great work, it must be very desirable to know how it was performed, and by what gradations it advanced to correctness. Of such an intellectual process the knowledge has very rarely been attainable; but happily there remains the original copy of the *Iliad* which, being obtained by Bolingbroke as a curiosity, descended from him to Mallet, and is now by the solicitation of the late Dr. Maty reposited in the Museum.

Between this manuscript (which is written upon accidental fragments of paper) and the printed edition, there must have been an intermediate copy that was perhaps destroyed as it returned from the press.

From the first copy I have procured a few transcripts, and shall exhibit first the printed lines, then, in a smaller print, those of the manuscripts with all their variations. Those words in the small print which are given in italics are cancelled in the copy, and the words placed under them adopted in their stead.

The beginning of the first book stands thus:

> The wrath of Peleus' son, the direful spring
> Of all the Grecian woes, O Goddess, sing;
> That wrath which hurled to Pluto's gloomy reign
> The souls of mighty chiefs untimely slain.

> The stern Pelides' *rage*, O Goddess, sing,
>   wrath

Mallet: David Mallet (1705?–65), miscellaneous writer.

Dr. Maty: Matthew Maty (1718–76), physician, writer, and librarian of the British Museum.

Peleus': in Greek mythology Peleus was the husband of Thetis and father of Achilles, the chief Greek hero of the Trojan War.

Pluto's: Pluto, the Greek god of Hades or the nether world.

> Of all the woes *of Greece* the fatal spring,
>   Grecian
> That strewed with *warriors* dead the Phrygian plain,
>   heroes
> And *peopled the dark hell with heroes* slain;
>   filled the shady hell with chiefs untimely

Whose limbs, unburied on the naked shore,
Devouring dogs and hungry vultures tore,
Since great Achilles and Atrides strove;
Such was the sovereign doom, and such the will of Jove.

> Whose limbs, unburied on the hostile shore,
> Devouring dogs and greedy vultures tore,
> Since first *Atrides* and *Achilles* strove;
> Such was the sovereign doom, and such the will of Jove.

Declare, O Muse, in what ill-fated hour
Sprung the fierce strife, from what offended Power!
Latona's son a dire contagion spread,
And heaped the camp with mountains of the dead;
The King of men his reverend priest defied,
And for the King's offence the people died.

> Declare, O Goddess, what offended Power
> Enflamed their *rage*, in that *ill-omened* hour:
>   anger   fatal, hapless
> Phoebus himself the *dire* debate procured,
>   fierce
> T' avenge the wrongs his injured priest endured;
> For this the God a dire infection spread,
> And heaped the camp with millions of the dead:
> The King of men the sacred sire defied,
> And for the King's offence the people died.

For Chryses sought with costly gifts to gain
His captive daughter from the Victor's chain;
Suppliant the venerable Father stands,
Apollo's awful ensigns grace his hands,
By these be begs, and, lowly bending down,
Extends the sceptre and the laurel crown.

> For Chryses sought by *presents to regain*
>   costly gifts to gain
> His captive daughter from the Victor's chain;
> Suppliant the venerable Father stands,
> Apollo's awful ensigns graced his hands,
> By these he begs, and lowly bending down
> *The golden sceptre* and the laurel crown,
> Presents the sceptre
> *For these as ensigns of his God he bare,*
> *The God that sends his golden shafts afar;*
> Then low on earth, the venerable man,
> Suppliant before the brother kings began.

Atrides: sons of Atreus (i.e. Agamemnon and Menelaus).

Latona's son: Apollo, whose priest Chryses had a daughter Chryseis who, on being taken prisoner, was given to Agamemnon. His refusal to let her father ransom her prompted Apollo to send a plague on the Greek camp.

He sued to all, but chief implored for grace
The brother kings of Atreus' royal race;
Ye kings and warriors, may your vows be crowned,
And Troy's proud walls lie level with the ground;
May Jove restore you, when your toils are o'er,
Safe to the pleasures of your native shore.

> To all he sued, but chief implored for grace
> The brother kings of Atreus' royal race.
> Ye *sons of Atreus*, may your vows be crowned,
>   kings and warriors
> *Your labours, by the Gods be all your labours crowned*;
> *So may the Gods your arms with conquest bless,*
> And Troy's proud walls lie level with the ground;
> *Till*   *laid*
> *And crown your labours with deserved success*;
> May Jove restore you, when your toils are o'er,
> Safe to the pleasures of your native shore.

But, oh! relieve a wretched parent's pain,
And give Chryseis to these arms again;
If mercy fail, yet let my present move,
And dread avenging Phoebus, son of Jove.

> But, oh! relieve a hapless parent's pain,
> And give my daughter to these arms again;
> *Receive my gifts*; if mercy fails, yet let my present move,
> And fear *the God that deals his darts around,*
>   avenging Phoebus, son of Jove.

The Greeks, in shouts, their joint assent declare
The priest to reverence, and release the fair.
Not so Atrides; he, with kingly pride,
Repulsed the sacred sire, and thus replied.

> He said, the Greeks their joint assent declare,
> *The father said; the gen'rous Greeks relent,*
> T' accept the ransom, and release the fair:
> *Revere the priest, and speak their joint assent:*
> Not so *the tyrant*, he, with kingly pride,
>   Atrides,
> Repulsed the sacred sire, and thus replied.
> [Not so the tyrant. DRYDEN.]

Of these lines and of the whole first book, I am told that there was
yet a former copy more varied, and more deformed with inter-
lineations.

The beginning of the second book varies very little from the printed
page, and is therefore set down without any parallel: the few slight
differences do not require to be elaborately displayed.

> Now pleasing sleep had sealed each mortal eye;
> Stretched in their tents the Grecian leaders lie;
> Th' Immortals slumbered on their thrones above,
> All but the ever-watchful eye of Jove.
> To honour Thetis' son he bends his care,
> And plunge the Greeks in all the woes of war.

Then bids an empty phantom rise to sight,
And thus *commands* the vision of the night:
     directs
Fly hence, delusive dream, and, light as air,
To Agamemnon's royal tent repair;
Bid him in arms draw forth th' embattled train,
March all his legions to the dusty plain.
Now tell the King 'tis given him to destroy
Declare ev'n now
The lofty *walls* of wide-extended Troy;
    towers
For now no more the Gods with Fate contend;
At Juno's suit the heavenly factions end.
Destruction *hovers* o'er yon devoted wall,
    hangs
And nodding Ilium waits th' impending fall.

Invocation to the Catalogue of Ships.

Say, Virgins, seated round the throne divine,
All-knowing Goddesses! immortal Nine!
Since earth's wide regions, heaven's unmeasured height,
And hell's abyss, hide nothing from your sight,
(We, wretched mortals! lost in doubts below,
But guess by rumour, and but boast we know)
Oh say what heroes, fired by thirst of fame,
Or urged by wrongs, to Troy's destruction came!
To count them all, demands a thousand tongues,
A throat of brass and adamantine lungs.

    Now, Virgin Goddesses, immortal Nine!
    That round Olympus' heavenly summit shine,
    Who see through heaven and earth, and hell profound,
    And all things know, and all things can resound;
    Relate what armies sought the Trojan land,
    What nations followed, and what chiefs command;
    (For doubtful Fame distracts mankind below,
    And nothing can we tell, and nothing know)
    Without your aid, to count th' unnumbered train,
    A thousand mouths, a thousand tongues were vain.

Book V. *v.* 1.

But Pallas now Tydides' soul inspires,
Fills with her force, and warms with all her fires:
Above the Greeks his deathless fame to raise,
And crown her hero with distinguished praise,
High on his helm celestial lightnings play,
His beamy shield emits a living ray;
Th' unwearied blaze incessant streams supplies,
Like the red star that fires th' autumnal skies.

    But Pallas now Tydides' soul inspires,
    Fills with her *rage*, and warms with all her fires;
        force,

Ilium: Troy.
Tydides: son of Tydeus (i.e. Diomedes).

O'er all the Greeks decrees his fame to raise,
Above the Greeks *her warrior's* fame to raise,
     his deathless
And crown her hero with *immortal* praise:
       distinguished
Bright from his beamy *crest* the lightnings play,
High on   helm
From his broad buckler flashed the living ray,
High on his helm celestial lightnings play,
His beamy shield emits a living ray.
The Goddess with her breath the flame supplies,
Bright as the star whose fires in Autumn rise;
Her breath divine thick streaming flames supplies,
Bright as the star that fires the autumnal skies:
Th' unwearied blaze incessant streams supplies,
Like the red star that fires th' autumnal skies.

When first he rears his radiant orb to sight,
And bathed in ocean shoots a keener light.
Such glories Pallas on the chief bestowed,
Such from his arms the fierce effulgence flowed;
Onward she drives him furious to engage,
Where the fight burns, and where the thickest rage.

 When fresh he rears his radiant orb to sight,
 And gilds old Ocean with a blaze of light,
 Bright as the star that fires th' autumnal skies,
 Fresh from the deep, and gilds the seas and skies.
 Such glories Pallas on her chief bestowed,
 Such sparkling rays from his bright armour flowed,
 Such from his arms the fierce effulgence flowed.
 Onward she drives him *headlong* to engage,
      furious
 Where the *war bleeds*, and where the *fiercest* rage.
    fight burns,   thickest

The sons of Dares first the combat sought,
A wealthy priest, but rich without a fault;
In Vulcan's fane the father's days were led,
The sons to toils of glorious battle bred;

 There lived a Trojan—Dares was his name,
 The priest of Vulcan, rich, yet void of blame;
 The sons of Dares first the combat sought,
 A wealthy priest, but rich without a fault.

Conclusion of Book VIII. *v.* 687.

As when the moon, refulgent lamp of night,
O'er heaven's clear azure spreads her sacred light;
When not a breath disturbs the deep serene,
And not a cloud o'ercasts the solemn scene;
Around her throne the vivid planets roll,
And stars unnumbered gild the glowing pole:
O'er the dark trees a yellower verdure shed,
And tip with silver every mountain's head;
Then shine the vales—the rocks in prospect rise,
A flood of glory bursts from all the skies;
The conscious swains, rejoicing in the sight,

Eye the blue vault, and bless the useful light.
So many flames before proud Ilion blaze,
And lighten glimmering Xanthus with their rays;
The long reflection of the distant fires
Gleam on the walls, and tremble on the spires:
A thousand piles the dusky horrors gild,
And shoot a shady lustre o'er the field;
Full fifty guards each flaming pile attend,
Whose umbered arms by fits thick flashes send;
Loud neigh the coursers o'er their heaps of corn,
And ardent warriors wait the rising morn.

As when in stillness of the silent night,
As when the moon in all lustre bright,
As when the moon, refulgent lamp of night,
O'er heaven's *clear* azure *sheds* her *silver* light;
        pure   spreads   sacred
As still in air the trembling lustre stood,
And o'er its golden border shoots a flood;
When *no loose gale* disturbs the deep serene,
     not a breath
And *no dim* cloud o'ercasts the solemn scene;
     not a
Around her silver throne the planets glow,
And stars unnumbered trembling beams bestow;
Around her throne the vivid planets roll,
And stars unnumbered gild the glowing pole:
Clear gleams of light o'er the dark trees are seen,
         o'er the dark trees a yellow sheds,
O'er the dark trees a yellower *green* they shed,
            gleam
            verdure
And tip with silver all the *mountain* heads:
           forest
And tip with silver every mountain's head.
The vallies open, and the forests rise,
The vales appear, the rocks in prospect rise,
Then shine the vales, the rocks in prospect rise,
All Nature stands revealed before our eyes;
A flood of glory bursts from all the skies.
The conscious shepherd, joyful at the sight,
Eyes the blue vault, and numbers every light.
The conscious *swains rejoicing at the* sight
         shepherds gazing with delight
Eye the blue vault, and bless the *vivid* light.
         glorious
         useful
So many flames before *the navy* blaze,
        proud Ilion
And lighten glimmering Xanthus with their rays,
Wide o'er the fields to Troy extend the gleams,
And tip the distant spires with fainter beams;
The long reflexions of the distant fires
Gild the high walls, and tremble on the spires,
Gleam on the walls, and tremble on the spires;
A thousand fires at distant stations bright,
Gild the dark prospect, and dispel the night.

Of these specimens every man who has cultivated poetry, or who

Xanthus: (alias 'Scamander') one of the rivers of the Trojan plain.

delights to trace the mind from the rudeness of its first conceptions to the elegance of its last, will naturally desire a greater number; but most other readers are already tired, and I am not writing only to poets and philosophers.

The *Iliad* was published volume by volume, as the translation proceeded; the first four books appeared in 1715. The expectation of this work was undoubtedly high, and every man who had connected his name with criticism, or poetry, was desirous of such intelligence as might enable him to talk upon the popular topic. Halifax who, by having been first a poet and then a patron of poetry, had acquired the right of being a judge, was willing to hear some books while they were yet unpublished. Of this rehearsal Pope afterwards gave the following account.

The famous Lord Halifax was rather a pretender to taste than really possessed of it. When I had finished the two or three first books of my translation of the *Iliad*, that lord desired to have the pleasure of hearing them read at his house. Addison, Congreve and Garth were there at the reading. In four or five places, Lord Halifax stopped me very civilly, and with a speech each time, much of the same kind, 'I beg your pardon, Mr. Pope, but there is something in that passage that does not quite please me. Be so good as to mark the place, and consider it a little at your leisure. I'm sure you can give it a little turn.' I returned from Lord Halifax's with Dr. Garth, in his chariot, and as we were going along, was saying to the Doctor that my Lord had laid me under a good deal of difficulty by such loose and general observations; that I had been thinking over the passages almost ever since, and could not guess at what it was that offended his lordship in either of them. Garth laughed heartily at my embarrassment; said I had not been long enough acquainted with Lord Halifax to know his way yet; that I need not puzzle myself about looking those places over and over when I got home. 'All you need do (says he) is to leave them just as they are, call on Lord Halifax two or three months hence, thank him for his kind observations on those passages, and then read them to him as altered. I have known him much longer than you have, and will be answerable for the event.' I followed his advice; waited on Lord Halifax some time after; said I hoped he would find his objections to those passages removed; read them to him exactly as they were at first; and his lordship was extremely pleased with them, and cried out, 'Ay, now they are perfectly right: nothing can be better.'

It is seldom that the great or the wise suspect that they are despised or cheated. Halifax, thinking this a lucky opportunity of securing immortality, made some advances of favour and some overtures of advantage to Pope, which he seems to have received with sullen coldness. All our knowledge of this transaction is derived from a single letter (Dec. 1, 1714) in which Pope says, 'I am obliged to you, both

the following account: Spence, § 204.
'*I am obliged*': *Pope: Corr.* i. 271 and n. 2.

for the favours you have done me, and those you intend me. I distrust neither your will nor your memory when it is to do good, and if I ever become troublesome or solicitous, it must not be out of expectation but out of gratitude. Your lordship may cause me to live agreeably in the town, or contentedly in the country, which is really all the difference I set between an easy fortune and a small one. It is indeed a high strain of generosity in you to think of making me easy all my life only because I have been so happy as to divert you some few hours; but if I may have leave to add it is because you think me no enemy to my native country, there will appear a better reason; for I must of consequence be very much (as I sincerely am) yours etc.'

These voluntary offers and this faint acceptance ended without effect. The patron was not accustomed to such frigid gratitude, and the poet fed his own pride with the dignity of independence. They probably were suspicious of each other. Pope would not dedicate till he saw at what rate his praise was valued; he would be 'troublesome out of gratitude, not expectation'. Halifax thought himself entitled to confidence, and would give nothing unless he knew what he should receive. Their commerce had its beginning in hope of praise on one side, and of money on the other, and ended because Pope was less eager of money than Halifax of praise. It is not likely that Halifax had any personal benevolence to Pope; it is evident that Pope looked on Halifax with scorn and hatred.

The reputation of this great work failed of gaining him a patron, but it deprived him of a friend. Addison and he were now at the head of poetry and criticism, and both in such a state of elevation that, like the two rivals in the Roman state, one could no longer bear an equal nor the other a superior. Of the gradual abatement of kindness between friends, the beginning is often scarcely discernible by themselves, and the process is continued by petty provocations and incivilities sometimes peevishly returned, and sometimes contemptuously neglected, which would escape all attention but that of pride, and drop from any memory but that of resentment. That the quarrel of those two wits should be minutely deduced is not to be expected from a writer to whom, as Homer says, 'nothing but rumour has reached, and who has no personal knowledge'.

Pope doubtless approached Addison, when the reputation of their wit first brought them together, with the respect due to a man whose abilities were acknowledged, and who, having attained that eminence to which he was himself aspiring, had in his hands the distribution of literary fame. He paid court with sufficient diligence by his prologue

'*nothing but rumour*': *Iliad*, ii. 486.

to *Cato*, by his abuse of Dennis, and with praise yet more direct by his poem on the *Dialogues on Medals*, of which the immediate publication was then intended. In all this there was no hypocrisy, for he confessed that he found in Addison something more pleasing than in any other man.

It may be supposed that as Pope saw himself favoured by the world, and more frequently compared his own powers with those of others, his confidence increased and his submission lessened, and that Addison felt no delight from the advances of a young wit who might soon contend with him for the highest place. Every great man, of whatever kind be his greatness, has among his friends those who officiously, or insidiously, quicken his attention to offences, heighten his disgust, and stimulate his resentment. Of such adherents Addison doubtless had many, and Pope was now too high to be without them.

From the emission and reception of the proposals for the *Iliad*, the kindness of Addison seems to have abated. Jervas the painter once pleased himself (Aug. 20, 1714) with imagining that he had re-established their friendship, and wrote to Pope that Addison once suspected him of too close a confederacy with Swift, but was now satisfied with his conduct. To this Pope answered, a week after, that his engagements to Swift were such as his services in regard to the subscription demanded, and that the Tories never put him under the necessity of asking leave to be grateful. 'But', says he, 'as Mr. Addison must be *the judge* in what regards himself, and seems to have no very just one in regard to me, so I must own to you I expect nothing but civility from him.' In the same letter he mentions Philips as having been busy to kindle animosity between them, but in a letter to Addison he expresses some consciousness of behaviour inattentively deficient in respect.

Of Swift's industry in promoting the subscription there remains the testimony of Kennett, no friend to either him or Pope.

Nov. 2, 1713, Dr. Swift came into the coffee-house, and had a bow from everybody but me, who, I confess, could not but despise him. When I came to the antechamber to wait before prayers, Dr. Swift was the principal man of talk and business, and acted as master of requests. Then he instructed a young nobleman that the 'best poet in England' was Mr. Pope (a Papist), who had begun a translation of Homer into English verse, for which 'he must have them all subscribe'; for, says he, the author *shall not* begin to print till *I have* 1,000 guineas for him.

he confessed: Spence, § 148.   *wrote to Pope*: *Pope: Corr*. i. 244.
Pope answered: ibid. i. 244–5.   *in a letter to Addison*: ibid. i. 263–4 (10 Oct. 1714).
Kennett: White Kennett (1660–1728), Bishop of Peterborough. Cf. *Swift: Corr.*
    v. 228–9.

About this time it is likely that Steele, who was, with all his political fury, good-natured and officious, procured an interview between these angry rivals which ended in aggravated malevolence. On this occasion, if the reports be true, Pope made his complaint with frankness and spirit, as a man undeservedly neglected or opposed; and Addison affected a contemptuous unconcern, and in a calm even voice reproached Pope with his vanity, and telling him of the improvements which his early works had received from his own remarks and those of Steele, said that he, being now engaged in public business, had no longer any care for his poetical reputation, nor had any other desire with regard to Pope than that his should not, by too much arrogance, alienate the public.

To this Pope is said to have replied with great keenness and severity, upbraiding Addison with perpetual dependence, and with the abuse of those qualifications which he had obtained at the public cost, and charging him with mean endeavours to obstruct the progress of rising merit. The contest rose so high that they parted at last without any interchange of civility.

The first volume of *Homer* was (1715) in time published, and a rival version of the first *Iliad*—for rivals the time of their appearance inevitably made them—was immediately printed with the name of Tickell. It was soon perceived that, among the followers of Addison, Tickell had the preference, and the critics and poets divided into factions. 'I', says Pope, 'have the town, that is, the mob, on my side; but it is not uncommon for the smaller party to supply by industry what it wants in numbers. . . . I appeal to the people as my rightful judges, and while they are not inclined to condemn me, shall not fear the high flyers at Button's.' This opposition he immediately imputed to Addison, and complained of it in terms sufficiently resentful to Craggs, their common friend.

When Addison's opinion was asked, he declared the versions to be both good, but Tickell's the best that had ever been written; and sometimes said that they were both good, but that Tickell had more of Homer.

Pope was now sufficiently irritated: his reputation and his interest were at hazard. He once intended to print together the four versions

if the reports: cf. Ayre, *Memoirs of Pope* (1745), pp. 100–2.
Tickell: Thomas Tickell (1686–1740), poet.
'*I*', *says Pope*: *Pope: Corr.* i. 306 (Pope to Craggs, 15 July 1715).
he declared: ibid. i. 305 (Gay to Pope, 8 July 1715).
He once intended: ibid. i. 298 (Lintot to Pope, 22 June 1715).

of Dryden, Maynwaring, Pope and Tickell, that they might be readily compared and fairly estimated. This design seems to have been defeated by the refusal of Tonson, who was the proprietor of the other three versions.

Pope intended at another time a rigorous criticism of Tickell's translation, and had marked a copy, which I have seen, in all places that appeared defective. But while he was thus meditating defence or revenge, his adversary sunk before him without a blow: the voice of the public were not long divided, and the preference was universally given to Pope's performance.

He was convinced, by adding one circumstance to another, that the other translation was the work of Addison himself; but if he knew it in Addison's lifetime, it does not appear that he told it. He left his illustrious antagonist to be punished by what has been considered as the most painful of all reflections, the remembrance of a crime perpetrated in vain.

The other circumstances of their quarrel were thus related by Pope.

Philips seemed to have been encouraged to abuse me in coffee-houses and conversations; and Gildon wrote a thing about Wycherley, in which he had abused both me and my relations very grossly. Lord Warwick himself told me one day that it was in vain for me to endeavour to be well with Mr. Addison, that his jealous temper would never admit of a settled friendship between us; and to convince me of what he had said, assured me that Addison had encouraged Gildon to publish those scandals, and had given him ten guineas after they were published. The next day, while I was heated with what I had heard, I wrote a letter to Mr. Addison to let him know that I was not unacquainted with this behaviour of his; that if I was to speak severely of him in return for it, it should be in such a dirty way that I should rather tell him, himself, fairly of his faults, and allow his good qualities; and that it should be something in the following manner; I then adjoined the first sketch of what has since been called my satire on Addison. Mr. Addison used me very civilly ever after.

The verses on Addison, when they were sent to Atterbury, were considered by him as the most excellent of Pope's performances, and the writer was advised, since he knew where his strength lay, not to suffer it to remain unemployed.

Maynwaring: Arthur Mainwaring (or Maynwaring) (1668–1712), auditor of imprests, whose translation of part of *Iliad* i appeared in 1704.
had marked a copy: cf. Warburton, iv. 27 n.
Philips seemed: Spence, §§ 165–6.
Gildon: Charles Gildon (1665–1724), author. Cf. Spence, ii. 625.
Lord Warwick: Edward Henry Rich (1698–1721), 7th Earl of Warwick.
my satire on Addison: cf. *Epistle to Arbuthnot*, ll. 193–214.
were considered by him: Pope: *Corr.* ii. 104–5 (Atterbury to Pope, 26 Feb. 1722).

This year (1715) being by the subscription enabled to live more by choice, having persuaded his father to sell their estate at Binfield, he purchased, I think only for his life, that house at Twickenham to which his residence afterwards procured so much celebration, and removed thither with his father and mother.[n]

Here he planted the vines and the quincunx which his verses mention, and being under the necessity of making a subterraneous passage to a garden on the other side of the road, he adorned it with fossil bodies, and dignified it with the title of a grotto—a place of silence and retreat from which he endeavoured to persuade his friends and himself that cares and passions could be excluded.

A grotto is not often the wish or pleasure of an Englishman, who has more frequent need to solicit than exclude the sun; but Pope's excavation was requisite as an entrance to his garden, and as some men try to be proud of their defects, he extracted an ornament from an inconvenience, and vanity produced a grotto where necessity enforced a passage. It may be frequently remarked of the studious and speculative that they are proud of trifles, and that their amusements seem frivolous and childish—whether it be that men conscious of great reputation think themselves above the reach of censure, and safe in the admission of negligent indulgences, or that mankind expect from elevated genius an uniformity of greatness, and watch its degradation with malicious wonder, like him who having followed with his eye an eagle into the clouds should lament that she ever descended to a perch.

While the volumes of his *Homer* were annually published, he collected his former works (1717) into one quarto volume, to which he prefixed a preface, written with great sprightliness and elegance, which was afterwards reprinted with some passages subjoined that he at first omitted; other marginal additions of the same kind he made in the later editions of his poems. Waller remarks that poets lose half their praise because the reader knows not what they have blotted. Pope's voracity of fame taught him the art of obtaining the accumulated honour both of what he had published and of what he had suppressed.

In this year his father died suddenly in his seventy-fifth year,[n] having passed twenty-nine years in privacy. He is not known but by the character which his son has given him. If the money with which he

which his verses mention: *Imit. Hor. Sat.* II. i. 130.
Waller remarks: 'Upon the Earl of Roscommon's Translation of Horace', ll. 41–2.
the character which: *Epistle to Arbuthnot*, ll. 388–403; *Imit. Hor. Ep.* II. ii. 54–67.

retired was all gotten by himself, he had traded very successfully in times when sudden riches were rarely attainable.

The publication of the *Iliad* was at last completed in 1720. The splendour and success of this work raised Pope many enemies that endeavoured to depreciate his abilities: Burnet, who was afterwards a judge of no mean reputation, censured him in a piece called *Homerides* before it was published; Duckett likewise endeavoured to make him ridiculous. Dennis was the perpetual persecutor of all his studies. But whoever his critics were, their writings are lost, and the names which are preserved are preserved in *The Dunciad.*

In this disastrous year (1720) of national infatuation, when more riches than Peru can boast were expected from the South Sea, when the contagion of avarice tainted every mind, and even poets panted after wealth, Pope was seized with the universal passion and ventured some of his money. The stock rose in its price, and he for a while thought himself 'the lord of thousands'. But this dream of happiness did not last long, and he seems to have waked soon enough to get clear with the loss only of what he once thought himself to have won, and perhaps not wholly of that.

Next year he published some select poems of his friend Dr. Parnell, with a very elegant dedication to the Earl of Oxford, who after all his struggles and dangers then lived in retirement, still under the frown of a victorious faction who could take no pleasure in hearing his praise.

He gave the same year (1721) an edition of Shakespeare.[n] His name was now of so much authority that Tonson thought himself entitled, by annexing it, to demand a subscription of six guineas for Shakespeare's plays in six quarto volumes; nor did his expectation much deceive him, for of 750 which he printed he dispersed a great number at the price proposed. The reputation of that edition indeed sunk afterwards so low that 140 copies were sold at sixteen shillings each.[n]

On this undertaking, to which Pope was induced by a reward of £217. 12*s*., he seems never to have reflected afterwards without vexation, for Theobald, a man of heavy diligence with very slender powers, first in a book called *Shakespeare Restored*, and then in a formal edition, detected his deficiencies with all the insolence of victory; and as he was now high enough to be feared and hated, Theobald had from others all the help that could be supplied by the desire of humbling a haughty character.

Burnet: Sir Thomas Burnet (1694–1753), co-author with George Duckett (d. 1732) of *Homerides* (1715).   '*the lord of thousands*': *Imit. Hor. Sat.* II. ii. 134.

From this time Pope became an enemy to editors, collators, commentators and verbal critics, and hoped to persuade the world that he miscarried in this undertaking only by having a mind too great for such minute employment.

Pope in his edition undoubtedly did many things wrong and left many things undone, but let him not be defrauded of his due praise. He was the first that knew, at least the first that told, by what helps the text might be improved. If he inspected the early editions negligently, he taught others to be more accurate. In his Preface he expanded with great skill and elegance the character which had been given of Shakespeare by Dryden, and he drew the public attention upon his works, which though often mentioned had been little read.

Soon after the appearance of the *Iliad*, resolving not to let the general kindness cool, he published proposals for a translation of the *Odyssey*, in five volumes, for five guineas. He was willing, however, now to have associates in his labour, being either weary with toiling upon another's thoughts, or having heard, as Ruffhead relates, that Fenton and Broome had already begun the work, and liking better to have them confederates than rivals.

In the patent, instead of saying that he had 'translated' the *Odyssey*, as he said of the *Iliad*, he says that he had 'undertaken' a translation; and in the proposals the subscription is said to be not solely for his own use, but for that of 'two of his friends who have assisted him in this work'.

In 1723, while he was engaged in this new version, he appeared before the Lords at the memorable trial of Bishop Atterbury, with whom he had lived in great familiarity and frequent correspondence. Atterbury had honestly recommended to him the study of the popish controversy in hope of his conversion, to which Pope answered in a manner that cannot much recommend his principles or his judgement. In questions and projects of learning they agreed better. He was called at the trial to give an account of Atterbury's domestic life and private employment, that it might appear how little time he had left for plots. Pope had but few words to utter, and in those few he made several blunders.

His letters to Atterbury express the utmost esteem, tenderness and

the character which: see above, p. 161.

he published proposals: cf. *Pope: Poems*, vii. *xliii*.

that Fenton and Broome: Ruffhead, pp. 205–6.

Atterbury had honestly: *Pope: Corr.* i. 451 (Atterbury to Pope, 8 Nov. 1717), 453–4 (Pope to Atterbury, 20 Nov. 1717).

gratitude: 'Perhaps', says he, 'it is not only in this world that I may have cause to remember the Bishop of Rochester'. At their last interview in the Tower, Atterbury presented him with a Bible.

Of the *Odyssey* Pope translated only twelve books; the rest were the work of Broome and Fenton; the notes were written wholly by Broome, who was not over-liberally rewarded. The public was carefully kept ignorant of the several shares, and an account was subjoined at the conclusion which is now known not to be true.[n]

The first copy of Pope's books, with those of Fenton, are to be seen in the Museum. The parts of Pope are less interlined than the *Iliad*, and the latter books of the *Iliad* less than the former. He grew dexterous by practice, and every sheet enabled him to write the next with more facility. The books of Fenton have very few alterations by the hand of Pope. Those of Broome have not been found, but Pope complained, as it is reported, that he had much trouble in correcting them.

His contract with Lintot was the same as for the *Iliad* except that only £100 were to be paid him for each volume.[n] The number of subscribers was 574, and of copies 819,[n] so that his profit when he had paid his assistants was still very considerable. The work was finished in 1725, and from that time he resolved to make no more translations.

The sale did not answer Lintot's expectation, and he then pretended to discover something of fraud in Pope, and commenced, or threatened, a suit in Chancery.

On the English *Odyssey* a criticism was published by Spence, at that time Prelector of Poetry at Oxford—a man whose learning was not very great, and whose mind was not very powerful. His criticism, however, was commonly just: what he thought he thought rightly, and his remarks were recommended by his coolness and candour. In him Pope had the first experience of a critic without malevolence, who thought it as much his duty to display beauties as expose faults, who censured with respect and praised with alacrity.

With this criticism Pope was so little offended that he sought the acquaintance of the writer, who lived with him from that time in great familiarity, attended him in his last hours, and compiled memorials of his conversation. The regard of Pope recommended him to the great

---

'*Perhaps*', *says he*: *Pope. Corr.* ii. 168 (20 Apr. 1723).

Pope complained: cf. Spence, § 206; *Pope: Corr.* ii. 356 (Pope to Broome, 30 Dec. 1725).

he resolved: *Pope: Corr.* ii. 321–2 (Pope to Swift, 14 Sept. 1725).

a suit in Chancery: ibid. ii. 290 (Pope to Fortescue, 18 Mar. 1725).

and powerful, and he obtained very valuable preferments in the Church.

Not long after Pope was returning home from a visit in a friend's coach, which in passing a bridge was overturned into the water; the windows were closed, and being unable to force them open, he was in danger of immediate death, when the postilion snatched him out by breaking the glass, of which the fragments cut two of his fingers in such a manner that he lost their use.

Voltaire, who was then in England, sent him a letter of consolation. He had been entertained by Pope at his table, where he talked with so much grossness that Mrs. Pope was driven from the room. Pope discovered by a trick that he was a spy for the Court, and never considered him as a man worthy of confidence.

He soon afterwards (1727) joined with Swift, who was then in England, to publish three volumes of *Miscellanies*, in which amongst other things he inserted the *Memoirs of a Parish Clerk*, in ridicule of Burnet's importance in his own *History*, and a 'Debate upon Black and White Horses', written in all the formalities of a legal process by the assistance, as is said, of Mr. Fortescue, afterwards Master of the Rolls. Before these *Miscellanies* is a preface signed by Swift and Pope, but apparently written by Pope, in which he makes a ridiculous and romantic complaint of the robberies committed upon authors by the clandestine seizure and sale of their papers. He tells, in tragic strains, how 'the cabinets of the sick and the closets of the dead have been broke open and ransacked'—as if those violences were often committed for papers of uncertain and accidental value which are rarely provoked by real treasures, as if epigrams and essays were in danger where gold and diamonds are safe. A cat hunted for his musk is, according to Pope's account, but the emblem of a wit winded by booksellers.

His complaint, however, received some attestation, for the same year the letters written by him to Mr. Cromwell, in his youth, were sold by Mrs. Thomas to Curll, who printed them.

In these *Miscellanies* was first published *The Art of Sinking in Poetry* which, by such a train of consequences as usually passes in literary quarrels, gave in a short time, according to Pope's account, occasion to *The Dunciad*.

a friend's: i.e. Bolingbroke's.   *a letter of consolation*: *Pope: Corr.* ii. 399.
the Memoirs: *Miscellanies. The Second Volume*, pp. 268–84.
a 'Debate': i.e. *Stradling versus Stiles*, ibid. pp. 292–6.
Mr. Fortescue: William Fortescue (1687–1749). Cf. Spence, § 137.
'the cabinets': *Miscellanies. The First Volume*, p. *xii*.
The Art: *Miscellanies. The Last Volume*, pp. 5–94 (of 1st series of pagination).

In the following year (1728) he began to put Atterbury's advice in practice, and showed his satirical powers by publishing *The Dunciad*, one of his greatest and most elaborate performances, in which he endeavoured to sink into contempt all the writers by whom he had been attacked, and some others whom he thought unable to defend themselves.

At the head of the Dunces he placed poor Theobald, whom he accused of ingratitude, but whose real crime was supposed to be that of having revised Shakespeare more happily than himself. This satire had the effect which he intended by blasting the characters which it touched. Ralph, who unnecessarily interposing in the quarrel got a place in a subsequent edition, complained that for a time he was in danger of starving as the booksellers had no longer any confidence in his capacity.

The prevalence of this poem was gradual and slow: the plan, if not wholly new, was little understood by common readers. Many of the allusions required illustration: the names were often expressed only by the initial and final letters, and if they had been printed at length, were such as few had known or recollected. The subject itself had nothing generally interesting, for whom did it concern to know that one or another scribbler was a dunce? If therefore it had been possible for those who were attacked to conceal their pain and their resentment, *The Dunciad* might have made its way very slowly in the world.

This, however, was not to be expected; every man is of importance to himself, and therefore, in his own opinion, to others, and supposing the world already acquainted with all his pleasures and his pains, is perhaps the first to publish injuries or misfortunes which had never been known unless related by himself, and at which those that hear them will only laugh—for no man sympathises with the sorrows of vanity.

The history of *The Dunciad* is very minutely related by Pope himself in a Dedication which he wrote to Lord Middlesex in the name of Savage.

I will relate the war of the 'Dunces' (for so it has been commonly called), which began in the year 1727, and ended in 1730.

whom he accused: cf. *Pope: Poems*, v. 75 n.
Ralph: James Ralph (1705?–62), miscellaneous writer, author of *Sawney, an Heroic Poem occasioned by the Dunciad* (1728). Cf. *Pope: Poems*, v. 165 and n.
Lord Middlesex: Charles Sackville (1711–69), Earl of Middlesex and 2nd Duke of Dorset.
I will relate: *A Collection of Pieces in Verse and Prose* (1732), pp. *iv–vii*.

When Dr. Swift and Mr. Pope thought it proper, for reasons specified in the Preface to their *Miscellanies*, to publish such little pieces of theirs as had casually got abroad, there was added to them the *Treatise of the Bathos*, or *The Art of Sinking in Poetry*. It happened that in one chapter of this piece the several species of bad poets were ranged in classes, to which were prefixed almost all the letters of the alphabet (the greatest part of them at random); but such was the number of poets eminent in that art, that someone or other took every letter to himself: all fell into so violent a fury that, for half a year or more, the common newspapers (in most of which they had some property, as being hired writers) were filled with the most abusive falsehoods and scurrilities they could possibly devise. A liberty no way to be wondered at in those people, and in those papers, that for many years, during the uncontrolled licence of the press, had aspersed almost all the great characters of the age—and this with impunity, their own persons and names being utterly secret and obscure.

This gave Mr. Pope the thought that he had now some opportunity of doing good by detecting and dragging into light these common enemies of mankind; since to invalidate this universal slander it sufficed to show what contemptible men were the authors of it. He was not without hopes that, by manifesting the dulness of those who had only malice to recommend them, either the booksellers would not find their account in employing them, or the men themselves, when discovered, want courage to proceed in so unlawful an occupation. This it was that gave birth to *The Dunciad*; and he thought it an happiness that, by the late flood of slander on himself, he had acquired such a peculiar right over their names as was necessary to this design.

On the 12th of March, 1729, at St. James's, that poem was presented to the King and Queen (who had before been pleased to read it) by the right honourable Sir Robert Walpole; and some days after the whole impression was taken and dispersed by several noblemen and persons of the first distinction.

It is certainly a true observation that no people are so impatient of censure as those who are the greatest slanderers, which was wonderfully exemplified on this occasion. On the day the book was first vended, a crowd of authors besieged the shop: entreaties, advices, threats of law and battery, nay cries of treason, were all employed to hinder the coming-out of *The Dunciad*; on the other side, the booksellers and hawkers made as great efforts to procure it. What could a few poor authors do against so great a majority as the public? There was no stopping a torrent with a finger, so out it came.

Many ludicrous circumstances attended it. The 'Dunces' (for by this name they were called) held weekly clubs, to consult of hostilities against the author; one wrote a letter to a great minister, assuring him Mr. Pope was the greatest enemy the government had, and another bought his image in clay to execute him in effigy, with which sad sort of satisfactions the gentlemen were a little comforted.

that poem was presented: i.e. the *Dunciad Variorum*. Cf. *Pope: Corr*. ii. 502 n. 3.

Sir Robert Walpole: (1676–1745), 1st Earl of Orford, first minister.

several noblemen: Oxford, Burlington, and Bathurst (*Pope: Poems*, v. *xxviii*).

Some false editions of the book having an owl in their frontispiece, the true one, to distinguish it, fixed in its stead an ass laden with authors. Then another surreptitious one being printed with the same ass, the new edition in octavo returned for distinction to the owl again. Hence arose a great contest of booksellers against booksellers, and advertisements against advertisements, some recommending the edition of the owl, and others the edition of the ass; by which names they came to be distinguished, to the great honour also of the gentlemen of *The Dunciad*.

Pope appears by this narrative to have contemplated his victory over the Dunces with great exultation; and such was his delight in the tumult which he had raised that for a while his natural sensibility was suspended, and he read reproaches and invectives without emotion, considering them only as the necessary effects of that pain which he rejoiced in having given.

It cannot however be concealed that by his own confession he was the aggressor, for nobody believes that the letters in the *Bathos* were placed at random; and it may be discovered that, when he thinks himself concealed, he indulges the common vanity of common men, and triumphs in those distinctions which he had affected to despise. He is proud that his book was presented to the King and Queen by the right honourable Sir Robert Walpole; he is proud that they had read it before; he is proud that the edition was taken off by the nobility and persons of the first distinction.

The edition of which he speaks was, I believe, that which, by telling in the text the names, and in the notes the characters, of those whom he had satirized, was made intelligible and diverting. The critics had now declared their approbation of the plan, and the common reader began to like it without fear: those who were strangers to petty literature, and therefore unable to decipher initials and blanks, had now names and persons brought within their view, and delighted in the visible effect of those shafts of malice which they had hitherto contemplated as shot into the air.

Dennis, upon the fresh provocation now given him, renewed the enmity which had for a time been appeased by mutual civilities, and published remarks, which he had till then suppressed, upon *The Rape of the Lock*.[n] Many more grumbled in secret, or vented their resentment in the newspapers by epigrams or invectives.

Duckett, indeed, being mentioned as loving Burnet with 'pious passion', pretended that his moral character was injured, and for some time declared his resolution to take vengeance with a cudgel. But Pope appeased him by changing 'pious passion' to 'cordial

'*pious passion*': *Dunciad*, iii. 176 (*Pope: Poems*, v. 169 and n.).

friendship', and by a note in which he vehemently disclaims the malignity of meaning imputed to the first expression.

Aaron Hill, who was represented as diving for the prize, expostulated with Pope in a manner so much superior to all mean solicitation that Pope was reduced to sneak and shuffle, sometimes to deny, and sometimes to apologize;[n] he first endeavours to wound and is then afraid to own that he meant a blow.

The Dunciad, in the complete edition, is addressed to Dr. Swift; of the notes, part was written by Dr. Arbuthnot, and an apologetical letter was prefixed signed by Cleland, but supposed to have been written by Pope.

After this general war upon dulness, he seems to have indulged himself awhile in tranquillity; but his subsequent productions prove that he was not idle. He published (1731) a poem *On Taste*, in which he very particularly and severely criticises the house, the furniture, the gardens, and the entertainments of Timon, a man of great wealth and little taste. By Timon he was universally supposed, and by the Earl of Burlington, to whom the poem is addressed, was privately said, to mean the Duke of Chandos—a man perhaps too much delighted with pomp and show, but of a temper kind and beneficent, and who had consequently the voice of the public in his favour.

A violent outcry was therefore raised against the ingratitude and treachery of Pope, who was said to have been indebted to the patronage of Chandos for a present of £1000,[n] and who gained the opportunity of insulting him by the kindness of his invitation.

The receipt of £1000 Pope publicly denied, but from the reproach which the attack on a character so amiable brought upon him, he tried all means of escaping. The name of Cleland was again employed in an apology, by which no man was satisfied, and he was at last reduced to shelter his temerity behind dissimulation, and endeavour to make that disbelieved which he never had confidence openly to deny. He wrote an exculpatory letter to the Duke, which was answered with great magnanimity as by a man who accepted his excuse without believing his professions.[n] He said that to have ridiculed his

Aaron Hill: (1685–1750), dramatist and poet.

is addressed: *Pope: Poems*, v. 62–3.

Dr. Arbuthnot: John Arbuthnot (1667–1735), physician and author.

Cleland: William Cleland (1674?–1741), commissioner of taxes and friend of Pope. Cf. Warburton, v. *xiv* n.

Earl of Burlington: Richard Boyle (1695–1753), 3rd Earl of Burlington and 4th Earl of Cork, statesman.

Duke of Chandos: James Brydges (1673–1744), 1st Duke of Chandos, M.P.

The name of Cleland: *Pope: Corr*. iii. 254–7 (Cleland to Gay, 16 Sept. 1731).

taste or his buildings had been an indifferent action in another man, but that in Pope, after the reciprocal kindness that had been exchanged between them, it had been less easily excused.

Pope, in one of his letters complaining of the treatment which his poem had found, 'owns that such critics can intimidate him, nay almost persuade him to write no more, which is a compliment this age deserves'. The man who threatens the world is always ridiculous, for the world can easily go on without him, and in a short time will cease to miss him. I have heard of an idiot who used to revenge his vexations by lying all night upon the bridge. 'There is nothing', says Juvenal, 'that a man will not believe in his own favour.' Pope had been flattered till he thought himself one of the moving powers in the system of life. When he talked of laying down his pen, those who sat round him entreated and implored, and self-love did not suffer him to suspect that they went away and laughed.

The following year deprived him of Gay, a man whom he had known early, and whom he seemed to love with more tenderness than any other of his literary friends. Pope was now forty-four years old—an age at which the mind begins less easily to admit new confidence, and the will to grow less flexible, and when therefore the departure of an old friend is very acutely felt.

In the next year he lost his mother—not by an unexpected death, for she had lasted to the age of ninety-three; but she did not die unlamented. The filial piety of Pope was in the highest degree amiable and exemplary; his parents had the happiness of living till he was at the summit of poetical reputation, till he was at ease in his fortune and without a rival in his fame, and found no diminution of his respect or tenderness. Whatever was his pride, to them he was obedient, and whatever was his irritability, to them he was gentle. Life has, among its soothing and quiet comforts, few things better to give than such a son.

One of the passages of Pope's life which seems to deserve some inquiry was a publication of letters between him and many of his friends, which falling into the hands of Curll, a rapacious bookseller of no good fame, were by him printed and sold. This volume containing some letters from noblemen, Pope incited a prosecution against him in the House of Lords for breach of privilege, and attended himself to stimulate the resentment of his friends. Curll

---

'*owns that*': *Pope: Corr*. iii. 266 (Pope to Burlington, Jan. 1732).
'*There is nothing*': *Satires*, iv. 70.
Gay: John Gay (1685–1732), poet and dramatist.
she did not die unlamented: cf. *Epistle to Arbuthnot*, ll. 408–13.

appeared at the bar, and knowing himself in no great danger, spoke of Pope with very little reverence. 'He has', said Curll, 'a knack at versifying, but in prose I think myself a match for him.'[n] When the orders of the House were examined, none of them appeared to have been infringed; Curll went away triumphant, and Pope was left to seek some other remedy.

Curll's account was that one evening a man in a clergyman's gown, but with a lawyer's band, brought and offered to sale a number of printed volumes, which he found to be Pope's epistolary correspondence; that he asked no name, and was told none, but gave the price demanded, and thought himself authorized to use his purchase to his own advantage.[n]

That Curll gave a true account of the transaction it is reasonable to believe because no falsehood was ever detected; and when some years afterwards I mentioned it to Lintot, the son of Bernard, he declared his opinion to be that Pope knew better than anybody else how Curll obtained the copies because another parcel was at the same time sent to himself, for which no price had ever been demanded, as he made known his resolution not to pay a porter, and consequently not to deal with a nameless agent.

Such care had been taken to make them public that they were sent at once to two booksellers: to Curll, who was likely to seize them as a prey, and to Lintot, who might be expected to give Pope information of the seeming injury. Lintot, I believe, did nothing; and Curll did what was expected. That to make them public was the only purpose may be reasonably supposed because the numbers offered to sale by the private messengers showed that hope of gain could not have been the motive of the impression.

It seems that Pope, being desirous of printing his letters, and not knowing how to do without imputation of vanity what has in this country been done very rarely, contrived an appearance of compulsion, that when he could complain that his letters were surreptitiously published, he might decently and defensively publish them himself.

Pope's private correspondence thus promulgated filled the nation with praises of his candour, tenderness and benevolence, the purity of his purposes, and the fidelity of his friendship. There were some letters which a very good or a very wise man would wish suppressed, but as they had been already exposed, it was impracticable now to retract them.

Lintot: Henry Lintot (1703–58), publisher.
the numbers offered: i.e. 650.

From the perusal of those letters Mr. Allen first conceived the desire of knowing him, and with so much zeal did he cultivate the friendship which he had newly formed that when Pope told his purpose of vindicating his own property by a genuine edition, he offered to pay the cost.

This however Pope did not accept, but in time solicited a subscription for a quarto volume, which appeared (1737), I believe with sufficient profit. In the preface he tells that his letters were reposited in a friend's library, said to be the Earl of Oxford's, and that the copy thence stolen was sent to the press. The story was doubtless received with different degrees of credit. It may be suspected that the preface to the *Miscellanies* was written to prepare the public for such an incident, and to strengthen this opinion James Worsdale, a painter, who was employed in clandestine negotiations but whose veracity was very doubtful, declared that he was the messenger who carried by Pope's direction the books to Curll.

When they were thus published and avowed, as they had relation to recent facts and persons either then living or not yet forgotten, they may be supposed to have found readers, but as the facts were minute, and the characters being either private or literary were little known or little regarded, they awakened no popular kindness or resentment: the book never became much the subject of conversation; some read it as contemporary history, and some perhaps as a model of epistolary language, but those who read it did not talk of it. Not much therefore was added by it to fame or envy; nor do I remember that it produced either public praise or public censure.

It had however in some degree the recommendation of novelty. Our language has few letters except those of statesmen. Howell indeed, about a century ago, published his *Letters*, which are commended by Morhof, and which alone of his hundred volumes continue his memory. Loveday's *Letters* were printed only once; those of

Mr. Allen: Ralph Allen (1694–1764), Mayor of Bath, philanthropist; cf. *Pope: Corr.* iv. 19 (Pope to Allen, 5 June 1736).

Earl of Oxford's: Edward Harley (1689–1741), 2nd Earl of Oxford, collector.

James Worsdale: (1692?–1767), portrait-painter and possible playwright, for an account of whom see W. R. Chetwood, *A General History of the Stage* (1749), pp. 249–50.

Morhof: Daniel George Morhof (1639–91), German author, professor of poetry and history at Kiel. Cf. *De Ratione Conscribendarum Epistolarum Libellus* (Lubeck, 1716), pp. 66–7.

Loveday: Robert Loveday (*fl.* 1655), translator, whose *Letters, Domestic and Foreign* went through seven impressions from 1659 to 1684.

Herbert and Suckling are hardly known.[n] Mrs. Philips's [Orinda's] are equally neglected; and those of Walsh seem written as exercises, and were never sent to any living mistress or friend. Pope's epistolary excellence had an open field: he had no English rival, living or dead.

Pope is seen in this collection as connected with the other contemporary wits, and certainly suffers no disgrace in the comparison; but it must be remembered that he had the power of favouring himself: he might have originally had publication in his mind and have written with care, or have afterwards selected those which he had most happily conceived or most diligently laboured—and I know not whether there does not appear something more studied and artificial in his productions than the rest, except one long letter by Bolingbroke, composed with all the skill and industry of a professed author. It is indeed not easy to distinguish affectation from habit: he that has once studiously formed a style rarely writes afterwards with complete ease. Pope may be said to write always with his reputation in his head, Swift perhaps like a man who remembered that he was writing to Pope, but Arbuthnot like one who lets thoughts drop from his pen as they rise into his mind.

Before these *Letters* appeared, he published the first part of what he persuaded himself to think a system of Ethics under the title of *An Essay on Man*, which, if his letter to Swift (of Sept. 14, 1725) be rightly explained by the commentator, had been eight years under his consideration, and of which he seems to have desired the success with great solicitude. He had now many open and doubtless many secret enemies. The Dunces were yet smarting with the war, and the superiority which he publicly arrogated disposed the world to wish his humiliation.

All this he knew and against all this he provided. His own name, and that of his friend to whom the work is inscribed, were in the first editions carefully suppressed, and the poem, being of a new kind, was ascribed to one or another as favour determined or conjecture wandered; it was given, says Warburton, to every man except him only who could write it. Those who like only when they like the author, and who are under the dominion of a name, condemned it;

Herbert: George Herbert (1593–1633), divine and poet, several of whose letters were printed in Isaac Walton's *Life of Mr. George Herbert* (1670), pp. 123–40.

Mrs. Philips's: Katherine Philips (1631–64), verse-writer, whose letters appeared in 1705.

those of Walsh: in *Letters and Poems, Amorous and Gallant* (1692).

one long letter: Pope: *Corr*. ii. 186–9.

be rightly explained: Warburton, ix. 36. Cf. Pope: *Corr*. ii. 321 n. 4.

his friend to whom: Bolingbroke.   *it was given*: Warburton, iv. 34 n.

and those admired it who are willing to scatter praise at random, which while it is unappropriated excites no envy. Those friends of Pope that were trusted with the secret went about lavishing honours on the new-born poet, and hinting that Pope was never so much in danger from any former rival.

To those authors whom he had personally offended, and to those whose opinion the world considered as decisive and whom he suspected of envy or malevolence, he sent his *Essay* as a present before publication that they might defeat their own enmity by praises which they could not afterwards decently retract.

With these precautions, in 1733 was published the first part of the *Essay on Man*. There had been for some time a report that Pope was busy upon a system of morality, but this design was not discovered in the new poem, which had a form and a title with which its readers were unacquainted. Its reception was not uniform: some thought it a very imperfect piece, though not without good lines. While the author was unknown, some, as will always happen, favoured him as an adventurer, and some censured him as an intruder, but all thought him above neglect; the sale increased, and editions were multiplied.

The subsequent editions of the first Epistle exhibited two memorable corrections. At first the poet and his friend

> Expatiate freely o'er this scene of man,
> A mighty maze *of walks without a plan.*

For which he wrote afterwards,

> A mighty maze, *but not without a plan*;   [l. 6]

for if there were no plan, it was in vain to describe or to trace the maze.

The other alteration was of these lines:

> And spite of pride, *and in thy reason's spite*,
> One truth is clear, whatever is, is right;

but having afterwards discovered, or been shown, that the 'truth' which subsisted 'in spite of reason' could not be very clear, he substituted

> And spite of pride, *in erring reason's spite.*   [l. 293]

To such oversights will the most vigorous mind be liable when it is employed at once upon argument and poetry.

The second and third Epistles were published, and Pope was, I believe, more and more suspected of writing them; at last in 1734 he avowed the fourth,[n] and claimed the honour of a moral poet.

In the conclusion it is sufficiently acknowledged that the doctrine of the *Essay on Man* was received from Bolingbroke, who is said to have ridiculed Pope, among those who enjoyed his confidence, as having adopted and advanced principles of which he did not perceive the consequence, and as blindly propagating opinions contrary to his own. That those communications had been consolidated into a scheme regularly drawn and delivered to Pope, from whom it returned only transformed from prose to verse, has been reported, but hardly can be true. The *Essay* plainly appears the fabric of a poet: what Bolingbroke supplied could be only the first principles; the order, illustration and embellishments must all be Pope's.

These principles it is not my business to clear from obscurity, dogmatism or falsehood, but they were not immediately examined; philosophy and poetry have not often the same readers, and the *Essay* abounded in splendid amplifications and sparkling sentences which were read and admired with no great attention to their ultimate purpose: its flowers caught the eye which did not see what the gay foliage concealed, and for a time flourished in the sunshine of universal approbation. So little was any evil tendency discovered that, as innocence is unsuspicious, many read it for a manual of piety.

Its reputation soon invited a translator. It was first turned into French prose, and afterwards by Resnel into verse.[n] Both translations fell into the hands of Crousaz, who first, when he had the version in prose, wrote a general censure, and afterwards reprinted Resnel's version with particular remarks upon every paragraph.

Crousaz was a professor of Switzerland eminent for his treatise of Logic and his *Examen de Pyrrhonisme*, and however little known or regarded here, was no mean antagonist. His mind was one of those in which philosophy and piety are happily united. He was accustomed to argument and disquisition, and perhaps was grown too desirous of detecting faults; but his intentions were always right, his opinions were solid, and his religion pure.

His incessant vigilance for the promotion of piety disposed him to look with distrust upon all metaphysical systems of theology, and all schemes of virtue and happiness purely rational, and therefore it was not long before he was persuaded that the positions of Pope, as

In the conclusion: iv. 373 ff.

Crousaz: Jean-Pierre de Crousaz (1663–1748), author of *Examen de l'Essai de M. Pope sur l'Homme* (1737), and *Commentaire sur la traduction en vers ... de l'Essai ... sur l'Homme* (1738).

treatise of Logic: *Système de réflexions ... ou Nouvel essai de logique* (1712; rev. 1720).

they terminated for the most part in natural religion, were intended to draw mankind away from Revelation, and to represent the whole course of things as a necessary concatenation of indissoluble fatality; and it is undeniable that in many passages a religious eye may easily discover expressions not very favourable to morals or to liberty.

About this time Warburton began to make his appearance in the first ranks of learning. He was a man of vigorous faculties, a mind fervid and vehement, supplied by incessant and unlimited inquiry, with wonderful extent and variety of knowledge which yet had not oppressed his imagination nor clouded his perspicacity. To every work he brought a memory full fraught, together with a fancy fertile of original combinations, and at once exerted the powers of the scholar, the reasoner and the wit. But his knowledge was too multifarious to be always exact, and his pursuits were too eager to be always cautious. His abilities gave him an haughty confidence which he disdained to conceal or mollify, and his impatience of opposition disposed him to treat his adversaries with such contemptuous superiority as made his readers commonly his enemies, and excited against the advocate the wishes of some who favoured the cause. He seems to have adopted the Roman Emperor's determination, *oderint dum metuant*: he used no allurements of gentle language, but wished to compel rather than persuade.

His style is copious without selection and forcible without neatness: he took the words that presented themselves; his diction is coarse and impure, and his sentences are unmeasured.

He had in the early part of his life pleased himself with the notice of inferior wits, and corresponded with the enemies of Pope. A letter was produced, when he had perhaps himself forgotten it, in which he tells Concanen: 'Dryden, I observe, borrows for want of leisure, and Pope for want of genius; Milton out of pride, and Addison out of modesty.'[n] And when Theobald published Shakespeare in opposition to Pope, the best notes were supplied by Warburton.

But the time was now come when Warburton was to change his opinion, and Pope was to find a defender in him who had contributed so much to the exaltation of his rival.

The arrogance of Warburton excited against him every artifice of offence, and therefore it may be supposed that his union with Pope was censured as hypocritical inconstancy; but surely to think differently, at different times, of poetical merit may be easily allowed. Such opinions are often admitted and dismissed without nice

oderint: Suetonius, *Caligula*, xxx. ('let them hate me so they but fear me').
Concanen: Matthew Concanen (1701–49), author.

examination. Who is there that has not found reason for changing his mind about questions of greater importance?

Warburton, whatever was his motive, undertook without solicitation to rescue Pope from the talons of Crousaz by freeing him from the imputation of favouring fatality or rejecting Revelation, and from month to month continued a vindication of the *Essay on Man* in the literary journal of that time called *The Republic of Letters*.[n]

Pope, who probably began to doubt the tendency of his own work, was glad that the positions of which he perceived himself not to know the full meaning could by any mode of interpretation be made to mean well, How much he was pleased with his gratuitous defender the following letter evidently shows:

24 March 1743

Sir,

I have just received from Mr. R. two more of your letters. It is in the greatest hurry imaginable that I write this; but I cannot help thanking you in particular for your third letter, which is so extremely clear, short and full, that I think Mr. Crousaz ought never to have another answer, and deserved not so good an one. I can only say you do him too much honour, and me too much right, so odd as the expression seems, for you have made my system as clear as I ought to have done, and could not. It is indeed the same system as mine, but illustrated with a ray of your own, as they say our natural body is the same still when it is glorified. I am sure I like it better than I did before, and so will every man else. I know I meant just what you explain, but I did not explain my own meaning so well as you. You understand me as well as I do myself; but you express me better than I could express myself. Pray accept the sincerest acknowledgements. I cannot but wish these letters were put together in one book, and intend (with your leave) to procure a translation of part, at least, of all of them into French; but I shall not proceed a step without your consent and opinion, etc.

By this fond and eager acceptance of an exculpatory comment, Pope testified that, whatever might be the seeming or real import of the principles which he had received from Bolingbroke, he had not intentionally attacked religion; and Bolingbroke, if he meant to make him without his own consent an instrument of mischief, found him now engaged with his eyes open on the side of truth.

It is known that Bolingbroke concealed from Pope his real opinions.

Sir: *Pope: Corr.* iv. 171–2 (Pope to Warburton, 11 Apr. [1739]).
Mr. R.: Jacob Robinson (ibid. n. 5).

He once discovered them to Mr Hooke, who related them again to Pope, and was told by him that he must have mistaken the meaning of what he heard; and Bolingbroke, when Pope's uneasiness incited him to desire an explanation, declared that Hooke had misunderstood him.

Bolingbroke hated Warburton, who had drawn his pupil from him, and a little before Pope's death they had a dispute from which they parted with mutual aversion.

From this time Pope lived in the closest intimacy with his commentator, and amply rewarded his kindness and his zeal, for he introduced him to Mr. Murray, by whose interest he became preacher at Lincoln's Inn, and to Mr. Allen, who gave him his niece and his estate, and by consequence a bishopric. When he died he left him the property of his works—a legacy which may be reasonably estimated at £4,000.[n]

Pope's fondness for the *Essay on Man* appeared by his desire of its propagation. Dobson, who had gained reputation by his version of Prior's *Solomon*, was employed by him to translate it into Latin verse, and was for that purpose some time at Twickenham; but he left his work, whatever was the reason, unfinished, and by Benson's invitation undertook the longer task of *Paradise Lost*. Pope then desired his friend to find a scholar who should turn his *Essay* into Latin prose, but no such performance has ever appeared.

Pope lived at this time 'among the great' with that reception and respect to which his works entitled him, and which he had not impaired by any private misconduct or factious partiality. Though Bolingbroke was his friend, Walpole was not his enemy, but treated him with so much consideration as, at his request, to solicit and obtain from the French Minister an abbey for Mr. Southcote, whom he considered himself as obliged to reward by this exertion of his interest for the benefit which he had received from his attendance in a long illness.

It was said that, when the Court was at Richmond, Queen Caroline had declared her intention to visit him. This may have been only a careless effusion, thought on no more; the report of such notice,

Mr. Hooke: Nathaniel Hooke (d. 1763), translator and historian.
Dobson: William Dobson (*fl.* 1734–50), classical scholar.
Pope then desired: Pope: *Corr.* iv. 251–2, 288 (Pope to Warburton, 24 June and 27 Oct. 1740).   '*among the great*': *Imit. Hor. Sat.* II. i. 133.
the French Minister: Cardinal Fleury (1653–1743).
Mr. Southcote: Thomas Southcote (or Southcott) (1670–1748), Catholic Jacobite priest.

however, was soon in many mouths, and if I do not forget or mis-apprehend Savage's account, Pope, pretending to decline what was not yet offered, left his house for a time, not, I suppose, for any other reason than lest he should be thought to stay at home in expectation of an honour which would not be conferred. He was therefore angry at Swift, who represents him as 'refusing the visits of a Queen', because he knew that what had never been offered had never been refused.

Beside the general system of morality supposed to be contained in the *Essay on Man*, it was his intention to write distinct poems upon the different duties or conditions of life—one of which is the *Epistle to Lord Bathurst* (1733) *on the Use of Riches*, a piece on which he declared great labour to have been bestowed.

Into this poem some incidents are historically thrown, and some known characters are introduced with others of which it is difficult to say how far they are real or fictitious; but the praise of Kyrle, the 'Man of Ross', deserves particular examination, who, after a long and pompous enumeration of his public works and private charities, is said to have diffused all those blessings from 'five hundred a year'. Wonders are willingly told and willingly heard. The truth is that Kyrle was a man of known integrity and active benevolence, by whose solicitation the wealthy were persuaded to pay contributions to his charitable schemes; this influence he obtained by an example of liberality exerted to the utmost extent of his power, and was thus enabled to give more than he had. This account Mr. Victor received from the minister of the place, and I have preserved it that the praise of a good man being made more credible may be more solid. Narrations of romantic and impracticable virtue will be read with wonder, but that which is unattainable is recommended in vain; that good may be endeavoured it must be shown to be possible.

This is the only piece in which the author has given a hint of his religion by ridiculing the ceremony of burning the Pope, and by mentioning with some indignation the inscription on the Monument.

When this poem was first published, the dialogue, having no letters of direction, was perplexed and obscure.[n] Pope seems to have

---

He was therefore angry: Pope: *Corr.* iii. 95 (Pope to Swift, 4 Mar. 1730).
'*refusing*': 'A Libel on D— D—', ll. 71–4.
on which he declared: Spence, § 312.   *Kyrle*: John Kyrle (1637–1724).
'*five hundred*': l. 280.
Mr. Victor: Benjamin Victor (d. 1778), theatrical manager, personally known to Johnson (*Life*, iv. 53).
by ridiculing: ll. 213–14.   *by mentioning*: ll. 339–40 and n.

written with no very distinct idea, for he calls that an 'Epistle to Bathurst' in which Bathurst is introduced as speaking.

He afterwards (1734) inscribed to Lord Cobham his *Characters of Men*, written with close attention to the operations of the mind and modifications of life. In this poem he has endeavoured to establish and exemplify his favourite theory of the 'ruling passion', by which he means an original direction of desire to some particular object, an innate affection which gives all action a determinate and invariable tendency, and operates upon the whole system of life either openly, or more secretly by the intervention of some accidental or subordinate propension.

Of any passion thus innate and irresistible the existence may reasonably be doubted. Human characters are by no means constant: men change by change of place, of fortune, of acquaintance; he who is at one time a lover of pleasure is at another a lover of money. Those indeed who attain any excellence commonly spend life in one pursuit, for excellence is not often gained upon easier terms. But to the particular species of excellence men are directed not by an ascendant planet or predominating humour, but by the first book which they read, some early conversation which they heard, or some accident which excited ardour and emulation.

It must be at least allowed that this 'ruling passion', antecedent to reason and observation, must have an object independent on human contrivance, for there can be no natural desire of artificial good. No man therefore can be born, in the strict acceptation, a lover of money, for he may be born where money does not exist; nor can he be born, in a moral sense, a lover of his country, for society, politically regulated, is a state contradistinguished from a state of nature, and any attention to that coalition of interests which makes the happiness of a country is possible only to those whom inquiry and reflection have enabled to comprehend it.

This doctrine is in itself pernicious as well as false: its tendency is to produce the belief of a kind of moral predestination or overruling principle which cannot be resisted; he that admits it is prepared to comply with every desire that caprice or opportunity shall excite, and to flatter himself that he submits only to the lawful dominion of nature in obeying the resistless authority of his 'ruling passion'.

Pope has formed his theory with so little skill that in the examples

Bathurst: Allen Bathurst (1685–1775), M.P., created Baron and later 1st Earl Bathurst.
Lord Cobham: Sir Richard Temple (1675–1749), Viscount Cobham and 4th Baronet of Stowe, general.

by which he illustrates and confirms it, he has confounded passions, appetites and habits.

To the *Characters of Men* he added soon after, in an Epistle supposed to have been addressed to Martha Blount, but which the last edition has taken from her, the *Characters of Women*. This poem, which was laboured with great diligence, and in the author's opinion with great success, was neglected at its first publication, as the commentator supposes because the public was informed by an advertisement that it contained 'no character drawn from the life'— an assertion which Pope probably did not expect or wish to have been believed, and which he soon gave his readers sufficient reason to distrust by telling them, in a note, that the work was imperfect because part of his subject was 'vice too high' to be yet exposed.

The time however soon came in which it was safe to display the Duchess of Marlborough under the name of Atossa, and her character was inserted with no great honour to the writer's gratitude.[n]

He published from time to time (between 1730 and 1740) imitations of different poems of Horace, generally with his name, and once, as was suspected, without it. What he was upon moral principles ashamed to own he ought to have suppressed. Of these pieces it is useless to settle the dates as they had seldom much relation to the times, and perhaps had been long in his hands.

This mode of imitation, in which the ancients are familiarized by adapting their sentiments to modern topics, by making Horace say of Shakespeare what he originally said of Ennius, and accommodating his satires on Pantolabus and Nomentanus to the flatterers and prodigals of our own time, was first practised in the reign of Charles II by Oldham and Rochester[n]—at least I remember no instances more ancient. It is a kind of middle composition between translation and original design, which pleases when the thoughts are unexpectedly applicable and the parallels lucky. It seems to have been Pope's favourite amusement, for he has carried it further than any former poet.

Martha Blount: (1690–1762).

in the author's opinion: *Pope: Corr*. iii. 349 (Pope to Swift, 16 Feb. 1733).

as the commentator supposes: Warburton, iii. 193 n.

'vice too high': n. to l. 199; cf. *Imit. Hor. Sat*. II. i. 60.

Duchess of Marlborough: Sarah Churchill (*née* Jennings) (1660–1744), Duchess of Marlborough.

and once: *Sober Advice from Horace* (1734) was published anonymously.

by making Horace: *Imit. Hor. Ep*. II. i. 69–72.

Ennius: (239–169 B.C.), Latin dramatist and poet.

accommodating his satires: *Imit. Hor. Sat*. II. i. 37–40.

Oldham: John Oldham (1653–83), poet, imitated poems by Horace and Juvenal.

He published likewise a revival, in smoother numbers, of Dr. Donne's *Satires*, which was recommended to him by the Duke of Shrewsbury and the Earl of Oxford. They made no great impression on the public. Pope seems to have known their imbecility, and therefore suppressed them while he was yet contending to rise in reputation, but ventured them when he thought their deficiencies more likely to be imputed to Donne than to himself.

The *Epistle to Dr. Arbuthnot*, which seems to be derived in its first design from Boileau's Address *à son Esprit*, was published in January 1735, about a month before the death of him to whom it is inscribed. It is to be regretted that either honour or pleasure should have been missed by Arbuthnot, a man estimable for his learning, amiable for his life, and venerable for his piety.

Arbuthnot was a man of great comprehension, skilful in his profession, versed in the sciences, acquainted with ancient literature, and able to animate his mass of knowledge by a bright and active imagination—a scholar with great brilliancy of wit, a wit who, in the crowd of life, retained and discovered a noble ardour of religious zeal.

In this poem Pope seems to reckon with the public. He vindicates himself from censures, and with dignity rather than arrogance enforces his own claims to kindness and respect.

Into this poem are interwoven several paragraphs which had been before printed as a fragment, and among them the satirical lines upon Addison, of which the last couplet has been twice corrected. It was at first,

> Who would not smile if such a man there be?
> Who would not laugh if Addison were he?

Then,

> Who would not grieve if such a man there be?
> Who would not laugh if Addison were he?

At last it is,

> Who but must laugh if such a man there be?
> Who would not weep if Atticus were he?

He was at this time at open war with Lord Hervey, who had distinguished himself as a steady adherent to the ministry, and being offended with a contemptuous answer to one of his pamphlets, had

Duke of Shrewsbury: Charles Talbot (1660–1718), 12th Earl and only Duke of Shrewsbury. Cf. *Pope: Poems*, iv. 3.   *Boileau's Address*: Satire ix.
which had been before printed: see *Pope: Poems*, vi. 144, 285.
Who would not: ll. 213–14.
Lord Hervey: John Hervey (1696–1743), Baron Hervey of Ickworth, pamphleteer and memoir-writer.

summoned Pulteney to a duel.[n] Whether he or Pope made the first attack perhaps cannot now be easily known; he had written an invective against Pope, whom he calls 'Hard as thy heart, and as thy birth obscure', and hints that his father was a 'hatter'.[n] To this Pope wrote a reply in verse and prose; the verses are in this poem, and the prose, though it was never sent, is printed among his letters, but to a cool reader of the present time exhibits nothing but tedious malignity.

His last satires of the general kind were two 'Dialogues', named from the year in which they were published *Seventeen Hundred and Thirty Eight*. In these poems many are praised and many are reproached. Pope was then entangled in the Opposition, a follower of the Prince of Wales, who dined at his house, and the friend of many who obstructed and censured the conduct of the ministers. His political partiality was too plainly shown: he forgot the prudence with which he passed, in his earlier years, uninjured and unoffending through much more violent conflicts of faction.

In the first 'Dialogue', having an opportunity of praising Allen of Bath, he asked his leave to mention him as a man not illustrious by any merit of his ancestors, and called him in his verses 'low-born Allen'. Men are seldom satisfied with praise introduced or followed by any mention of defect. Allen seems not to have taken any pleasure in his epithet, which was afterwards softened into 'humble Allen'.

In the second 'Dialogue' he took some liberty with one of the Foxes, among others—which Fox, in a reply to Lyttelton, took an opportunity of repaying by reproaching him with the friendship of a lampooner who scattered his ink without fear or decency, and against whom he hoped the resentment of the legislature would quickly be discharged.

About this time Paul Whitehead, a small poet, was summoned before the Lords for a poem called *Manners*, together with Dodsley his publisher. Whitehead, who hung loose upon society, skulked and escaped, but Dodsley's shop and family made his appearance

Pulteney: Sir William Pulteney (1684–1764), Earl of Bath, statesman.
the verses: ll. 305–33.
the prose: *A Letter to a Noble Lord* (Warburton, viii. 253–80).
he asked his leave: Pope: *Corr.* iv. 93 (28 Apr. 1738).
'low-born Allen': l. 135.
Fox: Henry Fox (1705–1774), 1st Baron Holland, statesman; see 'Dialogue II',
    ll. 166–79. Cf. 'Dialogue I', l. 71; *Lives*, ed. Hill, iii. 449.
Lyttelton: George Lyttelton (1709–73), 1st Baron Lyttelton.
Paul Whitehead: (1710–74), satirist.
Dodsley's: Robert Dodsley (1703–64), poet, dramatist, and bookseller.

necessary. He was, however, soon dismissed,[n] and the whole process was probably intended rather to intimidate Pope than to punish Whitehead.

Pope never afterwards attempted to join the patriot with the poet, nor drew his pen upon statesmen. That he desisted from his attempts of reformation is imputed by his commentator to his despair of prevailing over the corruption of the time. He was not likely to have been ever of opinion that the dread of his satire would countervail the love of power or of money; he pleased himself with being important and formidable, and gratified sometimes his pride and sometimes his resentment, till at last he began to think he should be more safe if he were less busy.

The *Memoirs of Scriblerus* published about this time, extend only to the first book of a work projected in concert by Pope, Swift and Arbuthnot, who used to meet in the time of Queen Anne, and denominated themselves the 'Scriblerus Club'. Their purpose was to censure the abuses of learning by a fictitious life of an infatuated scholar. They were dispersed, the design was never completed, and Warburton laments its miscarriage as an event very disastrous to polite letters.

If the whole may be estimated by this specimen, which seems to be the production of Arbuthnot with a few touches perhaps by Pope, the want of more will not be much lamented, for the follies which the writer ridicules are so little practised that they are not known; nor can the satire be understood but by the learned; he raises phantoms of absurdity and then drives them away. He cures diseases that were never felt.

For this reason this joint production of three great writers has never obtained any notice from mankind; it has been little read, or when read has been forgotten, as no man could be wiser, better or merrier by remembering it.

The design cannot boast of much originality, for besides its general resemblance to *Don Quixote*, there will be found in it particular imitations of *The History of Mr. Oufle*.[n]

Swift carried so much of it into Ireland as supplied him with hints for his *Travels*, and with those the world might have been contented though the rest had been suppressed.

Pope had sought for images and sentiments in a region not known to have been explored by many other of the English writers: he had

---

is imputed: Warburton, iv. 338.   *about this time*: actually in 1741.
Warburton laments: vi. 112 n.

consulted the modern writers of Latin poetry, a class of authors whom
Boileau endeavoured to bring into contempt, and who are too
generally neglected. Pope, however, was not ashamed of their
acquaintance, nor ungrateful for the advantages which he might have
derived from it. A small selection from the Italians who wrote in
Latin had been published at London about the latter end of the last
century by a man who concealed his name, but whom his preface
shows to have been well qualified for his undertaking.[n] This
collection Pope amplified by more than half, and (1740) published it
in two volumes, but injuriously omitted his predecessor's preface. To
these books, which had nothing but the mere text, no regard was paid:
the authors were still neglected, and the editor was neither praised nor
censured.

He did not sink into idleness; he had planned a work which he
considered as subsequent to his *Essay on Man*, of which he has given
this account to Dr. Swift.

25 March 1736

> If ever I write any more Epistles in verse, one of them
> shall be addressed to you. I have long concerted it, and
> begun it; but I would make what bears your name as
> finished as my last work ought to be, that is to say, more
> finished than any of the rest. The subject is large, and will
> divide into four Epistles, which naturally follow the
> *Essay on Man*, viz. 1. Of the Extent and Limits of Human
> Reason and Science. 2. A View of the useful and therefore
> attainable, and of the unuseful and therefore unattainable
> Arts. 3. Of the Nature, Ends, Application, and Use of
> different Capacities. 4. Of the Use of Learning, of the
> Science of the World, and of Wit. It will conclude with a
> satire against the misapplication of all these, exemplified
> by pictures, characters, and examples.

This work in its full extent, being now afflicted with an asthma and
finding the powers of life gradually declining, he had no longer
courage to undertake, but from the materials which he had provided,
he added at Warburton's request another book to *The Dunciad*, of
which the design is to ridicule such studies as are either hopeless or
useless, as either pursue what is unattainable or what, if it be attained,
is of no use.

When this book was printed (1742) the laurel had been for some
time upon the head of Cibber, a man whom it cannot be supposed

whom Boileau endeavoured: Oeuvres, iii. 60–1 (*Fragment d'un autre Dialogue*).
If ever I write: Pope: Corr. iv. 5.
at Warburton's request: see Warburton, i. *vii–viii*.

that Pope could regard with much kindness or esteem, though in one of the *Imitations of Horace* he has liberally enough praised *The Careless Husband*. In *The Dunciad*, among other worthless scribblers, he had mentioned Cibber, who in his *Apology* complains of the great poet's unkindness as more injurious 'because', says he, 'I never have offended him.'

It might have been expected that Pope should have been in some degree mollified by this submissive gentleness, but no such consequence appeared. Though he condescended to commend Cibber once, he mentioned him afterwards contemptuously in one of his *Satires*, and again in his *Epistle to Arbuthnot*, and in the fourth book of *The Dunciad* attacked him with acrimony to which the provocation is not easily discoverable. Perhaps he imagined that in ridiculing the laureate he satirized those by whom the laurel had been given, and gratified that ambitious petulance with which he affected to insult the great.

The severity of this satire left Cibber no longer any patience. He had confidence enough in his own powers to believe that he could disturb the quiet of his adversary, and doubtless did not want instigators who, without any care about the victory, desired to amuse themselves by looking on the contest. He therefore gave the town a pamphlet in which he declares his resolution from that time never to bear another blow without returning it, and to tire out his adversary by perseverance if he cannot conquer him by strength.

The incessant and unappeasable malignity of Pope he imputes to a very distant cause. After the *Three Hours after Marriage* had been driven off the stage by the offence which the mummy and crocodile gave the audience, while the exploded scene was yet fresh in memory it happened that Cibber played Bayes in *The Rehearsal*, and as it had been usual to enliven the part by the mention of any recent theatrical transactions, he said that he once thought to have introduced his lovers disguised in a mummy and a crocodile. 'This', says he, 'was received with loud claps, which indicated contempt of the play.' Pope, who was behind the scenes, meeting him as he left the stage, attacked him, as he says, with all the virulence of a 'wit out of his senses'; to which he replied 'that he would take no other notice of

he has liberally enough: Imit. Hor. Ep. II. i. 91–4.
In the Dunciad: Pope: Poems, v. 91, 184, 187.
'*because*', *says he*: Apology for the Life of Cibber (1740), p. 22.
he mentioned him: Imit. Hor. Sat. II. i. 34, 'Dialogue I', l. 115; Epistle to Arbuthnot, ll. 97, 373; Dunciad, iv. passim, esp. n. to l. 20.
a pamphlet: A Letter from Mr. Cibber to Mr. Pope (1742); see pp. 8, 17–19, 21–2, 47–9.   *exploded*: hissed off the stage.

what was said by so particular a man than to declare that, as often as he played that part, he would repeat the same provocation'.

He shows his opinion to be that Pope was one of the authors of the play which he so zealously defended, and adds an idle story of Pope's behaviour at a tavern.

The pamphlet was written with little power of thought or language, and if suffered to remain without notice, would have been very soon forgotten. Pope had now been enough acquainted with human life to know, if his passion had not been too powerful for his understanding, that from a contention like his with Cibber the world seeks nothing but diversion, which is given at the expense of the higher character. When Cibber lampooned Pope, curiosity was excited; what Pope would say of Cibber nobody inquired but in hope that Pope's asperity might betray his pain and lessen his dignity.

He should therefore have suffered the pamphlet to flutter and die, without confessing that it stung him. The dishonour of being shown as Cibber's antagonist could never be compensated by the victory. Cibber had nothing to lose: when Pope had exhausted all his malignity upon him, he would rise in the esteem both of his friends and his enemies. Silence only could have made him despicable: the blow which did not appear to be felt would have been struck in vain.

But Pope's irascibility prevailed, and he resolved to tell the whole English world that he was at war with Cibber, and to show that he thought him no common adversary, he prepared no common vengeance: he published a new edition of *The Dunciad* in which he degraded Theobald from his painful pre-eminence and enthroned Cibber in his stead. Unhappily the two heroes were of opposite characters, and Pope was unwilling to lose what he had already written; he has therefore depraved his poem by giving to Cibber the old books, the cold pedantry, and sluggish pertinacity of Theobald.

Pope was ignorant enough of his own interest to make another change, and introduced Osborne contending for the prize among the booksellers. Osborne was a man entirely destitute of shame, without sense of any disgrace but that of poverty. He told me when he was doing that which raised Pope's resentment that he should be put into *The Dunciad*; but he had the fate of Cassandra: I gave no credit to his prediction till in time I saw it accomplished. The shafts of satire

Osborne: Thomas Osborne (d. 1767), bookseller, and one-time employer of Johnson. Cf. *Dunciad*, ii. 167–78.

Cassandra: daughter of Priam and Hecuba who, having the gift of prophecy, foretold the doom of Troy, but had the misfortune to have her predictions go unheeded.

were directed equally in vain against Cibber and Osborne, being repelled by the impenetrable impudence of one, and deadened by the impassive dulness of the other. Pope confessed his own pain by his anger, but he gave no pain to those who had provoked him. He was able to hurt none but himself; by transferring the same ridicule from one to another he destroyed its efficacy, for by showing that what he had said of one he was ready to say of another, he reduced himself to the insignificance of his own magpie who from his cage calls cuckold at a venture.

Cibber, according to his engagement, repaid *The Dunciad* with another pamphlet which, Pope said, 'would be as good as a dose of hartshorn to him'; but his tongue and his heart were at variance. I have heard Mr. Richardson relate that he attended his father the painter on a visit when one of Cibber's pamphlets came into the hands of Pope, who said: 'These things are my diversion.' They sat by him while he perused it, and saw his features writhen with anguish, and young Richardson said to his father, when they returned, that he hoped to be preserved from such diversion as had been that day the lot of Pope.

From this time, finding his diseases more oppressive and his vital powers gradually declining, he no longer strained his faculties with any original composition, nor proposed any other employment for his remaining life than the revisal and correction of his former works, in which he received advice and assistance from Warburton, whom he appears to have trusted and honoured in the highest degree.

He laid aside his epic poem, perhaps without much loss to mankind, for his hero was Brutus the Trojan who, according to a ridiculous fiction, established a colony in Britain. The subject therefore was of the fabulous age: the actors were a race upon whom imagination has been exhausted and attention wearied, and to whom the mind will not easily be recalled when it is invited in blank verse, which Pope had adopted with great imprudence, and, I think, without due consideration of the nature of our language. The sketch is, at least in part, preserved by Ruffhead, by which it appears that Pope was thoughtless enough to model the names of his heroes with terminations not consistent with the time or country in which he places them.

his own magpie: *Epistle to Cobham*, ll. 5–6.

another pamphlet: *Another Occasional Letter from Mr. Cibber to Mr. Pope* (1744).

'would be as good': *Pope: Corr.* iv. 492 (Pope to Warburton, 12 Jan. 1744).

Mr. Richardson: Jonathan Richardson the younger (1694–1771), portrait-painter. Cf. *Richardsoniana*, pp. 311–12.

writhen: contorted.   *preserved by Ruffhead*: pp. 409 ff.

He lingered through the next year, but perceived himself, as he expresses it, 'going down the hill'. He had for at least five years been afflicted with an asthma and other disorders which his physicians were unable to relieve. Towards the end of his life he consulted Dr. Thomson, a man who had by large promises, and free censures of the common practice of physic, forced himself up into sudden reputation. Thomson declared his distemper to be a dropsy, and evacuated part of the water by tincture of jalap, but confessed that his belly did not subside. Thomson had many enemies, and Pope was persuaded to dismiss him.

While he was yet capable of amusement and conversation, as he was one day sitting in the air with Lord Bolingbroke and Lord Marchmont, he saw his favourite Martha Blount at the bottom of the terrace, and asked Lord Bolingbroke to go and hand her up. Bolingbroke, not liking his errand, crossed his legs and sat still, but Lord Marchmont, who was younger and less captious, waited on the lady, who when he came to her asked: 'What, is he not dead yet?' She is said to have neglected him with shameful unkindness in the latter time of his decay, yet of the little which he had to leave she had a very great part. Their acquaintance began early; the life of each was pictured on the other's mind; their conversation therefore was endearing, for when they met there was an immediate coalition of congenial notions. Perhaps he considered her unwillingness to approach the chamber of sickness as female weakness or human frailty, perhaps he was conscious to himself of peevishness and impatience, or though he was offended by her inattention might yet consider her merit as overbalancing her fault; and if he had suffered his heart to be alienated from her, he could have found nothing that might fill her place; he could have only shrunk within himself; it was too late to transfer his confidence or fondness.

In May 1744 his death was approaching; on the 6th he was all day delirious, which he mentioned four days afterwards as a sufficient humiliation of the vanity of man; he afterwards complained of seeing things as through a curtain and in false colours, and one day, in the presence of Dodsley, asked what arm it was that came out from the wall. He said that his greatest inconvenience was inability to think.[n]

Bolingbroke sometimes wept over him in this state of helpless

---

'*going down*': *Pope: Corr.* iv. 501 (Pope to Warburton, 21 Feb. 1744).

Dr. Thomson: Thomas Thompson (or Thomson) (d. 1763), physician.

Lord Marchmont: Hugh Hume (1708–94), 3rd Earl of Marchmont, politician, and Pope's literary executor.

She is said: Ruffhead, p. 548 n.

decay, and being told by Spence that Pope, at the intermission of his deliriousness, was always saying something kind either of his present or absent friends, and that his humanity seemed to have survived his understanding, answered: 'It has so.' And added: 'I never in my life knew a man that had so tender a heart for his particular friends, or more general friendship for mankind.' At another time he said: 'I have known Pope these thirty years, and value myself more in his friendship than . . .'—his grief then suppressed his voice.

Pope expressed undoubting confidence of a future state. Being asked by his friend Mr. Hooke, a Papist, whether he would not die like his father and mother, and whether a priest should not be called, he answered: 'I do not think it essential, but it will be very right; and I thank you for putting me in mind of it.'

In the morning, after the priest had given him the last sacraments, he said: 'There is nothing that is meritorious but virtue and friendship, and indeed friendship itself is only a part of virtue.'

He died in the evening of the 30th day of May, 1744, so placidly that the attendants did not discern the exact time of his expiration. He was buried at Twickenham, near his father and mother, where a monument has been erected to him by his commentator the Bishop of Gloucester.

He left the care of his papers to his executors, first to Lord Bolingbroke, and if he should not be living to the Earl of Marchmont, undoubtedly expecting them to be proud of the trust and eager to extend his fame. But let no man dream of influence beyond his life. After a decent time Dodsley the bookseller went to solicit preference as the publisher, and was told that the parcel had not been yet inspected; and whatever was the reason, the world has been disappointed of what was 'reserved for the next age'.

He lost, indeed, the favour of Bolingbroke by a kind of posthumous offence. The political pamphlet called *The Patriot King* had been put into his hands that he might procure the impression of a very few copies to be distributed according to the author's direction among his friends, and Pope assured him that no more had been printed than were allowed; but soon after his death, the printer brought and resigned a complete edition of 1,500 copies, which Pope had ordered him to print and to retain in secret. He kept, as was observed, his engagement to Pope better than Pope had kept it to his friend,[n] and nothing was known of the transaction till, upon the death of his employer, he thought himself obliged to deliver the books

expiration: 'the action of breathing one's last; death, decease. *Obs.*' (*OED*).
'*reserved for the next age*': *Imit. Hor. Sat.* II. i. 59–60.

to the right owner, who with great indignation made a fire in his yard and delivered the whole impression to the flames.

Hitherto nothing had been done which was not naturally dictated by resentment of violated faith—resentment more acrimonious as the violator had been more loved or more trusted. But here the anger might have stopped: the injury was private, and there was little danger from the example.

Bolingbroke, however, was not yet satisfied; his thirst of vengeance incited him to blast the memory of the man over whom he had wept in his last struggles, and he employed Mallet, another friend of Pope, to tell the tale to the public with all its aggravations. Warburton, whose heart was warm with his legacy and tender by the recent separation, thought it proper for him to interpose, and undertook, not indeed to vindicate the action, for breach of trust has always something criminal, but to extenuate it by an apology.[n] Having advanced, what cannot be denied, that moral obliquity is made more or less excusable by the motives that produce it, he inquires what evil purpose could have induced Pope to break his promise. He could not delight his vanity by usurping the work which, though not sold in shops, had been shown to a number more than sufficient to preserve the author's claim; he could not gratify his avarice, for he could not sell his plunder till Bolingbroke was dead—and even then, if the copy was left to another his fraud would be defeated, and if left to himself would be useless.

Warburton therefore supposes, with great appearance of reason, that the irregularity of his conduct proceeded wholly from his zeal for Bolingbroke, who might perhaps have destroyed the pamphlet which Pope thought it his duty to preserve even without its author's approbation. To this apology an answer was written in *A Letter to the most Impudent Man Living*.

He brought some reproach upon his own memory by the petulant and contemptuous mention made in his will of Mr. Allen, and an affected repayment of his benefactions. Mrs. Blount, as the known friend and favourite of Pope, had been invited to the house of Allen, where she comported herself with such indecent arrogance that she parted from Mrs. Allen in a state of irreconcilable dislike, and the door was for ever barred against her. This exclusion she resented with so much bitterness as to refuse any legacy from Pope unless he left the world with a disavowal of obligation to Allen. Having been long under her dominion, now tottering in the decline of life, and unable to resist the violence of her temper, or perhaps with the prejudice of a

Mrs. Allen: Elizabeth Allen (*née* Holder) (1698–1766).

lover, persuaded that she had suffered improper treatment, he complied with her demand and polluted his will with female resentment. Allen accepted the legacy, which he gave to the Hospital at Bath, observing that Pope was always a bad accomptant, and that if to £150 he had put a cipher more, he had come nearer to the truth.[n]

The person of Pope is well known not to have been formed by the nicest model. He has, in his account of the 'Little Club', compared himself to a spider, and by another is described as protuberant behind and before. He is said to have been beautiful in his infancy, but he was of a constitution originally feeble and weak, and as bodies of a tender frame are easily distorted, his deformity was probably in part the effect of his application. His stature was so low that, to bring him to a level with common tables, it was necessary to raise his seat. But his face was not displeasing, and his eyes were animated and vivid.

By natural deformity or accidental distortion, his vital functions were so much disordered that his life was a 'long disease'. His most frequent assailant was the headache, which he used to relieve by inhaling the steam of coffee, which he very frequently required.

Most of what can be told concerning his petty peculiarities was communicated by a female domestic of the Earl of Oxford, who knew him perhaps after the middle of life.[n] He was then so weak as to stand in perpetual need of female attendance, extremely sensible of cold, so that he wore a kind of fur doublet under a shirt of very coarse, warm linen with fine sleeves. When he rose, he was invested in bodice made of stiff canvas, being scarce able to hold himself erect till they were laced, and he then put on a flannel waistcoat. One side was contracted. His legs were so slender that he enlarged their bulk with three pair of stockings, which were drawn on and off by the maid, for he was not able to dress or undress himself, and neither went to bed nor rose without help. His weakness made it very difficult for him to be clean.

His hair had fallen almost all away, and he used to dine sometimes with Lord Oxford privately in a velvet cap. His dress of ceremony was black, with a tie-wig and a little sword.

The indulgence and accommodation which his sickness required had taught him all the unpleasing and unsocial qualities of a valetudinary man. He expected that everything should give way to his

compared himself: Guardian 92.
is described: Voltaire, *Oeuvres* (Paris 1819–25), xlii. 157.
He is said: Cf. Spence, §§ 8–9.   '*long disease*': *Epistle to Arbuthnot*, l. 132.

ease or humour, as a child whose parents will not hear her cry has an unresisted dominion in the nursery.

> C'est que l'enfant toujours est homme,
> C'est que l'homme est toujours enfant.

When he wanted to sleep he 'nodded in company', and once slumbered at his own table while the Prince of Wales was talking of poetry.

The reputation which his friendship gave procured him many invitations; but he was a very troublesome inmate. He brought no servant, and had so many wants that a numerous attendance was scarcely able to supply them. Wherever he was, he left no room for another because he exacted the attention and employed the activity of the whole family. His errands were so frequent and frivolous that the footmen in time avoided and neglected him, and the Earl of Oxford discharged some of the servants for their resolute refusal of his messages. The maids, when they had neglected their business, alleged that they had been employed by Mr. Pope. One of his constant demands was of coffee in the night, and to the woman that waited on him in his chamber he was very burdensome; but he was careful to recompense her want of sleep, and Lord Oxford's servant declared that in a house where her business was to answer his call, she would not ask for wages.

He had another fault easily incident to those who, suffering much pain, think themselves entitled to whatever pleasures they can snatch. He was too indulgent to his appetite: he loved meat highly seasoned and of strong taste, and at the intervals of the table amused himself with biscuits and dry conserves. If he sat down to a variety of dishes, he would oppress his stomach with repletion, and though he seemed angry when a dram was offered him, did not forbear to drink it.[n] His friends, who knew the avenues to his heart, pampered him with presents of luxury, which he did not suffer to stand neglected. The death of great men is not always proportioned to the lustre of their lives. Hannibal, says Juvenal, did not perish by a javelin or a sword; the slaughters of Cannae were revenged by a ring. The death of Pope was imputed by some of his friends to a silver saucepan in which it was his delight to heat potted lampreys.[n]

That he loved too well to eat is certain, but that his sensuality shortened his life will not be hastily concluded when it is remembered that a conformation so irregular lasted six and fifty years,

C'est que: a French proverb ('the child is ever a man, and the man ever a child').
'*nodded in company*': *Imit. Hor. Sat.* II. i. 13.
Hannibal: (247–182 B.C.), great Carthaginian general in the Second Punic War; see Juvenal, *Satires*, x. 164–6.

notwithstanding such pertinacious diligence of study and meditation.

In all his intercourse with mankind he had great delight in artifice,
and endeavoured to attain all his purposes by indirect and unsus-
pected methods. 'He hardly drank tea without a stratagem.' If at
the house of his friends he wanted any accommodation, he was not
willing to ask for it in plain terms, but would mention it remotely as
something convenient—though when it was procured he soon made
it appear for whose sake it had been recommended. Thus he teased
Lord Orrery till be obtained a screen. He practised his arts on such
small occasions that Lady Bolingbroke used to say, in a French
phrase, that 'he played the politician about cabbages and turnips'.[n]
His unjustifiable impression of *The Patriot King*, as it can be imputed
to no particular motive, must have proceeded from his general habit
of secrecy and cunning; he caught an opportunity of a sly trick, and
pleased himself with the thought of outwitting Bolingbroke.

In familiar or convivial conversation it does not appear that he
excelled. He may be said to have resembled Dryden as being not one
that was distinguished by vivacity in company. It is remarkable that
so near his time so much should be known of what he has written,
and so little of what he has said; traditional memory retains no
sallies of raillery, nor sentences of observation, nothing either
pointed or solid, either wise or merry. One apophthegm only stands
upon record. When an objection raised against his inscription for
Shakespeare was defended by the authority of Patrick, he replied—
horresco referens—that 'he would allow the publisher of a dictionary to
know the meaning of a single word, but not of two words put together'.

He was fretful and easily displeased, and allowed himself to be
capriciously resentful. He would sometimes leave Lord Oxford
silently, no one could tell why, and was to be courted back by more
letters and messages than the footmen were willing to carry. The
table was indeed infested by Lady Mary Wortley, who was the friend
of Lady Oxford, and who, knowing his peevishness, could by no
entreaties be restrained from contradicting him, till their disputes

'*He hardly drank*': Edward Young, *The Universal Passion: Satire VI*, l. 188.
Lord Orrery: John Boyle (1707–62), 5th Earl of Orrery, friend of Pope and Swift.
Lady Bolingbroke: Marie-Claire St. John (*c.* 1675–1750), Marquise de Villette,
    2nd w. of Bolingbroke.
Patrick: Samuel Patrick (1684–1748), scholar, published in 1727 rev. ed. of
    Hederich's Greek lexicon. Cf. Ruffhead, p. 205.
horresco referens: *Aeneid*, ii. 204 ('I shudder as I mention it').
Lady Mary Wortley: Lady Mary Wortley Montagu (1689–1762), letter-writer.
Lady Oxford: Henrietta Cavendish Harley (*née* Holles) (1694–1755), Lady Oxford.

were sharpened to such asperity that one or the other quitted the house.[n]

He sometimes condescended to be jocular with servants or inferiors, but by no merriment, either of others or his own, was he ever seen excited to laughter.

Of his domestic character, frugality was a part eminently remarkable. Having determined not to be dependent, he determined not to be in want, and therefore wisely and magnanimously rejected all temptations to expense unsuitable to his fortune. This general care must be universally approved; but it sometimes appeared in petty artifices of parsimony, such as the practice of writing his compositions on the back of letters, as may be seen in the remaining copy of the *Iliad*, by which perhaps in five years five shillings were saved; or in a niggardly reception of his friends and scantiness of entertainment, as, when he had two guests in his house, he would set at supper a single pint upon the table, and having himself taken two small glasses would retire and say, 'Gentlemen, I leave you to your wine.' Yet he tells his friends that 'he has a heart for all, a house for all, and, whatever they may think, a fortune for all'.

He sometimes, however, made a splendid dinner, and is said to have wanted no part of the skill or elegance which such performances require. That this magnificence should be often displayed, that obstinate prudence with which he conducted his affairs would not permit, for his revenue, certain and casual, amounted only to about £800 a year, of which however he declares himself able to assign one hundred to charity.

Of this fortune, which as it arose from public approbation was very honourably obtained, his imagination seems to have been too full: it would be hard to find a man so well entitled to notice by his wit that ever delighted so much in talking of his money. In his letters and in his poems, his garden and his grotto, his quincunx and his vines, or some hints of his opulence, are always to be found. The great topic of his ridicule is poverty: the crimes with which he reproaches his antagonists are their debts, their habitation in the Mint, and their want of a dinner. He seems to be of an opinion not very uncommon in the world that to want money is to want everything.

Next to the pleasure of contemplating his possessions seems to be that of enumerating the men of high rank with whom he was

---

'*Gentlemen*': *Swift: Corr.* iv. 39 (Swift to Gay, 10 July 1732).
'*he has a heart*': *Pope: Corr.* iv. 64 (Pope to Swift, 23 March 1737).
he declares himself: ibid. iii. 57. (Pope to Swift, 9 Oct. 1729).
the Mint: a sanctuary for insolvent debtors.

acquainted, and whose notice he loudly proclaims not to have been obtained by any practices of meanness or servility—a boast which was never denied to be true, and to which very few poets have ever aspired. Pope never set his genius to sale: he never flattered those whom he did not love, or praised those whom he did not esteem. Savage however remarked that he began a little to relax his dignity when he wrote a distich for 'his Highness's dog'.

His admiration of the great seems to have increased in the advance of life. He passed over peers and statesmen to inscribe his *Iliad* to Congreve with a magnanimity of which the praise had been complete had his friend's virtue been equal to his wit. Why he was chosen for so great an honour it is not now possible to know; there is no trace in literary history of any particular intimacy between them. The name of Congreve appears in the letters among those of his other friends, but without any observable distinction or consequence.

To his latter works, however, he took care to annex names dignified with titles, but was not very happy in his choice, for except Lord Bathurst, none of his noble friends were such as that a good man would wish to have his intimacy with them known to posterity; he can derive little honour from the notice of Cobham, Burlington or Bolingbroke.

Of his social qualities, if an estimate be made from his letters, an opinion too favourable cannot easily be formed: they exhibit a perpetual and unclouded effulgence of general benevolence and particular fondness. There is nothing but liberality, gratitude, constancy and tenderness. It has been so long said as to be commonly believed that the true characters of men may be found in their letters, and that he who writes to his friend lays his heart open before him. But the truth is that such were simple friendships of the Golden Age, and are now the friendships only of children. Very few can boast of hearts which they dare lay open to themselves, and of which, by whatever accident exposed, they do not shun a distinct and continued view; and certainly, what we hide from ourselves we do not show to our friends. There is, indeed, no transaction which offers stronger temptations to fallacy and sophistication than epistolary intercourse. In the eagerness of conversation the first emotions of the mind often burst out before they are considered; in the tumult of business, interest and passion have their genuine effect; but a friendly letter is a calm and deliberate performance, in the cool of leisure, in

he loudly proclaims: *Pope: Poems*, v. 18.   *a distich*: ibid. vi. 372.
It has been so long said: cf. Howell, *Familiar Letters* (ed. Jacobs), p. 647.

the stillness of solitude, and surely no man sits down to depreciate by design his own character.

Friendship has no tendency to secure veracity, for by whom can a man so much wish to be thought better than he is as by him whose kindness he desires to gain or keep? Even in writing to the world there is less constraint: the author is not confronted with his reader, and takes his chance of approbation among the different dispositions of mankind; but a letter is addressed to a single mind of which the prejudices and partialities are known, and must therefore please, if not by favouring them, by forbearing to oppose them.

To charge those favourable representations which men give of their own minds with the guilt of hypocritical falsehood, would show more severity than knowledge. The writer commonly believes himself. Almost every man's thoughts, while they are general, are right, and most hearts are pure while temptation is away. It is easy to awaken generous sentiments in privacy, to despise death when there is no danger, to glow with benevolence when there is nothing to be given. While such ideas are formed they are felt, and self-love does not suspect the gleam of virtue to be the meteor of fancy.

If the letters of Pope are considered merely as compositions, they seem to be premeditated and artificial. It is one thing to write because there is something which the mind wishes to discharge, and another to solicit the imagination because ceremony or vanity requires something to be written. Pope confesses his early letters to be vitiated with 'affectation and ambition'; to know whether he disentangled himself from these perverters of epistolary integrity, his book and his life must be set in comparison.

One of his favourite topics is contempt of his own poetry. For this, if it had been real, he would deserve no commendation, and in this he was certainly not sincere, for his high value of himself was sufficiently observed, and of what could he be proud but of his poetry? He writes, he says, when 'he has just nothing else to do'; yet Swift complains that he was never at leisure for conversation because he 'had always some poetical scheme in his head'. It was punctually required that his writing-box should be set upon his bed before he rose; and Lord Oxford's domestic related that, in the dreadful winter of '40, she was called from her bed by him four times in one night to supply him with paper lest he should lose a thought.

He pretends insensibility to censure and criticism, though it was observed by all who knew him that every pamphlet disturbed his

Pope confesses: *Pope: Corr.* i. xxxvii.　　　'*he has just*': cf. *Pope: Poems*, i. 6.
'*had always*': *Swift: Corr.* iv. 184 (Swift to Mrs. Caesar, 30 July 1733).

quiet, and that his extreme irritability laid him open to perpetual vexation; but he wished to despise his critics, and therefore hoped that he did despise them.

As he happened to live in two reigns when the Court paid little attention to poetry, he nursed in his mind a foolish disesteem of kings, and proclaims that 'he never sees Courts'. Yet a little regard shown him by the Prince of Wales melted his obduracy, and he had not much to say when he was asked by his Royal Highness 'how he could love a Prince while he disliked kings?'

He very frequently professes contempt of the world, and represents himself as looking on mankind sometimes with gay indifference, as on emmets of a hillock below his serious attention, and sometimes with gloomy indignation, as on monsters more worthy of hatred than of pity. These were dispositions apparently counterfeited. How could he despise those whom he lived by pleasing, and on whose approbation his esteem of himself was superstructed? Why should he hate those to whose favour he owed his honour and his ease? Of things that terminate in human life the world is the proper judge; to despise its sentence, if it were possible, is not just, and if it were just, is not possible. Pope was far enough from this unreasonable temper: he was sufficiently 'a fool to Fame', and his fault was that he pretended to neglect it. His levity and his sullenness were only in his letters; he passed through common life sometimes vexed and sometimes pleased, with the natural emotions of common men.

His scorn of the great is repeated too often to be real; no man thinks much of that which he despises; and as falsehood is always in danger of inconsistency, he makes it his boast at another time that he lives among them.

It is evident that his own importance swells often in his mind. He is afraid of writing lest the clerks of the Post Office should know his secrets; he has many enemies; he considers himself as surrounded by universal jealousy; 'after many deaths, and many dispersions, two or three of us', says he, 'may still be brought together, not to plot, but to divert ourselves, and the world too, if it pleases'—and they can live together and 'show what friends wits may be, in spite of all the fools in the world'. All this while it was likely that the clerks did not know his hand; he certainly had no more enemies than a public

'*he never sees Courts*': *Pope: Corr.* ii. 469 (Pope to Swift, ?Jan. 1728).
'*how he could*': Ruffhead, p. 535 n. Cf. *Life*, iv. 50.
'*a fool to Fame*': *Epistle to Arbuthnot*, l. 127.
'*after many deaths*': *Pope: Corr.* ii. 321 (Pope to Swift, 14 Sept. 1725).
'*show what*': ibid. iv. 64 (Pope to Swift, 23 March 1737).

character like his inevitably excites; and with what degree of friendship the wits might live, very few were so much fools as ever to inquire.

Some part of this pretended discontent he learned from Swift, and expresses it, I think, most frequently in his correspondence with him. Swift's resentment was unreasonable, but it was sincere; Pope's was the mere mimicry of his friend, a fictitious part which he began to play before it became him. When he was only twenty-five years old, he related that 'a glut of study and retirement had thrown him on the world', and that there was danger lest 'a glut of the world should throw him back upon study and retirement'. To this Swift answered with great propriety that Pope had not yet either acted or suffered enough in the world to have become weary of it. And, indeed, it must be some very powerful reason that can drive back to solitude him who has once enjoyed the pleasures of society.

In the letters both of Swift and Pope there appears such narrowness of mind as makes them insensible of any excellence that has not some affinity with their own, and confines their esteem and approbation to so small a number that whoever should form his opinion of the age from their representation would suppose them to have lived amidst ignorance and barbarity, unable to find among their contemporaries either virtue or intelligence, and persecuted by those that could not understand them.

When Pope murmurs at the world, when he professes contempt of fame, when he speaks of riches and poverty, of success and disappointment, with negligent indifference, he certainly does not express his habitual and settled sentiments, but either wilfully disguises his own character, or what is more likely, invests himself with temporary qualities, and sallies out in the colours of the present moment. His hopes and fears, his joys and sorrows, acted strongly upon his mind, and if he differed from others, it was not by carelessness; he was irritable and resentful; his malignity to Philips, whom he had first made ridiculous, and then hated for being angry, continued too long. Of his vain desire to make Bentley contemptible I never heard any adequate reason.[n] He was sometimes wanton in his attacks, and before Chandos, Lady Wortley and Hill, was mean in his retreat.

The virtues which seem to have had most of his affection were liberality and fidelity of friendship, in which it does not appear that he was other than he describes himself. His fortune did not suffer

'*a glut of study*': ibid. ii. 185 (Pope to Swift, ? Aug. 1723).
mean in his retreat: Warburton, viii. 264.

his charity to be splendid and conspicuous, but he assisted Dodsley with £100 that he might open a shop, and of the subscription of £40 a year that he raised for Savage, twenty were paid by himself. He was accused of loving money, but his love was eagerness to gain not solicitude to keep it.

In the duties of friendship he was zealous and constant: his early maturity of mind commonly united him with men older than himself, and therefore, without attaining any considerable length of life, he saw many companions of his youth sink into the grave; but it does not appear that he lost a single friend by coldness or by injury; those who loved him once continued their kindness. His ungrateful mention of Allen in his will was the effect of his adherence to one whom he had known much longer, and whom he naturally loved with greater fondness. His violation of the trust reposed in him by Bolingbroke could have no motive inconsistent with the warmest affection; he either thought the action so near to indifferent that he forgot it, or so laudable that he expected his friend to approve it.

It was reported, with such confidence as almost to enforce belief, that in the papers entrusted to his executors was found a defamatory Life of Swift which he had prepared as an instrument of vengeance to be used if any provocation should be ever given. About this I inquired of the Earl of Marchmont, who assured me that no such piece was among his remains.

The religion in which he lived and died was that of the Church of Rome, to which in his correspondence with Racine he professes himself a sincere adherent. That he was not scrupulously pious in some part of his life is known by many idle and indecent applications of sentences taken from the Scriptures—a mode of merriment which a good man dreads for its profaneness, and a witty man disdains for its easiness and vulgarity. But to whatever levities he has been betrayed, it does not appear that his principles were ever corrupted, or that he ever lost his belief of Revelation. The positions which he transmitted from Bolingbroke he seems not to have understood, and was pleased with an interpretation that made them orthodox.

A man of such exalted superiority, and so little moderation, would naturally have all his delinquencies observed and aggravated: those who could not deny that he was excellent would rejoice to find that he was not perfect.

---

was accused: cf. *Walpole: Corr.* xx. 61 (Walpole to Horace Mann, 17 May 1749).
Racine: Louis Racine (1692–1763), French poet; see *Pope: Corr.* iv. 416 and n.
   (Pope to Racine, 1 Sept. 1742). Cf. Spence, § 307.

Perhaps it may be imputed to the unwillingness with which the same man is allowed to possess many advantages that his learning has been depreciated. He certainly was in his early life a man of great literary curiosity, and when he wrote his *Essay on Criticism* had, for his age, a very wide acquaintance with books. When he entered into the living world, it seems to have happened to him as to many others that he was less attentive to dead masters; he studied in the academy of Paracelsus, and made the universe his favourite volume. He gathered his notions fresh from reality—not from the copies of authors but the originals of nature. Yet there is no reason to believe that literature ever lost his esteem: he always professed to love reading, and Dobson, who spent some time at his house translating his *Essay on Man*, when I asked him what learning he found him to possess, answered: 'More than I expected'. His frequent references to history, his allusions to various kinds of knowledge, and his images selected from art and nature, with his observations on the operations of the mind and the modes of life, show an intelligence perpetually on the wing, excursive, vigorous and diligent, eager to pursue knowledge, and attentive to retain it.

From this curiosity arose the desire of travelling, to which he alludes in his verses to Jervas, and which, though he never found an opportunity to gratify it, did not leave him till his life declined.

Of his intellectual character, the constituent and fundamental principle was good sense, a prompt and intuitive perception of consonance and propriety. He saw immediately, of his own conceptions, what was to be chosen and what to be rejected, and in the works of others, what was to be shunned and what was to be copied.

But good sense alone is a sedate and quiescent quality which manages its possessions well but does not increase them; it collects few materials for its own operations, and preserves safety, but never gains supremacy. Pope had likewise genius: a mind active, ambitious and adventurous, always investigating, always aspiring, in its widest searches still longing to go forward, in its highest flights still wishing to be higher, always imagining something greater than it knows, always endeavouring more than it can do.

To assist these powers he is said to have had great strength and exactness of memory. That which he had heard or read was not easily lost, and he had before him not only what his own meditation

---

Paracelsus: Theophrastus Bombast von Hohenheim (1493–1541), influential Swiss physician and scientist.

to which he alludes: ll. 23 ff.   *he is said*: cf. Spence, § 532.

suggested, but what he had found in other writers that might be accommodated to his present purpose.

These benefits of nature he improved by incessant and unwearied diligence: he had recourse to every source of intelligence, and lost no opportunity of information; he consulted the living as well as the dead; he read his compositions to his friends, and was never content with mediocrity when excellence could be attained. He considered poetry as the business of his life, and however he might seem to lament his occupation, he followed it with constancy; to make verses was his first labour, and to mend them was his last.

From his attention to poetry he was never diverted. If conversation offered anything that could be improved, he committed it to paper; if a thought, or perhaps an expression more happy than was common, rose to his mind, he was careful to write it; an independent distich was preserved for an opportunity of insertion, and some little fragments have been found containing lines, or parts of lines, to be wrought upon at some other time.

He was one of those few whose labour is their pleasure: he was never elevated to negligence nor wearied to impatience; he never passed a fault unamended by indifference, nor quitted it by despair. He laboured his works first to gain reputation, and afterwards to keep it.

Of composition there are different methods. Some employ at once memory and invention, and with little intermediate use of the pen form and polish large masses by continued meditation, and write their productions only when in their own opinion they have completed them. It is related of Virgil that his custom was to pour out a great number of verses in the morning, and pass the day in retrenching exuberances and correcting inaccuracies. The method of Pope, as may be collected from his translation, was to write his first thoughts in his first words, and gradually to amplify, decorate, rectify and refine them.

With such faculties and such dispositions, he excelled every other writer in poetical prudence: he wrote in such a manner as might expose him to few hazards. He used almost always the same fabric of verse, and indeed by those few essays which he made of any other, he did not enlarge his reputation. Of this uniformity the certain consequence was readiness and dexterity. By perpetual practice, language had in his mind a systematical arrangement: having always the same use for words, he had words so selected and com-

He considered poetry: cf. *Pope: Corr.* i. 42 (Pope to Cromwell, 18 March 1708).

bined as to be ready at his call. This increase of facility he confessed himself to have perceived in the progress of his translation.

But what was yet of more importance, his effusions were always voluntary and his subjects chosen by himself. His independence secured him from drudging at a task and labouring upon a barren topic: he never exchanged praise for money, nor opened a shop of condolence or congratulation. His poems, therefore, were scarce ever temporary. He suffered coronations and royal marriages to pass without a song, and derived no opportunities from recent events, nor any popularity from the accidental disposition of his readers. He was never reduced to the necessity of soliciting the sun to shine upon a birthday, of calling the Graces and Virtues to a wedding, or of saying what multitudes have said before him. When he could produce nothing new, he was at liberty to be silent.

His publications were for the same reason never hasty. He is said to have sent nothing to the press till it had lain two years under his inspection; it is at least certain that he ventured nothing without nice examination. He suffered the tumult of imagination to subside, and the novelties of invention to grow familiar. He knew that the mind is always enamoured of its own productions, and did not trust his first fondness. He consulted his friends, and listened with great willingness to criticism; and what was of more importance, he consulted himself, and let nothing pass against his own judgement.

He professed to have learned his poetry from Dryden whom, whenever an opportunity was presented, he praised through his whole life with unvaried liberality—and perhaps his character may receive some illustration if he be compared with his master.

Integrity of understanding and nicety of discernment were not allotted in a less proportion to Dryden than to Pope. The rectitude of Dryden's mind was sufficiently shown by the dismission of his poetical prejudices, and the rejection of unnatural thoughts and rugged numbers. But Dryden never desired to apply all the judgement that he had. He wrote, and professed to write, merely for the people, and when he pleased others he contented himself. He spent no time in struggles to rouse latent powers: he never attempted to make that better which was already good, nor often to mend what he must have known to be faulty. He wrote, as he tells us, with very little consideration; when occasion or necessity called upon him, he poured out what the present moment happened to supply, and when once it had passed the press, ejected it from

he confessed himself: Spence, § 203.   *He is said*: cf. ibid. § 98.
He professed: ibid. § 55.   *as he tells us*: see above, p. 153.

his mind—for when he had no pecuniary interest, he had no further solicitude.

Pope was not content to satisfy; he desired to excel, and therefore always endeavoured to do his best; he did not court the candour but dared the judgement of his reader, and expecting no indulgence from others, he showed none to himself. He examined lines and words with minute and punctilious observation, and retouched every part with indefatigable diligence till he had left nothing to be forgiven.

For this reason he kept his pieces very long in his hands while he considered and reconsidered them. The only poems which can be supposed to have been written with such regard to the times as might hasten their publication were the two satires of *Thirty Eight*, of which Dodsley told me that they were brought to him by the author that they might be fairly copied. 'Almost every line', he said, 'was then written twice over; I gave him a clean transcript, which he sent some time afterwards to me for the press, with almost every line written twice over a second time.'

His declaration that his care for his works ceased at their publication was not strictly true. His parental attention never abandoned them: what he found amiss in the first edition he silently corrected in those that followed. He appears to have revised the *Iliad* and freed it from some of its imperfections; and the *Essay on Criticism* received many improvements after its first appearance. It will seldom be found that he altered without adding clearness, elegance or vigour. Pope had perhaps the judgement of Dryden, but Dryden certainly wanted the diligence of Pope.

In acquired knowledge, the superiority must be allowed to Dryden, whose education was more scholastic, and who before he became an author had been allowed more time for study, with better means of information. His mind has a larger range, and he collects his images and illustrations from a more extensive circumference of science. Dryden knew more of man in his general nature, and Pope in his local manners. The notions of Dryden were formed by comprehensive speculation, and those of Pope by minute attention. There is more dignity in the knowledge of Dryden, and more certainty in that of Pope.

Poetry was not the sole praise of either, for both excelled likewise in prose; but Pope did not borrow his prose from his predecessor. The style of Dryden is capricious and varied, that of Pope is cautious and uniform; Dryden obeys the motions of his own mind, Pope constrains his mind to his own rules of composition. Dryden is sometimes

candour: see above, p. 110.   *His declaration*: *Guardian* 40.

vehement and rapid, Pope is always smooth, uniform and gentle. Dryden's page is a natural field, rising into inequalities and diversified by the varied exuberance of abundant vegetation; Pope's is a velvet lawn, shaven by the scythe and levelled by the roller.

Of genius, that power which constitutes a poet, that quality without which judgement is cold and knowledge is inert, that energy which collects, combines, amplifies and animates, the superiority must, with some hesitation, be allowed to Dryden. It is not to be inferred that of this poetical vigour Pope had only a little because Dryden had more, for every other writer since Milton must give place to Pope; and even of Dryden it must be said that if he has brighter paragraphs he has not better poems. Dryden's performances were always hasty, either excited by some external occasion or extorted by domestic necessity; he composed without consideration and published without correction. What his mind could supply at call, or gather in one excursion, was all that he sought and all that he gave. The dilatory caution of Pope enabled him to condense his sentiments, to multiply his images, and to accumulate all that study might produce or chance might supply. If the flights of Dryden therefore are higher, Pope continues longer on the wing. If of Dryden's fire the blaze is brighter, of Pope's the heat is more regular and constant. Dryden often surpasses expectation, and Pope never falls below it. Dryden is read with frequent astonishment, and Pope with perpetual delight.

This parallel will, I hope, when it is well considered, be found just; and if the reader should suspect me, as I suspect myself, of some partial fondness for the memory of Dryden, let him not too hastily condemn me, for meditation and inquiry may, perhaps, show him the reasonableness of my determination.

The works of Pope are now to be distinctly examined, not so much with attention to slight faults or petty beauties as to the general character and effect of each performance.

It seems natural for a young poet to initiate himself by pastorals which, not professing to imitate real life, require no experience, and exhibiting only the simple operation of unmingled passions, admit no subtle reasoning or deep inquiry. Pope's *Pastorals* are not however composed but with close thought: they have reference to the times of the day, the seasons of the year, and the periods of human life. The last, that which turns the attention upon age and death, was the author's favourite. To tell of disappointment and misery, to

The last: 'Winter'.

thicken the darkness of futurity and perplex the labyrinth of uncertainty, has been always a delicious employment of the poets. His
preference was probably just. I wish, however, that his fondness had
not overlooked a line in which the 'zephyrs' are made 'to lament in
silence'.

To charge these *Pastorals* with want of invention is to require what
never was intended.[n] The imitations are so ambitiously frequent that
the writer evidently means rather to show his literature than his wit.
It is surely sufficient for an author of sixteen not only to be able to
copy the poems of antiquity with judicious selection, but to have
obtained sufficient power of language and skill in metre to exhibit a
series of versification which had in English poetry no precedent, nor
has since had an imitation.

The design of *Windsor Forest* is evidently derived from *Cooper's
Hill*, with some attention to Waller's poem on 'The Park'; but Pope
cannot be denied to excel his masters in variety and elegance, and the
art of interchanging description, narrative and morality. The objection made by Dennis is the want of plan, of a regular subordination
of parts terminating in the principal and original design. There is this
want in most descriptive poems because as the scenes, which they
must exhibit successively, are all subsisting at the same time, the order
in which they are shown must by necessity be arbitrary, and more is
not to be expected from the last part than from the first. The attention, therefore, which cannot be detained by suspense must be
excited by diversity, such as this poem offers to its reader.

But the desire of diversity may be too much indulged; the parts of
Windsor Forest which deserve least praise are those which were
added to enliven the stillness of the scene—the appearance of Father
Thames, and the transformation of Lodona. Addison had in his
Campaign derided the 'rivers' that 'rise from their oozy beds' to tell
stories of heroes, and it is therefore strange that Pope should adopt
a fiction not only unnatural but lately censured. The story of Lodona
is told with sweetness, but a new metamorphosis is a ready and
puerile expedient: nothing is easier than to tell how a flower was
once a blooming virgin, or a rock an obdurate tyrant.

The Temple of Fame has, as Steele warmly declared, 'a thousand
beauties'. Every part is splendid: there is great luxuriance of orna-

---

'*zephyrs*': ll. 49–50.
Waller's poem: On St. James's Park, as lately Improved by his Majesty (1661).
The objection: Dennis, ii. 136.   *the appearance*: ll. 171 ff., 329 ff.
'*rivers*': The Campaign, l. 470; cf. Windsor Forest, l. 329.
'*a thousand beauties*': Pope: Corr. i. 152 (Steele to Pope, 12 Nov. 1712).

ments; the original vision of Chaucer was never denied to be much improved; the allegory is very skilfully continued, the imagery is properly selected and learnedly displayed; yet with all this comprehension of excellence, as its scene is laid in remote ages and its sentiments, if the concluding paragraph be excepted, have little relation to general manners or common life, it never obtained much notice, but is turned silently over, and seldom quoted or mentioned with either praise or blame.

That the 'Messiah' excels the 'Pollio' is no great praise if it be considered from what original the improvements are derived.

The 'Verses on the Unfortunate Lady' have drawn much attention by the illaudable singularity of treating suicide with respect; and they must be allowed to be written in some parts with vigorous animation, and in others with gentle tenderness; nor has Pope produced any poem in which the sense predominates more over the diction. But the tale is not skilfully told: it is not easy to discover the character of either the lady or her guardian. History relates that she was about to disparage herself by a marriage with an inferior; Pope praises her for the dignity of ambition, and yet condemns the uncle to detestation for his pride; the ambitious love of a niece may be opposed by the interest, malice or envy of an uncle, but never by his pride. On such an occasion a poet may be allowed to be obscure, but inconsistency never can be right.

The *Ode for St. Cecilia's Day* was undertaken at the desire of Steele; in this the author is generally confessed to have miscarried, yet he has miscarried only as compared with Dryden, for he has far outgone other competitors. Dryden's plan is better chosen: history will always take stronger hold of the attention than fable; the passions excited by Dryden are the pleasures and pains of real life, the scene of Pope is laid in imaginary existence; Pope is read with calm acquiescence, Dryden with turbulent delight; Pope hangs upon the ear, and Dryden finds the passes of the mind.

Both the odes want the essential constituent of metrical compositions—the stated recurrence of settled numbers. It may be alleged that Pindar is said by Horace to have written *numeris lege solutis*, but as no such lax performances have been transmitted to us, the meaning of that expression cannot be fixed; and perhaps the like return might properly be made to a modern Pindarist as Mr. Cobb

That the 'Messiah': cf. ibid. i. 146 (Steele to Pope, 1 June 1712); *Essay on Pope*, p. 11.   *'Pollio'*: see above, p. 187.
numeris: *Odes*, IV. ii. 11–12 ('in measures freed from rule').
Mr. Cobb: Samuel Cobb (1675–1713), translator and versifier.

received from Bentley, who, when he found his criticisms upon a Greek exercise which Cobb had presented refuted one after another by Pindar's authority, cried out at last: 'Pindar was a bold fellow, but thou art an impudent one.'

If Pope's ode be particularly inspected, it will be found that the first stanza consists of sounds well chosen indeed, but only sounds.

The second consists of hyperbolical commonplaces, easily to be found, and perhaps without much difficulty to be as well expressed.

In the third, however, there are numbers, images, harmony and vigour not unworthy the antagonist of Dryden. Had all been like this—but every part cannot be the best.

The next stanzas place and detain us in the dark and dismal regions of mythology, where neither hope nor fear, neither joy nor sorrow can be found; the poet however faithfully attends us: we have all that can be performed by elegance of diction or sweetness of versification; but what can form avail without better matter?

The last stanza recurs again to commonplaces. The conclusion is too evidently modelled by that of Dryden, and it may be remarked that both end with the same fault—the comparison of each is literal on one side and metaphorical on the other.

Poets do not always express their own thoughts; Pope, with all this labour in the praise of music, was ignorant of its principles and insensible of its effects.

One of his greatest though of his earliest works is the *Essay on Criticism* which, if he had written nothing else, would have placed him among the first critics and the first poets, as it exhibits every mode of excellence that can embellish or dignify didactic composition: selection of matter, novelty of arrangement, justness of precept, splendour of illustration, and propriety of digression. I know not whether it be pleasing to consider that he produced this piece at twenty, and never afterwards excelled it; he that delights himself with observing that such powers may be so soon attained, cannot but grieve to think that life was ever after at a stand.

To mention the particular beauties of the *Essay* would be unprofitably tedious, but I cannot forbear to observe that the comparison of a student's progress in the sciences with the journey of a traveller in the Alps is perhaps the best that English poetry can show.[n] A simile, to be perfect, must both illustrate and ennoble the subject, must show it to the understanding in a clearer view, and display it to the fancy with greater dignity; but either of these qualities may be sufficient to recommend it. In didactic poetry, of which the great

the comparison of each: see above, p. 192.

purpose is instruction, a simile may be praised which illustrates though it does not ennoble; in heroics, that may be admitted which ennobles though it does not illustrate. That it may be complete it is required to exhibit, independently of its references, a pleasing image, for a simile is said to be a short episode. To this antiquity was so attentive that circumstances were sometimes added which, having no parallels, served only to fill the imagination, and produced what Perrault ludicrously called 'comparisons with a long tail'. In their similes the greatest writers have sometimes failed: the ship-race compared with the chariot-race is neither illustrated nor aggrandised; land and water make all the difference; when Apollo, running after Daphne, is likened to a greyhound chasing a hare, there is nothing gained: the ideas of pursuit and flight are too plain to be made plainer, and a god and the daughter of a god are not represented much to their advantage by a hare and dog. The simile of the Alps has no useless parts, yet affords a striking picture by itself: it makes the foregoing position better understood, and enables it to take faster hold on the attention; it assists the apprehension and elevates the fancy.

Let me likewise dwell a little on the celebrated paragraph in which it is directed that 'the sound should seem an echo to the sense'—a precept which Pope is allowed to have observed beyond any other English poet.

This notion of representative metre, and the desire of discovering frequent adaptations of the sound to the sense, have produced, in my opinion, many wild conceits and imaginary beauties. All that can furnish this representation are the sounds of the words considered singly, and the time in which they are pronounced. Every language has some words framed to exhibit the noises which they express, as 'thump', 'rattle', 'growl', 'hiss'. These however are but few, and the poet cannot make them more; nor can they be of any use but when sound is to be mentioned. The time of pronunciation was in the dactylic measures of the learned languages capable of considerable variety, but that variety could be accommodated only to motion or duration, and different degrees of motion were perhaps expressed by verses rapid or slow, without much attention of the writer, when the image had full possession of his fancy; but our language having

---

Perrault: Charles Perrault (1628–1703), French writer of fairy-tales and literary controversialist; see his *Parallèle des Anciens et des Modernes*, ii. (Amsterdam ed., 1693), 41–2.   *the ship-race*: *Aeneid*, v. 129 ff.
when Apollo: Ovid, *Metamorphoses*, i. 533 ff.
'the sound': l. 365. Cf. *Rambler* 92.

little flexibility, our verses can differ very little in their cadence. The fancied resemblances, I fear, arise sometimes merely from the ambiguity of words: there is supposed to be some relation between a 'soft' line and a 'soft' couch, or between 'hard' syllables and 'hard' fortune.

Motion, however, may be in some sort exemplified; and yet it may be suspected that even in such resemblances the mind often governs the ear, and the sounds are estimated by their meaning. One of the most successful attempts has been to describe the labour of Sisyphus:

> With many a weary step, and many a groan,
> Up a high hill he heaves a huge round stone;
> The huge round stone, resulting with a bound,
> Thunders impetuous down, and smokes along the ground.

Who does not perceive the stone to move slowly upward and roll violently back? But set the same numbers to another sense:

> While many a merry tale, and many a song,
> Cheered the rough road, we wished the rough road long;
> The rough road then, returning in a round,
> Mocked our impatient steps, for all was fairy ground.

We have now surely lost much of the delay, and much of the rapidity.

But to show how little the greatest master of numbers can fix the principles of representative harmony, it will be sufficient to remark that the poet who tells us that

> When Ajax strives—the words move slow.
> Not so when swift Camilla scours the plain,
> Flies o'er th' unbending corn, and skims along the main,

when he had enjoyed for about thirty years the praise of Camilla's lightness of foot, tried another experiment upon 'sound' and 'time', and produced this memorable triplet:

> Waller was smooth; but Dryden taught to join ⎫
> The varying verse, the full-resounding line, ⎬
> The long majestic march, and energy divine. ⎭

Here are the swiftness of the rapid race, and the march of slow-paced majesty, exhibited by the same poet in the same sequence of syllables

Sisyphus: a legendary king of Corinth, who for his misdeeds on earth was condemned in Hades to roll a large stone to the top of a hill, which then rolled down again, thus making his punishment eternal.

With many: *Pope's Odyssey*, xi. 735–8.   *resulting*: moving quickly back.

When Ajax: *Essay on Criticism*, ll. 370 ff.

Camilla: a maiden-warrior, aily of Turnus (king of the Rutuli) in the *Aeneid*, and so swift-footed as to be able to run over a field of corn without bending the blades.   *Waller was smooth*: *Imit. Hor. Ep.* II. i. 267–9.

—except that the exact prosodist will find the line of 'swiftness' by one time longer than that of 'tardiness'.

Beauties of this kind are commonly fancied, and when real are technical and nugatory, not to be rejected and not to be solicited.

To the praises which have been accumulated on *The Rape of the Lock* by readers of every class, from the critic to the waiting-maid, it is difficult to make any addition. Of that which is universally allowed to be the most attractive of all ludicrous compositions, let it rather be now inquired from what sources the power of pleasing is derived.

Dr. Warburton, who excelled in critical perspicacity, has remarked that the preternatural agents are very happily adapted to the purposes of the poem. The heathen deities can no longer gain attention: we should have turned away from a contest between Venus and Diana. The employment of allegorical persons always excites conviction of its own absurdity; they may produce effects, but cannot conduct actions; when the phantom is put in motion it dissolves; thus Discord may raise a mutiny, but Discord cannot conduct a march, nor besiege a town. Pope brought into view a new race of beings, with powers and passions proportionate to their operation. The sylphs and gnomes act at the toilet and the tea-table what more terrific and more powerful phantoms perform on the stormy ocean or the field of battle; they give their proper help, and do their proper mischief.

Pope is said by an objector not to have been the inventor of this petty nation—a charge which might with more justice have been brought against the author of the *Iliad*, who doubtless adopted the religious system of his country; for what is there but the names of his agents which Pope has not invented? Has he not assigned them characters and operations never heard of before? Has he not, at least, given them their first poetical existence? If this is not sufficient to denominate his work original, nothing original ever can be written.

In this work are exhibited in a very high degree the two most engaging powers of an author. New things are made familiar, and familiar things are made new. A race of aerial people, never heard of before, is presented to us in a manner so clear and easy that the reader seeks for no further information, but immediately mingles with his new acquaintance, adopts their interests and attends their pursuits, loves a sylph and detests a gnome.

That familiar things are made new every paragraph will prove.

the preternatural agents: Warburton, i. 218–20 nn.; iv. 26 n.
Pope is said: *Essay on Pope*, p. 246.

The subject of the poem is an event below the common incidents of common life; nothing real is introduced that is not seen so often as to be no longer regarded, yet the whole detail of a female day is here brought before us invested with so much art of decoration that, though nothing is disguised, everything is striking, and we feel all the appetite of curiosity for that from which we have a thousand times turned fastidiously away.

The purpose of the poet is, as he tells us, to laugh at 'the little unguarded follies of the female sex'. It is therefore without justice that Dennis charges *The Rape of the Lock* with the want of a moral, and for that reason sets it below the *Lutrin*, which exposes the pride and discord of the clergy. Perhaps neither Pope nor Boileau has made the world much better than he found it; but if they had both succeeded, it were easy to tell who would have deserved most from public gratitude. The freaks and humours and spleen and vanity of women, as they embroil families in discord and fill houses with disquiet, do more to obstruct the happiness of life in a year than the ambition of the clergy in many centuries. It has been well observed that the misery of man proceeds not from any single crush of overwhelming evil, but from small vexations continually repeated.[n]

It is remarked by Dennis likewise that the machinery is superfluous, that by all the bustle of preternatural operation the main event is neither hastened nor retarded. To this charge an efficacious answer is not easily made. The sylphs cannot be said to help or to oppose, and it must be allowed to imply some want of art that their power has not been sufficiently intermingled with the action. Other parts may likewise be charged with want of connection: the game at ombre might be spared; but if the lady had lost her hair while she was intent upon her cards, it might have been inferred that those who are too fond of play will be in danger of neglecting more important interests. Those perhaps are faults; but what are such faults to so much excellence!

The 'Epistle of Eloise to Abelard' is one of the most happy productions of human wit: the subject is so judiciously chosen that it would be difficult, in turning over the annals of the world, to find another which so many circumstances concur to recommend. We regularly interest ourselves most in the fortune of those who most deserve our notice. Abelard and Eloise were conspicuous in their days for

---

to laugh at: Pope: *Poems*, ii. 142.   *that Dennis charges*: Dennis, ii. 330–1.
It is remarked: ibid. ii. 337.
Abelard: Peter Abelard (or Abailard) (1079–1142), theologian and philosopher, the most famous scholar of his day.
Eloise: Héloïse (c. 1098–1164), abbess of the Paraclete.

eminence of merit. The heart naturally loves truth. The adventures and misfortunes of this illustrious pair are known from undisputed history. Their fate does not leave the mind in hopeless dejection, for they both found quiet and consolation in retirement and piety. So new and so affecting is their story that it supersedes invention, and imagination ranges at full liberty without straggling into scenes of fable.

The story, thus skilfully adopted, has been diligently improved. Pope has left nothing behind him which seems more the effect of studious perseverance and laborious revisal. Here is particularly observable the *curiosa felicitas*, a fruitful soil and careful cultivation. Here is no crudeness of sense nor asperity of language.

The sources from which sentiments which have so much vigour and efficacy have been drawn, are shown to be the mystic writers by the learned author of the *Essay on the Life and Writings of Pope*, a book which teaches how the brow of criticism may be smoothed, and how she may be enabled with all her severity to attract and to delight.

The train of my disquisition has now conducted me to that poetical wonder, the translation of the *Iliad*, a performance which no age or nation can pretend to equal. To the Greeks translation was almost unknown; it was totally unknown to the inhabitants of Greece. They had no recourse to the Barbarians for poetical beauties, but sought for everything in Homer where, indeed, there is but little which they might not find.

The Italians have been very diligent translators, but I can hear of no version, unless perhaps Anguillara's *Ovid* may be excepted, which is read with eagerness. The *Iliad* of Salvini every reader may discover to be punctiliously exact, but it seems to be the work of a linguist skilfully pedantic, and his countrymen, the proper judges of its power to please, reject it with disgust.[n]

Their predecessors the Romans have left some specimens of translation behind them, and that employment must have had some credit in which Tully and Germanicus engaged; but unless we suppose, what is perhaps true, that the plays of Terence were versions of

curiosa felicitas: *Satyricon*, 118 ('studied felicity').
are shown to be: by Joseph Warton (1722–1800) in his *Essay on Pope*, p. 319.
Anguillara: Giovanni Andrea dell'Anguillara (b. 1517), Italian poet, author of *Le Metamorfosi d'Ovidio* (1561).
Salvini: Antonio Maria Salvini (1653–1729), Italian man of letters, author of *Iliade d'Omero tradotta dall'original Greco in versi sciolti* (1723).
Germanicus: (15 B.C.–A.D. 19), Roman general and poet, translated the *Phaenomena* and *Prognostica* of Aratus.
Terence: (195 or 185–159 B.C.), Roman comic dramatist.

Menander, nothing translated seems ever to have risen to high reputation. The French, in the meridian hour of their learning, were very
laudably industrious to enrich their own language with the wisdom of
the ancients, but found themselves reduced, by whatever necessity,
to turn the Greek and Roman poetry into prose. Whoever could read
an author could translate him. From such rivals little can be feared.

The chief help of Pope in this arduous undertaking was drawn from
the versions of Dryden. Virgil had borrowed much of his imagery
from Homer, and part of the debt was now paid by his translator.
Pope searched the pages of Dryden for happy combinations of heroic
diction; but it will not be denied that he added much to what he
found. He cultivated our language with so much diligence and art
that he has left in his *Homer* a treasure of poetical elegances to
posterity. His version may be said to have tuned the English tongue,
for since its appearance no writer, however deficient in other powers,
has wanted melody. Such a series of lines so elaborately corrected,
and so sweetly modulated, took possession of the public ear: the
vulgar was enamoured of the poem, and the learned wondered at the
translation.

But in the most general applause discordant voices will always be
heard. It has been objected by some who wish to be numbered among
the sons of learning, that Pope's version of Homer is not Homerical,
that it exhibits no resemblance of the original and characteristic
manner of the father of poetry as it wants his awful simplicity, his
artless grandeur, his unaffected majesty.[n] This cannot be totally
denied, but it must be remembered that *necessitas quod cogit defendit*
—that may be lawfully done which cannot be forborne. Time and
place will always enforce regard. In estimating this translation consideration must be had of the nature of our language, the form of our
metre, and above all, of the change which two thousand years have
made in the modes of life and the habits of thought. Virgil wrote in a
language of the same general fabric with that of Homer, in verses of
the same measure, and in an age nearer to Homer's time by eighteen
hundred years; yet he found, even then, the state of the world so much
altered, and the demand for elegance so much increased, that mere
nature would be endured no longer—and perhaps in the multitude
of borrowed passages very few can be shown which he has not embellished.

There is a time when nations emerging from barbarity, and falling
into regular subordination, gain leisure to grow wise, and feel the

Menander: (c. 342–c. 290 B.C.), Attic poet, the most famous writer of the New
Comedy.

shame of ignorance and the craving pain of unsatisfied curiosity. To this hunger of the mind plain sense is grateful: that which fills the void removes uneasiness, and to be free from pain for a while is pleasure; but repletion generates fastidiousness: a saturated intellect soon becomes luxurious, and knowledge finds no willing reception till it is recommended by artificial diction. Thus it will be found, in the progress of learning, that in all nations the first writers are simple, and that every age improves in elegance. One refinement always makes way for another, and what was expedient to Virgil was necessary to Pope.

I suppose many readers of the English *Iliad*, when they have been touched with some unexpected beauty of the lighter kind, have tried to enjoy it in the original, where, alas, it was not to be found. Homer doubtless owes to his translator many Ovidian graces not exactly suitable to his character, but to have added can be no great crime if nothing be taken away. Elegance is surely to be desired if it be not gained at the expense of dignity. A hero would wish to be loved as well as to be reverenced.

To a thousand cavils one answer is sufficient: the purpose of a writer is to be read, and the criticism which would destroy the power of pleasing must be blown aside. Pope wrote for his own age and his own nation: he knew that it was necessary to colour the images and point the sentiments of his author; he therefore made him graceful but lost him some of his sublimity.

The copious notes with which the version is accompanied, and by which it is recommended to many readers, though they were undoubtedly written to swell the volumes, ought not to pass without praise; commentaries which attract the reader by the pleasure of perusal have not often appeared; the notes of others are read to clear difficulties, those of Pope to vary entertainment.

It has however been objected, with sufficient reason, that there is in the commentary too much of unseasonable levity and affected gaiety, that too many appeals are made to the ladies, and the ease which is so carefully preserved is sometimes the ease of a trifler.[n] Every art has its terms and every kind of instruction its proper style; the gravity of common critics may be tedious, but is less despicable than childish merriment.

Of the *Odyssey* nothing remains to be observed; the same general praise may be given to both translations, and a particular examination of either would require a large volume. The notes were written by Broome, who endeavoured not unsuccessfully to imitate his master.

Of *The Dunciad* the hint is confessedly taken from Dryden's
Mac Flecknoe, but the plan is so enlarged and diversified as justly to
claim the praise of an original, and affords perhaps the best specimen
that has yet appeared of personal satire ludicrously pompous.

That the design was moral, whatever the author might tell either
his readers or himself, I am not convinced. The first motive was the
desire of revenging the contempt with which Theobald had treated his
Shakespeare, and regaining the honour which he had lost by crushing
his opponent. Theobald was not of bulk enough to fill a poem, and
therefore it was necessary to find other enemies with other names
at whose expense he might divert the public.

In this design there was petulance and malignity enough, but I
cannot think it very criminal. An author places himself uncalled
before the tribunal of criticism, and solicits fame at the hazard of
disgrace. Dulness or deformity are not culpable in themselves, but
may be very justly reproached when they pretend to the honour of
wit or the influence of beauty. If bad writers were to pass without
reprehension, what should restrain them? *impune diem consumpserit
ingens* Telephus; and upon bad writers only will censure have much
effect. The satire which brought Theobald and Moore into contempt
dropped impotent from Bentley, like the javelin of Priam thrown at
Neoptolemus.

All truth is valuable, and satirical criticism may be considered as
useful when it rectifies error and improves judgement; he that refines
the public taste is a public benefactor.

The beauties of this poem are well known; its chief fault is the
grossness of its images. Pope and Swift had an unnatural delight in
ideas physically impure, such as every other tongue utters with
unwillingness, and of which every ear shrinks from the mention.

But even this fault, offensive as it is, may be forgiven for the
excellence of other passages, such as the formation and dissolution
of Moore, the account of the Traveller, the misfortune of the Florist,
and the crowded thoughts and stately numbers which dignify the
concluding paragraph.

The alterations which have been made in *The Dunciad*, not always
for the better, require that it should be published, as in the last
collection, with all its variations.

impune diem: Juvenal, *Satires*, i. 4 ('An interminable *Telephus*, if allowed to pass
  uncensured, would waste the whole day').
Moore: James Moore Smythe (1702–34), playwright; see *Dunciad*, ii. 50.
like the javelin: *Aeneid*, ii. 544.
the formation: ii. 35–50, 109–20; iv. 293–336, 403–18, 627–36.

The *Essay on Man* was a work of great labour and long consideration, but certainly not the happiest of Pope's performances. The
subject is perhaps not very proper for poetry, and the poet was not
sufficiently master of his subject: metaphysical morality was to him
a new study; he was proud of his acquisitions, and supposing himself
master of great secrets, was in haste to teach what he had not learned.
Thus he tells us, in the first Epistle, that from the nature of the
Supreme Being may be deduced an order of beings such as mankind
because Infinite Excellence can do only what is best. He finds out
that these beings must be 'somewhere', and that 'all the question is
whether man be in a wrong place'. Surely if, according to the poet's
Leibnitian reasoning, we may infer that man ought to be only because he is, we may allow that his place is the right place because he
has it. Supreme Wisdom is not less infallible in disposing than in
creating. But what is meant by 'somewhere' and 'place', and 'wrong
place', it had been vain to ask Pope, who probably had never asked
himself.

Having exalted himself into the chair of wisdom, he tells us much
that every man knows, and much that he does not know himself:
that we see but little, and that the order of the universe is beyond our
comprehension (an opinion not very uncommon), and that there is a
chain of subordinate beings 'from infinite to nothing' of which
himself and his readers are equally ignorant. But he gives us one
comfort which, without his help, he supposes unattainable, in the
position 'that though we are fools, yet God is wise'.

This *Essay* affords an egregious instance of the predominance of
genius, the dazzling splendour of imagery, and the seductive powers
of eloquence. Never were penury of knowledge and vulgarity of sentiment so happily disguised. The reader feels his mind full, though he
learns nothing, and when he meets it in its new array, no longer
knows the talk of his mother and his nurse. When these wonder-
working sounds sink into sense, and the doctrine of the *Essay*, dis-
robed of its ornaments, is left to the powers of its naked excellence,
what shall we discover? That we are, in comparison with our
Creator, very weak and ignorant, that we do not uphold the chain of
existence, and that we could not make one another with more skill
than we are made. We may learn yet more: that the arts of human life
were copied from the instinctive operations of other animals; that if the
world be made for man, it may be said that man was made for geese.

He finds out: ll. 47–50.

Leibnitian: Gottfried Wilhelm Leibnitz (or Leibniz) (1646–1716), German
   philosopher and mathematician.   '*that though*': ii. 294.

To these profound principles of natural knowledge are added some moral instructions equally new: that self-interest, well understood, will produce social concord; that men are mutual gainers by mutual benefits; that evil is sometimes balanced by good; that human advantages are unstable and fallacious, of uncertain duration and doubtful effect; that our true honour is not to have a great part but to act it well; that virtue only is our own; and that happiness is always in our power.

Surely a man of no very comprehensive search may venture to say that he has heard all this before; but it was never till now recommended by such a blaze of embellishment, or such sweetness of melody. The vigorous contraction of some thoughts, the luxuriant amplification of others, the incidental illustrations, and sometimes the dignity, sometimes the softness of the verses, enchain philosophy, suspend criticism, and oppress judgement by overpowering pleasure.

This is true of many paragraphs; yet if I had undertaken to exemplify Pope's felicity of composition before a rigid critic, I should not select the *Essay on Man*, for it contains more lines unsuccessfully laboured, more harshness of diction, more thoughts imperfectly expressed, more levity without elegance, and more heaviness without strength, than will easily be found in all his other works.

The 'Characters of Men and Women' are the product of diligent speculation upon human life; much labour has been bestowed upon them, and Pope very seldom laboured in vain. That his excellence may be properly estimated, I recommend a comparison of his *Characters of Women* with Boileau's *Satire*; it will then be seen with how much more perspicacity female nature is investigated and female excellence selected, and he surely is no mean writer to whom Boileau shall be found inferior. The *Characters of Men*, however, are written with more, if not with deeper, thought, and exhibit many passages exquisitely beautiful. 'The gem and the flower' will not easily be equalled. In the women's part are some defects: the character of Atossa is not so neatly finished as that of Clodio, and some of the female characters may be found perhaps more frequently among men; what is said of Philomedé was true of Prior.[n]

In the *Epistles* to Lord Bathurst and Lord Burlington, Dr. Warburton has endeavoured to find a train of thought which was never in the writer's head, and to support his hypothesis has printed that first which was published last.[n] In one the most valuable passage

Boileau's Satire: i.e. no. X.   'The gem': ll. 93–100.

is perhaps the elogy on good sense, and the other the end of the Duke of Buckingham.

The *Epistle to Arbuthnot*, now arbitrarily called the 'Prologue to the Satires', is a performance consisting, as it seems, of many fragments wrought into one design, which by this union of scattered beauties contains more striking paragraphs than could probably have been brought together into an occasional work. As there is no stronger motive to exertion than self-defence, no part has more elegance, spirit or dignity than the poet's vindication of his own character. The meanest passage is the satire upon Sporus.

Of the two poems which derived their names from the year, and which are called the 'Epilogue to the Satires', it was very justly remarked by Savage that the second was in the whole more strongly conceived and more equally supported, but that it had no single passages equal to the contention in the first for the dignity of Vice, and the celebration of the triumph of Corruption.

The *Imitations of Horace* seem to have been written as relaxations of his genius. This employment became his favourite by its facility: the plan was ready to his hand, and nothing was required but to accommodate as he could the sentiments of an old author to recent facts or familiar images; but what is easy is seldom excellent; such imitations cannot give pleasure to common readers; the man of learning may be sometimes surprised and delighted by an unexpected parallel, but the comparison requires knowledge of the original, which will likewise often detect strained applications. Between Roman images and English manners there will be an irreconcilable dissimilitude, and the work will be generally uncouth and parti-coloured, neither original nor translated, neither ancient nor modern.

Pope had, in proportions very nicely adjusted to each other, all the qualities that constitute genius.[n] He had invention, by which new trains of events are formed and new scenes of imagery displayed, as in *The Rape of the Lock*, and by which extrinsic and adventitious embellishments and illustrations are connected with a known subject, as in the *Essay on Criticism*. He had imagination, which strongly impresses on the writer's mind, and enables him to convey to the reader the various forms of nature, incidents of life, and energies of passion, as in his 'Eloisa', *Windsor Forest*, and the *Ethic Epistles*.

---

the elogy: *Epistle to Burlington*, ll. 39–46; *elogy* (*obs.*): favourable characteri-
zation, expression of praise.   *the end*: *Epistle to Bathurst*, ll. 299–314.
arbitrarily called: This title was added by Warburton.
the satire upon Sporus: ll. 305–33.   *the contention*: ll. 113 ff., 141 ff.
seem to have been written: cf. *Pope: Corr.* iii. 353 (Pope to Caryll, 8 Mar. 1733).

He had judgement, which selects from life or nature what the present purpose requires, and by separating the essence of things from its concomitants, often makes the representation more powerful than the reality; and he had colours of language always before him, ready to decorate his matter with every grace of elegant expression, as when he accommodates his diction to the wonderful multiplicity of Homer's sentiments and descriptions.

Poetical expression includes sound as well as meaning; 'Music', says Dryden, 'is inarticulate poetry'; among the excellences of Pope, therefore, must be mentioned the melody of his metre. By perusing the works of Dryden he discovered the most perfect fabric of English verse, and habituated himself to that only which he found the best, in consequence of which restraint his poetry has been censured as too uniformly musical, and as glutting the ear with unvaried sweetness. I suspect this objection to be the cant of those who judge by principles rather than perception, and who would even themselves have less pleasure in his works if he had tried to relieve attention by studied discords, or affected to break his lines and vary his pauses.

But though he was thus careful of his versification, he did not oppress his powers with superfluous rigour. He seems to have thought with Boileau that the practice of writing might be refined till the difficulty should overbalance the advantage. The construction of his language is not always strictly grammatical; with those rhymes which prescription had conjoined he contented himself, without regard to Swift's remonstrances, though there was no striking consonance; nor was he very careful to vary his terminations, or to refuse admission at a small distance to the same rhymes.

To Swift's edict for the exclusion of alexandrines and triplets he paid little regard; he admitted them, but in the opinion of Fenton, too rarely; he uses them more liberally in his translation than his poems.

He has a few double rhymes, and always, I think, unsuccessfully, except once in *The Rape of the Lock*.

Expletives he very early ejected from his verses, but he now and then admits an epithet rather commodious than important. Each of the six first lines of the *Iliad* might lose two syllables with very little diminution of the meaning; and sometimes, after all his art and

'*Music*': *Dryden: Essays*, i. 139.
his poetry has been censured: cf. Charles Churchill, *The Apology*, ll. 368–75.
He seems to have thought: see *Pope: Poems*, i. 257–8 and n., 267 and n.
Swift's remonstrances: *Pope: Corr.* i. 301 (Swift to Pope, 28 June 1715); cf. ibid. iii. 366 (Pope to Swift, 20 Apr. 1733).
in the opinion of Fenton: see above, p. 199 and n.
except once: *Rape of the Lock*, iii. 153–4.

labour, one verse seems to be made for the sake of another. In his latter productions the diction is sometimes vitiated by French idioms, with which Bolingbroke had perhaps infected him.

I have been told that the couplet by which he declared his own ear to be most gratified was this:

> Lo, where Moeotis sleeps, and hardly flows
> The freezing Tanais through a waste of snows.

But the reason of this preference I cannot discover.

It is remarked by Watts that there is scarcely a happy combination of words or a phrase poetically elegant in the English language which Pope has not inserted into his version of Homer. How he obtained possession of so many beauties of speech it were desirable to know. That he gleaned from authors, obscure as well as eminent, what he thought brilliant or useful, and preserved it all in a regular collection, is not unlikely. When in his last years Hall's *Satires* were shown him, he wished that he had seen them sooner.

New sentiments and new images others may produce, but to attempt any further improvement of versification will be dangerous. Art and diligence have now done their best, and what shall be added will be the effort of tedious toil and needless curiosity.

After all this it is surely superfluous to answer the question that has once been asked, whether Pope was a poet,[n] otherwise than by asking in return: 'If Pope be not a poet where is poetry to be found?' To circumscribe poetry by a definition will only show the narrowness of the definer, though a definition which shall exclude Pope will not easily be made. Let us look round upon the present time and back upon the past, let us inquire to whom the voice of mankind has decreed the wreath of poetry, let their productions be examined and their claims stated, and the pretensions of Pope will be no more disputed. Had he given the world only his version, the name of poet must have been allowed him; if the writer of the *Iliad* were to class his successors, he would assign a very high place to his translator without requiring any other evidence of genius.

The following letter, of which the original is in the hands of Lord Hardwicke, was communicated to me by the kindness of Mr. Jodrell:

Lo, where: *Dunciad*, iii. 87–8.
Watts: Isaac Watts (1674–1748), hymn-writer; see his *Improvement of the Mind* (1741), pp. 357–8 (II. xxxvi. 3).
Lord Hardwicke: Philip Yorke (1720–90), 2nd Earl of Hardwicke.
Mr. Jodrell: Richard Paul Jodrell (1745–1831), classical scholar and dramatist, member of the Essex Head Club.

To Mr. Bridges, at the Bishop of London's at Fulham.

The favour of your letter, with your remarks, can never
be enough acknowledged; and the speed with which you
discharged so troublesome a task, doubles the obligation.

I must own you have pleased me very much by the
commendations so ill bestowed upon me; but, I assure you,
much more by the frankness of your censure, which I
ought to take the more kindly of the two, as it is more
advantageous to a scribbler to be improved in his judgement than to be soothed in his vanity. The greater part of
those deviations from the Greek, which you have observed,
I was led into by Chapman and Hobbes, who are (it seems)
as much celebrated for their knowledge of the original as
they are decried for the badness of their translations.
Chapman pretends to have restored the genuine sense of the
author, from the mistakes of all former explainers, in
several hundred places; and the Cambridge editors of the
large Homer, in Greek and Latin, attributed so much to
Hobbes that they confess they have corrected the old Latin
interpretation very often by his version.[n] For my part, I
generally took the author's meaning to be as you have explained it; yet their authority, joined to the knowledge of
my own imperfectness in the language, overruled me.
However, Sir, you may be confident I think you in the right,
because you happen to be of my opinion: for men (let them
say what they will) never approve any other's sense but as it
squares with their own. But you have made me much more
proud of and positive in my judgement, since it is strengthened by yours. I think your criticisms, which regard the
expression, very just, and shall make my profit of them; to
give you some proof that I am in earnest, I will alter three
verses on your bare objection, though I have Mr. Dryden's
example for each of them. And this, I hope, you will
account no small piece of obedience from one who values
the authority of one true poet above that of twenty critics
or commentators. But though I speak thus of commentators, I will continue to read carefully all I can procure, to
make up, that way, for my own want of critical understanding in the original beauties of Homer. Though the
greatest of them are certainly those of the invention and
design, which are not at all confined to the language; for
the distinguishing excellences of Homer are (by the consent of the best critics of all nations) first in the manners
(which include all the speeches, as being no other than the
representations of each person's manners by his words),
and then in that rapture and fire which carries you away
with him, with that wonderful force, that no man who has
a true poetical spirit is master of himself while he reads him.

Mr. Bridges: Ralph Bridges, nephew of Sir William Trumbull and chaplain to
Henry Compton (1632–1713), Bishop of London; see *Pope: Corr.* i. 43–5.

Homer makes you interested and concerned before you are aware, all at once; whereas Virgil does it by soft degrees. This, I believe, is what a translator of Homer ought principally to imitate; and it is very hard for any translator to come up to it, because the chief reason why all translations fall short of their originals is that the very constraint they are obliged to, renders them heavy and dispirited.

The great beauty of Homer's language, as I take it, consists in that noble simplicity which runs through all his works; and yet his diction, contrary to what one would imagine consistent with simplicity, is at the same time very copious. I don't know how I have run into this pedantry in a letter, but I find I have said too much, as well as spoken too inconsiderately; what farther thoughts I have upon this subject I shall be glad to communicate to you (for my own improvement) when we meet; which is a happiness I very earnestly desire, as I do likewise some opportunity of proving how much I think myself obliged to your friendship, and how truly I am, Sir,

Your most faithful, humble servant,

A. POPE

The criticism upon Pope's *Epitaphs*, which was printed in *The Visitor*, is placed here, being too minute and particular to be inserted in the Life.

Every art is best taught by example. Nothing contributes more to the cultivation of propriety than remarks on the works of those who have most excelled. I shall therefore endeavour at this 'visit' to entertain the young students in poetry with an examination of Pope's *Epitaphs*.

To define an epitaph is useless: everyone knows that it is an inscription on a tomb. An epitaph, therefore, implies no particular character of writing, but may be composed in verse or prose. It is indeed commonly panegyrical, because we are seldom distinguished with a stone but by our friends; but it has no rule to restrain or modify it except this, that it ought not to be longer than common beholders may be expected to have leisure and patience to peruse.

I

On Charles Earl of Dorset, in the Church of Withyham in Sussex.

Dorset, the grace of Courts, the Muse's pride,
Patron of arts, and judge of nature, died.

which was printed: *The Universal Visiter and Memorialist* (for 1756), pp. 207–19.
Earl of Dorset: Charles Sackville, 6th Earl of Dorset; see above, p. 118.

> The scourge of pride, though sanctified or great,
> Of fops in learning, and of knaves in state;
> Yet soft in nature, though severe his lay,
> His anger moral, and his wisdom gay.
> Blest satirist! who touched the mean so true,
> As showed vice had his hate and pity too.
> Blest courtier! who could king and country please,
> Yet sacred kept his friendship, and his ease.
> Blest peer! his great forefather's every grace
> Reflecting, and reflected on his race;
> Where other Buckhursts, other Dorsets shine,
> And patriots still, or poets, deck the line.

The first distich of this epitaph contains a kind of information which few would want, that the man for whom the tomb was erected 'died'. There are indeed some qualities worthy of praise ascribed to the dead, but none that were likely to exempt him from the lot of man, or incline us much to wonder that he should die. What is meant by 'judge of nature' is not easy to say. Nature is not the object of human judgement, for it is vain to judge where we cannot alter. If by nature is meant what is commonly called 'nature' by the critics —a just representation of things really existing, and actions really performed—nature cannot be properly opposed to 'art', nature being, in this sense, only the best effect of 'art'.

> The scourge of pride—

Of this couplet, the second line is not, what is intended, an illustration of the former. 'Pride' in the 'great' is indeed well enough connected with knaves in state, though 'knaves' is a word rather too ludicrous and light; but the mention of 'sanctified' pride will not lead the thoughts to 'fops in learning', but rather to some species of tyranny or oppression, something more gloomy and more formidable than foppery.

> Yet soft his nature—

This is a high compliment, but was not first bestowed on Dorset by Pope.[n] The next verse is extremely beautiful.

> Blest satirist!—

In this distich is another line of which Pope was not the author.[n] I do not mean to blame these imitations with much harshness; in long performances they are scarcely to be avoided, and in shorter they may be indulged because the train of the composition may naturally involve them, or the scantiness of the subject allow little

his great forefather's: see *Pope: Poems* vi. 336.

choice. However, what is borrowed is not to be enjoyed as our own, and it is the business of critical justice to give every bird of the Muses his proper feather.

> Blest courtier!—

Whether a courtier can properly be commended for keeping his 'ease sacred' may perhaps be disputable. To please king and country, without sacrificing friendship to any change of times, was a very uncommon instance of prudence or felicity, and deserved to be kept separate from so poor a commendation as care of his ease. I wish our poets would attend a little more accurately to the use of the word 'sacred', which surely should never be applied in a serious composition but where some reference may be made to a higher Being, or where some duty is exacted or implied. A man may keep his friendship 'sacred' because promises of friendship are very awful ties; but methinks he cannot, but in a burlesque sense, be said to keep his ease 'sacred'.

> Blest peer!—

The blessing ascribed to the 'peer' has no connection with his peerage: they might happen to any other man whose ancestors were remembered, or whose posterity were likely to be regarded.

I know not whether this epitaph be worthy either of the writer or of the man entombed.

II

On Sir William Trumbull, one of the principal Secretaries of State to King William III, who, having resigned his place, died in his retirement at Easthampstead in Berkshire, 1716.

> A pleasing form, a firm, yet cautious mind,
> Sincere, though prudent; constant, yet resigned;
> Honour unchanged, a principle professed,
> Fixed to one side, but moderate to the rest:
> An honest courtier, yet a patriot too,
> Just to his prince, and to his country true.
> Filled with the sense of age, the fire of youth,
> A scorn of wrangling, yet a zeal for truth;
> A generous faith, from superstition free;
> A love to peace, and hate of tyranny;
> Such this man was; who now, from earth removed,
> At length enjoys that liberty he loved.

In this epitaph, as in many others, there appears at the first view a fault which I think scarcely any beauty can compensate. The name is omitted.[n] The end of an epitaph is to convey some account of the dead, and to what purpose is anything told of him whose name is concealed? An epitaph and a history of a nameless hero are equally absurd, since the virtues and qualities so recounted in either are scattered at the mercy of fortune to be appropriated by guess. The name, it is true, may be read upon the stone; but what obligation has it to the poet, whose verses wander over the earth and leave their subject behind them, and who is forced, like an unskilful painter, to make his purpose known by adventitious help?

This epitaph is wholly without elevation and contains nothing striking or particular, but the poet is not to be blamed for the defects of his subject. He said perhaps the best that could be said. There are, however, some defects which were not made necessary by the character in which he was employed. There is no opposition between an 'honest courtier' and a 'patriot', for an 'honest courtier' cannot but be a 'patriot'.

It was unsuitable to the nicety required in short compositions to close his verse with the word 'too'; every rhyme should be a word of emphasis, nor can this rule be safely neglected except where the length of the poem makes slight inaccuracies excusable, or allows room for beauties sufficient to overpower the effects of petty faults.

At the beginning of the seventh line the word 'filled' is weak and prosaic, having no particular adaptation to any of the words that follow it.

The thought in the last line is impertinent, having no connection with the foregoing character, nor with the condition of the man described. Had the epitaph been written on the poor conspirator who died lately in prison after a confinement of more than forty years, without any crime proved against him, the sentiment had been just and pathetical; but why should Trumbull be congratulated upon his liberty who had never known restraint?

III

On the Hon. Simon Harcourt, only son of the Lord Chancellor Harcourt, at the Church of Stanton Harcourt in Oxfordshire, 1720.

> To this sad shrine, whoe'er thou art, draw near,
> Here lies the friend most loved, the son most dear:
> Who ne'er knew joy, but friendship might divide,
> Or gave his father grief but when he died.

the poor conspirator: John Bernardi (1657–1736), major, served under James II and was imprisoned after being captured at the Boyne (1690); see *GM*, vi. (1736), 553.

Simon Harcourt: (1684–1720), s. of Simon Harcourt (1661?–1727), 1st Viscount Harcourt.

How vain is reason, eloquence how weak!
If Pope must tell what Harcourt cannot speak.
Oh, let thy once-loved friend inscribe thy stone,
And with a father's sorrows mix his own!

This epitaph is principally remarkable for the artful introduction
of the name, which is inserted with a peculiar felicity to which chance
must concur with genius, which no man can hope to attain twice, and
which cannot be copied but with servile imitation.

I cannot but wish that of this inscription the two last lines had been
omitted, as they take away from the energy what they do not add to
the sense.

IV

On James Craggs, Esq. In Westminster Abbey.

JACOBVS CRAGGS,
REGI MAGNAE BRITANNIAE A SECRETIS
ET CONSILIIS SANCTIORIBVS,
PRINCIPIS PARITER AC POPVLI AMOR ET DELICIAE:
VIXIT TITVLIS ET INVIDIA MAJOR,
ANNOS HEV PAVCOS, XXXV.
OB. FEB. XVI. MDCCXX.[n]

Statesman, yet friend to truth! of soul sincere,
In action faithful, and in honour clear!
Who broke no promise, served no private end,
Who gained no title, and who lost no friend;
Ennobled by himself, by all approved,
Praised, wept and honoured by the Muse he loved.

The lines on Craggs were not originally intended for an epitaph,
and therefore some faults are to be imputed to the violence with
which they are torn from the poem that first contained them. We
may, however, observe some defects. There is a redundancy of words
in the first couplet: it is superfluous to tell of him who was 'sincere',
'true' and 'faithful' that he was 'in honour clear'.

There seems to be an opposition intended in the fourth line which
is not very obvious; where is the relation between the two positions
that he 'gained no title' and 'lost no friend'?

It may be proper here to remark the absurdity of joining in the
same inscription Latin and English, or verse and prose. If either
language be preferable to the other, let that only be used, for no
reason can be given why part of the information should be given in
one tongue, and part in another, on a tomb more than in any other
place on any other occasion; and to tell all that can be conveniently
told in verse, and then to call in the help of prose, has always the
were not originally intended: see *Pope: Poems*, vi. 204, 282.

appearance of a very artless expedient or of an attempt unaccomplished. Such an epitaph resembles the conversation of a foreigner who tells part of his meaning by words, and conveys part by signs.

V

Intended for Mr. Rowe. In Westminster Abbey.

> Thy relics, Rowe, to this fair urn we trust,
> And sacred, place by Dryden's awful dust:
> Beneath a rude and nameless stone he lies,
> To which thy tomb shall guide inquiring eyes.
> Peace to thy gentle shade, and endless rest!
> Blest in thy genius, in thy love, too, blest!
> One grateful woman to thy fame supplies
> What a whole thankless land to his denies.

Of this inscription the chief fault is that it belongs less to Rowe, for whom it was written, than to Dryden, who was buried near him—and indeed gives very little information concerning either.

To wish 'Peace to thy shade' is too mythological to be admitted into a Christian temple; the ancient worship has infected almost all our other compositions, and might therefore be contented to spare our epitaphs. Let fiction at least cease with life, and let us be serious over the grave.

VI

On Mrs. Corbett, who died of a Cancer in her Breast.

> Here rests a woman, good without pretence,
> Blest with plain reason, and with sober sense:
> No conquest she, but o'er herself desired;
> No arts essayed, but not to be admired.
> Passion and pride were to her soul unknown,
> Convinced that virtue only is our own.
> So unaffected, so composed a mind,
> So firm, yet soft, so strong, yet so refined,
> Heaven, as its purest gold, by tortures tried,
> The saint sustained [it], but the woman died.

I have always considered this as the most valuable of all Pope's epitaphs; the subject of it is a character not discriminated by any shining or eminent peculiarities, yet that which really makes, though not the splendour, the felicity of life, and that which every wise man will choose for his final and lasting companion in the languor of age, in the quiet of privacy, when he departs weary and disgusted from the ostentatious, the volatile and the vain. Of such a character, which the

a rude and: see above, p. 150; *Pope: Poems*, vi. 209.
one grateful woman: i.e. Rowe's widow, Anne.
Mrs. Corbett: Elizabeth Corbett (d. 1725).

dull overlook and the gay despise, it was fit that the value should be made known and the dignity established. Domestic virtue, as it is exerted without great occasions or conspicuous consequences, in an even unnoted tenor, required the genius of Pope to display it in such a manner as might attract regard and enforce reverence. Who can forbear to lament that this amiable woman has no name in the verses?

If the particular lines of this inscription be examined, it will appear less faulty than the rest. There is scarce one line taken from common-places, unless it be that in which 'only virtue' is said to be 'our own'. I once heard a lady of great beauty and excellence object to the fourth line that it contained an unnatural and incredible panegyric. Of this let the ladies judge.

VII

On the Monument of the Hon. Robert Digby, and of his Sister Mary, erected by their Father the Lord Digby, in the Church of Sherborne in Dorsetshire, 1727.[n]

> Go! fair example of untainted youth,
> Of modest wisdom, and pacific truth;
> Composed in sufferings, and in joy sedate,
> Good without noise, without pretension great.
> Just of thy word, in every thought sincere,
> Who knew no wish but what the world might hear;
> Of softest manners, unaffected mind,
> Lover of peace, and friend of human kind;
> Go, live! for heaven's eternal year is thine,
> Go, and exalt thy moral to divine.
>
> And thou, blest maid! attendant on his doom,
> Pensive hast followed to the silent tomb,
> Steered the same course to the same quiet shore,
> Not parted long, and now to part no more!
> Go, then, where only bliss sincere is known!
> Go, where to love and to enjoy are one!
>
> Yet take these tears, mortality's relief,
> And till we share your joys, forgive our grief:
> These little rites, a stone, a verse, receive,
> 'Tis all a father, all a friend can give!

This epitaph contains of the brother only a general indiscriminate character, and of the sister tells nothing but that she died. The difficulty in writing epitaphs is to give a particular and appropriate praise. This, however, is not always to be performed, whatever be

a lady of great beauty: Mary ('Molly') Aston (1706–c. 1765), Johnson's Lichfield friend.
Robert Digby: (d. 1726), and Mary (d. 1729), children of William Digby (1661–1752), 5th Baron Digby, M.P.

the diligence or ability of the writer, for the greater part of mankind 'have no character at all', have little that distinguishes them from others equally good or bad, and therefore nothing can be said of them which may not be applied with equal propriety to a thousand more. It is indeed no great panegyric that there is enclosed in this tomb one who was born in one year and died in another, yet many useful and amiable lives have been spent which yet leave little materials for any other memorial. These are however not the proper subjects of poetry, and whenever friendship or any other motive obliges a poet to write on such subjects, he must be forgiven if he sometimes wanders in generalities, and utters the same praises over different tombs.

The scantiness of human praises can scarcely be made more apparent than by remarking how often Pope has, in the few epitaphs which he composed, found it necessary to borrow from himself. The fourteen epitaphs which he has written comprise about 140 lines, in which there are more repetitions than will easily be found in all the rest of his works. In the eight lines which make the character of Digby, there is scarce any thought, or word, which may not be found in the other epitaphs.

The ninth line, which is far the strongest and most elegant, is borrowed from Dryden. The conclusion is the same with that on Harcourt, but is here more elegant and better connected.

VIII

On Sir Godfrey Kneller. In Westminster Abbey, 1723.

> Kneller, by heaven, and not a master taught,
> Whose art was nature, and whose pictures thought;
> Now for two ages, having snatched from fate
> Whate'er was beauteous, or whate'er was great,
> Lies crowned with princes' honours, poets' lays,
> Due to his merit, and brave thirst of praise.
>
> Living, great Nature feared he might outvie
> Her works; and dying, fears herself may die.

Of this epitaph the first couplet is good, the second not bad, the third is deformed with a broken metaphor, the word 'crowned' not being applicable to the 'honours' or the 'lays', and the fourth is not only borrowed from the epitaph on Raphael, but of very harsh construction.

'*have no character*': *Epistle to a Lady*, l. 2.
borrowed from Dryden: 'To the Pious Memory of Anne Killigrew', l. 15.
Sir Godfrey Kneller: (original name, Gottfried Kniller) (1646–1723), 1st Baronet, painter.
Raphael: (Raffaelo Santi or Sanzio) (1483–1520), famous painter, and architect; see *Opere del Cardinale Pietro Bembo* (Venice, 1729), iv. 354.

IX

On General Henry Withers. In Westminster Abbey, 1729.

> Here, Withers, rest! thou bravest, gentlest mind,
> Thy country's friend, but more of human kind,
> O! born to arms! O! worth in youth approved:
> O! soft humanity in age beloved!
> For thee the hardy veteran drops a tear,
> And the gay courtier feels the sigh sincere.
>
> Withers, adieu! yet not with thee remove
> Thy martial spirit, or thy social love!
> Amidst corruption, luxury, and rage,
> Still leave some ancient virtues to our age:
> Nor let us say (those English glories gone)
> The last true Briton lies beneath this stone.

The epitaph on Withers affords another instance of common-places, though somewhat diversified by mingled qualities and the peculiarity of a profession.

The second couplet is abrupt, general and unpleasing; exclamation seldom succeeds in our language, and I think it may be observed that the particle 'O!' used at the beginning of a sentence always offends.

The third couplet is more happy: the value expressed for him by different sorts of men raises him to esteem; there is yet something of the common cant of superficial satirists who suppose that the insincerity of a courtier destroys all his sensations, and that he is equally a dissembler to the living and the dead.

At the third couplet I should wish the epitaph to close, but that I should be unwilling to lose the two next lines, which yet are dearly bought if they cannot be retained without the four that follow them.

X

On Mr. Elijah Fenton. At Easthampstead in Berkshire, 1730.

> This modest stone, what few vain marbles can,
> May truly say, Here lies an honest man:
> A poet, blest beyond the poet's fate,
> Whom Heaven kept sacred from the proud and great:
> Foe to loud praise, and friend to learned ease,
> Content with science in the vale of peace.
> Calmly he looked on either life; and here
> Saw nothing to regret, or there to fear;
> From Nature's temperate feast rose satisfied;
> Thanked heaven that he had lived, and that he died.

The first couplet of this epitaph is borrowed from Crashaw. The

Henry Withers: (1651?–1729), lieutenant-general.
borrowed from Crashaw: 'Upon Mr. Ashton', ll. 1–4.

four next lines contain a species of praise peculiar, original and just.
Here, therefore, the inscription should have ended, the latter part
containing nothing but what is common to every man who is wise
and good. The character of Fenton was so amiable that I cannot
forbear to wish for some poet or biographer to display it more fully
for the advantage of posterity. If he did not stand in the first rank of
genius, he may claim a place in the second; and whatever criticism
may object to his writings, censure could find very little to blame in
his life.

XI

On Mr. Gay. In Westminster Abbey, 1732.

> Of manners gentle, of affections mild,
> In wit, a man, simplicity, a child;
> With native humour tempering virtuous rage,
> Formed to delight at once and lash the age;
> Above temptation in a low estate,
> And uncorrupted even among the great:
> A safe companion, and an easy friend,
> Unblamed through life, lamented in thy end.
> These are thy honours! not that here thy bust
> Is mixed with heroes, or with kings thy dust;
> But that the worthy and the good shall say,
> Striking their pensive bosoms—Here lies GAY.

As Gay was the favourite of our author, this epitaph was probably
written with an uncommon degree of attention; yet it is not more
successfully executed than the rest, for it will not always happen that
the success of a poet is proportionate to his labour. The same
observation may be extended to all works of imagination, which are
often influenced by causes wholly out of the performer's power, by
hints of which he perceives not the origin, by sudden elevations of
mind which he cannot produce in himself, and which sometimes rise
when he expects them least.

The two parts of the first line are only echoes of each other: 'gentle
manners' and 'mild affections', if they mean anything, must mean the
same.

That Gay was a 'man in wit' is a very frigid commendation: to have
the wit of a man is not much for a poet. The 'wit of man' and the
'simplicity of a child' make a poor and vulgar contrast, and raise no
ideas of excellence either intellectual or moral.

In the next couplet 'rage' is less properly introduced after the
mention of 'mildness' and 'gentleness', which are made the con-
stituents of his character; for a man so 'mild' and 'gentle' to 'temper'
his 'rage' was not difficult.

The next line is unharmonious in its sound and mean in its conception: the opposition is obvious, and the word 'lash' used absolutely, and without any modification, is gross and improper.

To be 'above temptation' in poverty and 'free from corruption among the great', is indeed such a peculiarity as deserved notice. But to be a 'safe companion' is praise merely negative, arising not from the possession of virtue but the absence of vice, and that one of the most odious.

As little can be added to his character by asserting that he was 'lamented in his end'. Every man that dies is, at least by the writer of his epitaph, supposed to be lamented, and therefore this general lamentation does no honour to Gay.

The first eight lines have no grammar: the adjectives are without any substantive and the epithets without a subject.

The thought in the last line, that Gay is buried in the bosoms of the 'worthy' and the 'good', who are distinguished only to lengthen the line, is so dark that few understand it, and so harsh, when it is explained, that still fewer approve.

XII

Intended for Sir Isaac Newton. In Westminster Abbey.

ISAACUS NEWTONIUS:
QUEM IMMORTALEM
TESTANTUR, TEMPUS, NATURA, CAELUM:
MORTALEM
HOC MARMOR FATETUR.

Nature, and Nature's laws, lay hid in night,
God said, 'Let Newton be!' and all was light.

Of this epitaph, short as it is, the faults seem not to be very few. Why part should be Latin and part English it is not easy to discover. In the Latin, the opposition of *immortalis* and *mortalis* is a mere sound or a mere quibble: he is not 'immortal' in any sense contrary to that in which he is 'mortal'.

In the verses the thought is obvious, and the words 'night' and 'light' are too nearly allied.

Sir Isaac Newton: (1642–1727), famous natural philosopher, who conceived the idea of universal gravitation. The Latin reads: Isaac Newton, whose immortality is attested by Time, Nature, and the Heavens, but whose mortality is confessed by this marble.

XIII

On Edmund Duke of Buckingham, who died in the 19th
Year of his Age, 1735.

> If modest youth, with cool reflection crowned,
> And every opening virtue blooming round,
> Could save a parent's justest pride from fate,
> Or add one patriot to a sinking state,
> This weeping marble had not asked thy tear,
> Or sadly told how many hopes lie here!
> The living virtue now had shone approved,
> The senate heard him, and his country loved.
> Yet softer honours, and less noisy fame,
> Attend the shade of gentle Buckingham;
> In whom a race, for courage famed and art,
> Ends in the milder merit of the heart;
> And chiefs or sages long to Britain given,
> Pays the last tribute of a saint to heaven.

This epitaph Mr. Warburton prefers to the rest, but I know not for
what reason. To 'crown' with 'reflection' is surely a mode of speech
approaching to nonsense. 'Opening virtues blooming round' is
something like tautology; the six following lines are poor and prosaic.
'Art' is in another couplet used for 'arts', that a rhyme may be had
to 'heart'. The six last lines are the best, but not excellent.

The rest of his sepulchral performances hardly deserve the notice
of criticism. The contemptible 'Dialogue' between HE and SHE
should have been suppressed for the author's sake.

In his last epitaph on himself, in which he attempts to be jocular
upon one of the few things that make wise men serious, he confounds
the living man with the dead:

> Under this stone, or under this sill,
> Or under this turf, etc.

When a man is once buried, the question under what he is buried
is easily decided. He forgot that though he wrote the epitaph in a
state of uncertainty, yet it could not be laid over him till his grave was
made. Such is the folly of wit when it is ill employed.

The world has but little new; even this wretchedness seems to have
been borrowed from the following tuneless lines:

> Ludovici Areosti humantur ossa
> Sub hoc marmore, vel sub hac humo, seu
> Sub quicquid voluit benignus haeres

Duke of Buckingham: Edmund Sheffield (1716–35), 2nd Duke of Buckingham and
    Normanby.
prefers to the rest: Warburton, vi. 85 n.
The contemptible 'Dialogue': 'Epitaph for Dr. Francis Atterbury'.

> Sive haerede benignior comes, seu
> Opportunius incidens viator;
> Nam scire haud potuit futura, sed nec
> Tanti erat vacuum sibi cadaver
> Ut urnam cuperet parare vivens,
> Vivens ista tamen sibi paravit.
> Quae inscribi voluit suo sepulchro
> Olim siquod haberet is sepulchrum.[n]

Surely Ariosto did not venture to expect that his trifle would have ever had such an illustrious imitator.

THOMSON[n]

James Thomson, the son of a minister well esteemed for his piety and diligence, was born September 7, 1700 at Ednam, in the shire of Roxborough, of which his father was pastor. His mother, whose name was Hume,[n] inherited as coheiress a portion of a small estate. The revenue of a parish in Scotland is seldom large, and it was probably in commiseration of the difficulty with which Mr. Thomson supported his family, having nine children, that Mr. Riccarton, a neighbouring minister, discovering in James uncommon promises of future excellence, undertook to superintend his education and provide him books.

He was taught the common rudiments of learning at the school of Jedburgh, a place which he delights to recollect in his poem of *Autumn*, but was not considered by his master as superior to common boys—though in those early days he amused his patron and his friends with poetical compositions, with which however he so little pleased himself that on every New Year's day he threw into the fire all the productions of the foregoing year.

From the school he was removed to Edinburgh, where he had not resided two years when his father died and left all his children to the care of their mother, who raised upon her little estate what money a mortgage could afford, and removing with her family to Edinburgh, lived to see her son rising into eminence.

The design of Thomson's friends was to breed him a minister. He lived at Edinburgh, as at school, without distinction or expectation till, at the usual time, he performed a probationary exercise by explaining a psalm. His diction was so poetically splendid that Mr. Hamilton, the professor of Divinity, reproved him for speaking language unintelligible to a popular audience, and he censured one of his expressions as indecent, if not profane.

This rebuke is reported to have repressed his thoughts of an ecclesiastical character, and he probably cultivated with new diligence his blossoms of poetry, which however were in some danger of a blast, for submitting his productions to some who thought themselves qualified to criticize, he heard of nothing but faults; but finding

a minister: Thomas Thomson (1666–1716).
September 7: The date usually accepted is 11 Sept. (Grant, p. 4).
His mother: Beatrix Thomson (*née* Trotter) (d. 1725).
Mr. Riccarton: Robert Riccaltoun (or Riccarton) (1691–1769), divine and author.
a place which: l. 891 (Oxford ed. of J. Logie Robertson, 1961 reprint).
a psalm: no. 104.   *Mr. Hamilton*: William Hamilton (d. 1733).
is reported: Murdoch, i. *v–vi*.

other judges more favourable, he did not suffer himself to sink into despondence.

He easily discovered that the only stage on which a poet could appear with any hope of advantage was London—a place too wide for the operation of petty competition and private malignity, where merit might soon become conspicuous, and would find friends as soon as it became reputable to befriend it. A lady who was acquainted with his mother advised him to the journey, and promised some countenance or assistance which at last he never received; however he justified his adventure by her encouragement, and came to seek in London patronage and fame.

At his arrival he found his way to Mr. Mallet, then tutor to the sons of the Duke of Montrose. He had recommendations to several persons of consequence which he had tied up carefully in his handkerchief, but as he passed along the street with the gaping curiosity of a newcomer, his attention was upon everything rather than his pocket, and his magazine of credentials was stolen from him.

His first want was of a pair of shoes. For the supply of all his necessities his whole fund was his *Winter*, which for a time could find no purchaser, till at last Mr. Millan was persuaded to buy it at a low price,[n] and this low price he had for some time reason to regret; but by accident Mr. Whatley, a man not wholly unknown among authors, happening to turn his eye upon it, was so delighted that he ran from place to place celebrating its excellence. Thomson obtained likewise the notice of Aaron Hill, whom, being friendless and indigent, and glad of kindness, he courted with every expression of servile adulation.[n]

Winter was dedicated to Sir Spencer Compton, but attracted no regard from him to the author till Aaron Hill awakened his attention by some verses addressed to Thomson, and published in one of the newspapers,[n] which censured the great for their neglect of ingenious men. Thomson then received a present of twenty guineas, of which he gives this account to Mr. Hill:

I hinted to you in my last that on Saturday morning I was with Sir Spencer

A lady: Lady Grizel Baillie (1665–1746), poetess.

countenance: 'patronage, support' (*Dict*.).

Duke of Montrose: James Graham (d. 1742), 4th Marquis and 1st Duke of Montrose of 2nd creation, privy councillor.

Mr. Millan: John Millan (or Millen) (d. 1784).

Mr. Whatley: either Thomas Whately (d. 1772), or Robert Whately (or Whatley), a divine.

Sir Spencer Compton: (1673?–1743), Earl of Wilmington, M.P. and Speaker of the House.　　*I hinted to you*: Thomson: *Letters*, pp. 32–3 (7 June 1726).

Compton. A certain gentleman, without my desire, spoke to him concerning me; his answer was that I had never come near him. Then the gentleman put the question, if he desired that I should wait on him? He returned, he did. On this, the gentleman gave me an introductory letter to him. He received me in what they commonly call a civil manner, asked me some commonplace questions, and made me a present of twenty guineas. I am very ready to own that the present was larger than my performance deserved, and shall ascribe it to his generosity, or any other cause, rather than the merit of the address.

The poem which, being of a new kind, few would venture at first to like, by degrees gained upon the public, and one edition was very speedily succeeded by another.

Thomson's credit was now high, and every day brought him new friends; among others Dr. Rundle, a man afterwards unfortunately famous, sought his acquaintance, and found his qualities such that he recommended him to the Lord Chancellor Talbot.

Winter was accompanied in many editions not only with a preface and a dedication, but with poetical praises by Mr. Hill, Mr. Mallet (then Malloch), and 'Mira', the fictitious name of a lady once too well known. Why the dedications are to *Winter* and the other seasons, contrarily to custom, left out in the collected works, the reader may inquire.

The next year (1727) he distinguished himself by three publications: of *Summer*, in pursuance of his plan; of *A Poem on the Death of Sir Isaac Newton*, which he was enabled to perform as an exact philosopher by the instruction of Mr. Gray; and of *Britannia*, a kind of poetical invective against the ministry, whom the nation then thought not forward enough in resenting the depredations of the Spaniards.[n] By this piece he declared himself an adherent to the Opposition, and had therefore no favour to expect from the Court.

Thomson, having been some time entertained in the family of the Lord Binning, was desirous of testifying his gratitude by making him the patron of his *Summer*; but the same kindness which had first

speedily succeeded: Four London editions of *Winter* appeared in 1726.

Dr. Rundle: Thomas Rundle (1688?–1743), Bishop of Derry, denied the see of Gloucester on the grounds of his alleged heresy, but probably the victim of ecclesiastical politics.

Lord Chancellor Talbot: Charles Talbot (1685–1737), Baron Talbot of Hensol.

'*Mira*': Martha Sansome (*née* Fowke) (d. 1736), for an account of whom see Dorothy Brewster, *Aaron Hill: Poet, Dramatist, Projector* (New York, 1913), pp. 188 ff. (The verses referred to first appeared in 2nd ed.)

Mr. Gray: John Gray (d. 1769), rector of Marischal College, Aberdeen.

Lord Binning: Charles Hamilton (1697–1733), Lord Binning, poet and Knight Marischal of Scotland.

disposed Lord Binning to encourage him determined him to refuse the dedication, which was by his advice addressed to Mr. Dodington, a man who had more power to advance the reputation and fortune of a poet.

Spring was published next year with a dedication to the Countess of Hertford, whose practice it was to invite every summer some poet into the country to hear her verses and assist her studies. This honour was one summer conferred on Thomson, who took more delight in carousing with Lord Hertford and his friends than assisting her ladyship's poetical operations, and therefore never received another summons.[n]

Autumn, the season to which the *Spring* and *Summer* are preparatory, still remained unsung, and was delayed till he published (1730) his works collected.

He produced in 1727 the tragedy of *Sophonisba*, which raised such expectation that every rehearsal was dignified with a splendid audience collected to anticipate the delight that was preparing for the public. It was observed however that nobody was much affected, and that the company rose as from a moral lecture.

It had upon the stage no unusual degree of success. Slight accidents will operate upon the taste of pleasure. There was a feeble line in the play:

> O Sophonisba, Sophonisba, O!

This gave occasion to a waggish parody,

> O, Jemmy Thomson, Jemmy Thomson, O!

which for a while was echoed through the town.[n]

I have been told by Savage that of the prologue to *Sophonisba* the first part was written by Pope, who could not be persuaded to finish it, and that the concluding lines were added by Mallet.

Thomson was not long afterwards, by the influence of Dr. Rundle, sent to travel with Mr. Charles Talbot, the eldest son of the Chancellor. He was yet young enough to receive new impressions, to have his opinions rectified and his views enlarged; nor can he be supposed to have wanted that curiosity which is inseparable from an active and comprehensive mind. He may therefore now be supposed to have

Mr. Dodington: George Bubb Dodington (1691–1762), Baron Melcombe, M.P. and literary patron.

the Countess of Hertford: Frances Thynne (1699–1754), m. Algernon Seymour (1684–1750), Earl of Hertford and 7th Duke of Dorset.

Mr. Charles Talbot: Charles Richard Talbot (d. 1733), set out with Thomson in Nov. 1730.

revelled in all the joys of intellectual luxury: he was every day feasted with instructive novelties; he lived splendidly without expense, and might expect when he returned home a certain establishment.

At this time a long course of opposition to Sir Robert Walpole had filled the nation with clamours for liberty of which no man felt the want, and with care for liberty which was not in danger. Thomson, in his travels on the Continent, found or fancied so many evils arising from the tyranny of other governments that he resolved to write a very long poem, in five parts, upon Liberty.

While he was busy on the first book, Mr. Talbot died, and Thomson, who had been rewarded for his attendance by the place of Secretary of the Briefs, pays in the initial lines a decent tribute to his memory.

Upon this great poem two years were spent, and the author congratulated himself upon it as his noblest work; but an author and his reader are not always of a mind. *Liberty* called in vain upon her votaries to read her praises and reward her encomiast: her praises were condemned to harbour spiders and to gather dust; none of Thomson's performances were so little regarded.

The judgement of the public was not erroneous; the recurrence of the same images must tire in time; an enumeration of examples to prove a position which nobody denied, as it was from the beginning superfluous, must quickly grow disgusting.

The poem of *Liberty* does not now appear in its original state, but when the author's works were collected after his death, was shortened by Sir George Lyttelton[n] with a liberty which, as it has a manifest tendency to lessen the confidence of society, and to confound the characters of authors by making one man write by the judgement of another, cannot be justified by any supposed propriety of the alteration or kindness of the friend. I wish to see it exhibited as its author left it.

Thomson now lived in ease and plenty, and seems for a while to have suspended his poetry; but he was soon called back to labour by the death of the Chancellor, for his place then became vacant; and though the Lord Hardwicke delayed for some time to give it away, Thomson's bashfulness, or pride, or some other motive perhaps not more laudable, withheld him from soliciting, and the new Chancellor would not give him what he would not ask.

He now relapsed to his former indigence, but the Prince of Wales was at that time struggling for popularity, and by the influence of

the author congratulated: Murdoch, i. *x*.
Lord Hardwicke: Philip Yorke (1690–1764), 1st Earl of Hardwicke.

Mr. Lyttelton professed himself the patron of wit; to him Thomson was introduced, and being gaily interrogated about the state of his affairs, said 'that they were in a more poetical posture than formerly', and had a pension allowed him of £100 a year.

Being now obliged to write, he produced (1738) the tragedy of *Agamemnon*, which was much shortened in the representation. It had the fate which most commonly attends mythological stories, and was only endured but not favoured. It struggled with such difficulty through the first night that Thomson, coming late to his friends with whom he was to sup, excused his delay by telling them how the sweat of his distress had so disordered his wig that he could not come till he had been refitted by a barber.[n]

He so interested himself in his own drama that, if I remember right, as he sat in the upper gallery he accompanied the players by audible recitation, till a friendly hint frighted him to silence.[n] Pope countenanced *Agamemnon* by coming to it the first night, and was welcomed to the theatre by a general clap; he had much regard for Thomson, and once expressed it in a poetical epistle sent to Italy, of which however he abated the value by transplanting some of the lines into his *Epistle to Arbuthnot*.

About this time the act was passed for licensing plays, of which the first operation was the prohibition of *Gustavus Vasa*, a tragedy of Mr. Brooke, whom the public recompensed by a very liberal subscription; the next was the refusal of *Edward and Eleonora*, offered by Thomson. It is hard to discover why either play should have been obstructed. Thomson likewise endeavoured to repair his loss by a subscription, of which I cannot now tell the success.[n]

When the public murmured at the unkind treatment of Thomson, one of the ministerial writers remarked that 'he had taken a *Liberty* which was not agreeable to *Britannia* in any *Season*'.

He was soon after employed, in conjunction with Mr. Mallet, to write the mask of *Alfred*, which was acted before the Prince at Cliveden House.

His next work (1745) was *Tancred and Sigismunda*, the most successful of all his tragedies, for it still keeps its turn upon the stage. It may be doubted whether he was, either by the bent of nature or habits of study, much qualified for tragedy. It does not appear that he had much sense of the pathetic, and his diffusive and descriptive style produced declamation rather than dialogue.

a poetical epistle: see *Pope: Corr.* iii. 226 n. 2.
Mr. Brooke: Henry Brooke (1703?–83), author. Cf. *Life*, i. 141 n. 1.
which was acted: on 1 Aug. 1740.

His friend Mr. Lyttelton was now in power, and conferred upon him the office of surveyor-general of the Leeward Islands,[n] from which, when his deputy was paid, he received about £300 a year.

The last piece that he lived to publish was *The Castle of Indolence*, which was many years under his hand, but was at last finished with great accuracy. The first canto opens a scene of lazy luxury that fills the imagination.

He was now at ease but was not long to enjoy it, for by taking cold on the water between London and Kew, he caught a disorder which, with some careless exasperation, ended in a fever that put an end to his life, August 27, 1748. He was buried in the church of Richmond without an inscription, but a monument has been erected to his memory in Westminster Abbey.

Thomson was of stature above the middle size, and 'more fat than bard beseems', of a dull countenance, and a gross, unanimated, uninviting appearance, silent in mingled company but cheerful among select friends, and by his friends very tenderly and warmly beloved.

He left behind him the tragedy of *Coriolanus*, which was, by the zeal of his patron Sir George Lyttelton, brought upon the stage for the benefit of his family,[n] and recommended by a prologue which Quin, who had long lived with Thomson in fond intimacy, spoke in such a manner as showed him 'to be', on that occasion, 'no actor'. The commencement of this benevolence is very honourable to Quin, who is reported to have delivered Thomson, then known to him only for his genius, from an arrest by a very considerable present; and its continuance is honourable to both, for friendship is not always the sequel of obligation. By this tragedy a considerable sum was raised, of which part discharged his debts, and the rest was remitted to his sisters whom, however removed from them by place or condition, he regarded with great tenderness, as will appear by the following letter which I communicate with much pleasure as it gives me at once an opportunity of recording the fraternal kindness of Thomson, and reflecting on the friendly assistance of Mr. Boswell, from whom I received it.

> *Hagley in Worcestershire*
> *4 October 1747*

> *My dear Sister,*
> I thought you had known me better than to interpret my

a monument: by Robert Adam, and unveiled May 1762.
'*more fat*': *The Castle of Indolence*, I. lxviii.
Quin: James Quin (1693–1766), actor. Cf. Prologue to *Coriolanus*, l. 8.
Mr. Boswell: James Boswell (1740–95), friend and biographer of Johnson.
My dear Sister: Mrs. Jean Thomson (d. 1781).

silence into a decay of affection, especially as your behaviour has always been such as rather to increase than
diminish it. Don't imagine, because I am a bad correspondent, that I can ever prove an unkind friend and
brother. I must do myself the justice to tell you that my
affections are naturally very fixed and constant; and if I
had ever reason of complaint against you (of which by the
by I have not the least shadow), I am conscious of so many
defects in myself as dispose me to be not a little charitable
and forgiving.

It gives me the truest heartfelt satisfaction to hear you
have a good kind husband, and are in easy contented circumstances; but were they otherwise, that would only
awaken and heighten my tenderness towards you. As our
good and tender-hearted parents did not live to receive any
material testimonies of that highest human gratitude I owed
them (than which nothing could have given me equal
pleasure), the only return I can make them now is by kindness to those they left behind them; would to God poor
Lizzy had lived longer, to have been a farther witness of the
truth of what I say, and that I might have had the pleasure
of seeing once more a sister who so truly deserved my esteem
and love. But she is happy, while we must toil a little longer
here below; let us however do it cheerfully and gratefully,
supported by the pleasing hope of meeting yet again on a
safer shore, where to recollect the storms and difficulties of
life will not perhaps be inconsistent with that blissful state.
You did right to call your daughter by her name, for you
must needs have had a particular tender friendship for one
another, endeared as you were by nature, by having passed
the affectionate years of your youth together, and by that
great softener and engager of hearts, mutual hardship.
That it was in my power to ease it a little I account one of
the most exquisite pleasures of my life. But enough of this
melancholy though not unpleasing strain.

I esteem you for your sensible and disinterested advice to
Mr. Bell, as you will see by my letter to him; as I approve
entirely of his marrying again, you may readily ask me
why I don't marry at all. My circumstances have hitherto
been so variable and uncertain in this fluctuating world as
induce to keep me from engaging in such a state; and now,
though they are more settled, and of late (which you will be
glad to hear) considerably improved, I begin to think myself too far advanced in life for such youthful undertakings,
not to mention some other petty reasons that are apt to

a good kind husband: Robert Thomson, master of Lanark Grammar School.
poor Lizzy: Elizabeth Bell (*née* Thomson) (d. *c.* 1746).
Mr. Bell: the Revd. Robert Bell (1702–81), formerly Elizabeth Thomson's
husband, m. Catherine Linning on 27 Aug. 1747.

startle the delicacy of difficult old bachelors. I am, however, not a little suspicious that was I to pay a visit to Scotland (which I have some thoughts of doing soon) I might
possibly be tempted to think of a thing not easily repaired
if done amiss. I have always been of opinion that none
make better wives than the ladies of Scotland; and yet, who
more forsaken than they while the gentlemen are continually running abroad all the world over? Some of them,
it is true, are wise enough to return for a wife. You see I am
beginning to make interest already with the Scots ladies.
But no more of this infectious subject. Pray let me hear
from you now and then; and though I am not a regular
correspondent, yet perhaps I may mend in that respect.
Remember me kindly to your husband, and believe me
to be,

Your most affectionate brother,

JAMES THOMSON

(Addressed) 'To Mrs. Thomson in Lanark'.

The benevolence of Thomson was fervid but not active: he would
give on all occasions what assistance his purse would supply, but the
offices of intervention or solicitation he could not conquer his
sluggishness sufficiently to perform. The affairs of others, however,
were not more neglected than his own. He had often felt the in-
conveniences of idleness, but he never cured it, and was so conscious
of his own character that he talked of writing an eastern tale of 'the
Man who loved to be in Distress'.

Among his peculiarities was a very unskilful and inarticulate
manner of pronouncing any lofty or solemn composition. He was
once reading to Dodington who, being himself a reader eminently
elegant, was so much provoked by his odd utterance that he snatched
the paper from his hand, and told him that he did not understand
his own verses.

The biographer of Thomson has remarked that an author's life is
best read in his works; his observation was not well-timed. Savage,
who lived much with Thomson, once told me how he heard a lady
remarking that she could gather from his works three parts of his
character: that he was 'a great lover', 'a great swimmer', and
'rigorously abstinent'; but, said Savage, he knows not any love but
that of the sex, he was perhaps never in cold water in his life, and he
indulges himself in all the luxury that comes within his reach. Yet
Savage always spoke with the most eager praise of his social qualities,
his warmth and constancy of friendship, and his adherence to his

The biographer: Patrick Murdoch (d. 1774), author; see Murdoch, i. *i.*

first acquaintance when the advancement of his reputation had left them behind him.

As a writer he is entitled to one praise of the highest kind: his mode of thinking and of expressing his thoughts is original. His blank verse is no more the blank verse of Milton, or of any other poet, than the rhymes of Prior are the rhymes of Cowley. His numbers, his pauses, his diction, are of his own growth, without transcription, without imitation. He thinks in a peculiar train, and he thinks always as a man of genius; he looks round on nature and on life with the eye which nature bestows only on a poet—the eye that distinguishes, in everything presented to its view, whatever there is on which imagination can delight to be detained, and with a mind that at once comprehends the vast and attends to the minute. The reader of *The Seasons* wonders that he never saw before what Thomson shows him, and that he never yet has felt what Thomson impresses.

His is one of the works in which blank verse seems properly used:[n] Thomson's wide expansion of general views, and his enumeration of circumstantial varieties, would have been obstructed and embarrassed by the frequent intersections of the sense which are the necessary effects of rhyme.

His descriptions of extended scenes and general effects bring before us the whole magnificence of nature, whether pleasing or dreadful. The gaiety of *Spring*, the splendour of *Summer*, the tranquillity of *Autumn*, and the horror of *Winter*, take in their turns possession of the mind. The poet leads us through the appearances of things as they are successively varied by the vicissitudes of the year, and imparts to us so much of his own enthusiasm that our thoughts expand with his imagery, and kindle with his sentiments. Nor is the naturalist without his part in the entertainment, for he is assisted to recollect and to combine, to arrange his discoveries, and to amplify the sphere of his contemplation.

The great defect of *The Seasons* is want of method, but for this I know not that there was any remedy. Of many appearances subsisting all at once, no rule can be given why one should be mentioned before another; yet the memory wants the help of order, and the curiosity is not excited by suspense or expectation.

His diction is in the highest degree florid and luxuriant, such as may be said to be to his images and thoughts 'both their lustre and their shade'—such as invests them with splendour through which

with the eye: cf. *Life*, i. 453; iii. 37.
'*both their lustre*': *Hudibras*, II. i. 908. Cf. *Life*, iii. 37.

perhaps they are not always easily discerned. It is too exuberant, and sometimes may be charged with filling the ear more than the mind.

These poems, with which I was acquainted at their first appearance, I have since found altered and enlarged by subsequent revisals,[n] as the author supposed his judgement to grow more exact, and as books or conversation extended his knowledge and opened his prospects. They are, I think, improved in general, yet I know not whether they have not lost part of what Temple calls their 'race'[n]—a word which, applied to wines in its primitive sense, means the flavour of the soil.

Liberty, when it first appeared, I tried to read, and soon desisted. I have never tried again, and therefore will not hazard either praise or censure.

The highest praise which he has received ought not to be suppressed: it is said by Lord Lyttelton in the prologue to his posthumous play that his works contained

> No line which, dying, he could wish to blot.[n]

'*race*': 'of speech, writing, etc.: a peculiar and characteristic style or manner, *esp*. liveliness, sprightliness, piquancy' (*OED*).

COLLINS

William Collins was born at Chichester on 25th December, about 1720.[n] His father was a hatter of good reputation. He was in 1733, as Dr. Warton has kindly informed me, admitted scholar of Winchester College, where he was educated by Dr. Burton. His English exercises were better than his Latin.

He first courted the notice of the public by some verses 'To a Lady weeping', published in the *Gentleman's Magazine*.[n]

In 1740 he stood first in the list of the scholars to be received in succession at New College, but unhappily there was no vacancy. This was the original misfortune of his life. He became a commoner of Queen's College, probably with a scanty maintenance, but was in about half a year elected a demy of Magdalen College,[n] where he continued till he had taken a Bachelor's degree, and then suddenly left the University, for what reason I know not that he told.

He now (about 1744) came to London a literary adventurer, with many projects in his head and very little money in his pocket. He designed many works; but his great fault was irresolution, or the frequent calls of immediate necessity broke his schemes and suffered him to pursue no settled purpose. A man doubtful of his dinner, or trembling at a creditor, is not much disposed to abstracted meditation or remote inquiries. He published proposals for a 'History of the Revival of Learning', and I have heard him speak with great kindness of Leo X, and with keen resentment of his tasteless successor. But probably not a page of the 'History' was ever written. He planned several tragedies, but he only planned them. He wrote now and then odes and other poems, and did something, however little.

About this time I fell into his company. His appearance was decent and manly, his knowledge considerable, his views extensive, his conversation elegant, and his disposition cheerful. By degrees I gained his confidence, and one day was admitted to him when he was immured by a bailiff that was prowling in the street. On this occasion recourse was had to the booksellers who, on the credit of a translation

His father: William Collins (d. 1733).

Dr. Warton: Joseph Warton, later headmaster of Winchester, was a schoolfellow of Collins.

Dr. Burton: John Burton (d. 1773), headmaster of Winchester (1724–66).

published proposals: cf. H. O. White *RES*, iii (1927), 16 n.; *Essay on Pope*, pp. 186–7.

Leo X: (1475–1521), succeeded by Adrian VI (1459–1523).

odes and other poems: *Persian Eclogues* (1742); *Odes on Several Descriptive and Allegoric Subjects* (1747).

of Aristotle's *Poetics* which he engaged to write with a large commentary, advanced as much money as enabled him to escape into the country. He showed me the guineas safe in his hand. Soon afterwards his uncle Mr. Martin, a lieutenant-colonel, left him about £2000, a sum which Collins could scarcely think exhaustible, and which he did not live to exhaust. The guineas were then repaid, and the translation neglected.[n]

But man is not born for happiness. Collins, who while he 'studied to live' felt no evil but poverty, no sooner 'lived to study' than his life was assailed by more dreadful calamities, disease and insanity.

Having formerly written his character while perhaps it was yet more distinctly impressed upon my memory, I shall insert it here.

Mr. Collins was a man of extensive literature, and of vigorous faculties. He was acquainted not only with the learned tongues, but with the Italian, French and Spanish languages. He had employed his mind chiefly upon works of fiction and subjects of fancy, and by indulging some peculiar habits of thought, was eminently delighted with those flights of imagination which pass the bounds of nature, and to which the mind is reconciled only by a passive acquiescence in popular traditions. He loved fairies, genii, giants and monsters: he delighted to rove through the meanders of enchantment, to gaze on the magnificence of golden palaces, to repose by the waterfalls of Elysian gardens.

This was however the character rather of his inclination than his genius: the grandeur of wildness and the novelty of extravagance were always desired by him, but were not always attained. Yet as diligence is never wholly lost, if his efforts sometimes caused harshness and obscurity, they likewise produced in happier moments sublimity and splendour. This idea which he had formed of excellence led him to oriental fictions and allegorical imagery, and perhaps while he was intent upon description he did not sufficiently cultivate sentiment. His poems are the productions of a mind not deficient in fire, nor unfurnished with knowledge either of books or life, but somewhat obstructed in its progress by deviation in quest of mistaken beauties.

His morals were pure and his opinions pious; in a long continuance of poverty, and long habits of dissipation, it cannot be expected that any character should be exactly uniform. There is a degree of want by which the freedom of agency is almost destroyed, and long

Mr. Martin: Edmund Martin (d. 1749).
'*studied to live*': cf. *The Works of Francis Bacon* (1803), vi. 332.

association with fortuitous companions will at last relax the strictness of truth and abate the fervour of sincerity. That this man, wise and virtuous as he was, passed always unentangled through the snares of life it would be prejudice and temerity to affirm; but it may be said that at least he preserved the source of action unpolluted, that his principles were never shaken, that his distinctions of right and wrong were never confounded, and that his faults had nothing of malignity or design, but proceeded from some unexpected pressure or casual temptation.

The latter part of his life cannot be remembered but with pity and sadness. He languished some years under that depression of mind which enchains the faculties without destroying them, and leaves reason the knowledge of right without the power of pursuing it. These clouds which he perceived gathering on his intellects he endeavoured to disperse by travel, and passed into France, but found himself constrained to yield to his malady and returned. He was for some time confined in a house of lunatics, and afterwards retired to the care of his sister in Chichester, where death in 1756 came to his relief.[n]

After his return from France, the writer of this character paid him a visit at Islington, where he was waiting for his sister whom he had directed to meet him; there was then nothing of disorder discernible in his mind by any but himself, but he had withdrawn from study and travelled with no other book than an English Testament, such as children carry to the school; when his friend took it into his hand out of curiosity to see what companion a man of letters had chosen, 'I have but one book', said Collins, 'but that is the best.'

Such was the fate of Collins, with whom I once delighted to converse, and whom I yet remember with tenderness.

He was visited at Chichester in his last illness by his learned friends Dr. Warton and his brother, to whom he spoke with disapprobation of his *Oriental Eclogues* as not sufficiently expressive of Asiatic manners, and called them his 'Irish Eclogues'. He showed them at the same time an ode inscribed to Mr. John Home on the superstitions of the Highlands, which they thought superior to his other works, but which no search has yet found.[n]

His disorder was not alienation of mind but general laxity and

---

his sister: Anne Collins (1705?–89).
his brother: Thomas Warton (1728–90), historian of English poetry.
to whom he spoke: *Works of Pope*, ed. Warton (1797), i. 61–2 n.
John Home: (1722–1808), dramatist.

feebleness—a deficiency rather of his vital than intellectual powers. What he spoke wanted neither judgement nor spirit, but a few minutes exhausted him so that he was forced to rest upon the couch till a short cessation restored his powers, and he was again able to talk with his former vigour.

The approaches of this dreadful malady he began to feel soon after his uncle's death, and with the usual weakness of men so diseased, eagerly snatched that temporary relief with which the table and the bottle flatter and seduce. But his health continually declined, and he grew more and more burdensome to himself.

To what I have formerly said of his writings may be added that his diction was often harsh, unskilfully laboured, and injudiciously selected. He affected the obsolete when it was not worthy of revival; and he puts his words out of the common order, seeming to think, with some later candidates for fame, that not to write prose is certainly to write poetry. His lines commonly are of slow motion, clogged and impeded with clusters of consonants. As men are often esteemed who cannot be loved, so the poetry of Collins may sometimes extort praise when it gives little pleasure.

Mr. Collins's first production is added here from the *Poetical Calendar*:

> To Miss Aurelia C—r,
> On her Weeping at her Sister's Wedding.
>
> Cease, fair Aurelia, cease to mourn;
>   Lament not Hannah's happy state;
> You may be happy in your turn,
>   And seize the treasure you regret.
>
> With Love united Hymen stands,
>   And softly whispers to your charms:
> 'Meet but your lover in my bands,
>   You'll find your sister in his arms'.

GRAY

Thomas Gray, the son of Mr. Philip Gray, a scrivener of London, was born in Cornhill, November 26, 1716.[n] His grammatical education he received at Eton under the care of Mr. Antrobus, his mother's brother, then assistant to Dr. George, and when he left school, in 1734, entered a pensioner at Peterhouse in Cambridge.

The transition from the school to the college is, to most young scholars, the time from which they date their years of manhood, liberty and happiness, but Gray seems to have been very little delighted with academical gratifications; he liked at Cambridge neither the mode of life nor the fashion of study, and lived sullenly on to the time when his attendance on lectures was no longer required. As he intended to profess the Common Law, he took no degree.[n]

When he had been at Cambridge about five years,[n] Mr. Horace Walpole, whose friendship he had gained at Eton, invited him to travel with him as his companion. They wandered through France into Italy, and Gray's letters contain a very pleasing account of many parts of their journey. But unequal friendships are easily dissolved; at Florence they quarrelled and parted, and Mr. Walpole is now content to have it told that it was by his fault.[n] If we look however without prejudice on the world, we shall find that men whose consciousness of their own merit sets them above the compliances of servility are apt enough in their association with superiors to watch their own dignity with troublesome and punctilious jealousy, and in the fervour of independence to exact that attention which they refuse to pay. Part they did, whatever was the quarrel, and the rest of their travels was doubtless more unpleasant to them both. Gray continued his journey in a manner suitable to his own little fortune, with only an occasional servant.

He returned to England in September 1741, and in about two months afterwards buried his father, who had, by an injudicious waste of money upon a new house, so much lessened his fortune that Gray thought himself too poor to study the law. He therefore retired to Cambridge, where he soon after became Bachelor of Civil Law,

Philip Gray: (d. 1741).

Mr. Antrobus: Robert Antrobus (d. 1730), b. of Dorothy Gray (d. 1753).

Dr. George: William George (1697–1756), Dean of Lincoln, formerly headmaster of Eton and Provost of King's College, Cambridge.

Horace (or Horatio) *Walpole*: (1717–97), 4th Earl of Orford, letter-writer and author of *The Castle of Otranto* (1764).

and where, without liking the place or its inhabitants, or professing to like them, he passed, except a short residence at London, the rest of his life.

About this time he was deprived of Mr. West, the son of a chancellor of Ireland, a friend on whom he appears to have set a high value, and who deserved his esteem by the powers which he shows in his letters, and in the 'Ode to May', which Mr. Mason has preserved, as well as by the sincerity with which, when Gray sent him part of *Agrippina*, a tragedy that he had just begun, he gave an opinion which probably intercepted the progress of the work, and which the judgement of every reader will confirm. It was certainly no loss to the English stage that *Agrippina* was never finished.

In this year (1742) Gray seems first to have applied himself seriously to poetry, for in this year were produced the 'Ode to Spring', his *Prospect of Eton*, and his 'Ode to Adversity'. He began likewise a Latin poem, 'De Principiis Cogitandi'.[n]

It may be collected from the narrative of Mr. Mason that his first ambition was to have excelled in Latin poetry; perhaps it were reasonable to wish that he had prosecuted his design, for though there is at present some embarrassment in his phrase and some harshness in his lyric numbers, his copiousness of language is such as very few possess, and his lines, even when imperfect, discover a writer whom practice would quickly have made skilful.

He now lived on at Peterhouse very little solicitous what others did or thought, and cultivated his mind and enlarged his views without any other purpose than of improving and amusing himself, when Mr. Mason, being elected fellow of Pembroke Hall,[n] brought him a companion who was afterwards to be his editor, and whose fondness and fidelity has kindled in him a zeal of admiration which cannot be reasonably expected from the neutrality of a stranger and the coldness of a critic.

In this retirement he wrote (1747) an ode on the 'Death of Mr. Walpole's Cat', and the year afterwards attempted a poem of more importance on 'Government and Education', of which the fragments which remain have many excellent lines.

His next production (1750) was his far-famed *Elegy in the Church-*

without liking: cf. 'Hymn to Ignorance'.

Mr. West: Richard West (1716–42), poet, s. of Richard West, senior (d. 1726), Lord Chancellor of Ireland (1725).

Mr. Mason: William Mason (1724–97), poet; see his memoir on Gray (1775), pp. 147–8.

he gave an opinion: Gray: *Corr.* i. 189–90 (West to Gray, 4 Apr. 1742).

It may be collected: Mason, p. 157.

yard which, finding its way into a magazine, first, I believe, made him known to the public.[n]

An invitation from Lady Cobham about this time gave occasion to an odd composition called 'A Long Story', which adds little to Gray's character.[n]

Several of his pieces were published (1753) with designs by Mr. Bentley, and that they might in some form or other make a book, only one side of each leaf was printed. I believe the poems and the plates recommended each other so well that the whole impression was soon bought. This year he lost his mother.

Some time afterwards (1756) some young men of the college, whose chambers were near his, diverted themselves with disturbing him by frequent and troublesome noises, and, as is said, by pranks yet more offensive and contemptuous.[n] This insolence, having endured it a while, he represented to the governors of the society, among whom perhaps he had no friends; and finding his complaint little regarded, removed himself to Pembroke Hall.

In 1757 he published 'The Progress of Poetry' and 'The Bard', two compositions at which the readers of poetry were at first content to gaze in mute amazement. Some that tried them confessed their inability to understand them, though Warburton said that they were understood as well as the works of Milton and Shakespeare, which it is the fashion to admire. Garrick wrote a few lines in their praise. Some hardy champions undertook to rescue them from neglect, and in a short time many were content to be shown beauties which they could not see.[n]

Gray's reputation was now so high that after the death of Cibber he had the honour of refusing the laurel, which was then bestowed on Mr. Whitehead.

His curiosity not long after drew him away from Cambridge to a lodging near the Museum,[n] where he resided near three years, reading and transcribing, and so far as can be discovered, very little affected by two odes on 'Oblivion' and 'Obscurity' in which his lyric performances were ridiculed with much contempt and much ingenuity.

When the professor of Modern History at Cambridge died, he

Lady Cobham: Anne (*née* Halsey) (d. 1760), w. of Sir Richard Temple, Viscount Cobham and 4th Baronet of Stowe.
Mr. Bentley: Richard Bentley (1708–82), miscellaneous writer.
refusing the laurel: see *Gray: Corr.* ii. 543–4 (Dec. 1757).
Mr. Whitehead: William Whitehead (1715–85).
two odes: George Colman and Robert Lloyd, *Two Odes* (1760).

was, as he says, 'cockered and spirited up' till he asked it of Lord Bute, who sent him a civil refusal; and the place was given to Mr. Brockett, the tutor of Sir James Lowther.

His constitution was weak, and believing that his health was promoted by exercise and change of place, he undertook (1765) a journey into Scotland, of which his account, so far as it extends, is very curious and elegant, for as his comprehension was ample, his curiosity extended to all the works of art, all the appearances of nature, and all the monuments of past events. He naturally contracted a friendship with Dr. Beattie, whom he found a poet, a philosopher, and a good man. The Mareschal College at Aberdeen offered him the degree of Doctor of Laws which, having omitted to take it at Cambridge, he thought it decent to refuse.

What he had formerly solicited in vain was at last given him without solicitation. The professorship of History became again vacant, and he received (1768) an offer of it from the Duke of Grafton. He accepted, and retained it to his death, always designing lectures but never reading them, uneasy at his neglect of duty, and appeasing his uneasiness with designs of reformation, and with a resolution which he believed himself to have made of resigning the office if he found himself unable to discharge it.

Ill health made another journey necessary, and he visited (1769) Westmorland and Cumberland. He that reads his epistolary narration wishes that to travel, and to tell his travels, had been more of his employment; but it is by studying at home that we must obtain the ability of travelling with intelligence and improvement.

His travels and his studies were now near their end. The gout, of which he had sustained many weak attacks, fell upon his stomach, and yielding to no medicines, produced strong convulsions which (July 30, 1771) terminated in death.

His character I am willing to adopt, as Mr. Mason has done, from

'*cockered*': *Gray: Corr.* ii. 787–8 (Gray to Wharton, 4 Dec. 1762). (The previous occupant of the Chair had been Shallet Turner.)

Lord Bute: John Stuart (1713–92), 3rd Earl of Bute.

Mr. Brockett: Lawrence Brockett (1724–68).

Sir James Lowther: (1736–1802), 1st Earl of Lonsdale and Viscount and Baron Lowther of Whitehaven, M.P.

his account: *Gray: Corr.* ii. 887–95 (Gray to Wharton, Sept. 1765).

Dr. Beattie: James Beattie (1735–1803), poet, philosopher, and divine.

having omitted: *Gray: Corr.* ii. 895 (Gray to Beattie, 2 Oct. 1765).

Duke of Grafton: Augustus Henry Fitzroy (1735–1811), 3rd Duke of Grafton. Cf. *Gray: Corr.* iii. 1034 (Gray to Grafton, July 1768).

his epistolary narration: ibid. iii. 1074 ff. and n. 1 (Gray to Wharton, 18 Oct. 1769).

a letter written to my friend Mr. Boswell by the Rev. Mr. Temple, rector of St. Gluvias in Cornwall, and am as willing as his warmest well-wisher to believe it true.

Perhaps he was the most learned man in Europe. He was equally acquainted with the elegant and profound parts of science, and that not superficially but thoroughly. He knew every branch of history, both natural and civil; had read all the original historians of England, France, and Italy; and was a great antiquarian. Criticism, metaphysics, morals, politics, made a principal part of his study; voyages and travels of all sorts were his favourite amusements; and he had a fine taste in painting, prints, architecture and gardening. With such a fund of knowledge, his conversation must have been equally instructing and entertaining; but he was also a good man, a man of virtue and humanity. There is no character without some speck, some imperfection; and I think the greatest defect in his was an affectation in delicacy, or rather effeminacy, and a visible fastidiousness, or contempt and disdain of his inferiors in science. He also had, in some degree, that weakness which disgusted Voltaire so much in Mr. Congreve:[n] though he seemed to value others chiefly according to the progress they had made in knowledge, yet he could not bear to be considered himself merely as a man of letters, and though without birth, or fortune, or station, his desire was to be looked upon as a private independent gentleman who read for his amusement. Perhaps it may be said: What signifies so much knowledge, when it produced so little? Is it worth taking so much pains to leave no memorial but a few poems? But let it be considered that Mr. Gray was, to others, at least innocently employed; to himself, certainly beneficially. His time passed agreeably; he was every day making some new acquisition in science; his mind was enlarged, his heart softened, his virtue strengthened; the world and mankind were shown to him without a mask; and he was taught to consider everything as trifling and unworthy of the attention of a wise man, except the pursuit of knowledge and practice of virtue in that state wherein God hath placed us.

To this character Mr. Mason has added a more particular account of Gray's skill in zoology. He has remarked that Gray's effeminacy was affected most 'before those whom he did not wish to please', and that he is unjustly charged with making knowledge his sole reason of preference as he paid his esteem to none whom he did not likewise believe to be good.

What has occurred to me, from the slight inspection of his letters in which my undertaking has engaged me, is that his mind had a large grasp, that his curiosity was unlimited and his judgement cultivated, that he was a man likely to love much where he loved at

Mr. Temple: William Johnston (or Johnson) Temple (1739–96), essayist and friend of Gray, became rector of St. Gluvias in 1776. (His name was first included in 1783 ed.)

Perhaps he was: cf. Mason, pp. 402–4; *Life*, ii. 515–16.

Mr. Mason has added: Mason, pp. 341, 402 n., 403 nn.

all, but that he was fastidious and hard to please. His contempt however is often employed where I hope it will be approved, upon scepticism and infidelity. His short account of Shaftesbury I will insert.

You say you cannot conceive how Lord Shaftesbury came to be a philosopher in vogue; I will tell you; first, he was a lord; secondly, he was as vain as any of his readers; thirdly, men are very prone to believe what they do not understand; fourthly, they will believe anything at all, provided they are under no obligation to believe it; fifthly, they love to take a new road, even when that road leads nowhere; sixthly, he was reckoned a fine writer, and seems always to mean more than he said. Would you have any more reasons? An interval of above forty years has pretty well destroyed the charm. A dead lord ranks with commoners: vanity is no longer interested in the matter, for a new road is become an old one.

Mr. Mason has added from his own knowledge that though Gray was poor he was not eager of money, and that out of the little that he had he was very willing to help the necessitous.

As a writer he had this peculiarity, that he did not write his pieces first rudely and then correct them, but laboured every line as it arose in the train of composition; and he had a notion, not very peculiar, that he could not write but at certain times or at happy moments—a fantastic foppery to which my kindness for a man of learning and of virtue wishes him to have been superior.

Gray's poetry is now to be considered, and I hope not to be looked on as an enemy to his name if I confess that I contemplate it with less pleasure than his life.

His 'Ode on Spring' has something poetical both in the language and the thought, but the language is too luxuriant, and the thoughts have nothing new. There has of late arisen a practice of giving to adjectives derived from substantives the termination of participles—such as the 'cultured' plain, the 'daisied' bank;[n] but I was sorry to see in the lines of a scholar like Gray the 'honied' spring. The morality is natural but too stale; the conclusion is pretty.

The poem on the 'Cat' was doubtless by its author considered as a trifle, but it is not a happy trifle. In the first stanza 'the azure flowers' that 'blow' show resolutely a rhyme is sometimes made when it cannot easily be found. Selima, the Cat, is called a nymph

Shaftesbury: Anthony Ashley Cooper (1671–1713), 3rd Earl of Shaftesbury, philosopher; see *Gray: Corr.* ii. 583 (Gray to Stonhewer, 18 Aug. 1758).
Mr. Mason has added: Mason, p. 335.
he had a notion: cf. *Gray: Corr.* ii. 571 (Gray to Wharton, 18 June 1758).
'*honied' spring*: l. 26.

with some violence both to language and sense; but there is good use made of it when it is done, for of the two lines,

> What female heart can gold despise?
> What cat's averse to fish?

the first relates merely to the nymph, and the second only to the cat. The sixth stanza contains a melancholy truth, that 'a favourite has no friend', but the last ends in a pointed sentence of no relation to the purpose: if 'what glistered' had been 'gold', the cat would not have gone into the water; and if she had, would not less have been drowned.

The *Prospect of Eton College* suggests nothing to Gray which every beholder does not equally think and feel. His supplication to father Thames to tell him who drives the hoop or tosses the ball is useless and puerile. Father Thames has no better means of knowing than himself. His epithet 'buxom health' is not elegant: he seems not to understand the word. Gray thought his language more poetical as it was more remote from common use; finding in Dryden 'honey redolent of spring', an expression that reaches the utmost limits of our language, Gray drove it a little more beyond common apprehension by making 'gales' to be 'redolent of joy and youth'.

Of the 'Ode on Adversity' the hint was at first taken from 'O Diva, gratum quae regis Antium', but Gray has excelled his original by the variety of his sentiments and by their moral application. Of this piece, at once poetical and rational, I will not by slight objections violate the dignity.

My process has now brought me to the 'wonderful Wonder of Wonders', the two Sister Odes, by which, though either vulgar ignorance or common sense at first universally rejected them, many have been since persuaded to think themselves delighted. I am one of those that are willing to be pleased, and therefore would gladly find the meaning of the first stanza of 'The Progress of Poetry'.

Gray seems in his rapture to confound the images of 'spreading sound' and 'running water'. A 'stream of music' may be allowed, but where does 'music', however 'smooth and strong', after having visited the 'verdant vales', 'roll down the steep amain' so as that

---

What female: ll. 23–4.   '*buxom health*': l. 45.
Gray thought: cf. *Gray: Corr.* i. 192–3 (Gray to West, Apr. 1742).
'*honey redolent*': 'Of the Pythagorean Philosophy', from *Metamorphoses* xv, l. 110.
'*redolent of joy*': l. 19.
'*O Diva*': Horace, *Odes*, i. 35 ('O goddess who rules pleasant Antium').

'rocks and nodding groves rebellow to the roar'? If this be said of 'music' it is nonsense; if it be said of 'water' it is nothing to the purpose.

The second stanza, exhibiting Mars's car and Jove's eagle, is unworthy of further notice. Criticism disdains to chase a schoolboy to his commonplaces.

To the third it may likewise be objected that it is drawn from mythology, though such as may be more easily assimilated to real life. Idalia's 'velvet-green' has something of cant. An epithet or metaphor drawn from nature ennobles art; an epithet or metaphor drawn from art degrades nature. Gray is too fond of words arbitrarily compounded. 'Many-twinkling' was formerly censured as not analogical; we may say 'many-spotted', but scarcely 'many-spotting'.[n] This stanza, however, has something pleasing.

Of the second ternary of stanzas, the first endeavours to tell something, and would have told it had it not been crossed by Hyperion; the second describes well enough the universal prevalence of poetry, but I am afraid that the conclusion will not rise from the premises. The caverns of the north and the plains of Chile are not the residences of 'Glory' and 'generous Shame'. But that poetry and virtue go always together is an opinion so pleasing that I can forgive him who resolves to think it true.

The third stanza sounds big with Delphi, and Aegean, and Ilissus, and Meander, and 'hallowed fountain' and 'solemn sound'; but in all Gray's odes there is a kind of cumbrous splendour which we wish away. His position is at last false: in the time of Dante and Petrarch, from whom he derives our first school of poetry, Italy was overrun by 'tyrant power' and 'coward vice'; nor was our state much better when we first borrowed the Italian arts.

Of the third ternary, the first gives a mythological birth of Shakespeare. What is said of that mighty genius is true, but it is not said happily: the real effects of his poetical power are put out of sight by the pomp of machinery. Where truth is sufficient to fill the mind, fiction is worse than useless; the counterfeit debases the genuine.

Idalia: a mountain city in Cyprus that was sacred to Venus.

Hyperion: in Greek mythology one of the Titans, the father of the Sun, or the Sun itself.

Delphi: an ancient oracular shrine sacred to Apollo, situated in a deep cleft on a spur of Mt. Parnassus.

Aegean: The island of Lesbos in the Aegean was the birthplace of Arion, Sappho, and Alcaeus.

Ilissus: a stream with its source on Mt. Hymettus, that descends through the plain of Attica.

His account of Milton's blindness, if we suppose it caused by study in the formation of his poem—a supposition surely allowable—is poetically true and happily imagined. But the 'car' of Dryden, with his 'two coursers', has nothing in it peculiar: it is a car in which any other rider may be placed.

'The Bard' appears at the first view to be, as Algarotti and others have remarked, an imitation of the prophecy of Nereus.[n] Algarotti thinks it superior to its original, and if preference depends only on the imagery and animation of the two poems, his judgement is right. There is in 'The Bard' more force, more thought, and more variety. But to copy is less than to invent, and the copy has been unhappily produced at a wrong time. The fiction of Horace was to the Romans credible, but its revival disgusts us with apparent and unconquerable falsehood. *Incredulus odi.*

To select a singular event, and swell it to a giant's bulk by fabulous appendages of spectres and predictions, has little difficulty, for he that forsakes the probable may always find the marvellous. And it has little use: we are affected only as we believe; we are improved only as we find something to be imitated or declined. I do not see that 'The Bard' promotes any truth, moral or political.

His stanzas are too long, especially his epodes: the ode is finished before the ear has learned its measures, and consequently before it can receive pleasure from their consonance and recurrence.

Of the first stanza the abrupt beginning has been celebrated, but technical beauties can give praise only to the inventor. It is in the power of any man to rush abruptly upon his subject that has read the ballad of 'Johnny Armstrong'.[n]

Is there ever a man in all Scotland—

The initial resemblances or alliterations, 'ruin', 'ruthless', 'helm nor hauberk', are below the grandeur of a poem that endeavours at sublimity.

In the second stanza the Bard is well described, but in the third we have the puerilities of obsolete mythology. When we are told that 'Cadwallo hushed the stormy main', and that 'Modred' made 'huge

it is a car: cf. *Life*, ii. 5.

Algarotti: Francesco Algarotti (1712–64), Italian scientist and essayist, honoured by Frederick the Great.

Nereus: an old sea-god, father of the Nereids, endowed with great wisdom and the gift of prophecy.

Incredulus odi: *Ars Poetica*, l. 188 ('I detest what I am unable to credit'). Cf. *Life*, iii. 229.

the abrupt beginning: Mason, p. 91 (2nd series of pagination); cf. *Life*, i. 403.

Plinlimmon bow his cloud-topped head', attention recoils from the repetition of a tale that, even when it was first heard, was heard with scorn.

The 'weaving' of the 'winding sheet' he borrowed, as he owns, from the northern bards, but their texture, however, was very properly the work of female powers, as the art of spinning the thread of life in another mythology. Theft is always dangerous: Gray has made weavers of his slaughtered bards by a fiction outrageous and incongruous. They are then called upon to 'Weave the warp, and weave the woof', perhaps with no great propriety, for it is by crossing the 'woof' with the 'warp' that men 'weave' the 'web' or piece; and the first line was dearly bought by the admission of its wretched correspondent, 'Give ample room and verge enough'. He has, however, no other line as bad.

The third stanza of the second ternary is commended, I think, beyond its merit. The personification is indistinct. Thirst and Hunger are not alike, and their features, to make the imagery perfect, should have been discriminated. We are told in the same stanza how 'towers' are 'fed'. But I will no longer look for particular faults; yet let it be observed that the ode might have been concluded with an action of better example—but suicide is always to be had without expense of thought.

These odes are marked by glittering accumulations of ungraceful ornaments: they strike rather than please; the images are magnified by affectation, the language is laboured into harshness. The mind of the writer seems to work with unnatural violence. 'Double, double, toil and trouble'. He has a kind of strutting dignity, and is tall by walking on tiptoe.[n] His art and his struggle are too visible, and there is too little appearance of ease and nature.

To say that he has no beauties would be unjust; a man like him, of great learning and great industry, could not but produce something valuable. When he pleases least it can only be said that a good design was ill directed.

His translations of Northern and Welsh poetry deserve praise: the imagery is preserved, perhaps often improved; but the language is unlike the language of other poets.

In the character of his *Elegy* I rejoice to concur with the common reader, for by the common sense of readers uncorrupted with literary

---

as he owns: see Gray's note.
texture: 'the process or art of weaving. *Obs*.' (*OED*).
is commended: cf. Mason, p. 93 (2nd series of pagination).
'*Double, double*': *Macbeth*, IV. i. 10, etc.

prejudices, after all the refinements of subtlety and the dogmatism of learning, must be finally decided all claim to poetical honours. The *Churchyard* abounds with images which find a mirror in every mind, and with sentiments to which every bosom returns an echo. The four stanzas beginning 'Yet even these bones' are to me original: I have never seen the notions in any other place; yet he that reads them here persuades himself that he has always felt them. Had Gray written often thus, it had been vain to blame, and useless to praise him.

Appendix

ON RELIGIOUS POETRY

It has been the frequent lamentation of good men that verse has been too little applied to the purposes of worship, and many attempts have been made to animate devotion by pious poetry; that they have very seldom attained their end is sufficiently known, and it may not be improper to inquire why they have miscarried.

Let no pious ear be offended if I advance, in opposition to many authorities, that poetical devotion cannot often please. The doctrines of religion may indeed be defended in a didactic poem, and he who has the happy power of arguing in verse will not lose it because his subject is sacred. A poet may describe the beauty and the grandeur of nature, the flowers of the spring, and the harvests of autumn, the vicissitudes of the tide, and the revolutions of the sky, and praise the Maker for His works in lines which no reader shall lay aside. The subject of the disputation is not piety, but the motives to piety; that of the description is not God, but the works of God.

Contemplative piety, or the intercourse between God and the human soul, cannot be poetical. Man admitted to implore the mercy of his Creator, and plead the merits of his Redeemer, is already in a higher state than poetry can confer.

The essence of poetry is invention, such invention as, by producing something unexpected, surprises and delights. The topics of devotion are few, and being few are universally known; but few as they are they can be made no more: they can receive no grace from novelty of sentiment, and very little from novelty of expression.

Poetry pleases by exhibiting an idea more grateful to the mind than things themselves afford. This effect proceeds from the display of those parts of nature which attract, and the concealment of those which repel the imagination; but religion must be shown as it is: suppression and addition equally corrupt it, and such as it is, it is known already.

From poetry the reader justly expects, and from good poetry always obtains, the enlargement of his comprehension and elevation of his fancy, but this is rarely to be hoped by Christians from metrical devotion. Whatever is great, desirable or tremendous, is comprised in the name of the Supreme Being. Omnipotence cannot be exalted; Infinity cannot be amplified; Perfection cannot be improved.

The employments of pious meditation are faith, thanksgiving, repentance and supplication. Faith, invariably uniform, cannot be invested by fancy with decorations. Thanksgiving, the most joyful of all holy effusions, yet addressed to a Being without passions, is confined to a few modes, and is to be felt rather than expressed. Repentance, trembling in the presence of the Judge, is not at leisure for cadences and epithets. Supplication of man to man may diffuse itself through many topics of persuasion; but supplication to God can only cry for mercy.

Of sentiments purely religious it will be found that the most simple expression is the most sublime. Poetry loses its lustre and its power because it is applied to the decoration of something more excellent than itself. All that pious verse can do is to help the memory and delight the ear, and for these purposes it may be very useful; but it supplies nothing to the mind. The ideas of Christian theology are too simple for eloquence, too sacred for fiction, and too majestic for ornament; to recommend them by tropes and figures is to magnify by a concave mirror the sidereal hemisphere.

(Life of Waller, pars. 134–41)

Notes

COWLEY

p. 1   Johnson considered this the best of his *Lives* because of its account of the 'metaphysical poets' (*Life*, iv. 38). For many of its biographical details he is indebted to Thomas Sprat, *An Account of the Life and Writings of Mr. Abraham Cowley* (prefixed to 1668 ed. of Cowley's *Works*, and reprinted in Spingarn, ii. 119–46) and to Anthony à Wood, *Fasti Oxonienses* (1721, 2nd rev. ed.), ii. 120–1 (the source of all subsequent references to Wood in this *Life*).

p. 1   Spingarn, ii. 121. Thomas Cowley described himself in his will as a citizen and stationer of London.

p. 1   Ibid. ii. 140.

p. 1   In his essay *Of Myself*, Cowley says that he found a copy of Spenser in his 'mother's parlour' (*Cowley: Essays*, pp. 457–8). Sir Joshua Reynolds told Edmond Malone that as a young boy he had eagerly read *The Jesuit's Perspective*, which 'happened to lie on the window-seat of his father's parlour'; see *The Works of Sir Joshua Reynolds* (1798, 2nd rev. ed.), i. *vii*. Johnson, who must have heard the same story, here transfers the detail of the window-seat to the house of Cowley's mother.

p. 2   Robert Vaughan's engraved portrait of Cowley, which appeared in *Poetical Blossomes* and is dated 1633, gives his age as 13. This must be the source of Johnson's error.

p. 2   Cowley was a scholar of Trinity College.

p. 3   For a contemporary reference to this event see C. H. Cooper, *Annals of Cambridge*, iii (1845), 321.

p. 3   Parliament effectively closed the theatres by resolving (2 Sept. 1642) to suppress stage plays. Further ordinances 'to suppress all public plays and playhouses' followed in 1647–8. For Cowley's statement that this play was sometimes acted privately see *Cowley: Essays*, p. 261.

p. 3   Cowley was one of the Fellows ejected from Trinity College on or after 8 Apr. 1644 under the terms of the Parliament's 'Ordinance for Regulating the University of Cambridge' (Cooper, *Annals of Cambridge*, iii. 369, 374, 379).

p. 3   *The Puritan and the Papist* was first included among Cowley's works in *The Works of the English Poets* introduced by Johnson's *Prefaces, Biographical and Critical*.

p. 3   Oxford opened its gates to the Parliamentary forces on 24 June 1646.

p. 5   One of Cowley's letters to Bennet is, however, dated 13 Sept. 1653.

p. 5   *Miscellanea Aulica, or A Collection of State-Treatises* (1702), p. 130. In Scotland Charles II had been proclaimed King on 4 Feb. 1649, and the Scottish parliament instructed its commissioners to negotiate with him at The Hague. Charles landed in Scotland in June 1650.

p. 5 Virgil came to be regarded with superstitious reverence as possessing miraculous powers. Attempts to foretell the future by opening his works at hazard (*sortes Virgilianae*) were made from an early date.

p. 6 For the passage later omitted see Spingarn, ii. 83–4. Cf. Sprat, ibid. ii. 124–6.

p. 7 *Poemata Latina: in quibus continentur, sex libri plantarum, viz. duo herbarum, florum, sylvarum* (1668).

p. 7 Milton and Cowley were not, of course, contemporaries at Cambridge.

p. 8 *Ode, upon the Blessed Restoration and Returne of His Sacred Majestie, Charls the Second* (1660).

p. 9 Cf. Hugh Macdonald, *A Journal from Parnassus* (1937), pp. *vii–viii*. Suckling's 'A Sessions of the Poets' (written 1637?) appeared in *Fragmenta Aurea* (1646), pp. 7–11.

p. 8 Commendatory verses by Cowley and others are prefixed to *The Adventures of Five Hours* (1664, 2nd ed.).

p. 10 It has been suggested that this person was 'a convivial country neighbour'; see William Stebbing, *Some Verdicts of History Reviewed* (1887), p. 78. Cf. Spence, § 449.

p. 11 Spingarn, ii. 145. For an eye-witness account of Cowley's funeral see *The Diary of John Evelyn*, ed. E. S. de Beer (Oxford, 1955), iii. 490.

p. 11 For discussions of this term see A. H. Nethercot, 'The Term "Metaphysical Poets" before Johnson', *MLN*, xxxvii (1922), 11–17; and my article, 'Locke as a Possible Source of Johnson's *Metaphysical*', *Johnsonian Studies*, ed. Magdi Wahba (Cairo, 1962), pp. 227–33.

p. 12 For the meaning of this phrase, which has puzzled modern critics, cf. George Cheyne, *The English Malady* (1733): 'It is well known to physicians what wonderful effects the passions, excited by lucky or unlucky accidents (which are justly reckoned intellectual or spiritual operations) have on the pulse . . .' (p. 68).

p. 13 The author of the ancient treatise *On the Sublime* had devoted a separate essay, now lost, to the 'pathetic'. Though in his discussion of sublimity he gave due prominence to 'the inspiration of vehement emotion', he also argued that 'many sublime passages are quite apart from emotion' (viii. 1, 2). For an account of these concepts in the eighteenth century see S. H. Monk, *The Sublime: A Study of Critical Theories in XVIII-Century England* (New York, 1935; repr. 1960).

p. 15 A genealogical tree derived from the *Introduction* to Logic by the Neoplatonic philosopher Porphyry (A.D. 233–c. 301) displays the genera to which man may be assigned below the *summum genus*. It also displays the differentiae by which each genus is distinguished within the genus next above it.

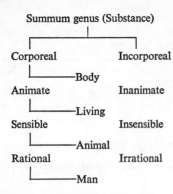

Summmum genus (Substance)

Corporeal   Incorporeal
└──────Body
Animate   Inanimate
└──────Living
Sensible   Insensible
└──────Animal
Rational   Irrational
└──────Man

This procedure by dichotomies led to the Porphyrian tree being taken as an example of dichotomy.

p. 21   *News from Newcastle* (1651), p. 2, a poem wrongly attributed to Cleveland in *J. Cleaveland Revived: Poems, Orations, Epistles* (1660, 2nd ed.), pp. 10–15.

p. 27   *Poetices libri septem* (Lyons, 1561), vi. 339A–B ('. . . quarum [Horace's *Odes*, iii. 9, iv. 3] similes malim composuisse, quam esse totius Tarraconensis rex').

p. 30   The poems by Cowley to which Addison alludes in this passage are 'The Vain Love', 'The Request', 'The Tree'.

p. 31   Jacopo Sannazaro, *Opera Latina* (Venice, 1535), sig. F3ᵛ ('Look, Vesbia, how I am distracted by the varying pains of love. I am inflamed and, oh, moisture drops from the fire of my passion. I am at once both Nile and Etna. O tears check my flames, or flame drink up my tears').

p. 31   Elys was the author of *An Exclamation to all those that Love the Lord Jesus in Sincerity, against an Apology written by an Ingenious Person for Mr. Cowley's Lascivious and Profane Verses* (1670).

p. 34   *Lyricorum libri tres* (Cologne, 1625), p. 6, 'Ad Crispum Levinium' ('At all seasons the ruler of the world fashions wings to be plied through the void. Some still lie hid in the nest, and grow for future years').

p. 36   Corbett Owen, *Carmen Pindaricum in Theatrum Sheldonianum in Solemnibus Magnifici Operis Encaeniis* (Oxford, 1669), was reprinted in *Musarum Anglicanarum Analecta* (Oxford), i (1692), 99–128.

p. 37   *Mac Flecknoe*, ll. 72–3, is a humorous reworking of Cowley's couplet from *Davideis*, i:
　　'Where their vast Courts the Mother-waters keep,
　　And undisturbed by Moons in silence sleep'.

p. 37   For Johnson's remarks on religious poetry in his *Life of Waller* see Appendix.

p. 38   'He looks around and sees a huge stone, a stone huge and ancient, which by chance was lying on the plain, and placed as a boundary-marker to settle disputes about property'.

p. 42   'Under whose feet (subjected to his grace)
        Sit nature, fortune, motion, time and place'   (E. FAIRFAX)

p. 46   In *Rambler* 88 Johnson had endorsed Dryden's view that 'a line of monosyllables is almost always harsh'.

p. 47   For the lines from the *Davideis* quoted in Cowley's note (*Poems*, p. 273) see ibid. pp. 243, 299, 304, 334, 374, 389.

p. 48   There are only two triplets in this poem's fifty-four lines (*Cowley: Essays*, pp. 373–4).

MILTON

p. 50   In his *Life of Fenton* Johnson refers to the 'Life' prefixed to Fenton's ed. of Milton's poems (1725) as 'short and elegant . . . written at once with tenderness and integrity'. Other sources on which he drew for material include: John Aubrey, 'Auctarium Vitarum à J. A. collectarum Aº Dom. 1681', Bodl. MS. Aubrey 8, ff. 63–8; Anthony à Wood, *Fasti Oxonienses* (1721), i. 261–6; Edward Phillips, *Letters of State, written by Mr. John Milton* (1694), pp. *i–xliv* ('The Life of Mr. John Milton'); John Toland, *A Complete Collection of the Historical, Political and Miscellaneous Works of John Milton* ('Amsterdam' [really London], 1698), i. *5–47* ('The Life of John Milton'); Jonathan Richardson the elder, *Explanatory Notes and Remarks on Milton's Paradise Lost*, by J. Richardson, Father and Son (1734), pp. *i–clxiii*; Thomas Birch, *A Complete Collection of the Historical, Political and Miscellaneous Works of John Milton* (1738), i. *i–lxiii* ('An Historical and Critical Account of the Life and Writings of Mr. John Milton'); Thomas Newton, *Paradise Lost . . . A New Edition* (1749), i. *i–lxi* ('The Life of Milton'). The accounts by Aubrey, Wood, Phillips, Toland and Richardson have been reprinted in *EL*. Birch's 'Life' was somewhat revised for the later, 1753 ed., though it seems certain that Johnson worked from the earlier ed.

p. 51   The Admission Register of Christ's College shows that Milton was formally admitted as a minor pensioner (not 'sizar') on 'ffeb. 12. 1624' (i.e. 12 Feb. 1624/5 or 1625). Cf. Parker, ii. 725. Being an Oxford not a Cambridge man, Johnson might have thought that a minor pensioner was the equivalent of a servitor (used to gloss 'sizar' in his *Dict.*) rather than a commoner. The date he gives also invites some comment. In his letter (22 July 1777) to Farmer, Johnson had said that the booksellers might be persuaded to employ 'a transcriber' to gather Cambridge material for the *Lives* (*Letters*, no. 530). In reckoning Milton's admission to the College as having taken place 'in the beginning of his sixteenth year', he could have either been working unthinkingly from a transcript, or assumed that the transcriber had already converted the date to New Style.

p. 51   Milton's first three *Elegies*, as well as 'In Obitum Procancellarii Medici' and 'In Obitum Praesulis Eliensis', were all composed in 1626.

p. 52   Haddon's Latin poems appeared in *Poemata . . . studio et labore T. Hatcheri collecta* (1567), and *Poematum . . . sparsim collectorum, libri duo* (1576). Ascham's Latin poems were added to his *Familiarum epistolarum libri tres* (1576).

p. 52   See *Poems of Mr. John Milton, both English and Latin, compos'd at several times* (1645).

p. 52   Despite his rustication, Milton was credited with keeping twelve terms between Feb. 1625 and Feb 1629. For the charge of expulsion, and Milton's denial, see Peter Du Moulin the younger, *Regii Sanguinis Clamor ad Coelum* (The Hague, 1652), p. 9; *Pro Populo Anglicano Defensio Secunda* (1654), *CM*, viii. 112–13.

p. 52   'I am in the city which the Thames washes with its tides; and it is not unwillingly that I stay in my sweet birthplace. I am not at present anxious to revisit the reedy Cam, or pining for the abode recently forbidden to me. . . . I do not like having continually to endure the threats of a harsh tutor and other things that my spirit will not bear. If this be exile—to be again in the paternal home and, free from care, to pursue welcome leisure—then I do not object to the name or fate of an exile, but gladly enjoy my state of banishment.'

p. 53   Johnson added this sentence in 1783.

p. 53   Milton supplicated for his B.A. early in 1629.

p. 54   *A Maske presented at Ludlow Castle* (1637) was first published with the title *Comus* in 1738.

p. 55   *Justa Edouardo King naufrago, ab Amicis Moerentibus* (Cambridge, 1638), containing Greek, Latin, and English poems, was the work of at least twenty-eight (and probably more) different hands.

p. 55   Cf. F. T. Prince, *The Italian Element in Milton's Verse* (Oxford, 1962, rev. ed.), pp. 71–88.

p. 55   The date of composition of 'Arcades' (published 1645), and of its first performance, is not known. Cf. Parker, ii. 755–8. There is, moreover, no evidence that the Countess Dowager ever entertained Milton as a guest.

p. 55   Milton's own account of his travels on the Continent is given in *Defensio Secunda*, *CM*, viii. 120–7.

p. 56   For the *testimonia* of Dati, Francini, and others see *CM*, i. 154–67. (Dati and Francini are mentioned in *Epitaphium Damonis*, l. 137.)

p. 57   For Milton's praise of Geneva, the seat of Protestant theology, see *Pro Se Defensio* (1655), *CM*, ix. 202–5.

p. 57   There is no evidence that Milton met Spanheim. Toland asserts, obviously erroneously, that Milton met Ezekiel Spanheim (1639–1710), Frederick's son (*EL*, p. 95)—a statement which, *mutatis mutandis*, might nevertheless have seemed to Johnson sufficient authority for mentioning a meeting between Milton and the father. Cf. *CM*, xii. 74–7.

p. 57   It is, however, clear from *Epitaphium Damonis* ('Argumentum' and ll. 12–17) that Milton had been abroad when he heard of Diodati's death. Cf. W. R. Parker, *MLN*, lxxii (1957), 486–8.

p. 58   *A Proposition for the Advancement of Experimental Philosophy* (1661), *Cowley: Essays*, pp. 245–58, esp. 252, 255–7. Cf. *Of Agriculture* (ibid. pp. 404–5); *Davideis*, i (*Cowley: Poems*, pp. 260–1).

p. 59   Johnson told Malone (*The Works of Samuel Johnson, LL.D.* (Oxford, 1825), vii. 77 n.) that he was alluding here, not to *Theatrum Poetarum, or A Compleat Collection of the Poets* (1675), but to *Tractatus de Carmine Dramatico Poetarum Veterum . . .*, which was first published in 17th ed. of J. Buchler's *Phrasium Poeticarum Thesaurus* (1669).

p. 59   Phillips mentions the works of Joannes Wollebius (d. 1629) and William Ames (1576–1633), an English Puritan divine who spent much of his life in Holland (*EL*, p. 61).

p. 60   The work of the five (not six) Presbyterian divines—Stephen Marshall (1594?–1655), Edmund Calamy (1600–66), Thomas Young, Matthew Newcomen (1610?–69), William Spurstow(e) (1605?–66)—was entitled *An Answer to a Book entitled An Humble Remonstrance*.

p. 60   *The Reason of Church Government*, of which the title-page is dated 1641, is thought to have been published in Jan. or Feb. 1641/2.

p. 60   This charge was made in the anonymous *A Modest Confutation of a Slanderous and Scurrilous Libell* (1642), sigg. *A3–A3ᵛ*.

p. 62   *The Doctrine and Discipline of Divorce* was published on or before 1 Aug. 1643, and 2nd ed. (extensively revised) on or before 2 Feb. 1644.

p. 62   *Colasterion: A Reply to a Nameless Answer against the Doctrine and Discipline of Divorce* (1645), *CM*, iv. 233 ff., 237–8. *An Answer to a Book, Intituled, the Doctrine and Discipline of Divorce* had appeared in 1644.

p. 63   Cf. *Areopagitica* (1644), *CM*, iv. 331; 'On the New Forcers of Conscience under the Long Parliament' (1646?), esp. l. 20.

p. 65   This move probably occurred about Aug. 1647 (Parker, i. 312; ii. 935 n. 58).

p. 65   For evidence that this aspersion is without foundation see Parker, ii. 964–6. For Pamela's prayer see *The Countesse of Pembroke's Arcadia*, *The Complete Works of Sir Philip Sidney*, ed. Albert Feuillerat (Cambridge, 1912–26), i. 382–3 (III. vi. 3). Milton's appointment as Secretary for the Foreign Tongues was confirmed on 15 March 1649.

p. 65   The passage to which Johnson alludes is that in 1738 ed., i. *lxxviii–lxxxiii*. Birch, however, had revised his view in 1753 ed. (i. *xxxiii–xxxiv*), which Johnson presumably did not consult.

p. 66   Cf. Samuel Butler, *Satires and Miscellaneous Poetry and Prose*, ed. René Lamar (Cambridge, 1928), pp. 76–7.

p. 67   Cf. *Defensio Secunda*, *CM*, viii. 68–9; Milton to Leonard Philaras (28 Sept. 1654), ibid. xii. 66–7; 'To Mr. Cyriack Skinner upon his Blindness'.

p. 67　For the reception abroad of Milton's *Pro Populo Anglicano Defensio* see *LR*, iii. 14, 22, 24–5; Parker, i. 386–8.

p. 67　Cf. *LR*, iii. 15–16, 19, for letters printed in *Sylloges Epistolarum a Viris Illustribus Scriptarum*, ed. Peter Burman (Leyden, 1727), iii. 595–6.

p. 67　For a recent view of this whole matter substantially in accordance with Johnson's own see *Complete Prose Works of John Milton*, ed. D. M. Wolfe *et al.* (New Haven, 1953–　), iv. 967 ff.

p. 67　In *Defensio Secunda*, *CM*, viii. 20–1, Milton seems to err in attributing to Salmasius reproach of his blindness. When Salmasius wrote *Defensio Regia* (1649), he could not have foreseen that Milton, who was anyway not yet blind, would be his antagonist. Milton probably had in mind a passage from the dedication to *Regii Sanguinis Clamor* which described him in the terms used of Polyphemus (*Aeneid*, iii. 658): *Monstrum, horrendum, informe, ingens, cui lumen ademptum* ('a hideous monster, ugly, huge, bereft of sight'). Rumours of his blindness had reached the continent by 1652.

p. 68　A majority of the Nominated or Barebones Parliament resigned on 12 Dec. 1653, and Cromwell was installed as Protector on 16th. The Rump Parliament had been dissolved the previous Apr.

p. 69　*Joannis Philippi Angli Responsio ad Apologiam Anonymi cujusdam Tenebrionis pro Rege & Populo Anglicano infantissimam* (1652).

p. 69　Johnson's note on this word is as follows: 'It may be doubted whether *gloriosissimus* be here used with Milton's boasted purity. *Res gloriosa* is an "illustrious thing"; but *vir gloriosus* is commonly a "braggart", as in *miles gloriosus.*'

p. 69　The full title of Milton's work is *Joannis Miltoni Angli Pro Se Defensio contra Alexandrum Morum, Ecclesiasten, Libelli famosi, cui titulus ' Regii Sanguinis Clamor ad Coelum adversus Parricidas Anglicanos', authorem recte dictum.* (During the previous year, 1654, there had come from More's pen the incomplete *Fides Publica contra calumnias Joannis Milton, Scurrae.*)

p. 70　Milton again entered into public controversy (see above, pp. 73–4) at the time of the events leading up to the Restoration.

p. 70　This work (*CM*, xiii. 509–63) was first attributed to Milton by Birch in 1738 (i. *xxxiv*). But cf. Parker, ii. 1039–40.

p. 70　Cf. Bulstrode Whitelocke, *Memorials of the English Affairs* (1682), p. 633; Samuel von Pufendorf, *De Rebus a Carolo Gustavo* (Nuremberg, 1696), p. 219.

p. 70　*Linguae Romanae Dictionarium Luculentum Novum. A New Dictionary, in five Alphabets . . . the Whole completed and improved from the several Works of Stephens, Cooper, Gouldman, Holyoke, Dr. Littleton, a Large Manuscript, in three Volumes of Mr. John Milton . . .* (Cambridge, 1693), sig. *A2ᵛ*.

p. 71　*Paradise Lost* (1725), pp. *x–xi*. Sir Richard Blackmore was the author of *Prince Arthur, an Heroic Poem* (1695), and *King Arthur, an Heroic Poem* (1697).

p. 71   For the draft outlines of *Paradise Lost* preserved in Trinity College Library see *John Milton's Complete Poetical Works* (reproduced in photographic facsimile), ed. H. F. Fletcher (Urbana, 1943–8), ii. 16–17, 26–7. The 'two plans' to which Johnson refers are four separate drafts. Cf. Phillips, *EL*, pp. 72–3; *PL*, iv. 32 ff. It should be added, in view of Johnson's statement, that 'allegorical persons' are characteristic of morality rather than miracle (or 'mystery') plays.

p. 72   Johnson's 1st ed. had read: 'After this, Lucifer appears, after his overthrow; bemoans himself....' In the MS. no punctuation mark occurs after 'appeares', where (in the light of Milton's practice immediately following) something like a full-stop is obviously intended.

p. 74   Within the space of a month or so, Milton's pamphlet was attacked in the following works: Roger L'Estrange, *Be Merry and Wise, or A Seasonable Word to the Nation*; *The Character of the Rump*; William Collinne, *The Spirit of the Fanatics Dissected*; *The Censure of the Rota*; George Starkey?, *The Dignity of Kingship Asserted*.

p. 74   Milton had moved with his family from Whitehall to Petty France in Dec. 1651.

p. 75   The date of the Act of Oblivion was 29 (not 19) Aug. 1660.

p. 75   *EL*, pp. 271–2. For the story of Davenant's being saved by Milton see Wood, *Athenae Oxonienses* (1721 ed.), ii. 412; cf. Parker, ii. 1017 n. 13. For Davenant's own account of his danger see *Gondibert, an Heroick Poem* (1651), sig. Kkk ('Postscript to the Reader').

p. 76   For a month or two before this move Milton had rented a house in Holborn.

p. 77   Johnson's source here is not Phillips (as he states) but Birch (1738 ed.), i. *lxii*.

p. 77   Johnson follows Wood (*EL*, p. 46) in giving the date of publication of this work as 1661 instead of 1669.

p. 78   *The History of the Life of Thomas Ellwood*, ed. Joseph Wyeth (1714), p. 135 (*CM*, xviii. 384).

p. 78   Parker, however, dates this move in 1669 or 1670 (i. 608; ii. 1125–6).

p. 78   F. D. White, *Voltaire's Essay on Epic Poetry: A Study and an Edition* (Albany 1915), pp. 130–1, where reference is made to Giovanni Battista Andreini's *L'Adamo*.

p. 80   For the Stoic and medieval concept of the world's decay cf. Jonson, 'To the World', ll. 13–14; Donne, 'The First Anniversary', ll. 191 ff.; Godfrey Goodman, *The Fall of Man, or the Corruption of Nature* (1616), esp. pts. II and III. For a list of modern works dealing with this subject see Parker, ii. 774 n. 79.

p. 81   Johnson here follows Birch's account of 1738 (i. *lxii*), which is based on the assertion of Elizabeth Foster. Aubrey, however, had stated that Deborah was

Milton's amanuensis (*EL*, p. 2). Both Mary and Deborah (who later became a schoolmistress) were taught by a governess, and their signatures survive. The crippled, eldest daughter Anne could only make a mark, and presumably never learnt to write.

p. 82 For another interpretation of this passage see J. B. Broadbent, *English Studies*, xxxvii (1956), 61–2.

p. 83 These details are given in the contract signed with Simmons, British Museum, Add. MS. 18861 (reproduced in *CM*, xviii. 422–4). This contract, mentioned by Fenton (p. *xxi*), was said by Birch in 1753 to be 'in the hands of Mr. Tonson the Bookseller' (i. *lvi*).

p. 83 This and the receipt of 21 Dec. 1680 are now in Christ's College Library, Cambridge.

p. 84 The First Folio was published in 1623, the Second in 1632, the Third in 1664.

p. 84 A folio ed. of *Paradise Lost* was published by subscription in 1688. For the poem's increased popularity see *The Poetical Works of Mr. John Milton*, i. *Paradise Lost* (1705, 7th ed.), sigg. *A–A*ᵛ.

p. 86 *Mr. John Milton's Character of the Long Parliament and Assembly of Divines* (1681), *CM*, xviii. 247–55. Cf. ibid. x. 317–25, 386. It was first 'inserted in its proper place' by Birch in *Complete Works of Milton* (1738), ii. 39–42.

p. 86 Newton, i. *xlii–xliii*. The elder Tonson had conjectured that 'Symonds might be dead'; see *The Manuscript of Milton's Paradise Lost Book I*, ed. Helen Darbishire (Oxford, 1931), p. *xii*.

p. 86 Johnson's source for this statement was Phillips or Toland (*EL*, pp. 75–6, 185), not Ellwood.

p. 87 *Joannis Miltonii Angli, Epistolarum Familiarum Liber Unus, quibus accesserunt, ejusdem, jam olim in Collegio adolescentis, Prolusiones Quaedam Oratoriae* (1674).

p. 88 The inscription on the monument to Milton in Westminster Abbey reads: 'In the year of Our Lord Christ One thousand seven hundred thirty and seven This bust of the Author of PARADISE LOST was placed here by William Benson Esquire One of the two Auditors of the Imprests to his Majesty King George the second formerly Surveyor General of the Works to his Majesty King George the first. *Rysbrack* was the Statuary who cut it.'

p. 89 Elizabeth Milton (d. 1727) was said by Newton (in 1749) to have died 'about twenty years ago' (i. *lvi*). Both he and Birch knew of these losses from Elizabeth Foster, who had heard of them from her mother, Milton's daughter Deborah. (Cf. Parker, ii. 1095 n. 73, where it is pointed out that the £2,000 reported lost as a result of Milton's dealings with the 'scrivener' may be the same £2,000 lost through the Excise bank.)

p. 90 Milton's copy of Euripides (Geneva, 1602) is now in the Bodleian Library. The annotation in his hand is printed in *CM*, xviii. 304–20.

p. 92   An old letter recording a meeting with Milton's daughter Deborah had been reproduced, two years before Johnson wrote this Life, in *GM*, xlvi (1776), 200. Cf. Birch (1738 ed.), i. *lxi–lxii*; Newton, i. *lviii*.

p. 93   Cf. *YJ*, vi. 240–1. The honour of suggesting such a benefit to Garrick was also Johnson's.

p. 93   This was probably Johnson's friend Giuseppe Baretti (1719–89), who nevertheless seems to have thought Milton's Italian poetry better in the conception than execution; see his *Account of the Manners and Customs of Italy* (1768), i. 108.

p. 93   'In Proditionem Bombardicam', three poems 'In eandem', 'In inventorem Bombardae', and 'In quintum Novembris'.

p. 94   For a description of the MS. volume in Trinity College Library see *Facsimile of the Manuscript of Milton's Minor Poems*, ed. W. A. Wright (Cambridge, 1899), pp. 3–4.

p. 98   For this prevailing neo-classical view see *Dryden: Essays*, ii. 95–6, 223.

p. 103   Johnson notes that 'Algarotti terms it *gigantesca sublimità Miltoniana*'. (An extensive search has so far failed to find this precise phrase in Algarotti's numerous volumes.)

p. 105   For a critical discussion of this sentence see J. H. Hagstrum, *PMLA*, lxiv (1949), 153–4, or *Samuel Johnson's Literary Criticism* (Minneapolis, 1952), p. 148.

p. 105   *Milton's Paradise Lost. A New Edition* (1732), esp. sigg. *a*ᵛ*–a2*.

p. 105   Cf. Jacob Tonson's letter to his nephew of the same name, *Manuscript of Paradise Lost Book I*, ed. Darbishire, p. *xiii*.

p. 106   Hagstrum, *Johnson's Literary Criticism*, p. 131, suggests that Johnson's terminology here has been influenced by Burke's *Philosophical Inquiry into the Origin of our Ideas of the Sublime and the Beautiful*.

p. 108   The allegorical personages appear at or near the beginning of each of these plays.

p. 111   *De Guiana, carmen Epicum*, printed in Lawrence Keymis, *A Relation of the Second Voyage to Guiana* (1596), sigg. *A*ᵛ*–A4*, was written by George Chapman.

p. 112   Mrs. Piozzi claimed to have told Johnson this, having learnt it herself from the actor Quin; see *Autobiography, Letters and Literary Remains of Mrs. Piozzi (Thrale)*, ed. A. Hayward (1861, 2nd rev. ed.), ii. 138.

DRYDEN

p. 114   Printed sources on which Johnson drew in writing this Life were: Thomas Birch's account of the poet in *A General Dictionary, Historical and*

Critical (based on the work of Pierre Bayle) (1734–41), iv. 676–87; Gerard Lang-baine, *An Account of the English Dramatick Poets* (Oxford, 1691), pp. 130–77 (reprinted in Spingarn, iii. 110–47); Samuel Derrick, *The Miscellaneous Works of John Dryden* (1760), i. *xiii–xxxiv* ('The Life of John Dryden').

p. 114   The Drydens were originally a Cumberland family and not (as Birch states) from Huntingdonshire.

p. 114   Dryden was admitted as a pensioner of Trinity College.

p. 115   Dryden was not on the Honours List of his year; nor (to judge from one surviving entry quoted by Ward, p. 14) was he always suitably deferential to the College authorities.

p. 115   *The Works of John Dryden*, ed. Walter Scott, rev. George Saintsbury (Edinburgh, 1882–93), xvii. 55.

p. 115   The verses of Dryden, Sprat, and Waller appeared together in *Three Poems upon the Death of his late Highnesse Oliver Lord Protector* (1659).

p. 115   Cf. *An Elegy on the Usurper O.C. by the Author of Absalom and Achito-phel, published to shew the Loyalty and Integrity of the Poet* (1681); see above, p. 145 and n.

p. 115   Cf. *Works of Dryden*, ed. Scott-Saintsbury, ix. 32 n.; Elkanah Settle, *Notes and Observations on the Empress of Morocco Revised* (1674), p. 3.

p. 116   *The Wild Gallant* (published 1669) was produced on 5 Feb. 1663, and revived in 1667. But a work on the subject of *The Duke of Guise*, 'damned in private' soon after the Restoration, had constituted Dryden's first attempt at writing a play. It has, moreover, been suggested that *The Wild Gallant* was not an original play by Dryden but an old play rewritten by him; see Alfred Harbage, *MLR*, xxxv (1940), 307–9.

p. 116   Cf. *The Critical and Miscellaneous Prose Work of John Dryden*, ed. Malone (1800), i. 56, 218; Osborn, p. 26.

p. 116   This is the reading of the 1st ed. The original intention had been to prefix Johnson's Life or 'Preface' to every author's works.

p. 116   *The General: A Tragi-Comedy* was the only play by Orrery actually performed before *The Rival Ladies*, though his second play *Henry the Fifth* was licensed on 3 Nov. 1663. Most of Dryden's *Rival Ladies* is written in blank-verse, not rhyme.

p. 117   For the pieces (later listed by Johnson) to which this argument between Dryden and Howard gave, rise see *Dryden & Howard 1664–1668*, ed. D. D. Arundell (Cambridge, 1929).

p. 118   Dryden's salary as Poet Laureate was £200 per year.

p. 118   *The Literary Works of Matthew Prior*, ed. H. B. Wright and M. K. Spears (Oxford, 1959), i. 249. But cf. Ward, pp. 343–4.

p. 120 Dennis referred to Dryden's jealousy in naming him one of the authors of this piece (*Dennis*, ii. 118); but Ward (pp. 328–9) considers its ascription to Dryden doubtful.

p. 124 *Tyrannic Love* was published in 1670 and *The Conquest of Granada* (the first part of which was acted at the end of that year) not until 1672. The latter play is mentioned in the preface to the former. One might, even so, have suggested that Johnson was misled by Langbaine's date of 1677 for the publication of *Tyrannic Love* had not the date of publication of *The Conquest of Granada* been given many pages earlier as 1678 (Spingarn, iii. 131, 144), and had not Johnson, as he states in his Advertisement to the 'Prefaces, Biographical and Critical', acknowledged Langbaine as his authority for the dates of Dryden's plays. Cf. above, p. 136.

p. 131 Dryden's *Vindication of the Duke of Guise* (1683) was prompted by a number of attacks: Thomas Hunt, *A Defence of the Charter* (1683), pp. 24 ff.; *The True History of the Duke of Guise* (1683); Thomas Shadwell, *Some Reflections upon the Pretended Parallel in the Play called the Duke of Guise* (1683).

p. 133 Pope considered *All for Love, Don Sebastian*, and *The Spanish Friar* to be Dryden's 'three best' dramas (Spence, § 64).

p. 134 Johnson's statement results from a misreading of the first sentence of Dryden's dedication to Halifax. *King Arthur* was performed in 1691. In 1783 the following sentence was added to this paragraph: 'When this was first brought upon the stage, news that the Duke of Monmouth had landed was told in the theatre, upon which the company departed, and *Arthur* was exhibited no more.' The piece interrupted by Monmouth's landing was, however, *Albion and Albanius*. Johnson's additional sentence, which is therefore erroneous, and also somewhat contradicts his previous statement, has been omitted from the text.

p. 134 Cf. *Dryden: DW*, vi. 403–4, where Dryden is, however, inclined to defend the 'catastrophe' of this play even though it flouts the rules of Aristotle.

p. 135 Malone mentions Southerne's two nights as a traditionally accepted fact (*Prose Works of Dryden*, i. 454 n. 5). It is uncertain when the sixth night's benefit became established practice, though it was certainly about the time that Southerne's *Sir Anthony Love* was performed (*c*. Sept. 1690). In the dedication to this play Southerne refers to 'the third and the sixth' performances, thereby suggesting a double benefit; see *The London Stage 1660–1800, Part I: 1660–1700*, ed. W. Van Lennep (Carbondale, 1965), p. *lxxxi*. I know of no printed authority for Johnson's statement that Rowe was the first dramatist to have three benefit nights—unless Nicholas Amhurst's reference to him as 'thrice honoured' ('On the Death of M. Rowe', *Musarum Lachrymae, or Poems to the Memory of Nicholas Rowe* (1719), p. 29) is to be so interpreted.

p. 135 For a discussion of this anecdote and the amounts involved see *Rare Prologues and Epilogues 1642–1700*, ed. A. N. Wiley (1940), pp. 67–9. Warburton (vi. 82) mentions figures of four and six guineas in recounting that Southerne told this story of Dryden to Pope and himself. Cf. *Essay on Pope*, p. 258. In *An Apology for the Life of Mr. Colley Cibber* (1740), Cibber mentions receiving two guineas for a prologue he had written (p. 114).

p. 136   *The Key to the Rehearsal, Miscellaneous Works, written by George, late Duke of Buckingham* (1704–5), ii. 3. Dryden had undertaken to furnish three plays a year, as documentary evidence proves (*Rehearsal*, pp. 87–8; Osborn, pp. 202 ff.).

p. 136   Langbaine, whom Johnson is here clearly following, assigns this date to all six plays. The dates of publication were, however, as follows: *All for Love*, 1678; *The Assignation*, 1673; *The Conquest of Granada* (both parts), 1672; *Sir Martin Mar-all*, 1668; *The State of Innocence*, 1677.

p. 136   These are the authors later named by Malone (*Prose Works of Dryden*, i. 95).

p. 136   Cf. Epilogue to *All for Love*, ll. 15–17; 'To Sir George Etherege', ll. 75–81; 'On the Duke of Bucks', stanzas 7 ff. (a poem attributed to Dryden in *Poems on Affairs of State* (1703), ii. 216–18).

p. 136   *Tyrannic Love, The Conquest of Granada*, and possibly *Marriage à la Mode* were, however, acted before the staging of *The Rehearsal*, of which, anyway, the 3rd ed. (1675) announces 'amendments and large additions by the author'.

p. 136   Cf. Malone, *Prose Works of Dryden*, i. 97–8.

p. 137   *The Key to the Rehearsal, Miscellaneous Works by Buckingham*, ii. *xii*.

p. 137   Rochester acted as a patron to Settle, and wrote a new prologue for *The Empress of Morocco*, at a time when he was also friendly with Dryden; cf. F. C. Brown, *Elkanah Settle: His Life and Works* (Chicago, 1910), pp. 52–3.

p. 137   *The Works of the Earls of Rochester and Roscommon, with some Memoirs of the Earl of Rochester's Life by Monsieur St. Evremont* (1709, 3rd ed.), sig. *b*8.

p. 138   Birch, following Wood (*Athenae Oxonienses*, ii. 804–5), had given this account of the affair, and described the attack as having taken place in Will's Coffee-house (*General Dictionary*, iv. 680). Derrick, quoting from a contemporary newspaper, showed that it had taken place in Rose Lane (i. *xxi*). It is unknown (cf. Ward, pp. 143–4) who was responsible for this attack on Dryden.

p. 138   *The Works of Lucian, translated from the Greek by several Eminent Hands* (1710–11); *Plutarch's Lives, translated from the Greek by Several Hands* (1683–6).

p.139   Dryden translated two (not one) on his own (*Heroides*, vii and xi), as well as one with Mulgrave (no. xvii).

p. 139   Jonson translated Horace's *Ars Poetica* (1640), and Sandys Ovid's *Metamorphoses* (see above, p. 48).

p. 139   Cf. Denham, 'To Sir Richard Fanshawe upon his Translation of Pastor Fido', esp. ll. 15 ff.; the preface to *The Destruction of Troy*; *Cowley: Poems*, pp. 155–6.

p. 140   Giles Jacob, *An Historical Account of the Lives and Writings of our most considerable English Poets* (1720), p. 193. Cf. *Pope: Poems*, iv. 105 n.; Osborn, pp. 146–7.

p. 140   *Athenae Oxonienses*, ii. 1078. Samuel Pordage (1633–91 ?) is now generally thought to have been the author of both *Azaria and Hushai* and *The Medal Reversed*. But cf. R. G. Ham, *MP*, xxv (1927–8), 413–15.

p. 142   In 1686 James had published by royal command *Copies of Two Papers written by the Late King Charles II; together with a Copy of a Paper written by the late Dutchess of York*. It was followed by Stillingfleet's *Answer to some Papers lately printed, concerning the Authority of the Catholick Church in Matters of Faith, and the Reformation of the Church of England* (1686); Dryden's *Defence of the Papers written by the Late King of Blessed Memory, and Duchess of York, against the Answer made to them* (1686); and Stillingfleet's *Vindication of the Answer to some Late Papers concerning the Unity and Authority of the Catholick Church, and the Reformation of the Church of England* (1687).

p. 142   Dryden translated Maimbourg's *History* in 1683–4, after the Rye House Plot.

p. 142   *The Late Converts Exposed, or the Reasons of Mr. Bays's Changing his Religion. Part the Second* (1690), pp. 33, 35.

p. 142   The *Answer* to Burnet's *Reflections on Mr. Varillas's History of the Revolutions that have happened in Europe in Matters of Religion* (Amsterdam, 1686) was by Varillas, not Dryden.

p. 145   *Mac Flecknoe* was, however, published more than six years before Dryden lost the laureateship.

p. 145   *Literary Works of Prior*, i. 254.

p. 147   Dryden translated *Georgics* iii late in 1693.

p. 148   Dryden's *Fables* appeared in March 1700.

p. 148   *Alexander's Feast*, reprinted in this volume, was first published in 1697. It is believed that the letter to Birch is no longer extant.

p. 148   Dryden died on 1 May 1700. Johnson presumably copied the wrong date from the account by Birch (*General Dictionary*, iv. 683), who had in turn been misled by the date Pope supplied for Dryden's tombstone (see *Pope: Poems*, vi. 209).

p. 148   Charles Wilson, *Memoirs of the Life, Writings and Amours of William Congreve* (1730), pt. II, pp. 3–9. This work was published by Curll, and Malone pointed out that the author of this 'wild story' was Elizabeth Thomas, whom Dryden once honoured with the name of 'Corinna', and who, at the time of writing it, was 'in the Fleet Prison, in great poverty and distress' (*Prose Works of Dryden*, i. 347–8). In *Biographia Britannica* (1747–66), ii. 1759 n. x, the original account is abridged. For an authentic account of Dryden's funeral see Ward, pp. 317–18.

p. 150   This paragraph was extensively revised by Johnson for 1783 ed., in which the reference to Farquhar was first added. He had, however, inserted in his

Advertisement to 1st ed.: 'I had been told that in the College of Physicians there is some memorial of Dryden's funeral, but my intelligence was not true. . . . There is in Farquhar's Letters an indistinct mention of it as irregular and disorderly, and of the oration which was then spoken. More than this I have not discovered.'

p. 155   The 'libel' to which Dryden refers may have been either the passage from *Prince Arthur*, vi (where Dryden is satirized in the character of Laurus), or the passage from *A Satyr against Wit*, which, though the title-page is dated 1700, was published on or before 23 Nov. 1699 (see Osborn, pp. 77 n. 20).

p. 156   Spingarn, iii. 142; *Late Converts Exposed* (1690), sig. ²*A* ('Preface to Mr. Bays').

p. 157   The two posts of Poet Laureate and Historiographer Royal were conferred on Dryden by Charles II, and the latter brought no increase in his salary.

p. 158   Since silver was the sole standard until 1816, the value of the gold guinea (first coined 1663, value 20s.) was subject to market fluctuations, and rose as high as 30s. in 1695.

p. 159   Wilson, *Memoirs of Congreve*, pt. I, pp. 24–31, a passage written long after the events themselves had taken place.

p. 162   *Praelectiones Poeticae* (Oxford, 1711–19), iii. 122. Cf. *Dryden: Essays*, ii. 290–1. The following translation of this passage has been adapted (with allowances for Johnson's minor misquotations) from that of Trapp's work (*Lectures on Poetry*) which appeared in 1742: 'We know Dryden's judgement about a poem of Chaucer's, truly beautiful, indeed, and worthy of praise, namely, that it was not only equal, but even superior to the *Iliad* and *Aeneid*. But we know likewise that his opinion was not always the most accurate, nor formed upon the severest rules of criticism. What was presently in hand was generally most in esteem; if it was uppermost in his thoughts, it was so in his judgement too' (p. 348).

p. 174   Diplomatic arrangements had been made with Denmark for the Dutch East India fleet to be attacked in Bergen harbour by an English force.

p. 177   'All things were laid to rest in the calm quiet of night.' This line, which is not Virgil's (as Johnson states), comes from a fragment of Varro.

p. 179   This passage probably resulted from a conflation in Johnson's mind of two separate episodes from *Don Bellianis*; see my note, *RES*, n.s. xvii (1966), 299.

p. 183   The Council of Nicaea, convoked by Constantine, and held in 325, was the first general council of the Christian Church.

p. 187   Dryden's translation of *Eclogue* iv first appeared in *Miscellany Poems* (1684), and was revised for his 1697 *Virgil*, as was also his translation of the two episodes from the *Aeneid*. These first appeared in *Sylvae, or the Second Part of Poetical Miscellanies* (1685).

p. 188   Milburne here quotes from the second translation of Virgil by Ogilby (1654, pp. 61, 63), the first having been published in 1649.

p. 190   Trapp's *Aeneis of Virgil* was published in 1718, and his *Works of Virgil* in 1731.

p. 192   *Dramatick Works of Dryden*, i. sig. *a11*.

p. 197   Cf. H. L. Piozzi, *Anecdotes of the late Samuel Johnson*, ed. S. C. Roberts (Cambridge, 1925), p. 106.

p. 199   *The Works of Alexander Pope ... with Notes and Illustrations by Joseph Warton, D.D. and Others* (1797), vii. 69 n.; cf. *Essay on Pope*, p. 147.

p. 200   Cf. *Dramatick Works of Dryden*, i. sig. *a11*. (I cannot find where Pope said this.)

p. 202   In the Advertisement to 1st ed. Johnson wrote: 'I have been told that Dryden's Remarks on Rymer have been printed before. The former edition I have not seen.' They had been printed by Tonson in 1711 ed. of Beaumont and Fletcher. Mr. J. C. Eade kindly informs me that they were omitted from 1750 ed. (which Johnson possessed) but were included in 1778 ed. Mr. George Watson in *Dryden: Essays*, i. 210–20, has followed and annotated Tonson's text, the sections of which are printed by Johnson in the following order: IV, VII, V, I, III, VI, II. Johnson's text is possibly more faithful to the original order of Dryden's jottings (Osborn, pp. 28–9, 283–5).

POPE

p. 210   The date of 21 May 1688 (confirmed by Pope's own written testimony) is now accepted as the date of the poet's birth (Spence, § 1 and n.). In writing this Life, Johnson drew mainly on the following sources: the MS. of Spence's *Anecdotes*; the notes (by both Pope and Warburton) and letters in *The Works of Alexander Pope*, ed. W. Warburton (1751); Joseph Warton, *An Essay on the Writings and Genius of Alexander Pope* (1756; rev. 1762); Owen Ruffhead, *The Life of Alexander Pope ... with a Critical Essay on his Writings and Genius* (1769).

p. 210   *Pope: Poems*, iv. 125 n. Cf. *GM*, iii (1733), 326. Pope's father was the grandson of a Richard Pope (d. 1633) who kept an inn at Andover.

p. 210   This name was given to Pope by Thomas Southerne; see John Boyle (Earl of Orrery), *Remarks on the Life and Writings of Dr. Jonathan Swift* (1752, 2nd rev. ed.), p. 145.

p. 211   The Popes did not move to Binfield till about 1700.

p. 211   The autograph of Pope's 'Ode on Solitude' dates, however, from 1709, and revision took place probably before, and certainly after, that date.

p. 212   Much of Pope's translation (published 1712) was, however, completed after 1709.

p. 216   Pope's *Essay* had, however, been published anonymously. Nor are ll. 585 ff. calculated to flatter Dennis's person.

p. 218   *Pope: Corr.* i. 117–19, 122, 128 (Pope to Caryll, 18, 25 June, 19 July 1711). Cf. *Essay on Criticism*, ll. 687–96.

p. 219   Johnson's inference seems to have been based on one or more passages from Pope's letters of 1711 (e.g. *Pope: Corr*. i. 119, 123, 130, 132). Cf. *Pope: Poems*, ii. 353–5 nn.

p. 219   Ruffhead in fact derived his account from that of William Ayre, *Memoirs of the Life and Writings of Alexander Pope* (1745), i. 75–6.

p. 222   Pope's *Temple of Fame* was published in 1715. Cf. *Pope: Corr*. i. 154 (Pope to Steele, 16 Nov. 1712).

p. 222   'Eloisa to Abelard' appeared in 1717, in 1st ed. of Pope's collected works.

p. 222   Cf., however, *Pope: Corr*. iii. 269 (Pope to Dr. William Cowper, 5 Feb. 1732).

p. 224   Pope copied Kneller's Betterton (*Pope: Corr*. i. 187 n. 2; Spence, § 108 n.).

p. 224   Johnson was probably informed of this by his friend Sir Joshua Reynolds, who also told Joseph Warton that Pope had poorly characterized the painters mentioned in ll. 37–8.

p. 225   For Pope's agreement with Lintot, which is now in the Bodleian Library, see *Pope: Poems*, x. 606.

p. 225   Cf. John Nichols, *Literary Anecdotes of the Eighteenth Century* (1812–15), i. 78, 109, 110 n.; viii. 169.

p. 226   These facts, as well as those in the last sentence of the subsequent paragraph, were derived from the ledgers of the printer William Bowyer (see ibid. i. 77–8).

p. 227   Despite Johnson's statement here, Boswell had previously read him a letter from Dr. Hugh Blair that reported, on Lord Bathurst's authority, Pope's adequate knowledge of Greek (*Life*, iii. 403).

p. 227   Chapman's translation appeared in 1611, Ogilby's in 1660, and Hobbes's in 1676.

p. 228   A Greek-Latin version of the first five books of the *Iliad*, with Eustathius's commentary on them, did not appear until 1730–5, at Florence. Cf. *Pope: Corr*. ii. 500 (Broome to Fenton, 15 June 1728).

p. 229   Dr. Mary Hyde, who owns the proof-sheets of the *Life of Pope*, kindly informs me that the numbers in this paragraph were added by John Nichols.

p. 230   In *The Works of Samuel Johnson* (1787), Sir John Hawkins mentions an annuity of £200 which Pope had purchased from either the late Duke of Buckingham or his mother, and which was charged on some part of the family estate, adding that 'the deed by which it was granted was some years in my custody' (iv. 95 n.). Cf. *Imit. Hor. Ep*. I. vii. 71.

p. 241   Pope probably leased the villa at Twickenham in 1718, and moved there in 1719, more than a year after his father's death.

p. 241   Alexander Pope senior was 71 when he died.

p. 242 Pope's undertaking was in this year (1721) made public, but his edition was not published until 1725.

p. 242 With the figures given here cf. *GM*, lvii (1787), 76, where some account is given of the sale of the effects of the younger Jacob Tonson in 1767.

p. 244 *Pope: Poems*, x. 378–9. Cf. ibid. p. 391; Sherburn, pp. 261–2. Broome translated books ii, vi, viii, xi-xii, xvi, xviii, xxiii, and Fenton i, iv, xix, xx.

p. 244 The figure of £100 given by Ruffhead (p. 205) is challenged by Sherburn, who points out (p. 254) that the total agreed upon for copy-money was less than Johnson states.

p. 244 In fact, 610 subscribers took 1,057 sets.

p. 248 *Remarks on Mr. Pope's Rape of the Lock; in several Letters to a Friend. With a Preface occasion'd by the late Treatise on the Profound, and the Dunciad* (1728).

p. 249 *Pope: Poems*, v. 136 n.; *Pope: Corr*. iii. 164–5 (Hill to Pope, 18 Jan. 1731), 165–6 (Pope to Hill, 26 Jan.), 166–9 (Hill to Pope, 28 Jan.), 169–72 (Pope to Hill, 5 Feb.).

p. 249 J. V. Guerinot, *Pamphlet Attacks on Alexander Pope 1711–1744* (1969), p. 227, points out that *An Epistle to the Little Satyrist of Twickenham* (1733), where a figure of £500 (not £1,000) is mentioned, might have been the source that prompted Pope to name the same figure in a note to his *Epistle to Arbuthnot*, l.375, as the present Welsted falsely accused him of receiving from Chandos. Cf. *Pope: Poems*, iv. 123 n.

p. 249 Cf. Spence, § 315 and n., where it is pointed out that modern scholarship has vindicated Pope. Chandos's surviving letter to Pope does not accord with Johnson's summary (see *Pope: Corr*. iii. 262–3).

p. 251 *Mr. Pope's Literary Correspondence. Volume the Second* (1735), p. *xvi* n. Curll was examined before the Lords on 14–15 May 1735. Contrary to his earlier advertisement, no letters of noblemen were found in those copies seized by the House.

p. 251 Ibid. p. 14 (1st series of pagination in arabic numerals).

p. 253 Suckling's letters, though never published separately, were regularly included in editions of his works.

p. 254 Pope's name did not appear on the editions of 1734, but his authorship had become an open secret.

p. 255 *Essai sur l'Homme*, trans. Etienne de Silhouette (London & Amsterdam, 1736); Du Resnel, *Les Principes de la morale* . . . (Paris, 1737).

p. 256 Warburton's letter (dated 2 Jan. 1727) became the property of the poet and physician Mark Akenside, and was eventually printed in J. and J. B. Nichols, *Illustrations of the Literary History of the Eighteenth Century* (1817–58), ii. 195–8.

p. 257   Warburton's vindication appeared in the *History of the Works of the Learned* (for 1738), ii. 425–36; (for 1739), i. 56–73, 89–105, 159–72, 330–58.

p. 258   Warburton printed Pope's will (ix. 367–72).

p. 259   For the eventual change to the form of a dialogue Warburton was responsible; see *Pope: Poems*, III. ii. 79–80.

p. 261   Modern scholarship, however, inclines to the view that this satire was directed against Katherine Darnley (1682?–1743), Duchess of Buckinghamshire. Cf. *Pope: Poems*, III. ii. 159 ff.

p. 261   Rochester wrote 'An Allusion to Horace: The Tenth Satire of the First Book'.

p. 263   Hervey probably wrote the dedication to Sir William Yonge's *Sedition and Defamation Displayed* (1731). Pulteney was the author of *A Proper Reply to a late Scurrilous Libel* (1731). The duel was fought on 25 Jan. 1731, neither combatant being much hurt (*GM*, i, 1731, 28).

p. 263   *Verses addressed to the Imitator of . . . Horace. By a Lady* [Lady Mary Wortley Montagu], [1733], p. 4; *An Epistle from a Nobleman to a Doctor of Divinity* (1733), p. 7.

p. 264   When the Lords adjudged the poem scandalous, Dodsley was ordered into custody and kept there a week; see *GM*, ix (1739), 104.

p. 264   Laurent Bordelon, *L'Histoire des imaginations extravagantes de M. Oufle* (Amsterdam/Paris, 1710). An English version appeared in 1711.

p. 265   Francis Atterbury was the editor of 'Ανθολογια, *seu selecta quaedam poemata Italorum qui Latine scripserunt* (1684).

p. 269   For the incidents recounted in this and the subsequent paragraph see Spence, §§ 633–4, 636, 638, 652–3, 655–6; cf. *Works of Pope* (1797), i. *lxiv*.

p. 270   Johnson here alludes to *Letters, on the Spirit of Patriotism, on the Idea of a Patriot King, and on the State of Parties at the Accession of King George the First* (1749), p. *vi*, where the number of 1,500 copies is also mentioned. The editor of this volume and author of the advertisement was David Mallet.

p. 271   Cf. *A Letter to the Editor of the Letters on the Spirit of Patriotism, the Idea of a Patriot-King, and the State of Parties* (1749), pp. 6 ff. (Pope had left Warburton the property of all his printed works and the profits arising from all subsequent unaltered editions.)

p. 272   Cf. *The Works of Alexander Pope*, ed. W. Elwin and W. J. Courthope (1871–89), viii. 523 (Orrery to Mallet, 14 July 1744).

p. 272   For her account, which includes most, but not all, of the details Johnson mentions, see *GM*, xlv (1775), 435.

p. 273   Cf. William King (whom Johnson knew and admired), *Political and Literary Anecdotes of his Own Times* (1818), pp. 12–13.

p. 275 Cf. ibid. p. 13; *Letters to and from Henrietta, Countess of Suffolk* (1824), ii. 84 (Lord Bathurst to Mrs. Howard, July 1734).

p. 274 Cf. *Life*, iii. 324, where Johnson is likened to Pope in being *un politique aux choux et aux raves*.

p. 275 Johnson is here following the account given by Oxford's domestic.

p. 279 For Pope's satire on Bentley see *Dunciad*, iv. 199 ff. Bentley was said, however, to have regarded Pope's *Iliad* as nothing like Homer; see *Pope: Poems*, vii. *xlii*; *Works of Pope* (1797), iv. 23 n.

p. 286 Warton had claimed that they contained no 'single rural image that is new' (*Essay on Pope*, p. 2).

p. 288 *Essay on Criticism*, ll. 219–32. Warton had attacked this simile (*Essay on Pope*, p. 139), and Johnson had defended it in his review of Warton's book in the *Literary Magazine* for 1756.

p. 292 Though it has been suggested that Johnson is perhaps here quoting himself (cf. *A Journey to the Western Islands of Scotland* (1775, 2nd rev. ed.), p. 212), both of his passages may have a common source.

p. 293 Cf. Giuseppe Baretti, *The Italian Library* (1757), pp. 127, 135.

p. 294 Cf. above, pp. 227, 279 and n.; *Dennis*, ii. 123–4, 134, 323, 363; Fielding, *Amelia*, VIII. 5; Young, *Conjectures on Original Composition* (1759), p. 58.

p. 295 Cf. *The Poet finish'd in Prose; being a Dialogue concerning Mr. Pope and his Writings* (1735), p. 37.

p. 298 *Epistle to a Lady*, ll. 69 ff. In his *Life of Prior* Johnson reproduced the passage from *Richardsoniana*, pp. 274–5, illustrating the poet's 'propensity to sordid converse'.

p. 298 Warburton, iii. 215–16 nn., 262 n. In the second volume of Pope's *Works* published in 1735, several years before he met his future editor, these *Epistles* appear in the order that Johnson here alleges is Warburton's. Cf. *Pope: Corr.* iii. 348 (Pope to Swift, 16 Feb. 1733).

p. 299 In assigning these qualities to Pope, Johnson was obviously indebted to Ruffhead, pp. 448–50; see my note, *Johnsonian News Letter*, XXVI. i (March, 1966), 10–11.

p. 301 In his *Essay on Pope*, Warton had challenged Pope's reputation as a poet.

p. 302 Pope was presumably referring to 4° ed. of 1689, published at Cambridge. But its reference to Hobbes (sig. *a4*), though complimentary, does not correspond with Pope's statement.

p. 304 Cf. Rochester, 'An Allusion to Horace: the Tenth Satire of the First Book', l. 60.

p. 304 Both Johnson's *Dict.* and the *OED* cite this couplet as Pope's. I have found no earlier occurrence of either line in English poetry.

p. 305   For the likely reason for this omission see *Pope: Poems*, vi. 170.

p. 307   'James Craggs, confidential and trusted secretary to the king of Great Britain, the favourite of the sovereign and people alike, lived above titles and envy for 35 years—alas, how few; and died on 16 February 1720.'

p. 309   This date suggests that the epitaph was first written for Robert alone, since Mary did not die until 1729 (see *Pope: Poems*, vi. 315).

p. 315   *Opere di M. Lodovico Ariosto* (Venice, 1730), ii. 399:

> 'The bones of Ludovico Ariosto are buried under this marble, or under this earth, or under whatever has been willingly provided by a kind heir, or a companion kinder than an heir, or by a traveller coming upon him more opportunely. For he could not know the future, but his lifeless body was not important enough to him to make him want to prepare a funeral urn in his lifetime; in his lifetime, however, he did prepare for himself the very verses which he wanted inscribed on his tomb, if at any date in the future he should have one.'

THOMSON

p. 316   In writing this Life, Johnson drew mainly on three printed accounts of the life of Thomson: that by Robert Shiels (or Shiells) in Cibber's *Lives of the Poets of Great-Britain and Ireland* (1753), v. 190–218; that by Patrick Murdoch, first prefixed to *The Works of James Thomson*, ed. Murdoch (1762, 4°); that prefixed to *The Seasons* (Edinburgh, 1768). The last two were mentioned to him by Boswell in a letter (9 June 1777) replying to a request for information about Thomson.

p. 316   Thomson's mother was the daughter of a woman whose maiden name was Hume. Boswell wrote to Johnson (18 June 1778), telling him that Murdoch (i. *ii*) was mistaken in giving Beatrix Thomson's maiden name as Hume; but Johnson perpetuated Murdoch's error.

p. 317   The sum mentioned was £3; see *The Seasons* ed. George Wright (1770?), p. *ix* n.; Benjamin Victor, *Original Letters, Dramatic Pieces, and Poems* (1776), iii. 27 n. This sum might, however, have been an advance to the author since Thomson did not surrender the copyright (Grant, pp. 48–9, 95 n. 1).

p. 317   Preface to *Winter* (1726, 2nd ed.), pp. 14, 18; *Thomson: Letters*, pp. 24–33 (letters to Hill, 5 Apr.–7 June 1726).

p. 317   'To Mr. Thomson, doubtful to what Patron he should address his Poem' was prefixed to the 2nd ed. of *Winter*. A letter praising the poem, and expressing the hope that the author's merit would find its just reward at the hands of the great, appeared in the *London Chronicle*, 4 June 1726, and is reprinted in A. D. McKillop, *The Background of Thomson's Seasons* (Minneapolis, 1942), pp. 175–7. Johnson could have run these two pieces together in his mind.

p. 318   *Britannia*, written in 1727, was published in 1729.

p. 319   For evidence that the Countess of Hertford showed a continuing interest in Thomson and his work see H. S. Hughes, *MP*, xxv (1927–8), 439–68.

p. 319   *Sophonisba* was, however, well received, as Shiels points out—though he includes the parody quoted by Johnson (Cibber's *Lives*, v. 209–10). *A Criticism on the New Sophonisba* (1730) contains the parody of Thomson's line in a form that seems likely to have been Johnson's source and the origin of this anecdote.

p. 320   Cf. *The Works of James Thomson*, ed. Lyttelton (1750), ii. sig. *C*. Thomson's text was restored by Murdoch in 1762.

p. 321   Various other accounts claim that *Agamemnon* was more favourably received than Johnson here suggests. Objection was made, however, to the epilogue, which had to be rewritten; and Thomas Davies, who tells the same story of Thomson's distress, notes that the audience showed 'displeasure' at certain scenes; see *Memoirs of the Life of David Garrick* (1780), ii. 33.

p. 321   Johnson had moved to London in 1737. Shiels attributes this incident to the first performance of *Sophonisba* (Cibber's *Lives*, v. 210).

p. 321   The number of copies printed indicates that the subscription was successful; see Grant, p. 189.

p. 322   Lyttelton became a lord of the Treasury in Dec. 1744. Murdoch says (i. *xi*) that Thomson enjoyed his surveyor-generalship for the last two years of his life—a statement supported by Birch's letter to Orrery of 30 Sept. 1748 (*Thomson: Letters*, p. 208).

p. 222   Completed in March 1747, this play was produced at Covent Garden on 13 Jan. 1749.

p. 325   Johnson expressed a comparable opinion with regard to *Paradise Lost* (see above, p. 112) and Young's *Night Thoughts*.

p. 326   For a table showing the number of lines added to every part of *The Seasons* from its first publication to 1746 (the date of Thomson's last revisions) see *The Seasons*, ed. Bolton Corney (1842), p. *xxix* n., *NQ*, 4th s. xi (1873), 419, or *Thomson's Seasons: Critical Edition*, ed. Otto Zippel (Berlin, 1908; *Palaestra*, vol. lxvi), pp. *x–xi*.

p. 326   *Upon the Gardens of Epicurus, or Of Gardening, Five Miscellaneous Essays by Sir William Temple*, ed. S. H. Monk (Ann Arbor, 1963), p. 29.

p. 326   Johnson added this last paragraph—which makes for a much more impressive conclusion—in 1783.

COLLINS

p. 327   Collins must have been born on 25 Dec. 1721 since he was baptised on 1 Jan. 1721/2. The year of his birth is correctly given in the biographical section of *Some Account of the Life and Writings of Mr. William Collins*, published in the *Poetical Calendar* (for Dec. 1763), xii. 107–12. To this Johnson was doubtless indebted for some details of the poet's life. He himself had contributed the latter portion (pp. 110–12), being described as 'a gentleman, deservedly eminent in the republic of letters' who knew Collins 'intimately well'.

p. 327 Printed at the end of this Life, these were not by Collins but by John Swan, as Johnson correctly intimates in a letter to Nichols (*Letters*, no. 652 and n.). Collins's first publication has been identified as 'On Hercules', a poem containing anti-Walpole satire, and published in *GM*, viii (1738), 45; see P. L. Carver, *The Life of a Poet: A Biographical Sketch of William Collins* (1967), pp. 15–16.

p. 327 Collins was admitted a commoner of Queen's on 21 March 1740, and elected to a Magdalen demyship on 29 July 1741.

p. 328 John Ragsdale, in his letter about Collins to William Hymers, said that he had been shown 'many sheets' of the translation of Aristotle which Collins, according to his own account, had 'fully employed himself about'; see *The Gleaner: A Series of Periodical Essays*, ed. Nathan Drake (1811), iv. 482–3.

p. 329 Collins died on 12 June 1759. The original *Account* had simply read '. . . where death at last came to his relief'. For the change the printer John Nichols was responsible, who wrote at the foot of a state of proof-sheets for this Life: 'There is no mention when Mr. Collins died. It was in 1756 at Chichester.' The misdating of Collins's death was therefore an error made by Nichols and not (as has been assumed) by Johnson.

p. 329 Dr. Alexander Carlyle, on reading Johnson's *Life of Collins*, was instrumental in bringing the poem to light again in 18th century, and it was published in 1788. Miss Claire Lamont has recently rediscovered the MS. at Aldourie Castle; see *RES*, n.s. xix (1968), 137–47.

GRAY

p. 331 Gray was born on 26 Dec. 1716 (see *Gray: Corr.* i. 261 and n. 20). The date is correctly given by William Mason in *Poems of Mr. Gray; to which are prefixed Memoirs of his Life and Writings*. Johnson owned a copy of this work (the first two editions of which were published in 1775 at York and London respectively), and drew upon it extensively in writing this Life.

p. 331 It was not necessary to take a degree in order to become a barrister; cf. *Walpole: Corr.* xiii. 115 and n. 1.

p. 331 Gray was admitted to Peterhouse on 4 July 1734, and went down in Sept. 1738.

p. 331 Walpole and Gray parted at Reggio, not Florence. Cf. Mason, pp. 40–1 and n.; *Walpole: Corr.* xxviii. 68–9 and n. 14 (Walpole to Mason, 2 March 1773).

p. 332 This date (1742) appears at the end of all three odes in Gray's Commonplace Book (Pembroke College, Cambridge). His Latin poem was begun at Florence in 1740, though the preface to the second book was composed in 1742.

p. 332 Though nominated in 1747, Mason's election to a fellowship did not take place until Feb. 1749.

p. 333 Gray sent a copy of his *Elegy* to Walpole on 12 June 1750, but it was not published until 15 Feb. 1751. The next day the *Magazine of Magazines* reprinted it, as did also the *London Magazine* and *Scots Magazine* the following month.

p. 333   Johnson had not been so outspoken in 1st ed., which had read: '... which, though perhaps it adds little to Gray's character, I am not pleased to find wanting in this collection. It will therefore be added to this Preface.'

p. 333   The last part of this sentence is not in 1st ed.; nor can Mason's version of the affair (pp. 241–2 n.) be regarded as its source. In *Illustrations of the Literary History of the Eighteenth Century* (1817–58) is reprinted a letter (dated 12 March 1756) in which the cruel hoax perpetrated on Gray of shouting 'Fire!' under his window is said to be 'much talked of' (vi. 805). An elaborately satirical account had been published by Archibald Campbell in his *Sale of Authors* (1767), but if Johnson knew of the story from an individual source, it was probably from Nichols, who owned the letter later reprinted. Both the letter and Campbell's account are reprinted in *Gray: Corr.* iii. 1216–20.

p. 333   *Gray: Corr.* ii. 519 (Gray to Hurd, 25 Aug. 1757), 532 (Gray to Wharton, 7 Oct. 1757), 535 n. 1; *Critical Review* (for Aug. 1757), iv. 167–70; Mason, pp. 86, 88–9, 91–5. Garrick's verses appeared first in the *London Chronicle* under 1 Oct. 1757.

p. 333   Gray's letter to Mason (23 July 1759) is inscribed: 'At Mr. Jauncey's, Southampton Row, Bloomsbury'.

p. 335   Voltaire, *Letters concerning the English Nation*, ed. Charles Whibley (1926), p. 140 (no. XIX, *On Comedy*).

p. 336   Cf. Shenstone, *Elegy* xxv. 18; Goldsmith, *The Traveller*, l. 236; Gay, *Dione*, I. i. 4.

p. 338   Cf. *The Letters of Horace Walpole*, ed. Mrs. Paget Toynbee (Oxford, 1903–5), iv. 85, where Walpole answers Lyttelton's objection to this phrase by quoting the authority of Mrs. Garrick. For Lyttelton's reply see *Supplement to the Letters of Horace Walpole*, ed. Paget Toynbee (Oxford, 1918–25), ii. 100–1. In his revisions of Thomson's poetry Lyttelton had made two changes in *Spring* that anticipate this later criticism. For 'many-twinkling', (l. 158, 1744 ed.) he printed 'ever-twinkling', and for 'Around him feeds his many-bleating flock' (l. 835) he printed 'Around him feeds dispersed his bleating flock'.

p. 339   Algarotti wrote to William Taylor How (26 Dec. 1762): 'La dirò bene all'orecchio che quel vaticinio mi sembra di gran lunga superiore al vaticinio di Nereo sopra lo eccidio di Troia' (Mason, p. 83). In the *Monthly Review* (for Sept. 1757), xvii. 239–43, Goldsmith said that Gray had imitated Horace's 'pastor cum traheret' (*Odes*, i. 15). This Gray denied in two letters to Wharton (7 Oct. 1757; Dec. 1758) not printed by Mason.

p. 339   For this ballad see *The English and Scottish Popular Ballads*, ed. F. J. Child (1956 reprint), iii. 368.

p. 340   Cf. Quintilian, II. iii. 8 (*statura breves in digitos eriguntur*).

Index

Abelard (Abailard), Peter, 292
Absalom Senior, 140
Adam, Robert, 322 n.
Addison, Joseph, 30, 92, 100–1,
    102 n., 110, 119, 139, 187, 216, 219,
    221, 223–6, 227 n., 236–40, 256,
    262, 286, 346
Adrian VI, Pope, 327
Aeschylus, 108
Agar, Thomas, 92
Akenside, Mark, 361
Alabaster, William, 52
Alexander, 27
Alfonso IV (Duke of Modena), 131 n.
Algarotti, Francesco, 339, 353, 367
allegory, 38, 94, 108, 179, 183, 291,
    328, 353. *See also* personification
Allen, Elizabeth (*née* Holder), 271
Allen, Ralph, 252, 258, 263, 271–2,
    280
Ames, William, 349
Amhurst, Nicholas, 355
Anacreon, 15, 29, 45
Andreini, Giovanni Battista, 351
Anglesey, Earl of. *See* Annesley,
    Arthur
Anguillara, Giovanni Andrea Dell',
    293
Anne, Queen, 264
Annesley, Arthur (Earl of Anglesey),
    86
Antipater of Sidon, 211 n.
Antrobus, Robert, 331
Aratus, 293 n.
Arbuthnot, John, 249, 253, 262, 264
Ariosto, Ludovico, 104, 109, 191,
    314–15, 364
Aristotle, 11, 101, 203–5, 219, 328,
    355, 366
Arminius, Jacobus, 90 n.
Arouet, François-Marie (Voltaire),
    78, 245, 272 n., 335, 351, 367
Ascham, Roger, 52, 347
Aston, Mary ('Molly'), 309
Atterbury, Francis, 88, 213, 240, 243–
    244, 246, 362
Aubrey, John, 347, 351
Augustus, 188 n., 200
Aurangzeb, 132
Aylmer, Brabazon, 83
Ayre, William, 239 n., 360
Azaria and Hushai, 140, 357

Bacon, Sir Francis, 25, 328 n.
Baillie, Lady Grizel, 317
Bannister, John, alias 'Taverner',
    210–11
Barberini, Francesco, Cardinal, 56
Baretti, Giuseppe, 353, 363
Barnes, Joshua, 4
Barrow, Samuel, 107
Bath, Earl of. *See* Pulteney, Sir
    William
Bathurst, Allen (Earl Bathurst),
    247 n., 260, 276, 298, 360, 363
Baudius, Dominic, 90
Bayle, Pierre, 354
Beattie, James, 334
Beaumont, Francis, 124, 359
Behn, Afra, 154
Bell, Elizabeth (*née* Thomson), 323
Bell, Robert, 323
Bembo, Pietro, Cardinal, 310 n.
Bennet, Henry (Earl of Arlington), 5,
    344
Benson, William, 88, 258, 352
Bentley, Richard, 28–9, 105, 109,
    288, 296, 363
Bentley, Richard (the younger), 333
Berkeley, George, 222
Berkshire, Earl of. *See* Howard,
    Thomas
Bernardi, John, 306
Berni, Francesco, 191
Beroald, Philip (the elder), 192
Betterton, Thomas, 76, 224
Binning, Lord. *See* Hamilton,
    Charles
Birch, Thomas, 7, 65, 148, 150 n.,
    347, 349–52, 356–7, 365
Blackborough, Hester, 63 n.
Blackborough, William, 63
Blackmore, Sir Richard, 147, 155–6,
    350
Blair, Hugh, 360
Blount, Martha, 261, 269, 271–2
Boccaccio, Giovanni, 191
Boiardo, Matteo Maria (Count of
    Scandiano), 191
Boileau-Despréaux, Nicholas, 146,
    148, 173–4, 262, 265, 292, 298,
    300
Bois, Mr., 10
Bolingbroke, Lady. *See* St. John,
    Marie-Claire

Bolingbroke, Viscount. *See* St. John, Henry

Bombast von Hohenheim, Theophrastus (Paracelsus), 281

Bond(e), Christiern (Count), 70

Bordelon, Laurent, 362

Boswell, James, 322, 335, 360, 364

Bouhours, Dominic, 142 n.

Bowyer, Sir William, 207

Bowyer, William, 360

Boyle, John (5th Earl of Orrery), 274, 359, 362, 365

Boyle, Richard (Earl of Burlington), 247 n., 249, 250 n., 276

Boyle, Roger (1st Earl of Orrery), 116–18, 354

Brady, Nicholas (the elder), 190

Bramhall, John, 68

Bridges, Ralph, 302

Bridgewater, Earl of. *See* Egerton, John

Brockett, Lawrence, 334

Brooke, Henry, 321

Broome, William, 228, 243–4, 295, 360–1

Brown, Thomas, 5, 142–4, 156

Browne, Sir George, 221

Browne, Sir Thomas, 182

Brydges, James (Duke of Chandos), 249, 279, 361

Bucer (or Butzer), Martin, 62

Buchler, J., 349

Buckingham, 2nd Duke of. *See* Villiers, George

Buckingham and Normanby, 1st Duke of. *See* Sheffield, John

Buckingham and Normanby, 2nd Duke of. *See* Sheffield, Edmund

Buckinghamshire, Duchess of. *See* Darnley, Katherine

Burke, Edmund, 353

Burlington, Earl of. *See* Boyle, Richard

Burman, Peter, 350

Burnet, Gilbert, 75, 142–3, 245, 357

Burnet, Thomas, 242, 248

Burton, John, 327

Busby, Richard, 114, 164

Bute, Earl of. *See* Stuart, John

Butler, James (Duke of Ormonde), 65, 137, 153

Butler, Samuel, 111, 136, 349

Caesar, Julius, 19 n., 69

Caesar, Mrs. Mary, 277 n.

Calamy, Edmund, 349

Caligula, 256

Campbell, Archibald, satirist, 367

Carlyle, Alexander, 366

Caroline (Queen of George II), 92, 247–8, 258

Carte, Thomas, 153

Cary, Lucius (Viscount Falkland), 3, 27

Caryll, John, Baron, 220–1

Caryll, John, friend of Pope, 217 n., 220 n., 221, 223 n., 226 n., 299 n., 359

Casimir. *See* Sarbiewski, Maciej Kazimierz

Cato (of 'Utica'), 102

Cavendish, Margaret (Duchess of Newcastle), 124

Cavendish, William (Duke of Newcastle), 123–4

Cecil, James (Earl of Salisbury), 134

Chandos, Duke of. *See* Brydges, James

Chapman, George, 163, 198, 227, 302, 353, 360

Charles I, 3, 8, 55, 57, 65, 68, 75–6, 78, 82, 118, 210

Charles II, 3, 5, 7–8, 11, 65, 74–5, 77, 82, 84, 114–15, 117, 124, 134, 139 n., 154 n., 165, 170–1, 174, 177, 179, 261, 344, 357–8

Chaucer, Geoffrey, 11, 162, 191, 212, 224, 287, 358

Cheke, Sir John, 52 n.

Chesterfield, 2nd Earl of. *See* Stanhope, Philip

Chetwood, Knightly, 187

Chetwood, W. R., 252

Cheyne, George, 345

Chillingworth, William, 141

Christinia of Sweden, 55, 67

Churchill, Charles, 300 n.

Churchill, Sarah (Duchess of Marlborough), 261

Cibber, Colley, 159, 265–8, 333, 355

Cicero, 162 n., 211–13, 293

Cinthio, Giambattista Giraldi, 124

Clarendon, Earl of. *See* Hyde, Edward

Clarges, Sir Thomas, 75

Clarke, Abraham, husband of Deborah Milton, 92

Clarke, Abraham, son of Caleb Clarke, 92 n.

Clarke, Caleb, 92

Clarke, Isaac, son of Caleb Clarke, 92 n.

Clarke, John, 100
Claudian, 163
Clavius, Christopher, 162
Cleland, William, 249
Clement XI, Pope, 150
Cleveland, John, 14, 19, 21, 346
Clifford, Hugh (2nd Baron Chudleigh), 147
Clifford, Martin, 125–6, 136
Cobb, Samuel, 287–8
Cobham, Viscount. *See* Temple, Sir Richard
Cobham, Anne, Dowager Viscountess, 333
Collier, Jeremy, 155
Collinne, William, 351
Collins, Anne, 329
Collins, William, father of the poet, 327
Collins, William, poet, 327–30, 365–366; 'On Hercules': 366; 'History of the Revival of Learning': 327; *Odes*: 327 n.; *Persian Eclogues*: 327 n., 329; trans. *Poetics*: 327–8, 366
Colman, George (the elder), 333 n.
Comber, Thomas, 3
Compton, Henry, 302 n.
Compton, Sir Spencer (Earl of Wilmington), 317–18
Concanen, Matthew, 256
Congreve, William, 148, 150–2, 159, 192, 236, 276, 335, 357
Cooper, Anthony Ashley (1st Earl of Shaftesbury), 139–40
Cooper, Anthony Ashley (3rd Earl of Shaftesbury), 336
Corbet, Owen, 346
Corbett, Elizabeth, 308–9
Corneille, Pierre, 133
Cowley, Abraham, 1 ff., 51, 58, 90, 94, 114, 129, 136, 139, 160, 164, 167, 194, 197–9, 214, 325, 344–7, 349; *Anacreontics*: 29–30; *Constantia and Philetus*: 2; *Cutter of Coleman Street*: 8; *Davideis*: 2–3, 36–42, 44, 46–8; *Discourse by way of Vision*: 7; *Guardian*: 3, 8; *Love's Riddle*: 2–3; *Miscellanies*: 26–9; *Mistress*: 4–5, 30–1, 43; *Naufragium Joculare*: 3; 'Ode: Upon Liberty': 46; *Pindaric Odes*: 31–6; *Poemata Latina ... sex libri plantarum*: 7, 345; *Poetical Blossomes*: 2, 344; *Puritan and the Papist*: 3, 344; *Tragical History of Pyramus and Thisbe*: 2

Cowley, Thomas, 1, 344
Cowley, Thomasine, 1–2
Cowper, William, physician and antiquary, 360
Cradock, Joseph, 90
Craggs, James (the younger), 229–30, 239, 307–8, 364
Crashaw, Richard, 29, 311
Creech, Thomas, 152, 186
Cromwell, Henry, 215, 245, 282 n.
Cromwell, Oliver, 6–7, 10 n., 48, 67, 69, 74, 77, 115, 169, 197, 350, 354
Cromwell, Richard, 74
Crousaz, Jean-Pierre de, 255, 257
Curll, Edmund, 215, 245, 250–2, 357, 361

Dacier, Anne Lefèvre, 227–8
Dalrymple, Sir John, 75
Dante, 338
Darnley, Katherine (Duchess of Buckinghamshire), 362
Dati, Carlo Roberto, 56, 348
Davenant, Sir William, 9 n., 28, 76, 118–19, 136–7, 169, 174, 351
Davies, Sir John, 200
Davies, Thomas, 365
Davis, Dr., 63
Deane, Thomas, 211
Demosthenes, 161
Denham, Sir John, 14, 42, 114, 139, 166–7, 197, 286, 356
Dennis, John, 8, 102 n., 152 n., 214, 216–18, 222–3, 227 n., 238, 242, 248, 286, 292, 355, 359, 363
Derby, Countess Dowager of. *See* Spencer, Alice
Derby, Earl of. *See* Stanley, Ferdinando
Derrick, Samuel, 114, 159, 186 n., 354, 356
Devereux, Robert (Earl of Essex), 61
Digby, Sir Kenelm, 3, 141
Digby, Mary, 309
Digby, Robert, 309–10
Digby, William (Baron Digby), 309
Diodati, Charles, 52, 57, 348
Diodati, Jean (or Giovanni), 57
Dobson, William, 258, 281
Dodington, George Bubb, 319, 324
Dodsley, Robert, 263, 269–70, 280, 284
Dolben, Sir Gilbert, 187 n.
Domenichi, Lodovico, 191
Donne, John, 12, 14–16, 18, 20–6, 43–4, 170, 262, 351

Don Quixote, 264
Dorset, 6th Earl of. *See* Sackville, Charles
Downe, Earl of. *See* Pope, William
Downes, John, 9
Drake, Nathan, 366
Drayton, Michael, 198
Dryden, Charles, 146, 148–50, 208
Dryden, Elizabeth (*née* Howard) 117 n., 148–50
Dryden, Sir Erasmus, 114
Dryden, Erasmus, 114
Dryden, Erasmus Henry, 150, 208
Dryden, John, 8, 12, 25, 28, 37, 48, 90, 102–3, 109, 114 ff., 212, 215, 243, 256, 274, 283–5, 287–8, 290, 294, 300, 302, 308, 310, 337, 339, 347, 353 ff. *Absalom* and *Achitophel*: 139–40, 145, 155, 178–9, 354; *Albion and Albanius*: 131, 355; *Alexander's Feast*: 148, 159, 181, 192, 208, 257; *All for Love*: 133, 136, 178, 355–6; *Amboyna*: 130; *Amphitryon*: 134; *Annus Mirabilis*: 117–18, 127, 129, 159–60, 173–8, 194, 196; *The Assignation*: 130, 136, 356; *Astraea Redux*: 115, 170–1, 197; *Aureng-Zebe*: 132–3, 178; *Britannia Rediviva*: 186; *Character of Polybius*: 138; *Cleomenes*: 134; *The Conquest of Granada*: 124–5, 127, 129, 136, 178, 195–6, 355–6; trans. *De Arte Graphica*: 147; *Defence of the Epilogue*: 125; *Defence of the Papers written by the Late King*: 357; *Discourse concerning Satire*: 146; *Don Sebastian*: 133–4, 146, 168, 178, 195, 355; *The Duke of Guise*: 131, 354–5; *Eleonora*: 181–2; trans. *Epistles* of Ovid: 139, 178, 356; *Essay of Dramatic Poesy*: 118, 160–1, 164; *Fables*: 148, 155–60, 163, 191–2, 212, 357; *Grounds of Criticism in Tragedy*: 130; *Heads of an Answer to Rymer*: 202–7, 359; 'Heroic Stanzas': 115, 169, 197, 354; *Hind and the Panther*: 143–5, 183–6, 196, 200; trans. *Histoire des révolutions*: 142; *History of the League*: 142, 357; trans. *Iliad* (bk. i): 148, 163; *The Indian Emperor*: 117–18, 126–7, 178; *The Indian Queen*: 117; trans. Juvenal: 146, 186; *King Arthur*: 134, 355; *Life of Lucian*: 138; *Life of Plutarch*: 115, 138;

Life of Xavier: 142; *Limberham, or the Kind Keeper*: 133; *Love Triumphant*: 134; *Mac Flecknoe*: 145, 296, 346, 357; *Marriage à la mode*: 130, 136, 356; *The Medal*: 140, 179–80; *The Mock Astrologer*: 123–4; *Notes and Observations on the Empress of Morocco*: 120–3, 355; *Oedipus*: 131, 133; trans. Persius: 146, 186–7; 'Prologue to the University of Oxford' ('Though Actors cannot'): 115; *Religio Laici*: 182–3; *Secret Love, or the Maiden Queen*: 119; *Sir Martin Mar-all*: 119, 136, 356; 'Song for St. Cecilia's Day': 181; *The Spanish Friar*: 130, 355; *The State of Innocence*: 131–2, 136, 178, 356; trans. Tacitus: 138; *The Tempest*: 119; *Threnodia Augustalis*: 165, 180; *To his Sacred Majesty*: 115, 171–2, 197; *To my Lord Chancellor*: 172–3; 'To Sir George Etherege': 356; 'To the Memory of Mrs. Anne Killigrew': 181, 192, 196, 310 n.; *Troilus and Cressida*: 130; *Tyrannic Love*: 124, 130, 136, 178, 193–5, 355–6; 'Upon the Death of Lord Hastings': 114; *Vindication of the Duke of Guise*: 354; trans. Virgil, 190–1, 208, 224, 358; (*Aeneid*: 147, 163, 187, 208, 358; *Eclogues*: 147, 187–8, 358; *Georgics*: 147, 156, 188–90); *The Wild Gallant*: 116, 354
Dryden, John, son of the poet, 146, 150
Duckett, George, 242, 248
Du Fresnoy, Charles Alphonse, 147
Du Moulin, Peter (the younger), 68–69, 348
Du Resnel, Jean-François de Bellay, 218, 255, 361

Egerton, Alice, 54
Egerton, John (Earl of Bridgewater), 54
Egerton, John, 54
Egerton, Thomas, 54
Elizabeth I, 55, 160, 198
Ellwood, Thomas, 77–8, 82, 86, 351–2
Eloise. *See* Héloïse
Elys, Edmund, 31, 346
Ennius, 261
Eobanus Hessus. *See* Hessus
epic poetry, 98 ff.

Epicurus, 13 n.
Erasmus, Desiderius, 81 n., 90, 218
Essex, Earl of. *See* Devereux, Robert
Euripides, 90, 92, 108, 203–5, 352
Eustathius, 228, 360
Evelyn, John, 345

Falkland, Viscount. *See* Cary, Lucius
Fanshawe, Sir Richard, 32 n., 139
Farmer, Richard, 347
Farquhar, George, 150, 357–8
Felltham, Owen, 167
Felton, Henry, 48
Fenton, Elijah, 50, 71, 199, 224, 228, 243–4, 300, 311–12, 347, 352, 360–1
Fermor, Arabella, 220–1
Fermor, Mrs., Abbess, 221
Fielding, Henry, 363
Fitzroy, Augustus Henry (Duke of Grafton), 334
Fletcher, John, 124, 204–6, 359
Fleury, Cardinal, 258
Fortescue, William, 244 n., 245
Foster, Elizabeth (*née* Clarke), 92–3, 351–2
Foster, Thomas, 92–3
Fox, Henry, 263
Francini, Antonio, 56, 348
Frederick the Great, 339 n.
Fuller, Thomas, 141 n.

Galileo, 57
Garrick, David, 202, 333, 353, 365, 367
Garrick, Mrs., 367
Garth, Samuel, 149, 236
Gay, John, 215 n., 226 n., 239 n., 249 n., 250, 275 n., 312–13, 367
Geoffrey of Monmouth, 85
George I, 218, 352, 362
George II, 247–8, 352
George, William, 331
Germanicus, 293
Gildon, Charles, 193 n., 240
Gill, Alexander (the elder), 51
Giraldi. *See* Cinthio
Goldsmith, 367
Goodman, Godfrey, 351
Goodwin, John, 75–6
Gorbuduc, 163
Gordon, Thomas, 138
Grafton, Duke of. *See* Fitzroy, Augustus Henry
Graham, James (Duke of Montrose), 317
Granville, George (Baron Lansdowne), 223

Gray, Dorothy, 331
Gray, John, 318
Gray, Philip, 331
Gray, Thomas, 331 ff., 366–7; *Agrippina*: 332; 'Alliance of Education and Government': 332; 'The Bard': 333, 339–40; 'Ode on the Death of a Favourite Cat': 332, 336–7; 'De Principiis Cogitandi': 332; *Elegy written in a Country Churchyard*: 332–3, 340–1, 366; *Ode on a Distant Prospect of Eton College*: 332, 337; 'Hymn to Adversity': 332, 337; 'Hymn to Ignorance': 332 n.; Letters: 331, 334; 'A Long Story': 333; 'The Progress of Poesy': 333, 337–9; 'Ode on the Spring': 332, 336
Gregory, David, 88
Gregory XIII, Pope, 19 n.
Griffith, Matthew, 74
Grotius, Hugo, 43, 55
Guardian, 134
Gustavus Adolphus, 55 n.
Gwyn, Eleanor, 154

Haddon, Walter, 52, 347
Halifax, Marquis of. *See* Savile, Sir George
Halifax, Earl of. *See* Montagu, Charles
Hall, Joseph, 60, 198, 301
Hamilton, Anthony, 218
Hamilton, Charles (Lord Binning), 318–19
Hamilton, William, 316
Hampton, James, 51
Hannibal, 273
Harcourt, Simon (Viscount), 306
Harcourt, Simon, son of the above, 306–7, 310
Hardwicke, 1st Earl of. *See* Yorke, Philip
Hardwicke, 2nd Earl of. *See* Yorke, Philip
Harley, Edward (2nd Earl of Oxford), 247 n., 252, 272, 274, 277
Harley, Henrietta Cavendish (Lady Oxford), 274
Harley, Robert (1st Earl of Oxford), 225, 229, 242, 262
Harrington, James, political theorist, 74 n.
Harte, Walter, 178, 224
Hartlib, Samuel, 53, 77
Harvey, William, 27, 94

Hastings, Henry, Lord, 114
Hawkins, Sir John, 360
Hederich, Benjamin, 247 n.
Héloïse, 292
Henri IV of France, 3 n.
Henrietta Maria, 3, 10
Herbert, George, 253
Hertford, Countess of. *See* Seymour, Frances
Hertford, Earl of. *See* Seymour, Algernon
Hervey, John (Baron Hervey of Ickworth), 262–3, 362
Hessus, Helius Eobanus, 227
Hill, Aaron, 249, 279, 317–18, 361, 364
History of Mr. Oufle, 264, 362
Hobbes, Thomas, 66, 194 n., 227, 302, 360, 363
Hobson (*née* Ley), Lady Margaret, 62
Hobson, Thomas, 14
Holstenius, Lucas, 56
Holyday, Barten, 139, 167, 186
Home, John, 329
Homer, 54, 90, 92, 102, 148, 187, 203, 226–7, 237–9, 294, 300–3, 363; *Iliad*: 41, 162, 224, 228–9, 291, 293; *Odyssey*: 41, 59 n., 104 n., 174 n.
Hooke, Nathaniel, 258, 270
Hooker, Richard, 219
Horace, 28 n., 34 n., 80 n., 152–3, 167–8, 181 n., 194 n., 200 n., 261, 287, 337, 339, 346, 356, 362–3, 367
How, William Taylor, 367
Howard, Lady Elizabeth. *See* Dryden, Elizabeth
Howard, Henrietta (Countess of Suffolk), 363
Howard, Henry (Earl of Surrey), 111
Howard, Sir Robert, 117–18, 137, 145 n., 208, 354
Howard, Thomas (Earl of Berkshire), 150
Howell, James, 62, 252, 276 n.
Hume, Hugh (Earl of Marchmont), 269–70, 280
Hunt, Thomas, 355
Hurd, Richard, 44, 367
Hyde, Edward (Earl of Clarendon), 43–4, 172
Hymers, William, 366

Innocent XII, Pope, 146 n.

Jacob, Giles, 356
James I, 55

James II, 50, 84, 131, 141, 146, 157, 186, 220, 306 n., 357
Jeffreys, George (1st Baron Jeffreys of Wem), 141, 148
Jeffreys, John (2nd Baron Jeffreys of Wem), 148–50
Jermyn, Henry (Earl of St. Albans), 3, 5, 10
Jervas, Charles, 224, 238, 281
Jodrell, Richard Paul, 301
Johnson, Michael, 139
Jonson, Ben, 14, 44, 96, 111, 118, 124, 139, 160, 167, 170, 351, 356
Jortin, John, 228
Juvenal, 67, 130, 139 n., 146, 151, 155, 186, 250, 261 n., 273, 296 n.
Juxon, William, 65

Kennett, White, 238
Ker, John, 66
Kéroualle, Louise Renée de (Duchess of Portsmouth), 138
Keymis, Lawrence, 353
King, Edward, 54–5, 348
King, Sir John, 54
King, William, 158, 362
Kneller, Sir Godfrey, 310, 360
Kyrle, John, 259

Lamotte, Charles, 137
Langbaine, Gerard (the younger), 118–19, 130, 133, 136, 156, 354–6
Lansdowne, Baron. *See* Granville, George
La Valterie, Abbé de, 227
Le Bossu, René, 99
Lee, Nathaniel, 131, 133
Leibnitz, Gottfried Wilhelm, 297 n.
Leo X, Pope, 327
L'Estrange, Sir Roger, 74, 351
Ley, Lady Margaret. *See* Hobson, Lady Margaret
Linning, Catherine, 323 n.
Lintot, Barnaby Bernard, 223 n., 225–6, 239 n., 244, 251, 360
Lintot, Henry, 251
Lloyd, Robert, 333 n.
Locke, John, 213
Locke, William, 112
Longinus, 161, 345
Lonsdale, Earl of. *See* Lowther, Sir James
Loveday, Robert, 252
Lowther, Sir James (1st Earl of Lonsdale), 334
Lucan, 102

Lucian, 138, 356
Lucretius, 152, 221 n.
Lyttleton, Sir George (Baron Lyttleton), 263, 320–2, 326, 365, 367

MacSwinney, Owen, 159
Maecenas, 188, 201
Maimbourg, Louis, 142, 357
Mainwaring (Maynwaring), Arthur, 240
Malherbe, François de, 171
Mallet, David, 230, 271, 317–19, 321, 362
Malone, Edmond, 344, 349, 355–7
Manilius, 12 n.
Mann, Horace, 280 n.
Mannock, Williams, 211 n.
Mansfield, Earl of. *See* Murray, William
Manso, Giovanni Battista (Marquis of Villa), 56–7
Marchmont, Earl of. *See* Hume, Hugh
Marino, Giambattista, 14
Marlborough, Duchess of. *See* Churchill, Sarah
Marshall, Stephen, 349
Martial, 47 n.
Martin, Edmund, 328, 330
Marvell, Andrew, 75, 131
Mary I, Queen, 198
Mary of Modena (Queen of James II), 131–2, 142, 220–1
Mason, William, 332, 334–5, 366–7
Masson, David, 56 n.
Maty, Matthew, 230
May, Thomas, 8, 48
Medal Reversed, The, 140, 357
Menander, 294
'metaphysical poets', 11 ff., 344–5
Middlesex, Earl of. *See* Sackville, Charles
Milbourne, Luke, 147, 155–6, 187–190, 200, 358
Millan, John, 317
Milton, Anne, daughter of the poet, 68, 85, 92, 352
Milton, Anne, sister of the poet, 50–1
Milton, Catherine, 92
Milton, Sir Christopher, 50, 92
Milton, Deborah, 68, 85, 92, 351–3
Milton (*née* Minshull), Elizabeth, 76–7, 83, 89, 352
Milton, John, father of the poet, 50–51, 54–5, 58, 61

Milton, John, poet, 2, 7–8, 14, 29, 43–4, 50 ff., 131, 164, 174, 214, 256, 285, 325, 333, 339, 345, 347 ff.; *Accidence commenced Grammar*: 77, 351; 'Ad Patrem': 50; *Animadversions*: 60; *Apology against a Pamphlet*: 60–1; 'Arcades': 55, 348; *Areopagitica*: 63, 349; *Artis Logicae Plenior Institutio*: 86–7; *Brief Notes upon a Late Sermon*: 74; *Character of the Long Parliament*: 86, 352; *Colasterion*: 349; *Comus*: 54, 93, 96–8, 111, 348; *Considerations touching the likeliest Means*: 53, 74; *Defensio 'Prima'*: 66–7, 89, 350; *Defensio Secunda*: 69–70, 75, 348–50; diction: 93–4, 110–11; *Doctrine and Discipline of Divorce*: 62, 349; 'Elegia Prima': 52–3; *Epitaphium Damonis*: 57, 348; *Familiar Epistles*: 87, 352; *History of Britain*: 70–1, 85–6; *Judgement of Martin Bucer*: 62; 'L'Allegro' and 'Il Penseroso': 64, 95–6; 'Lycidas': 54–5, 94–5; 'Mansus': 57; *Observations on the Articles of Peace*: 65; *Of Education*: 53; *Of Prelatical Episcopacy*: 60; *Of Reformation*: 60; *Of True Religion*: 87; 'On the New Forcers of Conscience': 349; *Paradise Lost*: 51, 60, 71–3, 77–86, 93, 98 ff., 111–13, 351–2, 365 ('fable', 99; 'characters', 99–102, 104–6; 'sentiments', 102–4; 'defects' 105–9; versification, 111–112); *Paradise Regained*: 86, 110; 'The Passion': 93; *Pro Se Defensio*: 348; *Ready and Easy Way*: 74; *Reason of Church Government*: 60, 349; *Samson Agonistes*: 86, 110; Sonnets: 63, 68, 98; *Tenure of Kings*: 65; *Tetrachordon*: 62; 'To Mr. Cyriack Skinner upon his Blindness': 74 n.; *Treatise of Civil Power*: 73–4
Milton (*née* Woodcock), Katherine, 68, 77
Milton (*née* Powell), Mary, 61–4, 68, 77
Milton, Mary, daughter of the poet, 68, 92, 352
Milton, Mary, daughter of Christopher Milton, 92
Milton, Richard, 50
Milton (*née* Jeffrey), Sarah, 50, 55

Milton, Thomas, 92
Molière. *See* Poquelin, Jean-Baptiste
Monck, George (Duke of Albemarle), 75 n., 117, 170
Monmouth, Duke of. *See* Scott, James
Montagu, Charles (Earl of Halifax), 143, 148–9, 183, 236–7
Montagu, Lady Mary Wortley, 274, 279, 362
Montrose, Duke of. *See* Graham, James
Moore Smythe, James. *See* Smythe, James Moore
More, Alexander, 68–70, 350
Morhof, Daniel, 252
Morrice, Sir William, 75
Moyle, Walter, 159
Mulgrave, Earl of. *See* Sheffield, John
Murdoch, Patrick, 324, 364–5
Murray, William (Earl of Mansfield), 224, 258
mythology, 95, 104, 171, 288, 308, 338–40

'nature', 94, 193, 304
Newcastle, Duchess of. *See* Cavendish, Margaret
Newcastle, Duke of. *See* Cavendish, William
Newcastle (Newcastle-upon-Tyne and Newcastle-under-Lyme), Duke of. *See* Pelham-Holles, Sir Thomas
Newcomen, Matthew, 349
Newton, Sir Isaac, 313, 318
Newton, Thomas, 93, 347, 352
Nichols, John, 360–1, 366
Nichols, John Bowyer, 361
Norfolk, James, 76
Northcote, James, 1 n.

Ogilby, John, 188–90, 210–11, 227, 358, 360
Oldham, John, 261
Orford, 1st Earl of. *See* Walpole, Sir Robert
Orford, 4th Earl of. *See* Walpole, Horace
Ormonde, Duchess of. *See* Somerset, Lady Mary
Ormonde, Duke of. *See* Butler, James
Orrery, 1st Earl of. *See* Boyle, Roger
Orrery, 5th Earl of. *See* Boyle, John

Osborne, Thomas, 267–8
Osorio da Fonseca, Jerome, 52 n.
Otway, Thomas, 193
Ovid, 17 n., 66 n., 90, 92, 139, 163–4, 178, 189, 211–13, 293, 295
Oxford, 1st Earl of. *See* Harley, Robert
Oxford, 2nd Earl of. *See* Harley, Edward
Oxford, Lady. *See* Harley, Henrietta Cavendish

Paget, Nathan, 76
Palmer, Sir Geoffrey, 75
Panciroli, Guido, 31
Paracelsus. *See* Bombast von Hohenheim, Theophrastus
Parnell, Thomas, 198 n., 229, 242
pastoral: 2, 57, 94–5
Patrick, Samuel, 274
Pausanius, 211 n.
Peacham, Henry, 144 n.
Peck, Francis, 10
Pelham-Holles, Sir Thomas (Duke of Newcastle-upon-Tyne and Newcastle-under-Lyme), 150
Pepys, Samuel, 10 n.
Percy, Thomas, 125
Perrault, Charles, 289
Persius, 139 n., 146, 186
personification, 115–16, 340. *See also* allegory
Petrarch, Francesco, 4, 338
Petre, Robert (Baron Petre), 220
Petronius, 174 n., 293 n.
Phaer, Thomas, 198
Philaras, Leonard, 349
Philips, Ambrose, 216, 223–4, 238, 240, 279
Philips, John, 88
Philips, Katherine, 253
Phillips, Edward (the elder), 50 n., 51, 92
Phillips, Edward (the younger), 51, 57, 59, 61–4, 70–1, 77, 79, 85, 92, 347, 349, 351–2
Phillips, John, 51, 57, 68, 92, 350
Pindar, 4, 31–3, 35–6, 45, 211, 187–8
Piozzi (Thrale), H. L., 353, 359
Plato, 17 n.
Plautus, 134
Plutarch, 115, 138, 356
'poetical diction', 166–7
Poliziano (Politian), Angelo, 51
Pollio, Gaius Asinius, 187 n.
Polybius, 51

Pope, Alexander, father of the poet, 210–11, 241, 359–60

Pope, Alexander, poet, 2, 12, 27, 29, 75, 140, 147, 166 n., 168 n., 183, 187, 190, 197, 199–200, 210 ff., 319, 321, 329 n., 355, 357, 359 ff.; 'Alcander': 213; *Art of Sinking in Poetry*: 245, 247–8; trans. Donne's *Satires*: 262; *Dunciad*: 145, 242, 245 ff., 265–9, 296, 301 n., 361, 363; 'Eloisa to Abelard': 222, 292–3, 299, 360; *Epistle to a Lady*: 261, 298, 310 n.; *Epistle to Arbuthnot*: 210 n., 211 n., 240 n., 250 n., 262–3, 266, 272 n., 278 n., 299, 321, 361; *Epistle to Bathurst*: 259–60, 298–9; *Epistle to Burlington*: 249, 298–9; *Epistle to Cobham*: 260–1, 268 n., 298; 'Epistle to Mr. Jervas': 224, 281; *Epitaphs*: 303 ff.; *Essay on Criticism*: 12, 216–19, 281, 284, 288–290, 299, 363; *Essay on Man*: 99 n., 253 ff., 265, 281, 297–8; trans. *Iliad*: 144 n., 224 ff., 244, 275, 284, 293–5, 300, 302; *Imitations of Horace*; 197 n., 241 n., 242 n., 261, 266, 270 n., 290 n., 299; 'January and May': 212; Letters: 215, 245, 250 ff., 276–9; *Letter to a Noble Lord*: 263; *Memoirs of a Parish Clerk*: 245; *Memoirs of Scriblerus*: 264–5; 'Messiah': 219, 287; *Narrative concerning the Frenzy of John Dennis*: 223; *Ode for St. Cecilia's Day*: 287–8; 'Ode on Solitude': 212, 359; trans. *Odyssey*: 163, 243 ff., 295; *One Thousand Seven Hundred and Thirty Eight*: 263, 284, 299; *One Thousand Seven Hundred and Thirty Eight: Dialogue II*: 263, 284, 299; 'On Silence': 213; *Pastorals*: 214–16, 223, 285–6; Prologue to *Cato*: 223, 237; *Rape of the Lock*: 220–2, 248, 291–2, 299–300; 'Sappho to Phaon': 212–13; ed. Shakespeare: 242–3, 296; *Stradling versus Stiles*: 245; *Temple of Fame*: 222, 286, 360; trans. *Thebaid*: 212; *Three Hours after Marriage*: 266–7; 'To Mr. Addison occasioned by his Dialogues on Medals': 238; 'Verses to the Memory of an Unfortunate Lady': 219, 287; 'Wife of Bath her Prologue':

212–13; *Windsor Forest*: 223, 286, 239

Pope (*née* Turner), Editha, 210, 241, 245

Pope, Richard, 359

Pope, William (Earl of Downe), 210

Poquelin, Jean-Baptiste (Molière), 134

Pordage, Samuel, 357

Porphyry, 345–6

Portsmouth, Duchess of. *See* de Kéroualle, Louise Renée de

Powell, Richard, 61

Prince of Wales (Frederick Louis), 263, 273, 278, 320–1

Prior, Matthew, 35, 143, 145, 183, 222, 258, 298, 325, 354, 357, 363

Pufendorf, Samuel von, 350

Pulteney, Sir William (Earl of Bath), 263, 362

Puttenham, George, 160 n.

Puttenham, Richard, 160

Quin, James, 322, 353

Quintilian, 102, 164, 367

Racine, Jean, 132

Racine, Louis, 280

Rackett, Magdalen, 210

Ragsdale, John, 366

Rainolds, John, 141

Rainolds, William, 141

Raleigh, Sir Walter, 73, 111

Ralph, James, 246

Ramus, Petrus (Pierre de La Ramée), 87

Raphael, 310

Rapin, René, 202–3, 205

Ravenscroft, Edward, 145 n.

Rehearsal, The, 117, 136–7, 266

Reynolds, Sir Joshua, 1, 344, 360

Riccaltoun (or Riccarton), Robert, 316

Rich, Edward Henry (Earl of Warwick), 240

Richardson, Jonathan (the elder), 1, 75, 78, 81, 88, 268, 347

Ricardson, Jonathan (the younger), 268, 347

Robinson, Jacob, 257

Robothon, John, 218

Rochester, Earl of. *See* Wilmot, John

Rowe, Anne, 308

Rowe, Nicholas, 135, 308, 355

Rowland, John, 68 n.

Ruffhead, Owen, 219, 243, 268, 359–361, 363
Rundle, Thomas, 318–19
Rupert, Prince, 117
Russell, Mr., tailor, 57
Russell, William, Mr., 149
Rymer, Thomas, 37, 41–2, 117, 130, 161–2, 202–7, 359
Rysbrack, John Michael, 352

Sacheverell, Henry, 139
Sackville, Charles (Earl of Dorset), 118, 145–6, 303–5
Sackville, Charles (Earl of Middlesex and Duke of Dorset), 246
St. Albans, Earl of. *See* Jermyn, Henry
St. Genevieve, 213
St. John, Henry (Viscount Bolingbroke), 158, 230, 245, 253, 255, 257–8, 269–70, 276, 280, 301
St. John, Marie-Claire, 274
Salisbury, Earl of. *See* Cecil, James
Salmasius (Saumaise, Claude de), 65–7, 350
Salvini, Antonio Maria, 293
Salzilli, Giovanni, 56
Sandys, George, 48, 139, 167, 210–11
Sannazaro, Jacopo, 31 (quoted), 346
Sansome, Martha, 318
Sarbiewski, Maciej Kazimierz, 34
Savage, Richard, 222, 246, 259, 276, 280, 299, 319, 324
Savile, Sir George (Marquis of Halifax), 134, 355
Scaliger, Joseph Justus, 162
Scaliger, Julius Caesar, 27, 43
Scarburgh, Sir Charles, 6
Scott, James (Duke of Monmouth), 139, 355
Scriblerus Club, 264
Scudamore, John (Viscount Scudamore), 55
Sedley, Sir Charles, 130
Selvaggi, 56
Seneca (the elder), 177
Seneca (the younger), 133, 164, 168
Settle, Elkanah, 119–23, 126 ff., 137, 140–1, 154, 354, 356
Sewell, George, 163
Seymour, Algernon (Earl of Hertford and Duke of Dorset), 319
Seymour, Frances (*née* Thynne) (Countess of Hertford), 319, 364
Shadwell, Thomas, 145, 355

Shaftesbury, 1st Earl of. *See* Cooper, Anthony Ashley
Shaftesbury, 3rd Earl of. *See* Cooper, Anthony Ashley
Shakespeare, William, 43, 84, 90, 95 n., 96, 103 n., 119, 124, 130, 161, 191, 203–6, 242–3, 246, 256, 261, 274, 333, 338; quotations from plays: *Love's Labour Lost*, 81; *Macbeth*, 340; *A Midsummer Night's Dream*, 4; *Twelfth Night*, 144
Sheeres, Sir Henry, 138
Sheffield, Edmund (2nd Duke of Buckingham and Normanby), 314
Sheffield, John (Earl of Mulgrave and 1st Duke of Buckingham and Normandy), 132, 138–9, 147, 150, 178, 230, 356
Sheldon, Gilbert, 83 n.
Shenstone, William, 367
Sherburne, Sir Edward, 168
Shields, Robert, 364–5
Shrewsbury, Duke of. *See* Talbot, Charles
Sidney, Sir Philip, 65, 349
Silhouette, Etienne de, 361
simile, 288–9
Simmons, Samuel, 83, 86, 352
Smythe, James Moore, 296
Socrates, 59
Somers, John (Baron Somers), 140, 150
Somerset, Lady Mary (Duchess of Ormonde), 159
Sophocles, 133, 203–5
Southcote, Thomas, 258
Southerne, Thomas, 135, 155, 355, 359
Spanheim, Ezekiel, 348
Spanheim, Frederick, 57, 348
Spectator, 37
Spence, Joseph, 163, 244, 270, 359
Spencer, Alice (Countess Dowager of Derby), 55, 348
Spenser, Edmund, 1, 11, 36, 43, 90, 111, 198, 344
Sprat, Thomas, 1–2, 5–6, 8–11, 30, 36, 48, 88, 125, 136, 148–9, 344, 354
Spurstow(e), William, 349
Stanhope, Philip (2nd Earl of Chesterfield), 147
Stanley, Ferdinando (Earl of Derby), 55 n.
Stapleton (Stapylton), Sir Robert, 186

Starkey, George, 351
Starkey, John, 86
Statius, 36, 163, 215
Stebbing, William, 345
Steele, Sir Richard, 219, 222–3, 226, 239, 286, 287 n., 360
Steward, Elizabeth, 148 n.
Stillingfleet, Edward, 142, 357
Stonhewer, Richard, 336 n.
Stuart, John (Earl of Bute), 334
sublimity, 13, 103, 105
Suckling, Sir John, 9, 14, 28, 253, 345, 361
Suetonius, 200 n., 256 n.
Suffolk, Countess of. *See* Howard, Henrietta
Surrey, Earl of. *See* Howard, Henry
Swan, John, 366
Swift, Jonathan, 135, 147 n., 199, 238, 244 n., 245, 247, 249, 253, 261 n., 264–5, 275 n., 277, 278 n., 279, 296, 300, 359, 363

Tacitus, 138–9
Talbot, Charles (Lord Chancellor, Baron Talbot of Hensol), 318–20
Talbot, Charles (Duke of Shrewsbury), 262
Talbot, Charles Richard, son of Baron Talbot, 319–20
Tasso, Torquato, 41–2, 57; *Gerusalemme Liberata*: 41–2, 104, 146
Tate, Nahum, 179
'Taverner'. *See* Bannister, John
Temple, Sir Richard (Viscount Cobham), 260, 276, 333 n.
Temple, Sir William, 213, 326, 365
Temple, William Johnston, 335
Terence, 10 n., 293
Theobald, Lewis, 95, 242, 246, 256, 267, 296
Theron, 32
Thirlby, Styan, 228
Thomas, Elizabeth, 215, 245, 357
Thompson (or Thomson), Thomas, physician, 269
Thomson (*née* Trotter), Beatrix, 316, 364
Thomson, James, 316 ff., 364–5; *Agamemnon*: 321; *Alfred*: 321; *Britannia*: 318, 364; *Castle of Indolence*: 322; *Coriolanus*: 322, 365; *Edward and Eleonora*: 321; *Liberty*: 320, 326; *Poem on the Death of Sir Isaac Newton*: 318; *Seasons*: 325, 365 (*Autumn*: 316, 325; *Spring*: 319, 325; *Summer*: 318–19, 325; *Winter*: 317–18, 325, 364); *Sophonisba*: 319, 365; *Tancred and Sigismunda*: 321
Thomson, Mrs. Jean, 322–4
Thomson, Robert, 323
Thomson, Thomas, 316
Tickell, Thomas, 239–40
Timotheus, 192
Toland, John, 74, 79, 347–8, 352
Tomkyns, Thomas, 83
Tonson, Jacob, 83, 93, 157–8, 208, 216, 240, 242, 352–3, 359
Tonson, Jacob, great-nephew of the above, 93, 157, 352–3, 361
translation (and 'imitation'), 139, 167–8, 261, 293–4, 299
Trapp, Joseph, 156, 162, 190, 358
Trissino, Giangiorgio, 111
Trumbull, Sir William, 214, 302 n., 305–6
Tuke, Sir Samuel, 9
Turner, Elizabeth, 210
Turner, Shallet, 334 n.
Turner, William, 210
Tyers, Thomas, 210

Urban VIII, Pope, 56 n.
Ussher, James, 60

Varillas, Antoine, 142–3, 357
Vaughan, Robert, 344
Vavasseur, Francis, 66 n.
Vega Carpio, Lope de, 136
Victor, Benjamin, 259, 364
Villiers, George (2nd Duke of Buckingham), 10, 136, 299
Virgil, 5, 36, 38, 47–8, 111, 147, 163, 169, 177, 187, 189, 190, 196, 203, 282, 294–5, 303, 345, 358; *Aeneid*: 162, 187, 190, 198, 296 n., 358; *Eclogues*: 190 ('Pollio', 187, 287, 358); *Georgics*: 156, 187–90
Voiture, Vincent de, 119
Voltaire. *See* Arouet, François-Marie
Vyse, Dr. William, 207

Waller, Edmund, 14, 45, 114, 139, 166–7, 174, 197, 241, 286, 290, 354
Waller, Sir William, 64
Walpole, Horace (4th Earl of Orford), 280 n., 331, 366–7
Walpole, Sir Robert (1st Earl of Orford), 247–8, 258, 320
Walsh, William, 215, 217–18, 253

Walton, Isaac, 253 n.
Warburton, William, 218, 253, 256–8, 261, 264–5, 268, 269 n., 270–1, 291, 298, 299 n., 314, 359, 361–3
Warton, Joseph, 293, 327, 329, 359–360
Warton, Thomas, 329
Warwick, Earl of. *See* Rich, Edward Henry
Watts, Isaac, 301
Webbe, William, 160
Welsted, Leonard, 361
West, Richard (the elder), 332
West, Richard, poet and friend of Gray, 332, 337 n.
Wharton, Thomas, 334 n., 336 n., 367
Whately (or Whatley), Mr., 317
Whiston, William, 29 n.
Whitehead, Paul, 263–4
Whitehead, William, 333
Whitelocke, Bulstrode, 350
William III, 208, 305
Wilmot, John (Earl of Rochester), 130, 136–8, 213, 261

Wilson, Charles, 357–8
Wilson, John, 145 n.
Winstanley, William, 128
wit, 11 ff., 27, 30–1 ('mixed wit'), 33–4, 194, 217
Withers, Henry, 311
Wollebius, Joannes, 349
Wood, Anthony à, 1, 3, 6–9, 62, 79, 140, 344, 347, 351
Woodcock, William, 68
Worsdale, James, 252
Wotton, Sir Henry, 27, 43, 55
Wright, George, 364
Wycherley, William, 155, 214, 240
Wyeth, Joseph, 351

Xavier, St. Francis, 142

Yonge, Sir William, 362
Yorke, Philip (1st Earl of Hardwicke), 320
Yorke, Philip (2nd Earl of Hardwicke), 301
Young, Edward, 274 n.
Young, Thomas, 51, 349

DATE DUE

SEP 14 2012	

GAYLORD   PRINTED IN U.S.A.